Atypical Cognitive Deficits in Developmental Disorders:
Implications for Brain Function

ATYPICAL COGNITIVE DEFICITS IN DEVELOPMENTAL DISORDERS
Implications for Brain Function

Edited by

Sarah H. Broman
Jordan Grafman
National Institute of Neurological Disorders and Stroke

LEA LAWRENCE ERLBAUM ASSOCIATES, PUBLISHERS
1994 Hillsdale, New Jersey   Hove and London

Lawrence Erlbaum Associates, Inc., Publishers
365 Broadway
Hillsdale, New Jersey 07642

Library of Congress Cataloging-in-Publication Data
Atypical cognitive deficits in developmental disorders : implications
  for brain function / edited by Sarah H. Broman, Jordan Grafman.
      p. cm.
   Includes bibliographical references and index.
   ISBN 0-8058-1180-X (alk. paper)
      1. Developmental disabilities—Congresses.   2. Cogniton disorders
in children—Congresses.   3. Developmental neurology—Congresses.
4. Developmental neurophysiology—Congresses.   I. Broman, Sarah H.
II. Grafman, Jordan.
   [DNLM: 1. Autism—in infancy & childhood—congresses.   2. Child
Development Disorders—congresses.   3. Cognition Disorders—
congresses.   4. Turner's Syndrome—congresses.   WM 203.5 A887
1994]
RJ506.D47A89   1994
155.45'2—dc20
DNLM/DLC
for Library of Congress   93-12499
                                                                      CIP

Books published by Lawrence Erlbaum Associates are printed on acid-free paper, and their
bindings are chosen for strength and durability.

Printed in the United States of America
10 9 8 7 6 5 4 3 2 1

Contents

Part IV: Commentary

Contributors

Dr. Natacha A. Akshoomoff, Neuropsychology Research Laboratory, Children's Hospital, San Diego, CA 92123

Dr. Mark Appelbaum, Department of Human Development, George Peabody College, Vanderbilt University, Nashville, TN 37203

Dr. Elizabeth Bates, Department of Pediatrics, University of California at San Diego, La Jolla, CA 92093

Dr. Ursula Bellugi, Laboratory for Language and Cognitive Studies, The Salk Institute for Biological Studies, San Diego, CA 92138

Dr. Bruce G. Bender, National Jewish Center for Immunology and Respiratory Medicine, Denver, CO 80206

Dr. Sarah H. Broman, Developmental Neurology Branch, Division of Convulsive, Developmental, and Neuromuscular Disorders, National Institute of Neurological Disorders and Stroke, Bethesda, MD 20892

Dr. Eric Courchesne, Neuropsychology Research Laboratory, Children's Hospital, San Diego, CA 92123

Dr. Martha Bridge Denckla, Department of Developmental Cognitive Neurology, The Kennedy-Krieger Institute, Baltimore, MD 21205

Mr. Brian Egaas, Neuropsychology Research Laboratory, Children's Hospital, San Diego, CA 92123

Dr. Jack M. Fletcher, Department of Pediatrics, University of Texas Medical School at Houston, Houston, TX 77225

Dr. Patricia S. Goldman-Rakic, Section of Neurobiology, Yale School of Medicine, New Haven, CT 06510

Dr. Jordan Grafman, Cognitive Neuroscience Section, Medical Neurology Branch, National Institute of Neurological Disorders and Stroke, Bethesda, MD 20892

Dr. Richard H. Haas, Department of Neurology, University of California at San Diego Medical Center, La Jolla, CA 92093

Dr. Hector E. James, Neuropsychology Research Laboratory, Children's Hospital, San Diego, CA 92123

Dr. Terry L. Jernigan, Departments of Psychiatry and Radiology, University of California at San Diego, La Jolla, CA 92093

Dr. Ray Johnson, Jr., Cognitive Neuroscience Section, Medical Neurology Branch, National Institute of Neurological Disorders and Stroke, Bethesda, MD 20892

Dr. Alan J. Lincoln, Neuropsychology Research Laboratory, Children's Hospital, San Diego, CA 92123

Dr. Mary G. Linden, National Jewish Center for Immunology and Respiratory Medicine, Denver, CO 80206

Dr. Lewis P. Lipsitt, Department of Psychology, Brown University, Providence, RI 02912

Dr. Debra L. Mills, Laboratory for Neuropsychology, The Salk Institute for Biological Studies, San Diego, CA 92138

Dr. James W. Murakami, Neuropsychology Research Laboratory, Children's Hospital, San Diego, CA 92123

Dr. Helen J. Neville, Laboratory for Neuropsychology, The Salk Institute for Biological Studies, San Diego, CA 92138

Dr. Gary A. Press, Department of Neuroradiological Imaging, Kaiser Hospital, San Diego, CA 92120

Dr. Isabelle Rapin, Department of Neurology, Albert Einstein College of Medicine, Bronx, NY 10461

Dr. Arthur Robinson, National Jewish Center for Immunology and Respiratory Medicine, Denver, CO 80206

Dr. Judith L. Ross, Department of Pediatrics, Medical College of Pennsylvania, Philadelphia, PA 19129

Dr. Osamu Saitoh, Neuropsychology Research Laboratory, Children's Hospital, San Diego, CA 92123

Dr. Eric Schopler, Department of Psychiatry, University of North Carolina Medical School, Chapel Hill, NC 27599

Dr. Laura Schreibman, Department of Psychology, University of California at San Diego, La Jolla, CA 92093

Dr. Marian Sigman, Neuropsychiatric Institute, University of California at Los Angeles, Los Angeles, CA 90024

Dr. Jean P. Townsend, Neuropsychology Research Laboratory, Children's Hospital, San Diego, CA 92123

Dr. Lynn Waterhouse, Child Behavior Study, Trenton State College, Trenton, NJ 08650

Dr. Beverly White, Cytogenetics Unit, Laboratory of Chemical Biology, National Institute of Diabetes, Digestive, and Kidney Diseases, Bethesda, MD 20892

Dr. Paul P. Wang, Laboratory for Language and Cognitive Studies, The Salk Institute for Biological Studies, San Diego, CA 92138

Ms. Rachel Yeung-Courchesne, Neuropsychology Research Laboratory, Children's Hospital, San Diego, CA 92123

Foreword

Monographs of conference proceedings are rarely considered must-read publications: Their interest is often limited mostly to the participants in the conference and to a relatively narrow audience of investigators working in that field. Moreover, conference proceedings are often relatively unedited, disparate, and undigested, and may contain redundancies or even unaddressed contradictions.

This monograph grew out of a conference, but these were no routine conference proceedings. Readers must not be put off by the fact that relatively esoteric conditions—autism, Turner and Williams syndromes—were discussed. These conditions, fascinating in their own right, provided the unique scaffolding for a sophisticated and entirely modern exploration of the complex relationships of brain maturation and its aberrations to the abilities and behaviors of children. The contributors discuss in depth the biologic (genetic, anatomic, electrophysiologic), neuropsychologic, and behavioral complexities of each condition in order to highlight its unique heuristic contribution to furthering the understanding of brain–mind relations in children. Each condition yields the opportunity for one or more tightly reasoned essays that transcend that condition and address such theoretical issues as classification research, the complementary contributions of studies of children with focal lesion versus diffuse lesions versus developmental aberrations, the insights and pitfalls of investigations that use large samples versus single cases, and the value of integrating insights from research in primates and in man.

Far from being an ephemeral summary of a conference on a heterogeneous group of topics by a heterogeneous group of investigators, this mongraph provides incisive, insightful, broad but focused epistemologic discussions of issues that investigators of children's cognition, language, social ability, and other behaviors, and their relation to underlying brain maturation, ignore at their peril. Held at the start of the Decade of the Brain, the conference on *Atypical Cognitive Deficits in Developmental Disorders: Implications for Brain Function* aptly sets the scene for the Decade by laying out the requirements for conceptually, methodologially, and technologically sound multidisciplinary research in this area. It provides investigators with thoughtful and rich essays they will want to ponder, return to, and discuss throughout the Decade of the Brain.

ISABELLE RAPIN

Preface

I begin this preface by commenting with great enthusiasm on the treatment of methodology throughout all the chapters in this volume. It is an exhilarating experience to have methodology and statistical analysis made as interesting as they are in the chapter by Elizabeth Bates and Mark Appelbaum. These authors believe that our styles of data collection and our procedures for drawing inferences from the data are among the most exciting aspects of our work; these are the facets of the scientific enterprise that lend credibility to our factual assertions when the study is finished. It is also exciting because there is a certain amount of risk involved. You put your money (literally, in the case of grant-giving agencies) on a set of protocols, a certain frame of reference, and an anticipation of outcomes that are only probable. After all, if you knew at the outset how the study was going to come out, there would be no need to do it. One's capacity for scientific prediction and even one's ego are on the line. It is extremely rewarding to run the risk of a long-shot hypothesis with impeccably defensible methodology on your side—and then win.

Along with conveying this excitement, which Bates and Appelbaum temper with appropriate cautions and deep respect for the empirical data, this conference led to magnificent insights into some newly identified or recently investigated neurocognitive deficits. Also exhilarating were the surroundings in which the conference took place—the campus of the National Institutes of Health—and the presence of several people I had known during the late 1950s and early 1960s when we were all associated with the Collaborative Perinatal Project of the National Institute of Neurological Disorders and Stroke. The objective of that longitudinal study of some 50,000 births was to discover the prenatal and birth hazards that "caused" cerebral palsy, mental retardation, and other neurological and psychological disorders. Some of those at the conference were connected with that study, as I was, from its earliest days.

The largest study of human development ever undertaken in the history of the life sciences to that date, the Collaborative Perinatal Project that eventually involved 12 major universities and their associated hospitals, paved the way, I believe, for the meticulous attention given at this conference to empirical documentation of subtle clinical signs and neurological deficits. The planning for the Collaborative Project was underway in 1957; data collection, following pretesting of instruments, was begun in 1959. New births were enrolled in the study over a 7-year period, and the children were followed to at least 7 years of age. Some of us, we at Brown University included, are still following those children. For its day, the study was very expensive, involving interdisciplinary, long-term investigation of prenatal conditions and delivery room practices, and requiring extensive pediatric, neurological, and eventually psychological and speech and hearing examinations. The protocols were elaborate constructions, calling for more precision of measurment than most of the disciplines were accustomed to or aspired to, and the requirements of quality control in examinations and records-keeping were stringent.

Today we might say that the "take" from the Collaborative Perinatal Project was not great for the energy, time, and funds expended. For example, some obstetrical procedures extant in those days are no longer current. Also, because newer technologies insure that more infants with very low birth-weights survive, some findings are not applicable to new births. As a native of coastal Massachusetts, I'd say that was a day of hard digging for only a few quahogs (note: thick-shelled American clams). Some seeds were laid as we dug, however, and a new generation of ideas, methods, and investments has arisen as a direct benefit of that study. This conference, organized by Sally Broman, one of the pioneers of the Collaborative Perinatal Project, is unquestionably one of them. Her experience with an N of 50,000 infants may have even led to her inviting the article on the methods and art of studying the small sample!

There are other continuities between the setting for this conference and the work supported by the National Institute of Neurological Disorders and Stroke 30 years ago. There were major findings—now virtual truisms—that came from the Collaborative Perinatal Project. For example, it was one of the first major research programs to report a relationship between smoking behavior and health deficits. One early finding was that mothers who smoked were more likely to give birth prematurely and to have smaller babies. Small and premature babies, in turn, were documentably at greater risk for other adverse conditions of development.

Ghosts in the nursery, or the influence of experiences of long ago on our behavior today, may well have affected the conference organizer who, with her colleagues, reported some of the most interesting and surprising findings of the Collaborative Perinatal Project. Recall that the principal goal of that study was to document the *prenatal and birth conditions* that contribute to birth defects and developmental disabilities. Quite unexpectedly, it turned out that the factor accounting for most of the variability in intelligence as measured at 4 years of age was *socio-economic level* (Broman, Nichols, & Kennedy, 1975). Poverty was a more influential determinant of at least this (very important) facet of developmental functioning than any physiological or medical antecedent. Similarly, Lee Willerman, then of the National Institute of Neurological Disorders and Stroke, and his colleagues showed that intelligence as an outcome is a complex variable and that early manifestations of retarded intellect resulting from constitutional insufficiencies occasioned by birth hazards can be abated by later conditions of felicitous family life indexed as higher socio-economic level (Willerman, Broman, & Fiedler, 1970). These findings about the socio-cultural-familial nurturing of intelligence in young children were real eye-openers for their time because the *Zeitgeist* was more inclined to assume that hereditary and other constitutional determinants were the largest contributors to intellectual or cognitive deficit. In this respect, there is an important promissory note contained in the results of the Collaborative Perinatal Project. The present conference, for all of its wondrous discoveries about fascinating aberrations of development that are clearly biological in origin, needs to be followed by another that will address the environmental and experiential processes contributing to deficits in human learning and cognition.

I must make another comment on the historical context of this conference on neurocognitive aspects of development, which has much to do with its value. The conference presentations and papers in this book emphasize individual differences and neurological or constitutional underpinnings of aberrations in memory, acquisition of language, and other cognitive processes, and hence, intellectual and cognitive deficits. Research in these areas was but a gleam in the eyes of many psychologists initially involved in the Collaborative Perinatal Project. However, during planning sessions to select assessments for developmental follow-ups in meetings that included neurologists and pediatricians, behavioral measures proposed to tap sensory and learning capacities, including those of the newborn, were not approved. The disciplines of pediatrics and psychology were *status* oriented then, still under the spell of the Gesellian influence. The point of developmental testing was to find out what the infant or child can do (or knows) and when he or she can do it. There was little emphasis on *process*:

The Collaborative Perinatal Project, however, helped to strengthen a new view of infancy, which is one relating to the importance of sociocultural factors in the determination of developmental destinies. It is a view concerning the reciprocities between brain and behavior, or between constitutional determinants and the developmental milieu. It is this view that has led to so much discussion in this conference of the "context" of development. Genetic promise becomes potentiated in socio-environmental contexts, and these "surrounding conditions" can make all the difference in the world. The old view in developmental psychology was that heredity and congenital conditions dictate and that environmental acquiesces. The Collaborative Perinatal Project produced good evidence, reported in the Broman et al. (1975) volume, that social conditions are of great importance in the unfolding of the child's intelligence, regardless of other predisposing conditions. Based on this conclusion, no future study can ever be done without attention to that side of the developmental coin.

A newly emerging aspect of development emphasized in this volume on characteristics and correlates of autism is the crucially important early establishment of reciprocating interpersonal dialogues between the infant or child and his or her parents, teachers, observers, or other important persons in the environment. Explaining the autistic child's often observed diminished capacity for engaging in such interactions would be a major step toward solving the puzzle of the disorder. Measures or indices of the development of reciprocity, empathy, and identification with others would also, of course, be important additions to normative studies of development.

How much we have changed in our view of what our disciplines are about and in terms of what we can now do, professionally and scientifically. I take to heart the statement made at the outset of this conference by Dr. F. J. Brinley, Jr. of the National Institute of Neurological Disorders and Stroke, that just because something is doable does not mean that you have to do it. One has to be selective, and one has to count on the worth of the promissory notes handed down from our predecessors in our respective disciplines. At the same time, I would insist that a bit of vision and the willingness to take some risk in the name of scientific creativity can often enhance the value of the promissory notes.

We have not explored the potential of behavior science for illuminating brain function as much as we should have. This is despite the fact that more young people die from behavioral misadventures, such as accidents and homicide, than from all diseases combined and that social and behavioral mishaps, such as dangerous driving and excessive maternal drug-taking, cause developmental neurological aberrations.

The investigators contributing to this volume have adopted an information-processing orientation to their work. That is, the processing of information in the brain is carried out by topographically and psychologically distinct components that operate on separate features of the information. These operations can be selectively impaired or dissociated by different forms of brain damage. Developmental neurological disorders such as Williams syndrome, autism, and Turner syndrome, by virtue of their lesion location, have selective and persistent deleterious effects on the operations of specific information-processing components. At this level of description, biology and genetics play a major role in the pattern of cognitive deficits and strengths in an individual. Socio-environmental conditions, however, may affect the richness of information contained in the intact components and may help to develop the impaired components to their functional limits.

In summary, we do not know enough about the natural reciprocities between brain function and behavior, or about the conditions that could help to thwart brain dysfunction and developmental disabilities. The reciprocities of which I speak are honored in this symposium in a very enlightening way, and I hope this program is a landmark, a bellwether. The Decade of the Brain, celebrated from now until the year 2000, should have been called the Decade of the Brain and Behavior.

LEWIS P. LIPSITT

REFERENCES

Broman, S. H., Nichols, P. L., & Kennedy, W. A. (1975). *Preschool IQ: Prenatal and early developmental correlates*. Hillsdale, NJ: Lawrence Erlbaum Associates.

Willerman, L., Broman, S. H., & Fiedler, M. (1970). Infant development, preschool IQ, and social class. *Child Development, 41,* 69–77.

Introduction

Sarah H. Broman
Jordan Grafman
National Institute of Neurological Disorders and Stroke

Fascinating but often catastrophic experiments of nature occur that alter brain function. When these events are studied carefully, they can reveal not only therapeutic strategies to be used against the disabling conditions, but new information about basic biological and behavioral processes in human development. Promising examples are childhood syndromes of genetic, congenital, or still undefined eitiologies whose effects include cognitive and other behavioral deficits that are clearly selective. In addition to using neuropsychological assessment to define these specific patterns of deficit, the noninvasive techniques of brain structural imaging, brain functional imaging, and electrophysiological recording can aid in localizing the affected cognitive functions in the brain and identifying underlying neural mechanisms. This multidisciplinary and multifactorial examination of developmental disorders can help to develop more complete models of brain-behavior relations and, at the same time, identify more specific interventions for different etiological groups.

To examine what was known about the neuropsychology and brain structure and function in three syndromes currently under investigation, and to evaluate the utility of such models as research tools, a workshop was convened at the National Institutes of Health in the spring of 1991 under the sponsorship of the National Institute of Neurological Disorders and Stroke. This volume is a collection of the papers presented there.

The goal of the workshop and of this volume is to add to the knowledge base of cognitive neuroscience within a developmental framework. Much of what we know about the neurological basis of cognitive function in humans has been learned from studies of central nervous system trauma or disease in adults. Certain neurodevelopmental disorders affect the central nervous system in unique ways by producing specific as opposed to generalized cognitive deficit. Studies of these disorders using neurobiological and neuropsychological techniques show that they can yield new insights into the localization of cognitive processes in the brain and the developmental course of atypical cognitive profiles.

This book focuses on three developmental disorders: Williams syndrome, autism, and Turner syndrome. The multidisciplinary approaches, methods, techniques, and findings reported here are at the cutting edge of cognitive neuroscience research on complex behavioral processes and their neural substrates. Although each of the disorders is accompanied by some degree of general cognitive impairment or mental retardation, least severe in Turner syndrome, of greater interest are the atypical deficits in which a cognitive function is spared, such as language in Williams syndrome, or is disproportionately depressed as are spatial discrimination skills and visual-motor coordination in Truner syndrome. Drastically reduced or seemingly absent language capabilities and little social interaction characterize the core autism syndrome.

The book is divided into four parts with Part 2 subdivided into three sections devoted to the three developmental disorders that are the focus of this volume. In Part 1, localization of higher cognitive functions in the central nervous system, a key issue in cognitive neuroscience, is discussed by Patricia Goldman-Rakic and illustrated by results from her experimental studies in monkeys of the role of the prefrontal cortex in working memory.

Part 2 presents findings from behavioral and neurobiological studies of Williams syndrome, autism, and Turner syndrome in 10 chapters. The general plan was to present an overview of each syndrome followed by special studies in, for example, neuroanatomy and neurophysiology. The format differs for each syndrome, however. The overview chapters for Williams syndrome and for autism were written from a behavioral perspective by Ursula Bellugi and colleagues and by Eric Schopler, respectively. The overview of Turner syndrome by Beverly White focuses primarily on genetic issues. In the case of Williams syndrome, probably the most well-developed of the three models within a cognitive neuroscience framework, Terry Jernigan and Ursula Bellugi present neuroanatomic findings from magnetic resonance imaging studies of affected children and Helen Neville and colleagues examine electrophysiologic correlates of linguistic development. In the section on autism, a disorder not immune from controversy, Eric Courchesne and colleagues report on their work on neuroanatomic abnormalities found in the neocerebellum of autistic patients, which were found to be associated with an inability to shift attention rapidly and accurately. This compromised ability to control shifts of attention, present in autistic infants, may, in turn, be a key factor in the verbal and social interaction deficits in autism. In the two other chapters on autism, definitional problems are discussed in the context of the authors' research. Marian Sigman addresses the issue of what the core deficits in autism are (the usual controversy focusing on the seemingly artificial dichotomy of intellectual versus social-emotional impairment), and Lynn Waterhouse discusses severity of behavioral impairment as a factor in the diagnosis of autism as opposed to autistic spectrum disorders, and proposes a neurological model to account for variation in the severity of behavioral abnormalies. For the third developmental disorder under consideration, Bruce Bender and colleagues describe the varied behavioral characteristics associated with Turner syndrome. Then Ray Johnson and Judith Ross report on their elegant studies of event-related electrophysiological indices of brain activity in Turner syndrome.

Part 3 of the book takes up methodological issues; in particular, the ability to make reliable inferences from studies of small samples, relevant here because of the rareness of most of the developmental disorders of interest. A comprehensive and critical discussion by Elizabeth Bates and Mark Appelbaum of appropriate statistical techniques is illustrated with examples from studies of small groups and single subjects in neurolinguistics and related fields. The fourth and last part of the book consists of commentary in chapters by Martha Denckla, a behavioral neurologist, and Jack Fletcher, a neuropsychologist who wrote the Afterword in this volume. Each of these contributions provides a different view of the advantages, pitfalls, theories, and methods of a developmental approach to the central problems of cognitive neuroscience.

Although open to the charge of reductionism revisited because of attempts to map cognition onto a neural substrate, this volume shows that the study of developmental disorders can make a major contribution to the knowledge base of cognitive neuroscience.

Part I

COGNITION AND NEUROSTRUCTURE

1

Specification of Higher Cortical Functions

Patricia S. Goldman-Rakic
Yale School of Medicine

One of the dramatic aspects of the behavioral profiles in autism, Turner, and Williams syndromes is that glaring deficits in one cognitive domain coexist with remarkable performance in another. The dissociation of capacity can be striking, as for instance in the capacity of Williams syndrome children to recognize faces and objects in noncanonical views although failing utterly to copy the simplest pictures of ordinary items (Bellugi, Klima, & Sipple, 1989). Understanding of how cerebral cortex is organized both anatomically and functionally can aid in interpreting the apparent contradictions on behavioral capacity and perhaps shed light on the etiology of disorders by identifying the structures, systems, circuits, and perhaps cell classes involved in a particular condition. Such information would lead to theories of why a particular subset of structures is more vulnerable than others to a genetic or epigenetic event.

A major issue in neurobiology of particular relevance to these developmental disorders is the degree to which specific functions are strictly localized in the central nervous system. The answer to this question has varied widely over this century. Earlier in this century, Lashley (1929) was impressed with the lack of specificity of cortical mechanisms because relatively large lesions rarely resulted in lasting behavioral deficits. Although few neuroscientists today would deny localization of function, many still view the cortex as capable of considerable restructuring as a basis for sparing of function after cortical damage. Another school of thought adheres to the more traditional view that the brain is essentially hard-wired and its plasticity limited. Whatever view is held, it is clear that the true degree of neural and behavioral plasticity requires a thoroughgoing analysis of function allocation in the normal brain and the detailed mechanisms underlying the latitude of these functions. Yet our understanding of normative structure-function relationships often falls far short of this prerequisite, particularly in the cerebral cortex.

Understanding of structure-function relationships is most advanced in the sensory cortices, particularly the primary visual and somatosensory areas. However, even with our knowledge of the anatomical and physiological organization of sensory cortices (Edelman, Gall, & Cowan, 1984), there is little consensus on the degree of their reorganization in the face of lesions and, in my opinion, only suggestive evidence that lost sensory functions can be reconstituted after damage to specified areas. Indeed, one of the currently more dramatic examples of cortical plasticity is the expansion of the face representation in the somatosensory cortex following deafferentation by dorsal rhizotomy in the rhesus monkey (Pons et al., 1991). This example demonstrates that intact functions can be enlarged but it does not show that lost functions can be recovered; in this case, an enlarged facial representation is at the expense of a diminished hand representation. Finally, in this widely publicized example of plasticity, it is by no means clear that the cortex rather than the lower centers has been reorganized.

It is of considerable importance that issues of functional and structural organization be examined in a variety of cortical areas. It is often tacitly assumed that the association areas would be those areas of the cortex most advanced with respect to plastic mechanisms. These uncharted territories have long been considered to be less specific in their organization and more adaptive to environmental contingencies. This chapter is about one area of prefrontal cortex—the principal sulcus—that has been the subject of intense study over several decades (Fuster, 1989; Goldman-Rakic, 1987). Our studies provide an opportunity to examine functional localization. The example from our work concerns critical aspects of spatial cognition, a complex cognitive domain that can be studied very well in monkeys and a domain that I believe demonstrates that higher cortical functions depend on specific processing mechanisms that are organized in a manner analogous to the more rigidly specified sensorimotor functions of the brain. Additionally, these studies reveal a remarkably strong relationship between the behavioral, anatomical, and physiological organization of a brain region and its function.

AREAL LOCALIZATION

To understand the contribution of the cerebral cortex to behavior and higher cortical function, we have used the strategy of focusing on a particular area referred to in Brodmann's and others' cytoarchitectonic maps as Area 46 (Fig. 1.1). This area is adjacent to Area 9 and is one of many subdivisions in the prefrontal cortex. It is our conviction that if this area could be better

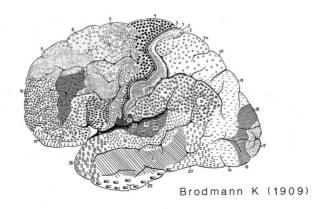

Brodmann K (1909)

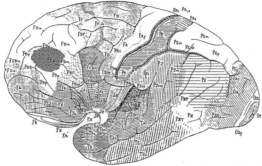

Economo C von, Koskinas GN (1925)

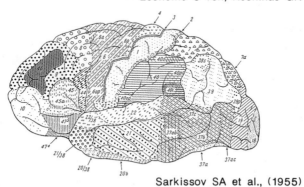

Sarkissov SA et al., (1955)

FIG. 1.1. Lateral views of classical cytoarchitectonic maps of human cerebral cortex with Area 46 shaded on each. Top: Brodmann's map; Middle: von Economo and Koskinas (1925); Lower: Sarkissov, Filimonoff, & Kononova, (1955). Note that the shape and size of Area 46 is somewhat different in each map.

understood in terms of anatomical circuitry, neurotransmitters, and their receptors and essential functions, we should be able to explain other prefrontal areas including Areas 44, 45, 11, 10, 9, 8, and all of the different subdivisions in the human prefrontal cortex that are thought to subserve the distinctively human capacities of reasoning, planning, and conceptual ability.

Figure 1.1 shows three classical maps of the human frontal lobe, one of Brodmann, one of von Economo's, and one of Sarkissov's. Examination of these maps reveals that Area 46 is slightly different in each of the maps. However, recently in my laboratory we reconstructed this area in a number of human brains on the basis of very specific cytometric criteria (Rajkowska & Goldman-Rakic, in press). To our surprise, we found that each of the first three brain reconstructions (not shown) conformed nicely to each of the three cytoarchitectonic maps, leading us to conclude that the classical anatomists were really quite accurate in their maps; they were just looking at different brains. Our findings thus emphasize that there are individual differences among humans in the size and shape of Area 46. On the other hand, we can emphasize the similarities in all of the brains we have examined, as Area 46 is always in the dorsolateral sector of the frontal lobe, occupying the middle frontal gyrus to one degree or other, and it is nearly always distinguishable from surrounding or neighboring regions by the distinctness of its inner granular IVth layer. Thus this area exists in roughly the same location in every normal human.

WORKING MEMORY

A vast clinical and experimental literature supports the conclusion that Area 46 and other areas in the prefrontal cortex are highly specialized for a particular kind of memory function (Goldman-Rakic, 1987). Although that function has been given different names, I favor the descriptive term *working memory* to denote a memory process defined by temporary coding and dynamic processing of memoranda in the workspace of the mind (see Baddeley, 1983; Carpenter & Just, 1988). Simply stated, working memory is the ability to hold information in mind, to internalize information, and use that information to guide behavior without the aid of or in the absence of reliable external cues. Working memory is a central concept in the study of language, comprehension, and reasoning (Baddeley, 1983; Carpenter & Just, 1988). An important point is that working memory is a very different process than associative memory, which is the process of acquiring knowledge by repetition and by reinforcement (see Goldman-Rakic, 1987, for further discussion of this point). Working memory to a large extent presupposes knowledge; it is a dynamic process that operates on the products of associative learning (Fig. 1.2).

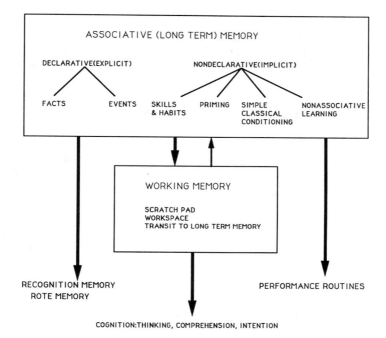

FIG. 1.2. Diagrammatic representation of the relationship between Associative Memory and Working Memory Systems. Declarative and Nondeclarative Memory as partitioned by Squire (1991) is treated as one domain of behavioral control defined by dependence on the repetition of constant relationships over time. In this scheme, facts and events are remembered through memorial or actual repetition, as are habits. The contents of associative memory stores is the source of the material upon which working memory operates. Associative memory is the grist and working memory the mill. Information that is directly retrieved from associative memory stores is expressed as recognition and/or routine performance. However, if that information is processed dynamically, it can lead to comprehension, thought, and intentionality.

Can working memory be studied in animals? I have posited that the process referred to as working memory in humans is measured by classical delayed-response tasks given to experimental primates. In these tasks, a monkey watches an experimenter place a food morsel into one of two wells and a delay is imposed by lowering a screen and preventing the animal from orienting to the food well. After a delay, which can be as brief as a few seconds, the screen is raised. The animal has to select which of the two food wells contains the reward.

The important point that illustrates the nature of the distinction between working and associative memory is that at the time the animal must make its response, there is no information in the environment to guide the response. There is no cue, no signal, no differential discriminative stimulus in the situation external to the animal. The information that guides the response is in the animal's "mind." To achieve correct performance, it has to base its response on an internalized representation of a stimulus presented seconds before. The interposition of the delay between the input and the output forces the animal to use internalized information to guide its response.

LESIONS OF AREA 46

Bilateral removal of Area 46 produces a profound impairment on delayed-response tasks, particularly spatial delayed-response tasks, which require the animal to remember where an object is placed (for review, see Goldman-Rakic, 1987). It is important to recognize that the impairment is restricted to this task and similar tasks that require the animal to base its response on remembered spatial cues. Thus, monkeys with lesions of the principal sulcus are not at all impaired on cued spatial responses, for example (Goldman & Rosvold, 1970; Passingham, 1975). Furthermore, monkeys with dorsolateral prefrontal lesions are not impaired on any number of other tasks, in which the stimuli are external to the animals, are nonspatial, or require any association between stimuli and responses that is repeatedly reinforced (Goldman-Rakic, 1987). Similarly, patients with frontal lobe lesions can perform a wide range of associatively learned skills and may even achieve normal scores on IQ tests, reflecting that the store of associatively acquired knowledge is relatively intact (Hebb, 1949). In spite of an intact long-term memory system, the frontal lobe patient is deficient in using his knowledge to guide behavior in a coherent, goal-directed manner. Thus, the frontally damaged monkey and human provide strong examples of a remarkable dissociation between associative memory that is relatively intact and working memory that is deficient.

OCULOMOTOR DELAYED RESPONSE

The classical delayed response has been used for decades to test spatial memory, and it has been instrumental in elucidating basic principals of brain and behavior. However, modern versions of this task have provided the opportunity for a more detailed analysis of brain-behavior relationships. In our laboratory, we employ an oculomotor version of the classical delayed-response task, which requires the monkey to fixate a small spot on the center of a cathode ray tube throughout a trial (Funahashi, Bruce, & Goldman-Rakic, 1989). As shown in Fig. 1.3, a trial consists of presenting a target in one of eight locations. The target is presented briefly, for half a second, and then goes off. As in the classical spatial delayed-response task, a delay is

OCULOMOTOR DELAYED-RESPONSE

memory-guided

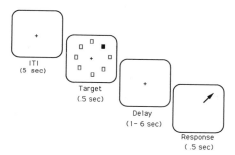

sensory-guided

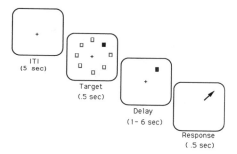

FIG. 1.3. This figure diagrams the oculomotor delayed-response task in its memorial version (top) and sensory-guided (bottom) versions. In the memory-guided version, the stimulus to be remembered (right, upper quadrant) disappears before the delay and the animal makes a response in the absence of an external cue when the fixation spot extinguishes at the end of the delay. In the sensory-guided task, the cue remains on during the delay and is present to guide the response at the end of the delay.

introduced. At the end of the delay, the fixation spot goes off, instructing the animal to direct its gaze to where the target had been. Important to note, as in the manual version, no information to guide the response is available at the end of the delay and the animal must base its response on an internalized cue. This task allows us not only to test the animal's ability to keep in mind a previous event, but to differentiate memoranda of the exact X-Y coordinates of that event, that is, whether it was located at 90°, 45°, 135°, and so forth. In a fundamental way, the oculomotor delayed-response (ODR) paradigm allows manipulation of the contents of the animal's memory on every trial. Further, given that the position of the target to be remembered is randomly varied from trial to trial, the test requires the animal to continuously update this information on a moment-to-moment basis. Finally, notice that if the target is left on during the delay period and is present at the end of the delay, we can compare the same responses when they are sensory guided as opposed to memory guided (lower panel, Fig. 1.3).

MNEMONIC SCOTOMATA

In a recent study in our laboratory, rhesus monkeys received unilateral lesions around the principal sulcus or the adjacent frontal eyefields after they had learned to perform the ODR task at high levels (90% correct or better). All monkeys were impaired in making saccadic eye movements to remembered cues presented in the visual field contralateral to the hemisphere in which the lesion was placed. When a second lesion was added in the opposite hemisphere, the deficit was enlarged to include the remaining hemifield. The degree of impairment was related to the length of the delay; that is, it was exacerbated as the delay increased and errors consisted of eye movements in inappropriate directions. Significantly, the prefrontal lesions had no effect on eye movements that were sensory guided in the control task, even though those eye movements were of identical polarity to those that were impaired in the memory-guided version of the task. It is remarkable that lesions in the prefrontal cortex produce deficits only on the memory-guided version and not the sensory-guided version of the ODR task, proving once again that the functions affected by the lesion are mnemonic and not sensorimotor (Fig. 1.4; Funashashi, Bruce, & Goldman-Rakic, 1993). It bears further emphasis that the memory deficit is lateralized; that is, memory for visual cues in each hemifield is processed largely in the contralateral hemisphere. Most important, these findings provide evidence for the concept of a mnemonic scotoma, that is, a memory deficit for a particularly visual field location, unaccompanied by simple sensory or motor deficits.

SUBAREAL AND COMPARTMENTAL LOCALIZATION OF MNEMONIC UNITS

Lesion studies have revealed that the cortical center for spatial working memory is localized within the principal sulcus. As this anatomical organization has come under closer scrutiny, it is abundantly clear that the principal sulcus, Area 46, is not a homogeneous area but has subareas and columnar compartments (for review, see Goldman-Rakic, 1984). Figure 1.5 summarizes the results of several recent tracing studies in our laboratory, revealing the columnar compartmentalization of the principal sulcus. In the example given, the projections from the posterior parietal cortex are illustrated. By virtue of its direct innervation from secondary visual areas, this posterior

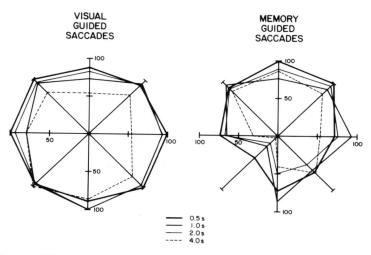

FIG. 1.4. This figure displays percent correct performance on an octagonal graph under delays of different duration (lines of different stripe) before and after a unilateral lesion involving the posterior dorsolateral prefrontal cortex. Performance is unimpaired in the sensory-guided task and is selectively impaired on the memory-guided task, particularly in the lower left quadrant of the visual field contralateral to the lesion. This finding indicates that the impairment is mnemonic and not due to sensory or motor deficits. From Goldman-Rakic (1987). Reprinted by permission.

parietal cortex is concerned particularly with spatial and motion vision as well as with oculomotor and eye-hand coordination. It is divisible into several subdivisions reflecting this functional and anatomical diversity and serves as a relay center from the sensory periphery to the prefrontal cortex. As shown in Fig. 1.5, the medial parietal, Area 7b, which itself is connected to a subset of somatosensory related areas, projects to the ventral bank of the principal sulcus (PS); the parietal cortex buried in the intraparietal sulcus, Area 7ip, projects to the caudal (fundus) region of the PS near the frontal eyefield; Area 7a, which is concerned with eye-hand coordination, projects to the depths of the PS; and the cortex on the medial wall of the parietal lobe, Area 7m, which receives both somatosensory and visual information, projects to the dorsal rim of the PS. The point of this illustration is to indicate that the PS may be decomposed into subareas with possibly different subfunctions related respectively to ocular, manual, and eye-hand coordination. Moreover, each of the inputs is defined by a few or at most a set of columns of fibers that are suggestive of ocular dominance columns. Do these columns represent physiological or functional units? This issue is of particular interest in our laboratory and is currently under investigation.

Although most of the neuropsychological literature is concerned with the behavioral consequences of larger surgical lesions of varying sizes and contours, recent methodological advances have allowed the production of

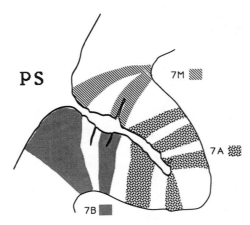

FIG. 1.5. Schematic drawing of a section through the prefrontal cortex displaying the parcellation of the prefrontal cortex by its projections from the posterior parietal cortex; the figure also reveals the columnar nature of the parietal inputs to the prefrontal cortex.

reversible lesions and some of these methods permit investigators to inactivate small territories, for example, volumes of approximately $2mm^3$. Recently in my laboratory, Sawaguchi injected microquantities of SCH23390 and raclopride, compounds that block D1 and D2 dopamine receptors, respectively, into the principal sulcus. An example of our findings are shown in Fig. 1.6. Before the injection, the monkeys performed at greater than 90% correct performance; the monkeys could easily remember targets in all polar directions. However, shortly after an intracerebral injection of SCH23390, the monkeys begin to exhibit a loss of memory for one and only one target location. At this location, the animal made more than numerous errors while continuing to perform excellently at all other target locations. More remarkably, the animal performed nearly perfectly on the sensory-guided control version of the task, even for the target location that was affected in the memory-guided ODR task. These findings dramatically illustrate once again that behavior is altered by prefrontal dysfunction only if it is memory guided and not if it is externally guided; and the memory mechanisms for a given part of space are localized in a circumscribed zone of cortex not greater than approximately $2mm^3$.

CELLULAR LOCALIZATION

Working memory can also be localized at the cellular level. In a remarkable set of studies, neurophysiologists have observed neuronal activity in precise registration with the cue, the delay, or response periods of a delayed-response task, suggesting that separate and distinct neuronal populations encode the

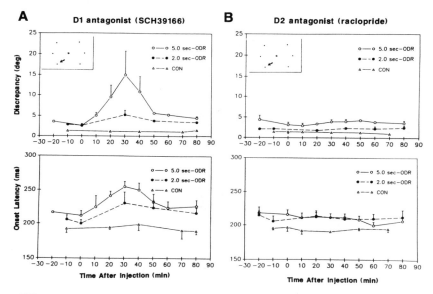

FIG. 1.6. This figure illustrates that injection of a drug (SCH23390) that antagonizes D1 receptors into the prefrontal cortex and produces a deficit restricted to one location in the visual field (arrow) approximately 20–40 min after injection; the effect is delay-dependent. Latency of response is also affected. However, in the sensory-guided task conducted in the same session, the animal's accuracy and latency are unimpaired. From Sawaguchi and Goldman-Rakic (1991). Reprinted by permission.

input, mnemonic, and output functions required in these tasks (Fuster, 1973; Kubota & Niki, 1971; Niki, 1974). These results confirm, at a neuronal level, what could be analytically derived; namely that performance on a delayed-response task involves several levels of information processing—sensory encoding, temporary storage of information, and response execution. I have hypothesized that the prefrontal cortex contains multiple working memory circuits, each dedicated to a different information-processing domain, and that, within these centers, specific classes of neuron are specialized for carrying out the subfunctions necessary to accomplish an integrated memory-driven act (Goldman-Rakic, 1987, 1988).

Several classes of neurons have been recorded in and around the principal sulcus. One of these responds only to the presentation of the cue in the ODR task (Fig. 1.7.) Most neurons of this class gave a phasic excitatory response following cue onset, with a median latency of 116 msec (see Funahashi, Bruce & Goldman-Rakic, 1990, for details). Although similar neurons have been recorded previously in manual delayed-response tasks (e.g., Fuster, 1973), the use of visual perimetry (i.e., presenting the visual cue in a number of positions throughout the visual field) enabled us to show that over 95% of these cells are directionally selective; that is, they increased their firing rate only for one or a few positions of the cue in the ODR task. Furthermore, most neurons had

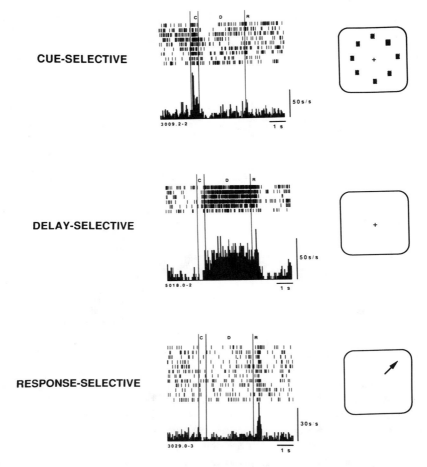

CUE-SELECTIVE

DELAY-SELECTIVE

RESPONSE-SELECTIVE

FIG. 1.7. Summary of major neuronal responses observed in neurons recorded from the dorsolateral prefrontal cortex. This cell at the top responds in a phasic manner to the presentation of the sensory cue but returns to baseline during the period of the delay. The cell in the middle panel increases its discharge dramatically when the cue disappears from view and fires tonically throughout the delay, ceasing abruptly when the response is initiated. The cell in the lowest panel is responding phasically in relation to the response. A large majority of cells of each class are directionally selective, responding only to cues from a particular radial direction.

their "best directions" (the target to which the neuron responded most strongly) in the visual field contralateral to the recording. Thus, a class of prefrontal neuron in and near the principal sulcus accesses specific information about the spatial coordinates of objects in the visual world and all polar directions within the peripheral visual fields are represented.

The largest class of task-related neurons in the prefrontal cortex are those that increase or decrease their discharge in a directionally selective pattern during the delay period (Fig. 1.7, middle). Such neurons discharge most vigorously (or are inhibited) when the to-be-remembered stimulus disappears from view and during the period that motor action is deferred, thus making them particularly relevant to the memory process. Indeed, a given neuron is consistently activated during the delay period for only one or a few locations in space, and different neurons code different locations. For example, a neuron may be activated during the delay only when the monkey had to remember the target at the 270° location. The same neuron's activity is suppressed at the 90° location and does not differ significantly from baseline firing when the target was presented at all other locations. We have termed the neuron's activation to a specific best direction its *memory field* in analogy to the receptive fields of sensory cortical neurons (Funahashi et al., 1989). When we plotted the best directions for the entire sample of neurons with directional memory fields in polar coordinates, we discovered that different neurons coded different locations preferentially, and that there was a bias for representing the contralateral visual field in memory (Funahashi et al., 1989).

Almost one fourth of task-related neurons are related to the motor response, with latencies ranging from −192 msec to 460 msec within the initiation of the saccadic responses required in the ODR task (Funahashi, Bruce & Goldman-Rakic, 1991). The majority of the oculomotor responses are postsaccadic; that is, they increased firing after the initiation of the eye movement, although a smaller percentage are also presaccadic, discharging in advance of the response. Both presaccadic and postsaccadic responses, like delay-period and cue-period activity, are directionally specific, again favoring contralateral fields. Oculomotor activity was registered in neurons unaccompanied by cue- and delay-period activity, again indicating that separate neurons code different events in the task. However, it should be underscored that a neuron's response can be related to more than one event in the ODR task. For example, many neurons with delay-period activity also responded in relation to the cue, to the response, or to both cue and response.

CONCLUSIONS

The ability of a monkey to keep a location of an object in mind is not unlike the ability of humans to keep a phone number or the name of a person in mind. If, as we have argued, the classical and contemporary versions of delayed-response tasks measure working memory processes in nonhuman primates, then these cellular responses must be considered essential elements of local circuits designed to carry out this process. As reviewed here, a spatial cognitive center is located in and around the principal sulcus of the prefrontal cortex. Furthermore, memory cells for specific target locations appear to be organized in a type of memory map in which small territories of cortex, possibly cortical columns or modules, mediate the memory function of one or a few polar directions. Finally, memories can be located at the cellular level with a given cell coding one or a few target locations and different cells coding different locations. There is every reason to believe that similar neurons play some role in the integrated process that underlies spatial memory functions in humans and that these cells subserve spatial comprehension, spatial thought, and spatial problem solving in humans. Indeed, frontal lobe patients have been shown to be impaired on a range of other tasks requiring working memory (Milner, Petrides, & Smith, 1985).

Finally, we have proposed that the prefrontal cortex is generally concerned with guiding behavior based on internal representations of the outside world. For the most part, those representations are formed and stored in multiple segregated portions of the parietal and temporal lobes. The prefrontal cortex provides the mechanism needed to draw upon that knowledge, bring it "on line" to bear on current decisions and to guide behavior at the moment. Different portions of prefrontal cortex match up with different representational systems, such that we could say that different regions of the prefrontal cortex are involved in regulating behavior by different representational domains. If the prefrontal cortex is damaged severely and bilaterally, an animal will guide its behavior correctly only if there are reliable stimuli in the outside world to provide external guidance. Otherwise, the behavior will be disconnected from the knowledge base and it will be incoherent, fragmented, and erratic. It will be impulsive and the animal will be highly distracted by environmental stimuli, because the mechanism of behavioral guidance will be drawn to the outside, rather than the inside. Most relevant for conditions like Williams syndrome, basic neurobiological considerations allow that guidance in one knowledge domain can be spared whereas behavior in another domain could be impaired. The developmental basis of the disorder is thus not likely to be a generalized condition affecting the entire cortical mass but a set of factors that target one or a few subsystems specifically. It is difficult to imagine that a system as precisely organized as the spatial cognitive system described earlier could be replaced by areas specialized for other functions, but this matter is now open for study on an informed basis.

REFERENCES

Baddeley, A. D. (1983). Working memory. *Philosophical Transactions Royal Society London B Biological Sciences*, 302, 311–324.

Bellugi, U., Klima, E. S., & Siple, P. (1989). Remembering in signs. *Cognition*, 3, 93–125.

Carpenter, P. A., & Just, M. A. (1988). The role of working memory in language comprehension. In D. Klahr & K. Kotovsky (Eds.), *Complex information processing: The impact of Herbert A. Simon*. Hillsdale, NJ: Lawrence Erlbaum Associates.

Economo, C. von, & Koskinas, G. N. (1925). *Die cytoarchitectonic der Hirnrinde des erwachsenen Menschen*. Berlin:Springer.

Edelman, G. M., Gall, E. W., & Cowan, W. M. (1984). Dynamic aspects of neocortical function. New York: Wiley.

Funahashi, S., Bruce, C. J., & Goldman-Rakic, P. S. (1989). Mnemonic coding of visual space in the monkey's dorsolateral prefrontal cortex. *Journal of Neurophysiology, 61,* 331–349.

Funahashi, S., Bruce, C. J., & Goldman-Rakic, P. S. (1990). Visuospatial coding in primate prefrontal neurons revealed by oculomotor paradigms. *Journal of Neurophysiology, 63,* 814–831.

Funahashi, S., Bruce C. J., & Goldman-Rakic, P. S. (1991). Neuronal activity related to saccadic eye movements in the monkey's dorsolateral prefrontal cortex. *Journal of Neurophysiology, 65*(6), 1464–1483.

Funahashi, S., Bruce, C. J., & Goldman-Rakic, P. S. (1993) *Dorsolateral prefrontal lesions and oculomotor delayed-response performance: Evidence for mnemonic scotoma. Journal of Neuroscience, 13,* 1479–1497.

Fuster, J. M. (1973). Unit activity in prefrontal cortex during delayed-response performance: Neuronal correlates of transient memory. *Journal of Neurophysiology, 36,* 61–78.

Fuster, J. M. (1989). *The prefrontal cortex* (2nd ed.). New York: Raven.

Goldman, P. S., & Rosvold, H. E. (1970). Localization of function within the dorsolateral prefrontal cortex of the rhesus monkey. *Experimental Neurology, 27,* 291–304.

Goldman-Rakic, P. S. (1984). Modular organization of prefrontal cortex. *Trends in Neuroscience, 7,* 419–424.

Goldman-Rakic, P. S. (1987). Circuitry of the prefrontal cortex and the regulation of behavior by representational knowledge. In F. Plum & V. Mountcastle (Eds.), *Handbook of physiology,* (Vol. 5, p. 373). Bethesda, MD: American Physiological Society.

Goldman-Rakic, P. S. (1988). Topography of cognition: Parallel distributed networks in primate association cortex. *Annual Review of Neuroscience, 11,* 137–156.

Hebb, D. O. (1949). *Organization of behavior*. New York: Wiley.

Kubota, K., & Niki, H. (1971). Prefrontal cortical unit activity and delayed cortical unit activity and delayed alternation performance in monkeys. *Journal of Neurophysiology, 34,* 337–347.

Lashley, K. S. (1929). *Brain mechanisms and intelligence: A quantitative study of injuries to the brain*. Chicago: University of Chicago Press.

Milner, B., Petrides, M., & Smith, M. L. (1985). Frontal lobes and the temporal organization of memory. *Human Neurobiology, 4,* 137–142.

Niki, H. (1974). Differential activity of prefrontal units during right and left delayed response trials. *Brain Research, 70,* 346–349.

Passingham, R. (1975). Delayed matching after selective prefrontal lesions in monkeys (*Macaca mulatta*). *Brain Research, 92,* 89–102.

Pons, T. P., Garraghty, P. E., Ommaya, A. K., Kaas, J. H., Taub, E., & Mishkin, M. (1991). Massive cortical reorganization after sensory deafferentation in adult monkeys. *Science, 252,* 1857–1860.

Rajkowska, G. & Goldman-Rakic, P. S. (in press-a). Cytoarchitectonic definition of prefrontal areas in the normal human cortex: I: Cytoarchitectonics remapping using quantitative criteria. Cerebral Cortex, 1994.

Rajkowska, G. & Goldman-Rakic, P. S. (in press-b). Cytoarchitectonic definition of prefrontal areas in the normal human cortex: II: Variability in locations of Areas 9 and 46 and relationship to the talairach coordinate system. Cerebral Cortex, 1994.

Sarkissov, S. A., Filimonoff, I. N., Kononova, I. P., (1955). *Preobrazenskaja NS, Kukueva LA* [Atlas of the cytoarchitectonics of the human cerebral cortex]. Moscow: Medgiz.

Sawaguchi, T. & Goldman-Rakic, P. S. (1991) D1 dopamine receptors in prefrontal cortex: Involvement in working memory, Science, 251, 947–950.

Squire, L. R. & Zola-Morgan, S. (1991) The medial temporal lobe memory system. Science, 1380–1386.

Part II

STUDIES OF DEVELOPMENTAL DISORDERS

Section 1

WILLIAMS SYNDROME

2

Williams Syndrome: An Unusual Neuropsychological Profile

Ursula Bellugi
The Salk Institute for Biological Studies

Paul P. Wang
The Salk Institute for Biological Studies

Terry L. Jernigan
Veterans Affairs Medical Center and UCSD School of Medicine

As a genetic experiment of nature, Williams syndrome (WS) is expressed on multiple biological levels. Ultimately, WS presents an unusual neurobehavioral profile, affording the opportunity to study both neurobiology and neuropsychology within a single, genetically defined paradigm. The Salk Institute's Laboratory for Cognitive Neuroscience (LCN) has been engaged in a comprehensive program of study that spans multiple biological levels in WS. These levels include the linguistic, the neuropsychological, the neuroanatomic, the neurophysiologic, and the genetic. The fundamental goal of these combined investigations is to help elucidate the brain bases of behavior.

In this chapter, we first present the unusual neuropsychological profile of WS, a profile of peaks and valleys of abilities within and across domains of higher cognitive functioning. We then review the results of recent studies on the neuroanatomic basis of WS and its neurophysiological characteristics, and the implications of this research program for an understanding of the neural systems that subserve language and cognitive functioning. A more complete discussion of the neuroanatomic and neurophysiologic investigations in WS is presented in the chapters that follow. Important to note, these cross-disciplinary studies are all carried out on the same subjects, and thus give us the unusual opportunity to relate findings from cognitive, neuroanatomical, and neurophysiological levels.

OVERVIEW OF WILLIAMS SYNDROME

Williams syndrome is a rare genetic disorder, first identified in 1961 by the cardiologist Williams and his associates (Williams, Barratt-Boyes, & Lowe, 1961). They described four children with supravalvar aortic stenosis in association with mental retardation and a characteristic facial appearance. It is now recognized that the syndrome also commonly includes other abnormalities of the cardiovascular system, as well as of the renal, musculoskeletal, endocrine, and other organ systems (Jones & Smith, 1975; Martin, Snodgrass, & Cohen, 1984; Morris, Demsey, Leonard, Dilts, & Blackburn, 1988). The overall incidence of WS has been estimated at a rare 1 in 25,000 live births. Early medical observers remarked anecdotally on the "friendly and loquacious" personality of WS subjects and their "unusual command of language" (Von Arnim & Engel, 1964), but no systematic investigation of specific cognitive domains was undertaken until recently.

A psychophysical feature of this genetic disorder is an unusual sensitivity to certain environmental sounds, manifested in specific ways: (a) an awareness of sounds before others in the environment, and (b) an aversion to sounds not usually considered aversive in normal populations (Bellugi, Bihrle, Doherty, Neville, & Damasio, 1989; Udwin, Yule, & Martin, 1987). The implications of WS subjects' sensitivity to sounds is considered in chapter 4 of this volume.

The genetic basis of WS has been established recently by Morris' identification of a father–son pair, both with Williams syndrome (C. Morris personal communication, October 1991). The mode of transmission is therefore likely to be autosomal dominant, with most cases representing new mutations. According to McKusick (1988), WS is an autosomal dominant disorder characterized by supravalvar aortic stenosis, peripheral pulmonary stenosis, elfin facies, mental retardation, statural deficiencies, characteristic dental malformations, and hypercalcemia. The hypercalcemia of Williams syndrome is associated with abnormal regulation of serum calcitonin (Culler, Jones, & Deftos, 1985), and, we have hypothesized, possible abnormalities related to the neuropeptide CGRP (calcitonin-gene related peptide) (Bellugi, Bihrle, Jernigan, Trauner, & Doherty, 1990). Molecular studies are underway to determine the specific location and nature of the gene responsible for WS.

Previous Studies. Mental retardation is probably the most common feature of WS, next to the defining facies. Large surveys have shown a prevalence of 95%, with full-scale IQs usually falling in the range of mild to moderate retardation (Arnold, Yule, & Martin, 1985; Jones & Smith, 1975; Morris et al., 1988; Udwin et al., 1987). This retardation is evident also in the adaptive behavior of WS subjects. They uniformly require special educational placements, and their academic accomplishment lags far behind that of age-matched peers. Even in adulthood, the vast majority of WS subjects have only rudimentary skills in reading, writing, and arithmetic (Udwin, 1990). As a consequence, WS adults generally reside with their parents or in supervised group homes.

To date, most published research on WS children's neuropsychological functioning was based primarily on standard achievement tests and IQ measures with little attempt to probe specific domains of cognitive functions, with uneven or no controls, and across different age groups. Behavioral studies that have appeared show conflicting outcomes and report inconsistent findings. For example, although some studies report that verbal abilities surpass nonverbal performance abilities, others report the opposite, concluding that linguistic abilities are not superior to nonlinguistic abilities (Arnold et al., 1985; Crisco & Dobbs, 1988; Kataria, Goldstein, & Kushnick, 1984). One limitation of these studies is that verbal abilities are assessed by instruments that confound linguistic with other cognitive processing, and thus do not permit differential assessment of specific domains of functioning.

SUBJECTS AND PROGRAM

The results we report here represent multidisciplinary studies with carefully selected adolescent WS subjects. We chose to begin our studies with WS subjects at a point at which many of the basic milestones of language and cognitive functioning had been attained, and thus these studies were conducted with subjects 10 years of age and above. Subject selection criteria were both inclusive and exclusive and were strictly observed, requiring diagnosis by a medical geneticist with confirmation by dysmorphologist Dr. Kenneth Lyons Jones, a colleague at the University of California at San Diego, who has long been involved in important studies delineating the consistent features of WS for purposes of diagnosis (Jones & Smith, 1975). Moreover, the clinical diagnosis was confirmed where possible with the use of a neuroendocrine marker developed by Dr. Floyd Culler (Bellugi & Culler, 1987; Culler et al., 1985).

Over 100 WS subjects have been tested by the LCN, to date. The results presented here focus primarily on a core group of 10 adolescents, ranging in age from 10 to 20 years (Bellugi et al., 1990; Bellugi, Bihrle, Neville, Jernigan, & Doherty, 1992). They are contrasted with Down syndrome (DS) subjects, matched for age, sex, and mental function on IQ measures. (Mean full scale IQs were 50.8 for the WMS group, and 48.8 for the DS group. Mean ages were 14.4 and 15.4 years, respectively.) In addition, subjects from each group were generally in similar classrooms for educable mentally retarded students. The DS adolescents were chosen to provide a relatively homogeneous control group of mentally retarded subjects, although further studies are showing that this group also may exhibit a specific and nonuniform profile of neurobehavioral abilities.

In order to evaluate components of language and cognition in WS, we are engaged in a program of systematic studies of the neurobehavioral profile of adolescents and adults. A number of these studies are undertaken in the context of a multiinstitutional, multidisciplinary National Institutes of Health-sponsored Center for the Study of the Neurological Bases of Language and Communication Disorders. The WS and DS subjects undergo neurological examination (Trauner, Bellugi, & Chase, 1989), metabolic screening, and diagnostic behavioral screening. These same subjects have had magnetic resonance imaging (MRI; Jernigan & Bellugi, 1990; see also chapter 3 of this volume), and take part in neurophysiological studies (Bellugi et al., 1992; see also chapter 4 of this volume), as well as our battery of neurobehavioral studies. Moreover, the WS subjects are involved in our studies of the neurobiological basis of the disorder. These investigations apply experimental probes to test the specific abilities of WS subjects, as well as subjects with specific language impairment, certain metabolic disorders, and children with focal lesions to the right or left hemisphere.

EQUIVALENT COGNITIVE IMPAIRMENT IN WS AND DS

Studies from the LCN show not only that WS and DS subjects are equivalently low on IQ tests, but also that they characteristically fail on other cognitive probes, including Piagetian tests of conservation skills (for number, weight, and substance) and seriation skills (Bellugi, Marks, Bihrle, & Sabo, 1988; Bellugi, Sabo, & Vaid, 1988). These tasks tap general cognitive ability and are normally mastered early in the course of cognitive development. Figure 2.1a illustrates an example of conservation of volume: A quantity of water transferred from one container to another retains the same volume regardless of the shape of the container. Figure 2.1b shows the uniformly poor performance of WS adolescents: Whereas mental age-matched controls have full command of the concept of conservation, WS subjects exhibit no evidence of such mastery. We note that their matched DS counterparts fail similarly on the same tasks.

Equivalent deficits in WS and DS in the general cognitive skills needed for concept formation are exhibited on the Reitan-Indiana version of the Category Test (Bellugi et al., 1992). This test requires subjects to note similarities and differences in stimuli and to formulate hypotheses regarding the principles used to organize the stimuli. Although normal subjects readily discern these organizational principles, the matched WS and DS adolescents require markedly more training in the task, do not seem able to benefit from examiner feedback, and ultimately perform well below their chronological

a.

Conservation of Liquid

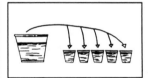

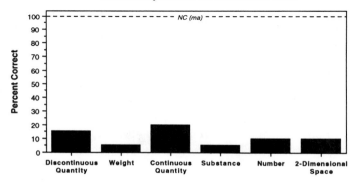

b.

Williams Performance on Conservation Tasks

FIG. 2.1. Understanding of the Piagetian concept of conservation in WMS. (a) Illustration of the Piagetian concept of conservation. The total quantity of water remains the same regardless of the shape of the container. (b) Williams syndrome subjects perform at very low levels on tasks of conservation, equivalent to the level of 4- or 5-year-olds. Normal children show near perfect performance by 8 years of age.

age, at the level of 7-year-olds. In summary, both WS and DS subjects in our sample are markedly impaired on a range of purely cognitive tasks such as conservation, concept formation, and problem solving, despite differences in performance on linguistic probes (see following discussion).

SPARED LANGUAGE ABILITIES IN WS BUT NOT DS

In the setting of this general cognitive impairment, the expressive language of WS adolescent subjects is dramatically different from the language of matched DS subjects. Consider, for example, an excerpt from the spontaneous and fluent speech of an 18-year-old WS subject (IQ of 49) as she described her aims in life. She said, "You are looking at a professional bookwriter. My books will be filled with drama, action, and excitement. And everyone will want to read them. . . . I am going to write books, page after page, stack after stack. I'm going to start on Monday.'' This young WS woman shows great facility with language and is even able to weave vivid stories of imaginary events and to compose lyrics to a love song. However, she fails all Piagetian seriation and conservation tasks, has academic skills comparable to those of a first-grader, and requires a babysitter for supervision. This unusual dissociation of language from other cognitive functions forms the basis for this series of studies. Here, we discuss tests of grammatical ability, semantic skills, and the interplay of linguistics with expression of affect.

Sparing of Syntax in WS

Language is not a unitary phenomenon. Rather it is composed of distinct components whose separate workings can be seen most clearly under unusual circumstances. WS subjects provide a powerful vehicle for investigating the separability of linguistic and cognitive functioning, and even the components of language itself. Until now, there have been very few investigations of the linguistic capacities of WS subjects. Results from our studies suggest that although our WS and DS subjects are comparably impaired cognitively, and in fact are selected on the basis of equivalent IQ scores, the differences between the two groups are highly marked in the linguistic domain, with WS subjects showing an unusual profile of dissociations. Analyses of their language production indicates that lexical and grammatical abilities are remarkably spared in adolescent WS subjects, given the extent of their cognitive deficits (Bellugi, Marks, Bihrle, & Sabo, 1988; Bellugi, Sabo, & Vaid, 1988).

The grammatical facility of WS subjects—and their difference from IQ- and age-matched DS subjects—is apparent on formal tests of comprehension. The WS adolescents perform much better than their DS matches, and nearly at ceiling on tests of comprehension of passive sentences, negation, and conditionals (Fig. 2.2a) (Bellugi et al., 1990). For example, on a test of comprehension of passive sentences, the WS subjects perform at a mean of above 90%, choosing correctly among the possible pictorial representations of the test sentences. The test sentences employed, semantically reversible passives, such as ''the horse is chased by the man,'' cannot be solved solely from the knowledge of word meanings. They require an understanding of the underlying syntax of the sentence. Although DS subjects characteristically do poorly on such tests, WS subjects give evidence of good syntactic comprehension and processing.

The ability to detect and correct anomalies in the syntax of a sentence depends on knowledge of syntactic constraints and the ability to reflect upon grammatical form. These are sophisticated metalinguistic abilities that may be mastered considerably after the acquisition of grammar and may never fully

Language Processing Tasks

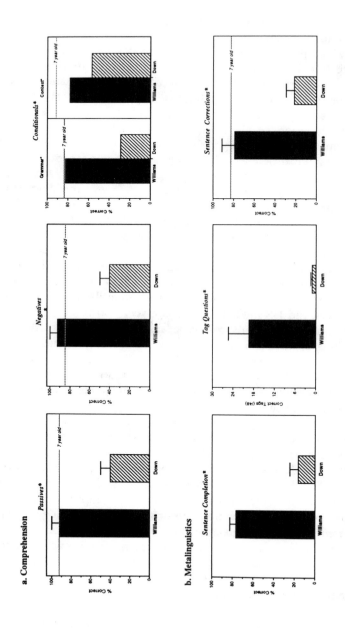

FIG. 2.2. Performance on sentence-processing tasks in WS and DS. Williams syndrome subjects show significantly better performance than Down syndrome subjects on (a) tests of sentence comprehension, and (b) metalinguistic tasks requiring the subject to correct ungrammatical sentences or to otherwise manipulate sentences.

develop in certain at-risk populations. We are finding that the WS subjects' remarkable linguistic abilities extend to tests of metalinguistic abilities in language as well (Bellugi et al., 1992). Fig. 2.2b shows results from tests of sentence completion, sentence correction, and the correct completion of syntactically complex tag questions. Such probes require the subjects to contemplate language as an object, by asking them to massage a stimulus sentence into new grammatical forms or to correct ungrammatical sentences. The "tag question" task requires subjects to supply a specific syntactic form, which serves as a request for confirmation, as in "John and Mary like apples, *don't they?*" Provision of tag questions involves mastery of the rules of question formation, the auxiliary verb system, pronoun usage, and negation, all for a trifling semantic effect. WS subjects show good performance on a probe for the linguistic ability to form tag questions, whereas DS subjects are essentially unable to perform this linguistic task. On a metalinguistic task involving sentence correction, subjects are presented with sentences that may be ungrammatical, for example, "I hope you to eat all your supper." Subjects are asked to monitor and correct ungrammatical examples. Although one WS subject correctly responded, "I hope that you will eat all your supper," the DS match was unable to provide a correct answer, and instead responded, "Chicken." There were significant differences across the board between the two groups on these linguistic and metalinguistic probes, with WS subjects performing well and DS subjects performing very poorly.

Analysis of the spontaneous expressive language of adolescent WS subjects shows that they characteristically produce well-formed, grammatically correct sentences. They characteristically employ a rich variety of grammatically complex forms, including passive sentences, conditional clauses, and embedded relative clauses, although there are occasional errors and even some systematic ones (Rubba & Klima, 1991).

Important to note then, the WS subjects are able to manipulate, process, and comprehend complex grammatical structures, and they also are able to monitor and correct ungrammatical sentences. Despite the occasional errors, WS subjects generally use morphological markers appropriately and correctly, including markers for tense and aspect, as well as auxiliaries and articles. By contrast, the language of the matched DS subjects is simpler and less varied in construction, often with errors and omissions in both morphology and syntax. These differences in linguistic competence, on both production and comprehension tasks, evidence a remarkable preservation of linguistic knowledge in WS, in the context of otherwise widespread general cognitive impairment.

Unusual Semantic Organization

WS adolescents clearly show that they have understanding of words and are able to provide appropriate contexts of use. Unlike DS subjects, they often use unusual words in spontaneous conversation, exhibiting considerable knowledge about words, that belies their lack of cognitive understanding of the world. The WS subjects' knowledge of the meanings of words is exhibited on standard tests of word knowledge, such as the Peabody Picture Vocabulary Test (Fig. 2.3). The WS subjects were often able to correctly match a word to one of four possible pictures, even with advanced items such as

"Show me cooperation."

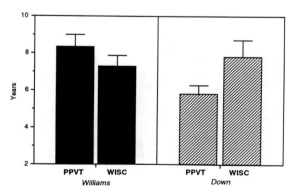

b. *Vocabulary vs. Mental Age*

FIG. 2.3. Comparison of semantic knowledge and IQ in WS and DS. (a) Example of an item from the Peabody Picture Vocabulary Tests, testing knowledge of the word *cooperation*. (b) In Williams syndrome, semantic knowledge (given as age-equivalent score) often surpasses IQ-age, whereas semantic knowledge is significantly lower than IQ-age in matched Down syndrome subjects.

abrasive, *cooperation*, and *solemn*. As the figure shows, the WS subjects characteristically score above their mental age, whereas the DS counterparts typically score below their mental age, accentuating the differences between the two groups.

However, studies from LCN have found that WS subjects show both a preservation of ability and a possible deviance in that ability (Bellugi et al., 1992). For example, the spontaneous language of WS adolescents often includes unusual word choices, such as "The bees abort the beehive" (meaning "they leave the hive") and "I'll have to evacuate the glass" (meaning "empty the glass"). This unusual semantic organization is also seen on tests of word fluency (Bellugi et al., 1990). When asked to name as many animals as they can in a minute, WS subjects provide significantly more responses than DS subjects do (Fig. 2.4). Whereas DS responses are typically fewer, and more often involve perseverations or category errors (e.g., *horsie*, *dog*, *ice cream*), WS responses are nearly all within category; moreover, they are peppered with unusual items such as *weasel*, *newt*, *salamander*, *chihuahua*, *ibex*, and *yak*. We have found that WS adolescents give a larger number of uncommon responses than do control children who are matched on the number of common responses. (Here, commonality refers to the frequency with which a word appears in reading materials [Carrol, Davies, & Richman, 1971].) Only normals who give a greater number of common responses give as many uncommon items as WS adolescents. Thus, WS subjects show a proclivity for unusual words that is not seen in either matched normal or DS subjects.

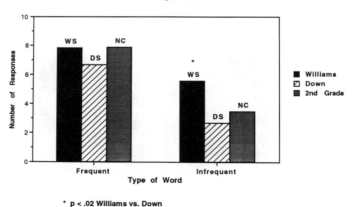

Semantic   Organization

* p < .02 Williams vs. Down
p < .05 Williams vs. 2nd Grade

FIG. 2.4.   Unusual semantic organization in WS. WS, DS, and second-grade control children give similar numbers of frequent items, but WS children give significantly more infrequent items.

Preservation of Narrative in WS Subjects

Beyond the abilities needed for the production and comprehension of syntactically well-formed sentences lie narrative and discourse abilities. They include the ability to structure a story and the skills necessary for fluent and cohesive conversation. Moreover, the components of good storytelling include both paralinguistic devices (e.g., affective prosody) and lexically encoded devices (references to affective states, other frames of mind, causal connectors, etc.) that allow the narrator to highlight particularly significant developments in the stories and are relevant to the capacity to engage an audience's interest and maintain it. The abilities of WS and DS subjects in these areas were assessed on a story telling task (Reilly, Klima, & Bellugi, 1991). A wordless picture book *Frog, Where Are You?* (Mayer, 1969) illustrates in pictures the adventures of a boy and a dog during their search for a lost frog. (A sample illustration appears in Fig. 2.5a.) Subjects are asked to tell a story from the pictures as they progress page by page through the book. No framework is provided to the subjects beyond the pictures themselves.

On analysis of their responses to this task, marked differences were found between the matched WS and DS subjects. The number of WS utterances was on average three times that obtained from the DS subjects, and the mean length of utterance by WS subjects averaged three to four times longer than for the DS subjects. The spontaneous language displayed by WS subjects was phonologically and syntactically sophisticated and also effective in using subordinate clauses to foreground and background information. This is in stark contrast to language samples from the matched DS counterparts. Characteristically, DS subjects provided minimal descriptions of the individual pictures, often in simple fragments that were not well-formed sentences. Moreover, the DS subjects frequently failed to establish an orientation for the story and provided no cohesion from one picture to the next. Many of these subjects failed to explain that the boy and the dog were searching for the frog. In short, they often seemed to miss the point of the story. By way of contrast, WS subjects characteristically provide well-structured narrations, establishing a clear orientation, introducing time, characters, and their states and behaviors ("Once upon a time, when it was dark at night"), stating the problem ("Next morning . . . there was no frog to be found"), and including a resolution ("Lo and behold, they find him"). In short, the WS subjects' narratives, in contrast to those of the DS, tended to be well-formed stories, with well-formed story grammar and a variety of narrative enrichment devices, as we explain next.

Narratives as a Context for Affective Expression in WS

The modulation of voice tone and stress, evident in linguistic expressions such as "OH, my POOOOOOR little wabbit," is a paralinguistic affective

a.

b.

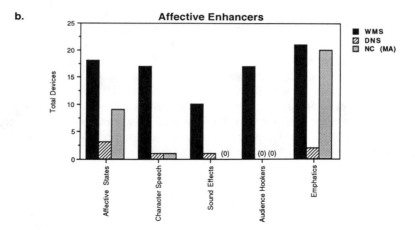

FIG. 2.5. Use of affective enhancers in narration. (a) Schematic of a page from the picture book narration task, reported in Reilly, Klima and Bellugi, 1991. (b) WS subjects use a greater number of various linguistic devices to affectively enrich their narrations than do DS or control children. From Reilly et al. (1991). Adapted by permission.

device. Language may be emotionally enriched through the use of such devices, as well as through the use of lexically encoded devices (i.e., the use of words that refer to emotion and affect). We examined the ability of WS and DS subjects to use such devices to express affect and to engage the audience on the same frog story narration task (Reilly et al., 1991).

In their frog story narrations, WS subjects were found to use affective prosody far more frequently than either DS matches or normal children with a higher mental age. In fact, WS subjects continued to use high levels of affective prosody even on second and third retellings of the story. (In this respect, their expressivity contrasts markedly with both normal child behavior and that of disordered populations such as autistic subjects). This extensive use of prosody by WS subjects confirms observations of affective expressivity in their casual conversations as well as in their storytelling.

The affective richness of the WS narratives was also reflected in their lexical choices. Their narratives included frequent comments on the affective state of the characters in the stories (e.g., "And ah! he was amazed" or "The dog gets worried and the boy gets mad"), as well as the use of dramatic devices such as sound effects and character speech ("And BOOM, millions of bees came out and tried to sting him" or "He goes, 'Ouch! oh uh get outta here bumblebees' "). These devices were notably absent in the DS subjects' tellings. The attention of WS narrators to the state of their storytelling audience was evident through their use of exclamatory phrases and other audience engagement devices that convey surprise to the listener, such as "Suddenly splash! The water came up" or "Lo and behold" and "Gadzooks! The boy and the dog start flipping over." The unique proclivity for WS narrators to employ a wide variety of affective enhancers is shown in Fig. 2.5b, compared to DS subjects and controls.

In summary the WS stories are replete with narrative enhancement devices, which contribute immensely to the drama and immediacy of the story and to the impression that adolescents with WS are extremely expressive. It is clear that despite their mental retardation and severe cognitive deficits, WS subjects are able to employ paralinguistic and linguistic devices for expressive purposes and to maintain audience interest. The contrast between children with WS, children with DS, and autistic children is marked and illuminating. The fact that the WS subjects continue to use the same level of expressivity regardless of how many times they have told the story, and irrespective of their audience, suggests that their extreme expressivity may turn out to be aberrant. In general, these findings corroborate the anecdotal experience of parents and professional caretakers of WS subjects. WS adolescents appear acutely attentive to the emotional state of others and often express exquisite emotions themselves. In contrast to the flatter affectual appearance of DS subjects, WS subjects are animated and vivid in their everyday deportment.

PEAKS AND VALLEYS OF ABILITY IN SPATIAL COGNITION IN WS

Unlike language, which includes the well-defined components of phonology, morphology, syntax, semantics, and prosody, spatial cognition has resisted fractionation into components (Stiles-Davis, Kritchevsky, & Bellugi, 1988).

Studies from the LCN are showing, however, that WS subjects display a markedly nonuniform pattern even within the domain of spatial cognition. The WS subjects' pattern of peaks and valleys of spatial performance may provide insight into the structural components of spatial cognition. Here we review the remarkable profile of preservation and impairment in spatial cognition in WS, in contrast with matched DS counterparts.

Marked Dissociation Between Linguistic and Spatial Cognition in WS

On many visuospatial tasks, we have found that WS subjects perform poorly (Bellugi et al., 1990; Bellugi, Sabo, & Vaid, 1988). For example, WS subjects show tremendous difficulty on a simple test of spatial perception—the Benton Line Orientation Test. This test requires subjects to designate which of several slanted lines matches the orientation of model lines. Both WS and DS subjects fail on this task, characteristically unable to complete even the practice items correctly. On a standardized visuoconstructive measure, the Developmental Test of Visuo-Motor Integration, subjects are required to copy a series of figures (lines, triangles, and combinations of forms). On this task, both WS and DS subjects are markedly impaired, with WS subjects at a mean age equivalent of 4;8 years and DS at 5;6 years. We note that WS subjects appeared to show a selective disability on items that required integration of component parts (a triangle made out of circles).

The dramatic dissociation between WS visuospatial skills and their linguistic abilities is clearly illustrated in Fig. 2.6, which compares the drawing of an elephant with the verbal description of one by a WS subject, age 18 years with an IQ of 49. The drawing shown is typical of the impoverished and disorganized drawings produced by the WS adolescents in our studies. Without the subject's verbal labels, the drawing would be unrecognizable. By contrast, the linguistic description is fluent and rich (what an elephant is, what an elephant does, and what an elephant has . . . "It has long grey ears, fan ears, ears that can blow in the wind. It has a long trunk that can pick up grass or pick up hay"). Indeed, WS subjects often seem to talk their way through drawings, as if using their verbal skills to mediate the severely impaired act of drawing, although the results often belie this effort (Fig. 2.6). In general, WS subjects, like right-hemisphere-damaged patients with lesions in the parietal lobe, often depict the parts of an object scattered on the page, with no attempt at integration into functional objects, and fail to represent spatial orientation, perspective, or depth (Bellugi, Poizner, & Klima, 1989; Bihrle, 1990; Bihrle, Bellugi, Delis, & Marks, 1989).

Local and Global Modes of Processing

In the context of their low-scoring results on some visuospatial tasks, an analysis of the characteristics of WS versus DS responses is highly revealing.

Contrast Between Visuo-Spatial and Language Abilities in Williams Syndrome

a.

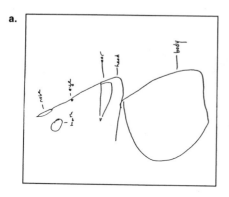

b.

And what an elephant is, it is one of the animals. And what the elephant does, it lives in the jungle. It can also live in the zoo. And what it has, it has long gray ears, fan ears, ears that can blow in the wind. It has a long trunk that can pick up grass, or pick up hay....If they're in a bad mood it can be terrible...If the elephant gets mad it could stomp;   It could charge, like a bull can charge.   They have long big tusks.   They can damage a car...It could be dangerous. When they're in a pinch, when they're in a bad mood it can be terrible.   You don't want an elephant as a pet.   You want a cat or a dog or a bird...

FIG. 2.6. Contrast between visuospatial and language abilities in WS. (a) Drawing of an elephant by an 18-year-old WS woman, whose IQ is 49. (b) Her verbal description of an elephant.

Consider the Block Design subtest of the Wechsler Intelligence Scale for Children–Revised (WISC–R), where both WS and DS subjects score extremely poorly. When we examine the final performance on the designs, we find that the processes by which they arrive at their poor scores demonstrate remarkably different approaches (Bihrle, 1990; Bihrle et al., 1989). Although they fail to provide correct designs, DS subjects generally adhere to the overall configuration of the block arrangements, with internal configurations of the designs incorrect. WS subjects, by contrast, fail to adhere to the global conformation of the designs, appearing biased to the details of the designs, as shown in Fig. 2.7. We note that the DS responses, with errors of internal detail, resemble the performance of left-hemisphere-damaged patients, whereas the WS responses exhibit a fragmented approach as is typical of right-hemisphere-damaged patients on this task. Thus the two groups show marked processing differences between them with respect to parts and wholes of objects.

An experimental task that distinguishes local and global features more rigorously was employed to investigate and characterize these visuoconstructive impairments. In the Delis Hierarchical Processing Test (Fig. 2.8a) each stimulus item is composed of local components that together take a recognizable global form (i.e., a big *D* made up of little *Y*s). When asked to copy these items, WS subjects reliably draw only the local features and do not configure them in the correct global arrangement. DS subjects on the other hand draw the global figure correctly, but omit all of the local detail (Bihrle, 1990; Bihrle et al., 1989). These results (see Fig. 2.8b) suggest an unusual processing pattern in WS, a specific pattern identifiable within the context of poor overall performance.

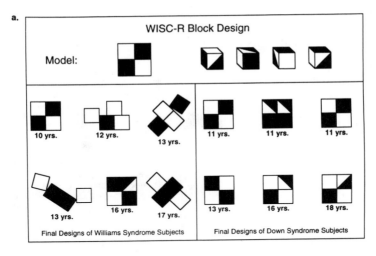

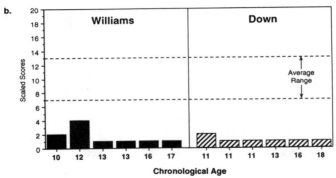

FIG. 2.7. Contrasting block design performance in WS and DS. (a) On the Block Design subtest of the WISC–R, both WS and DS designs reveal striking differences in their errors. WS subjects uniquely fail to reproduce the correct global configuration of blocks. (b) However, these differences are not reflected in quantitative scores, which are comparably low. From Bihrle, Bellugi, Delis, and Marks (1989). Adapted by permission. Also from Bihrle (1990). Adapted by permission.

Facial Recognition: An Island of Sparing in WS

Despite their spatial cognitive dysfunctions, there exist realms within spatial cognition where WS subjects display selective preservation of abilities. The WS subjects (but not the DS subjects) demonstrate a dramatic ability to discriminate unfamiliar faces (Bellugi et al., 1992). The Benton Test of Facial Recognition asks subjects to match either one or three of six pictures of faces with an original target photograph. The six stimulus pictures show faces at different angles and in different lighting conditions (Fig. 2.9a). On this test,

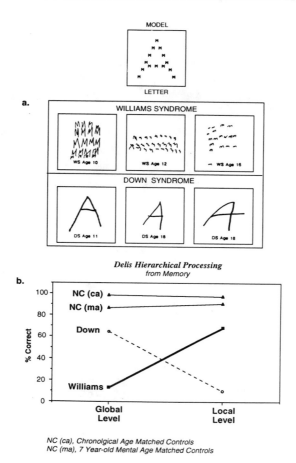

FIG. 2.8. Different error patterns in WS and DS on the Delis Hierarchical Processing Task. (a) In their reproduction of the model figure, WS subjects produce the correct local detail but omit the global configuration. DS subjects perform oppositely. (b) Quantitative assessment of these errors patterns reveals significant differences between WS and DS. From Bihrle, Bellugi, Delis, and Marks (1989). Reprinted by permission. Also from Bihrle (1990). Reprinted by permission.

WS subjects perform significantly better than their DS matches, and were significantly different from the adult control group (Fig. 2.9b). The difference between WS and DS is also found on an inverted version of the Benton Faces task, where the six match pictures are presented upside down. The DS subjects did not vary on the upright and inverted task, scoring equally poorly on both. Although the WS subjects do show a decrement on the inverted task, as do normals, they still show unusual preservation of performance.

On the Mooney Closure Test (Lansdell, 1968, Mooney, 1957); subjects are

a.

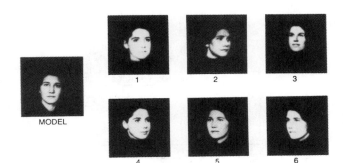

b.

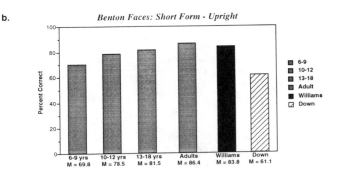

FIG. 2.9. Spared discrimination of unfamiliar faces in WS. (a) Sample items from the Benton Test of Facial Recognition. Subjects must match the picture at the left to one of the other six. (b) WS subjects perform significantly better than DS subjects on this task, and just as well as adult normal controls.

required to identify whether pictures like that in Fig. 2.10a depict a male or female person, and whether that person is young, middle-age, or old. Performance on this test has been shown to factor with closure ability rather than face recognition ability in studies of adult stroke populations (Wasserstein, Zappulla, Rosen, Gestman, & Rock, 1987). Surprisingly however, WS subjects perform very well on this task (Fig. 2.10b), even though they do poorly on other visual closure tests using nonface stimuli (Bellugi, Sabo, & Vaid, 1988). The biological organization of spatial cognition therefore appears to be different in WS than in the adult populations previously studied. The neurobiological discovery that certain cells in the superior temporal sulcus respond selectively to visually presented faces (Perrett, Rolls, & Caan, 1982) gives biological plausibility to the pattern of abilities found in WS.

WS subjects also do well in the identification of objects that are shown

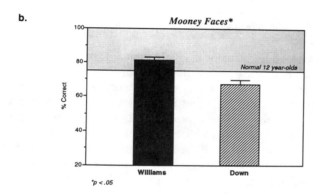

FIG. 2.10.   Mooney Closure Test. Subjects must decide whether each face is of a young, middle-age, or old man or woman. (b) WS subjects perform significantly better than DS subjects on this task, and just as well as adult normal controls.

from unusual perspectives (Bellugi & Doherty, 1990). The Canonical/Noncanonical Views Test (R. Diamond & S. Carey, personal communication, March, 1991) draws on this ability, by presenting objects either in a canonical orientation (e.g., a watering can from the side) or a noncanonical orientation (e.g., a teapot from above). On canonical orientations, WS and DS groups perform equally well, proving that they know the objects pictured. However, WS subjects perform significantly better than DS matches on noncanonical views. Results from these tests taken together suggest that WS adolescents exhibit an unusual pattern of peaks as well as valleys of abilities within spatial cognition. We discuss later the possibility that these peaks are not randomly occurring, but that they reflect the preservation of (or overreliance on) one particular cognitive processing mode.

DISSOCIATIONS IN MEMORY FUNCTION IN WS

The memory abilities of WS and DS subjects are also coming under scrutiny in the LCN, in studies of both short- and long-term memory. The digit span subtest of the WISC–R served as a starting point for these studies. It taps phonological short-term memory. Results from the same WS and DS subjects described previously show a significant difference between the two groups on digit span (Wang & Bellugi, in preparation), as shown in Fig. 2.11. On forward repetition of the digits, every WS subject was able to correctly repeat a sequence of at least 4 digits. Most DS subjects had a span of 1–3 digits, with only two subjects able to repeat a sequence of 4. On backwards repetition, WS subjects averaged 2.5 digits, but DS subjects averaged only 1.6. These group differences were observed even when subjects were not required to repeat the digits in the exact order of presentation, suggesting that the results are not accounted for by sequential ordering abilities.

Explicit Versus Implicit Memory

Long-term memory is thought to be divisible into at least two independent components. These are explicit and implicit memory. Explicit memory, also referred to as declarative memory, refers to the ability to store and retrieve information in a form that can be consciously reflected upon and expressed verbally (e.g., remembering a phone number). Implicit or nondeclarative memory refers to a heterogeneous collection of abilities, including motor skills (riding a bike), perceptual skills (reading something in a mirror), and some cognitive skills (solving certain types of puzzle problems). These different types of memory have been shown to be dissociated in particular disorders. For example, adults with Huntington's disease show preservation

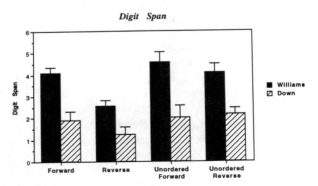

FIG. 2.11.   Digit span subtest of the WISC–R. WS subjects score significantly higher than DS subjects on both forward and reverse digit span, regardless of serial ordering considerations.

of explicit memory, but degradation of implicit motor skills, whereas Alzheimer's subjects may show the opposite pattern (Heindel, Salmon, Shults, Walicke, & Butters, 1989). Studies at the LCN are examining both explicit and implicit components of long-term memory.

Explicit skills in WS and DS were assessed with the California Verbal Learning Test–Children's Version (CVLT–C). Here, WS subjects demonstrated better preserved memory abilities than did DS subjects. In a finding related to linguistic skills, WS subjects used semantic clustering strategies in memory more often than DS subjects did. That is, presented with a list of items from three categories (e.g., toys, clothes, fruit), WS subjects are more likely to group items from the same category together when asked to recall all the items. More extensive tests of long-term explicit memory are in progress.

We have begun studies on implicit memory using a rotor pursuit task. This test of implicit motor learning requires subjects to maintain contact between a hand-held stylus and a small metallic disk that revolves on a turntable. As a pure motor task, it does not admit verbally mediated cognitive strategies. Pilot results from groups of 5 WS and 5 DS subjects suggest that WS and DS subjects have comparable initial levels of performance on this task. With practice, however, it appears that DS subjects learn more quickly and reach a higher level of performance than do WS subjects. These results suggest that at least one type of nonverbal memory and learning, as evidenced by performance benefit, is superior in DS, showing an opposite pattern of abilities than on the tests of explicit memory described earlier. However, confirmation of these results and the double dissociation of explicit and implicit mnestic abilities, will require further testing.

CONTRASTING SYNDROMIC PROFILES: BRAIN IMPLICATIONS

A general goal of our research is to relate cognitive functions to underlying neural substrates. In the case of WS, our studies show marked and specific alterations in behavioral development, pointing to the dissociability of various linguistic and cognitive functions. The resulting neuropsychological profiles of adolescent WS subjects clearly point to the possibility of abnormal development of neural systems, and the potential implications for understanding both brain function and brain structure. Such syndromic patterns of neurocognitive deficits may provide insight into the development of the neural systems underlying higher cognitive functions.

Contrast Between Linguistic and Cognitive Functions in WS

WS and DS present interesting contrasts in both language and spatial cognition. First, the language profiles in these two syndromes suggest that certain linguistic skills may become functionally independent from general cognitive ability. As the data presented earlier suggest, WS subjects are far superior to DS subjects on both receptive and expressive grammatical abilities, despite similar levels of general cognitive impairment. This broad argument for the dissociation of cognitive and linguistic skills is iterated at a more specific level, in the relationship between particular cognitive and linguistic abilities. It has been argued that mastery of the Piagetian concept of conservation, which embodies ideas of reversibility and transitivity, is a prerequisite to the full understanding of passive sentences in language and co-occurs in development in the normal child (Berlin, 1975). However, despite their manifest inability to conserve, WS subjects correctly produce and comprehend semantically reversible passive sentences (such as ''The horse is chased by the man'') without difficulty.

Semantic knowledge, which allows us to attribute meaning to words and phrases, intuitively seems dependent on our understanding of the world, items in it, and relationships among those items. In WS, we are finding evidence of semantic deviance as well as preservation, supporting the notion that semantic knowledge may depend on general cognition. So too, prosody and discourse rely on knowledge of cultural expectations, on affective astuteness, and on other aspects of cognition. WS subjects' performance on the frog stories tended to show deviantly persistent use of affective prosody. Grammar, by contrast, can more readily be construed as an independent, formal system. Thus, it would seem less likely for grammatical skill to depend on some nonlinguistic ability. The selective, nondeviant preservation of grammar in WS suggests that this may be the case.

WS, DS, and Lateralization of Brain Function

The pattern of linguistic preservation and marked spatial cognitive deficit found in WS is suggestive of the effects of right-hemisphere damage on these domains. Focal lesions (e.g., strokes) to the right hemisphere frequently spare most core linguistic functions, while severely disrupting spatial skills (Bellugi et al., 1989). This spatial cognitive disruption may consist of preservation of some spatial skills but loss of others, as in WS. The contrast between WS and DS in their respective proclivities for local and global modes of spatial processing is also reminiscent of the effects of left- and right-hemisphere damage (Delis & Bihrle, 1989; Delis, Kiefner, & Fridlund, 1988; Lamb, Robertson, & Knight, 1989). Right-hemisphere damage tends to result in a bias toward local spatial processing, as in WS. Left-hemisphere damage results in a bias toward global processing, as in DS. However, the MRI studies of Jernigan and Bellugi show no pattern of focal cerebral lesions, right or left, in either WS or DS (see chapter 3 of this volume). These studies find that dissociations between language and spatial cognition and differential modes of processing (parts vs. wholes) can arise even in the absence of lateralized focal lesions.

In WS and DS, these processing preferences presumably result from aberrant neural organization. It would be unlikely for this aberrant organization to mimic perfectly the left- and right-hemisphere differences seen in adults with focal lesions. In fact, WS teaches us something new about the behavioral patterns that may arise in a neurodevelopmental disorder. For example, in WS there is preservation of facial discrimination ability despite their other deficits and biases in spatial processing, and despite the usual pattern of right-hemisphere specialization for these tasks. In the case of the Mooney Closure Task, where we have seen that subjects with WS perform surprisingly well, it has been shown that neurological patients do worse after removal of the right temporal lobe than after removal of the left (Lansdell, 1968, 1970). Thus, the genetic paradigm that is WS results in aberrant neurodevelopment and a behavioral pattern that is distinct from the pattern revealed by split-brain and focal lesion paradigms.

We note that there are also aspects of WS language that demonstrate preservation where right-hemisphere-damaged subjects fail. The first of these is in semantic processing. As discussed previously, WS subjects make frequent use of semantic clustering strategies in verbal memory tasks. Right-hemisphere-damaged subjects, on the other hand, are impaired in their ability to use semantic clustering strategies (Villardita, 1987). This distinction is also evident on semantic fluency tasks, where subjects are asked to name as many members of a category as they can (e.g., all the animals they can think of). As discussed, WS subjects provide far more responses than DS subjects matched for IQ. Right-hemisphere-damaged subjects, however, perform worse than matched controls on semantic fluency, despite normal performance on other fluency tasks (e.g., name all the words starting with an "s" sound; Laine & Niemi, 1988).

A second distinction between WS and right-hemisphere dysfunction is in affective prosody. Several studies of adults with focal cerebral lesions have shown that the right hemisphere is specialized for affective prosody. Subjects with right-hemisphere damage have difficulty expressing and comprehending different emotional tones of voice (Heilman, Bowers, Speedie, & Coslett, 1984; Tucker, Watson, & Heilman, 1977). However, the speech of WS subjects evidences good command and frequent utilization of affective prosodic devices, as discussed before. Third, right-hemisphere-damaged subjects are poor at organizing narrative into a coherent whole, and they often show a tendency to miss the gist or moral of a story (Wapner, Hamby, & Gardner, 1981). The frog story data on WS subjects, by contrast, show particular preservation of this ability and its absence in the comparison DS group. Three domains of WS language thus display preservation despite their usual right-hemispheric dependence. Rather than mimicking right hemisphere, WS presents a consistent but new and different biologically determined neurobehavioral pattern.

WS and Autism: Syndromic Contrasts

To date, a distillation of the neurobehavioral profile of WS yields what appear to be three notable features. We suggest that on all three of these axes an intriguing syndromic contrast to WS might be found in autism, although the same studies have not been done across both groups. The first of these contrasts is in the area of language. Although WS language is spontaneously fluent and engaging, the *Diagnostic and Statistical Manual of Mental Disorders* (3rd ed. rev.) (*DSM–III–R*) definition of autism cites impairments in verbal and nonverbal communication (American Psychiatric Association, 1987). As Rapin (1991) reviewed, children with autism show a wide range of competence on tests of specific linguistic skills, and a wide range of deficits as well. These deficits can include comprehension deficiencies, semantic irregularities, and prosodic peculiarities. It seems then that at least a large fraction of subjects with autism fail to employ language in the effective, communicative manner of the WS adolescents in our studies (Reilly et al., 1991).

Sigman and her colleagues emphasized the role that social interaction (and its perturbation) has in the aberrant language development of children with autism (chapter 7 of this volume). In this realm of social interaction and emotional affect, we suggest that WS and autism may pose an even more dramatic contrast. Evidence from their frog story narrations suggests that WS subjects are acutely attentive to the affect of others and reflect this affectual concern in their language. During social interactions, WS adolescents can be lively and engaging. Sigman et al. (Mundy & Sigman, 1989; Mundy, Sigman, & Kasari, 1990) have demonstrated that children with autism characteristically show deficits in joint social attention and affective sharing. The *DSM–III–R* definition of autism summarized these features as a marked lack of awareness of the existence and feelings of others and a unique "aloneness" (APA, 1987). Courchesne (Akshoomoff, Courchesne, & Press, 1990; see also chapter 6 of this volume) suggested that the basis for these behavioral distinctions may lie in neocerebellar structures, on which WS and autistic subjects show divergent morphology (Jernigan & Bellugi, 1990). He argued that these structures are integral to the mechanisms necessary for attentional shifting. The third distinctive finding in WS—the excellent facial recognition ability—would seem to bear on these issues of sociability. In informal situations, we have noted that WS subjects attend intensely to their social partners' faces, seeming receptive and responsive to any and all facial cues. Children with autism are thought to be unresponsive to such cues, failing to notice another person's distress, for example (American Psychiatric Association, 1987). Additionally, it has been found that Fragile X subjects characteristically avoid eye contact during social greetings (Wolff, Gardner, Pacia, & Lappen, 1989).

A strong distinction between WS and autism also is found on a formal test of spatial cognitive skill—the Block Design subtest of the WISC–R. The poor and fractionated performance of WS subjects on this measure has been reviewed. Conversely, it has been reported that autistic subjects display a performance peak on Block Design, actually solving the designs faster than normal subjects of the same age (Shah & Frith, 1983). In a recent study, we contrast matched WS, DS, and autistic subjects on a block design task (Chen, 1992), Fig. 2.12. We found striking differences between the subjects, with the WS subject using a fragmented piecemeal approach, never gaining the correct overall configuration, requiring multiple trials even on simple designs, including many counterproductive isolating movements (in which one block is isolated from the others, rather than brought together with the other blocks), and trying to talk their way through the task. By contrast, the matched autistic subject solves the puzzles rapidly and with great economy of effort, making very few unnecessary or nonproductive manipulations, never making isolating moves, and working with almost mechanical precision and accuracy (Chen, 1992).

NEUROPHYSIOLOGICAL STUDIES OF BRAIN FUNCTION IN WS

We report on a series of studies with Neville and colleagues (Neville, Holcomb, & Mills, 1989; see also chapter 4 of this volume) to assess the

WISC-R Block Design

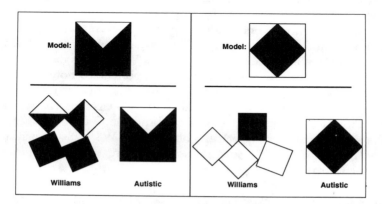

FIG. 2.12.   Comparison between autistic and WS subjects on WISC–R Block Design. Comparison of performance between an autistic subject (perfect performance, very rapidly executed) and a matched WS subject (poor performance, fragmented, and slow). From Chen (1992). Reprinted by permission.

timing and organization of neural systems active during sensory, cognitive and language processing in Williams syndrome subjects. These studies employ the event-related potential (ERP) technique, one of few noninvasive techniques that permits a millisecond by millisecond monitoring of brain activity that precedes, accompanies, and/or follows particular types of cognitive processing. In this chapter, we mention studies of two characteristics of the WS behavioral profile. First, we examine their auditory recovery cycle for indices that might provide clues to the basis of their apparent hyperacusis (i.e., increased sensitivity to sounds). Is there evidence for hyperexcitability at any stage along the auditory pathway? Second, we examine auditory sentence processing. Are the relatively preserved language capabilities of these otherwise mentally retarded adolescent WS subjects mediated by brain systems that resemble or differ in some principled manner from those that are active in normal age-matched control subjects?

Auditory and Visual Recovery Paradigm.   As mentioned previously, a psychophysical feature of WS is an unusual sensitivity to specific classes of environmental sounds, manifested in specific ways. In subjects tested to date, auditory brainstem evoked responses are normal in WS subjects, suggesting that hyperexcitability does not occur at the brainstem level. However, the auditory recovery data suggest a possible cortical mechanism subserving the apparent sensitivity to sounds. As Neville et al. (1989) reported, WS and normal subjects listened to tones presented at different repetition rates (monitoring for frequency shifts) in order to index the rate of recovery or refractory period of the auditory sensory evoked response. The overall morphology of the ERP to tone stimuli (i.e., the N100–P200 response) was very similar in WS and control subjects over both hemispheres. However, WS subjects displayed larger responses at high repetition rates than did controls, suggesting that their responses were less refractory (i.e., more excitable) than in normals. This effect is only evident over temporal cortex and only occurs to auditory stimuli. These data suggest that although similar brain systems are activated by tones in WS and normal subjects, WS subjects display hyperexcitability compared with normal controls. Important to note, on a visual recovery cycle paradigm, the same WS subjects showed results that were indistinguishable from those of normal controls, suggesting that the hyperexcitability effect is specific to auditory information. Taken together, these studies suggest that the hyperacusis observed in WS subjects may reflect specific mechanisms in the cortical areas that are utilized in processing acoustic information.

Abnormal Brain Function During Language Processing.   In studies with WS subjects, ERPs were recorded to auditorily presented words that formed sentences. Responses to open and closed class words in sentence medial position were compared. In addition, one half of the sentences were highly contextually constrained, ending with an expected word (semantically appropriate), and the other half ending with an anomalous unexpected word (semantically inappropriate), as in "I take my coffee with cream and paper." Normal subjects show a large negative response at 400 msec (N400) to semantically unprimed words, which is thought to be an index of how the mental lexicon is organized. Results from this study are highly revealing. Analysis of the responses to sentence-middle words (i.e., not the semantically primed words) revealed that WS subjects displayed responses that were highly abnormal within the first 200–300 ms following word onset. The abnormality consisted of a large positivity not apparent in control subjects at any age. This effect, only apparent over temporal brain regions, may relate to the hyperacusis these subjects display. Furthermore, the WS responses do not display the asymmetry (left temporal regions more negative than right) that is normally apparent by about 7 years of age, suggesting that there may be an unusual pattern of brain organization underlying language.

Hypersemanticity.   In the same studies, the N400 response to the semantically anomalous sentence endings is similar in WS and control subjects; there is a large negative peak around 400 msec just as in the normal subjects. However, the effect of the semantic priming appears to be larger in WS than in controls. An abnormally large effect of semantic priming may be related to behavioral findings discussed earlier, in which these same WS subjects tend to generate low frequency and nonprototypical lexical responses. The effect of greater priming may indicate an abnormally large degree of activation, which extends to less frequent and nonprototypical items within the mental lexicon.

These neurophysiological studies raise the possibility that at least some of the brain systems that mediate the remarkably preserved language in the WS population differ from those that mediate language in the normal population. Implications from these studies are discussed in chapter 4 of this volume. Further studies of WS will help to clarify the role of different factors in the development of functional differentiation in the brain.

Implications for Biological/Behavioral Correlation

These studies on neurophysiological function in WS raise an important caveat for the study of biological/functional relationships in our populations or in other disordered populations. They point out that the neural systems employed by WS subjects for sensory, cognitive, or language processing need not be identical to the systems employed by the normal population for the same tasks.

Semantic processing in WS is a case in point. The coincidence of well-preserved word knowledge, good semantic fluency, and volume preservation of frontal brain regions (see discussion that follows and chapter 3 of this volume) might imply the existence of an intact and normal neurobiolo-gical substrate for semantic function in WS. However, the unusual semantic organization evident in the fluency behavior of WS subjects and the deviant ERP patterns on semantic priming suggest that the underlying brain systems may be deviant as well. The aberrant ERP patterns seen for open and closed class words remind us that the brain systems mediating WS behavior may be either an aberrantly organized deviation from the normal or a system that is mechanistically and anatomically distinct from the system usually responsible for a given task in the normal population.

The facial recognition abilities of WS subjects and their proclivity for a local mode of processing provide a second illustration of this caveat. The local processing mode pervades the spatial constructions of WS subjects, from tests specifically designed to elicit this trait to free drawing. Verbal clues given by the WS subjects during testing suggest that they may employ a related processing mode during the facial recognition task. That is, rather than forming and utilizing a gestalt impression of the faces, as normal subjects do, WS subjects may rely exclusively on a feature-by-feature analysis, responding that two items match because they have the same nose or same eyebrows. The same strategy may effect good performance on the canonical/noncanonical object identification task as well. If this alternative strategy obtains, then the neurobiological system underlying WS performance may once again be distinct from that operating in normals during these particular tasks. These distinctions should not, however, dissuade us from studying these cognitive processes in abnormal populations. They merely point out the necessity of careful dissection of the cognitive processes whose neural mechanisms are sought.

MRI STUDIES OF BRAIN STRUCTURE IN WS AND DS

As described earlier, the neurobehavioral results from WS disclose a unique profile of cognitive skill. Because a genetic etiology underlies this fascinating neurobehavioral and neurophysiologic profile, the opportunity exists to examine its neurobiological underpinnings on multiple levels, from the genetic to the neuroanatomic and the neurophysiologic. Despite the caveats that we identify in the previous section, and that Neville and colleagues reiterate (chapter 4 of this volume), we find the opportunity posed by WS to be provocative.

Within cognitive neuroscience, it is the neuroanatomical correlations to neuropsychology that are best studied. On the basis of this body of knowledge, one might expect that both WS and DS subjects would exhibit microcephaly, as often is seen in mental retardation. As Jernigan details in chapter 3 of this volume, this is indeed the case (Jernigan & Bellugi, 1990;

Wang, Doherty, Hesselink, & Bellugi 1992; Wang, Hesselink, Jernigan, Doherty, & Bellugi, 1992). More interesting is the pattern of regional cortical anatomy that might be predicted from the neurobehavioral evidence. We suggest that regions within the temporal lobe could be expected to show relative structural integrity in WS, on the basis of multiple behavioral evidence. First, the pattern of spared affective and emotional ability argues for relatively good function of the limbic system. Similarly, the relatively stronger explicit memory skill of WS subjects (as compared to DS subjects) also suggests that the hippocampus and related mesial temporal structures would be preserved.

A second neuroanatomic prediction may be found in the psychological dichotomy between explicit and implicit memory processes. It has been proposed that whereas explicit/declarative memory is mediated through the medial temporal lobe (Squire & Zola-Morgan, 1991), the motor learning subset of the implicit processes may be mediated by the basal ganglia (Heindel et al., 1989). Therefore, considering the superior behavioral results on motor learning, it would be intriguing if DS subjects show greater integrity of the subcortical nuclei than WS subjects.

The role of frontal brain regions in language, and especially in lexical and semantic processing, is increasingly supported by a number of lines of evidence. The Broca's aphasia that results from damage to specific frontal regions is well known; evidence from well-studied subjects with frontal brain lesions is also telling (Damasio, 1990). Electrophysiologic and positron emission tomographic studies also suggest that frontal brain regions play a critical role in semantic processing (Petersen, Fox, Posner, Mintun, & Raichle, 1989). The relatively strong performance of WS subjects on semantic and fluency tasks is compatible with the suggestion that their frontal areas may be better preserved than in DS.

As Jernigan reviews in chapter 3 of this volume, MRI studies of the brain in WS, DS, and control subjects are consonant with some of the correlations postulated here. For example, the superior performance of WS subjects on semantic fluency may be associated with proportional preservation of frontal volume, despite a decrease in overall cerebral volume relative to controls. Also, Wang et al. (1992) showed that the most rostral fifth of the corpus callosum is better preserved in WS than in DS (Wang, Doherty, Hesselink, Bellugi, 1992). Studies of partial commisurotomy patients suggest that this region of the callosum is important for the interhemispheric transfer of semantic information (Gazzaniga, Kutas, VanPetten, & Fendrich, 1989; Sidtis, Volpe, Holtzman, Wilson, & Gazzaniga, 1981).

A major neuroanatomical contrast between WS and autism is found in the cerebellum—a part of the brain that, until recently, was thought to contribute significantly only to motor function. In WS, a particular portion of the midline cerebellar vermis is significantly larger in cross-section than in either DS or normal controls (Jernigan & Bellugi, 1990). That portion, lobules VI and VII, comprises the neo-cerebellar part of the vermis. In proportion to a phylogenetically more ancient part of the vermis (lobules I–V), the neo-cerebellar vermis is again significantly larger in WS than in either of the other groups. Although its role is not yet conclusively established, a growing body of evidence suggests that the neocerebellum participates in higher cognitive function, including possibly the coordination of the many cognitive resources necessary for fluent speech (Leiner, Leiner, & Dow, 1989). For example, animal studies have shown that lesion to the vermis may result in abnormalities in certain types of learning and in social interaction and approach behavior (Bernston & Schumacher, 1980). Courchesne et al.'s earlier demonstration of neocerebellar vermal hypoplasia in autism (Courchesne, Yeung-Courchesne, Press, Hesselink, & Jernigan, 1988) is interesting along these latter lines. The contrast between autism and WS in communicative and affective behavior mirrors their differences in neocerebellar morphology. We thus find the neo-cerebellar findings in WS particularly stimulating (Wang, Hesselink, Jernigan, Doherty, & Bellugi, 1992). They represent the dynamic potential of the cross-level neuroscientific investigations in which we are engaged.

CURRENT AND FUTURE DIRECTIONS

Research in our laboratory is continuing along a number of promising lines. Critical among these is the exploration of the developmental trajectory of language and cognitive abilities in our special populations. Preliminary results from a survey of development in WS suggests that their language and the language of DS children are equivalently delayed at a young age. Continued longitudinal follow-up of these subjects will be needed to define when and in what manner the linguistic abilities of these subjects diverge from purported cognitive underpinnings. Investigations of nonlinguistic cognitive development in the same children will allow us to address hypotheses on the cognitive correlates or prerequisites for language.

We also continue to explore the spatial cognitive abilities of WS subjects. Their pattern of strengths and weaknesses provides a new hint about the nature of spatial cognition. Despite the efforts of many investigators, a broadly applicable nosology of visual-spatial cognition has been difficult to construct. We believe that the unique profile of visual-spatial abilities in WS is founded biologically and therefore may have broad implications. Our primary caveat, that some performance peaks may derive from nonstandard performance strategies, will actually help guide our explorations, as long as it is kept in theoretical mind.

The biological foundation of WS will permit invaluable study of the brain bases of behavior. The work reported by Jernigan and Neville marks the first major effort to illuminate the neural systems underlying the unique neuro-behavioral profile of WS as contrasted with other populations. With the advancing capabilities of noninvasive neuroimaging and neurophysiological probes, we will garner a more and more detailed account of the structures and mechanisms of the WS brain (Damasio & Frank, in press). Also, we have recently obtained an autopsy brain specimen from a WS subject. This will allow us to extend our biological explorations to the microscopic level of cortical organization and neuronal morphology. Last, investigations on the genetic basis of WS are gathering speed, with the identification of the first certified family pedigree of WS cases. We hope and expect eventually to give a full account of cognition in WS, from the molecular biological level to the behavioral level.

ACKNOWLEDGMENTS

This work was supported in part by National Institutes of Health Grants DC00146, HD26022, P50NS22343, P01DC01289, the Axe Houghton Foundation, and the MacArthur Foundation Research Network. Paul P. Wang is a William T. Grant Foundation fellow of the Pediatric Scientist Development Program. We are very grateful to the children and parents who have taken part in our studies of the Neuropsychological and Neurobiological Bases of Williams and Down syndromes. Diane Niles is parent coordinator for these studies. We thank the National Williams Syndrome Association, several Regional Williams Syndrome Associations, the Canadian Association for Williams Syndrome, and the Parents of Down Syndrome Association for their cooperation. We are grateful to Dr. Michael Rossen, Dr. Sally Doherty, Judy Goodman, Dr. Amy Bihrle, Naomi Singer, and Valerie Loewe for their help in these studies.

REFERENCES

Akshoomoff, N. A., Courchesne, E., & Press, G. A. (1990). The contribution of the cerebellum to neuropsychological functioning: Evidence from a case of cerebellar degenerative disorder. Poster presented at the meeting of the International Neuropsychological Society, Orlando, FL. *Journal of Clinical and Experimental Neuropsychology, 12,* 69.

American Psychiatric Association. (1987). *Diagnostic and statistical manual of mental disorders* (3rd rev. ed.,). Washington, DC: Author.

Arnold, R., Yule, W., & Martin, N. (1985). The psychological characteristics of infantile hypercalcaemia: A preliminary investigation. *Developmental Medicine and Child Neurology, 27,* 49–59.

Beilin, H. (1975). *Studies in the cognitive basis of language development.* New York: Academic.

Bellugi, U., Bihrle, A., Doherty, S., Neville, H., & Damasio, A. (1989, February). *Neural correlates of higher cortical functioning in a neurodevelopmental disorder.* Symposium conducted at the meeting of the International Neuropsychological Society, Vancouver, British Columbia, Canada.

Bellugi, U., Bihrle, A., Jernigan, T., Trauner, D., & Doherty, S. (1990). Neuropsychological, neurological, and neuroanatomical profile of Williams syndrome. *American Journal of Medical Genetics*, *6*, 115–125.

Bellugi, U., Bihrle, A., Neville, H., Jernigan, T., & Doherty, S. (1992). Language, cognition, and brain organization in a neurodevelopmental disorder. In M. Gunnar & C. Nelson (Eds.), *Developmental behavioral neuroscience* (pp. 201–232). Hillsdale, NJ: Lawrence Erlbaum Associates.

Bellugi, U., & Culler, F. (1987). *Gene coding and behavioral expression in Williams syndrome children*. Colloquium, UCLA Medical Center, Genetics and Dysmorphology, Los Angeles, CA.

Bellugi, U., & Doherty, S. (1990). [Orientation-invariant object identification in Williams and Down syndromes]. Unpublished observations.

Bellugi, U., Marks, S., Bihrle, A., & Sabo, H. (1988). Dissociation between language and cognitive functions in Williams syndrome. In D. Bishop & K. Mogford (Eds.), *Language development in exceptional circumstances* (pp. 177–189). London: Churchill Livingstone.

Bellugi, U., Poizner, H., & Klima, E. S. (1989). Language, modality and the brain. *Trends in Neurosciences*, *10*, 380–388.

Bellugi, U., Sabo, H., & Vaid, J. (1988). Spatial deficits in children with Williams syndrome. In J. Stiles-Davis, M. Kritchevsky, & U. Bellugi (Eds.), *Spatial cognition: Brain bases and development* (pp. 273–298). Hillsdale, NJ: Lawrence Erlbaum Associates.

Bernston, G., & Schumacher, K. (1980). Effects of cerebellar lesions on activity, social interactions, and other motivated behaviors in the rat. *Journal of Comparative Physiological Psychology*, *94*, 706–717.

Bihrle, A. M. (1990). *Visuospatial processing in Williams and Down syndrome*. Unpublished doctoral dissertation, University of California and San Diego State University, San Diego.

Bihrle, A. M., Bellugi, U., Delis, D., & Marks, S. (1989). Seeing either the forest or the trees: Dissociation in visuospatial processing. *Brain and Cognition*, *11*, 37–49.

Carroll, J. B., Davies, P., & Richman, B. (1971). *Word frequency book*. New York: American Heritage Publishing.

Chen, S. Y. (1992). *Differential processing: Block design test in Williams syndrome, Down syndrome, and autism*. Unpublished manuscript, The Salk Institute, La Jolla, CA.

Courchesne, E., Yeung-Courchesne, R., Press, G., Hesselink, J., & Jernigan, T. (1988). Hypoplasia of cerebellar vermal lobules VI and VII in autism. *New England Journal of Medicine*, *318*, 1349–1354.

Crisco, J. J., & Dobbs, J. M. (1988). Cognitive processing of children with Williams syndrome. *Developmental Medicine and Child Neurology*, *5*, 650–656.

Culler, F., Jones, K., & Deftos, L. (1985). Impaired calcitonin secretion in patients with Williams syndrome. *Journal of Pediatrics*, *107*, 720–723.

Damasio, A. R. (1990). Category-related recognition defects as a clue to the neural substrates of knowledge. *Trends in Neurosciences*, *13*(3), 95–98.

Damasio, H., & Frank, R. (in press). Three dimensional in vivo mapping of brain lesions in humans. *Archives of Neurology*.

Delis, D. C., & Bihrle, A. M. (1989). Fractionation of spatial cognition following focal and diffuse brain damage. In A. Ardila & F. Ostrosky-Solis (Eds.), *Brain organization of language and cognitive processes*. (pp. 17–35). New York: Plenum.

Delis, D., Kiefner, M., & Fridlund, A. (1988). Visuospatial functioning following unilateral brain damage: Dissociations in hierarchical and hemispatial analysis. *Journal of Clinical Experimental Neuropsychology*, *10*, 421–431.

Gazzaniga, M., Kutas, M., VanPetten, C., & Fendrich, R. (1989). Human callosal function: MRI-verified neuropsychological functions. *Neurology*, *39*, 942–946.

Heilman, K., Bowers, D., Speedie, L., & Coslett, H. (1984). Comprehension of affective and non-affective prosody. *Neurology*, *34*, 917–921.

Heindel, W., Salmon, D., Shults, C., Walicke, P., & Butters, N. (1989). Neuropsychological evidence for multiple implicit memory systems: A comparison of Alzheimer's, Huntington's, and Parkinson's disease patients. *Journal of Neuroscience, 9*(2), 582–587.

Jernigan, T., & Bellugi, U. (1990). Anomalous brain morphology on magnetic resonance images in Williams syndrome and Down syndrome. *Archives of Neurology, 47*, 529–533.

Jones, K., & Smith, D. (1975). The Williams elfin facies syndrome: A new perspective. *Journal of Pediatrics, 86*, 718–723.

Kataria, S., Goldstein, D. J., & Kushnick, T. (1984). Developmental delays in Williams elfin facies syndrome. *Applied Research in Mental Retardation, 5*, 419–423.

Laine, M., & Niemi, J. (1988). *Word fluency production strategies of neurological patients: Semantic and phonological processing*. Conference proceedings of the International Neuropsychological Society Meeting, New Orleans.

Lamb, M., Robertson, L., & Knight, R. (1989). Attention and interference in the processing of global and local information: Effects of unilateral temporal–parietal junction lesions. *Neuropsychologia, 27*, 471–483.

Lansdell, H. (1968). Effect of extent of temporal lobe ablations on two lateralized deficits. *Physiology and Behavior, 3*, 271–273.

Lansdell, H. (1970). Relation of extent of temporal removals to closure and visuomotor factors. *Perceptual and Motor Skills, 31*, 491–498.

Leiner, H., Leiner, A., & Dow, R. (1989). Reappraising the cerebellum: What does the hindbrain contribute to the forebrain? *Behavioral Neuroscience, 103*, 998–1008.

Martin, N., Snodgrass, G., & Cohen, R. (1984). Idiopathic infantile hypercalcaemia: A continuing enigma. *Archives of Diseases in Children, 59*, 605–613.

Mayer, M. (1969). *Frog, Where Are You?* New York: Dial Books for Young Readers.

McKusick, V. (1988). *Mendelian inheritance in man: Catalogs of autosomal dominant, autosomal recessive and X-linked phenotypes*. Baltimore: Johns Hopkins University Press.

Mooney, C. M. (1957). Age in the development of closure ability in children. *Canadian Journal of Psychology, 11*, 216–226.

Morris, C., Demsey, S., Leonard, C., Dilts, C., & Blackburn, B. (1988). Natural history of Williams syndrome: Physical characteristics. *Journal of Pediatrics, 113*, 318–326.

Mundy, P., & Sigman, M. (1989). The theoretical implications of joint-attention deficits in autism. *Development and Psychopathology, 1*, 173–183.

Mundy, P., Sigman, M., & Kasari, C. (1990). A longitudinal study of joint attention and language development in autistic children. *Journal of Autism and Development Disorders, 20*(1), 115–128.

Neville, H. J., Holcomb, P., & Mills, D. (1989, February). *Neural correlates of higher cortical functioning in a neurodevelopmental disorder*. Symposium conducted at the meeting of the International Neuropsychological Society, Vancouver, British Columbia, Canada.

Perrett, D., Rolls, E., & Caan, W. (1982). Visual neurons responsive to faces in the monkey temporal cortex. *Experimental Brain Research, 47*, 329–342.

Peterson, S., Fox, P., Posner, M., Mintun, M., & Raichle, M. (1989). Positron emission tomographic studies of the processing of single words. *Journal of Cognitive Neuroscience, 1*(2), 153–170.

Rapin, I. (1991). Autistic children: Diagnosis and clinical features. *Pediatrics, 87*, 751–760.

Reilly, J., Klima, E. S., & Bellugi, U. (1991). Once more with feeling: Affect and language in atypical populations. *Development and Psychopathology, 2*, 367–391.

Rubba, J., & Klima, E. S. (1991). Preposition use in a speaker with Williams syndrome: Some cognitive grammar proposals. *Center for Research on Language Newsletter*, University of California at San Diego, 5(3), 3–12.

Shah, A., & Frith, U. (1983). An islet of ability in autistic children: A research note. *Journal of Child Psychology and Psychiatry, 24*, 613–620.

Sidtis, J., Volpe, B., Holtzman, J., Wilson, D., & Gazzaniga, M. (1981). Cognitive interaction after staged callosal section: Evidence for transfer of semantic activation. *Science, 212*, 344–346.

Squire, L., & Zola-Morgan, S. (1991). The medial temporal lobe memory system. *Science*, *253*, 1380–1386.

Stiles-Davis, J., Kritchevsky, M., & Bellugi, U. (Eds.) (1988). *Spatial cognition: Brain bases and development*. Hillsdale, NJ: Lawrence Erlbaum Associates.

Trauner, D., Bellugi, U., & Chase, C. (1989). Neurologic features of Williams and Down syndromes. *Pediatric Neurology*, *5*(3), 166–168.

Tucker, D., Watson, R., & Heilman, K. (1977). Affective discrimination and evocation in patients with right parietal disease. *Neurology 27*, 947–950.

Udwin, O. (1990). A survey of adults with Williams syndrome and idiopathic infantile hypercalcaemia. *Developmental Medicine and Child Neurology*, *32*, 129–141.

Udwin, O., Yule, W., & Martin, N. (1987). Cognitive abilities and behavioral characteristics of children with idiopathic infantile hypercalcaemia. *Journal of Child Psychology and Psychiatry*, *28*, 297–309.

Villardita, C. (1987). Verbal memory and semantic clustering in right brain-damaged patients. *Neuropsychologia*, *25*, 277–280.

Von Arnim, G., & Engel, P. (1964). Mental retardation related to hypercalcemia. *Developmental Medicine and Child Neurology*, *6*, 366–377.

Wang, P., & Bellugi, U. (in preparation). *Working memory for verbal and for visual-spatial information is doubly-dissociated in two genetic syndromes*.

Wang, P., Doherty, S., Hesselink, J., & Bellugi, U. (1992). Callosal morphology concurs with neurobehavioral and neuropathological findings in two neurodevelopmental syndromes. *Archives of Neurology*, *49*, 407–411.

Wang, P. P., Hesselink, J. R., Jernigan, T. L., Doherty, S., & Bellugi, U. (1992). Specific neurobehavioral profile of Williams syndrome is associated with neocerebellar hemispheric preservation. *Neurology*, *42*, 1999–2002.

Wapner, W., Hamby, S., & Gardner, H. (1981). The role of the right hemisphere in the apprehension of complex linguistic materials. *Brain and Language*, *14*, 15–33.

Wasserstein, J., Zappulla, R., Rosen J., Gerstman, L., & Rock, D. (1987). In search of closure: subjective contour illusions, gestalt completion tests, and implications. *Brain and Cognition*, *6*, 1–14.

Williams, J., Barratt-Boyes, B., & Lowe, J. (1961). Supravalvular aortic stenosis. *Circulation*, *24*, 1311–1318.

Wolff, P., Gardner, J., Pacia, J., & Lappen, J. (1989). The greeting behavior of Fragile X males. *American Journal of Mental Retardation*, *93*(4), 406–411.

3

Neuroanatomical Distinctions Between Williams and Down Syndromes

Terry L. Jernigan
Veterans Affairs Medical Center and University of California, San Diego

Ursula Bellugi
The Salk Institute for Biological Studies

Williams syndrome (WS) is a rare developmental disorder characterized by mental retardation (Jones & Smith, 1975; Preus, 1984; von Arnim & Engel, 1964; Williams, Barrett-Boyes, & Lowe, 1961). Several reports have appeared describing some of the neuropsychological deficits observed in WS subjects (Crisco, Dobbs, & Mulhern, 1988; MacDonald & Roy, 1988; Udwin & Yule, 1991). Although these studies present conflicting results, most note their particularly poor visuospatial and visuomotor abilities. These studies have generally contrasted the performance of WS subjects on standardized tests to those of normal children or IQ-matched controls with mixed or nonspecific developmental disorders. In a series of recent neurobehavioral investigations, the unusual profile of higher cognitive functions in WS subjects has been illuminated (Bellugi, Bihrle, Jernigan, Trauner, & Doherty, 1990; Bellugi, Bihrle, Neville, Jernigan, & Doherty, 1992; Bellugi, Sabo, & Vaid, 1988; see also chapter 2 of this volume).

Studies under the Neurodevelopmental Research Center focus on carefully selected WS children who have been clearly diagnosed as WS by genetic or metabolic markers, who are all in a similar age range (10 years and above), and who are contrasted with another well-defined genetically based disorder of mental retardation, Down syndrome (DS). The two groups are matched in age, gender, educational background, and IQ. Both groups of subjects undergo magnetic resonance imaging (MRI), neurological exams, and a battery of experimental measures across disciplines, including linguistic, visuospatial, cognitive, and affective functions, as well as studies of brain function using event-related potentials. Highly distinct and contrasting neuropsychological profiles for WS versus DS have emerged from these studies (Bellugi, 1991; Bellugi et al., 1992; Bihrle, Bellugi, Delis, & Marks, 1989; Reilly, Kilma, & Bellugi, 1990; see also chapter 2 of this volume). The first and most striking characteristic of WS is the contrast between linguistic and other cognitive abilities, including striking visuospatial deficits. Although measures of language that conflate general cognitive and linguistic abilities, such as the Vocabulary subtest from the Wechsler Intelligence Scale for Children–Revised (WISC–R; which requires well-formed definitions), reveal equally severe deficits in both WS and DS, experimental probes of specifically linguistic processing yield striking differences between the two groups. The WS subjects show a significant advantage on measures of lexical knowledge, and other measures of syntactic and semantic competence, whereas DS are markedly impaired. Moreover, the WS adolescent subjects' language is peppered with unusual vocabulary, and word fluency tasks reveal a nearly normal (age-matched) performance but with a proclivity for nonprototypical items (*ibex, chihuahua, saber-toothed tiger, unicorn*) (Bellugi et al., 1990).

In the visuospatial domain, although global tests such as Developmental Test of Motor Integration (Beery & Buktenica, 1967) and the WISC–R Block Design subtest suggest similar deficits in DS and WS, it is the DS subjects who show an advantage on tests involving spatial integration (Bellugi et al., 1992). Experimental studies of visuospatial function have revealed intriguing qualitative differences between the performances of WS and DS subjects (Bihrle, 1990; Bihrle et al., 1989). Using a paradigm employing hierarchical stimuli with information at both the global and local processing levels (see Delis & Bihrle, 1989; Delis, Kiefner, & Fridlund, 1988; Delis, Robertson, & Efron, 1986), WS subjects were shown to utilize local form information disproportionately, whereas DS subjects showed an advantage for global forms. Again, this pattern emerged in the context of equally impaired overall performance in the two groups. Interestingly, previous neuropsychological studies with this task have suggested a larger role for the left hemisphere in the processing of local form information, and right-hemisphere superiority for the processing of global forms.

Another interesting contrast occurs on tests of facial discrimination. WS subjects demonstrate a selective ability to discriminate unfamiliar faces, whereas DS subjects are markedly impaired (Bellugi et al., 1992; see also chapter 2 of this volume). Preservation of this function in WS is surprising in light of the severe impairment they show on other tasks requiring the integration of visuospatial information.

Finally, recently completed studies of the use of affect in language suggest further dramatic differences between the groups (Reilly et al., 1990). The WS subjects make abundant use of affective prosody and other affective linguistic devices in their narratives, perhaps even more than normal subjects, whereas the DS subjects employ very few.

Our brain-imaging studies of these subjects have attempted to identify anatomical distinctions between the groups that might shed some light on the neural bases of these differences in behavioral profile. In our first report (Jernigan & Bellugi, 1990), we described several gross brain morphologic distinctions on MRI between these two disorders. Although the cerebral hypoplasia observed was of equal degree in our two IQ-matched groups, cerebellar size was entirely normal in the WS subjects, whereas cerebellar hypoplasia was at least as severe in DS as was cerebral hypoplasia. In addition, measurements of vermal lobules in WS and controls suggested that whereas paleocerebellar lobules tended to subtend a smaller area on midsagittal sections, neocerebellar lobules were actually larger. These results suggested important distinctions between Ws and DS in terms of the action and anatomical targets of factors that alter brain development in these syndromes. We then conducted a second study on somewhat larger groups of subjects. The focus of the second study was on morphological features within the cerebrum. A number of differences emerged between WS and DS cerebra, in spite of roughly equivalent overall cerebral size in the two groups. Before the results are described, the morphometric techniques used are outlined briefly.

MAGNETIC RESONANCE IMAGING AND IMAGE ANALYSIS

MRI was performed with a 1.5 Tesla superconducting magnet. Two spatially registered images were obtained simultaneously for each section, using an asymmetrical, multiple-echo sequence to obtain images of the entire brain in the axial plane.

Three subcortical structures and three cortical regions were examined. The volumes of caudate nuclei, lenticular nuclei, and the thalamic and hypothalamic (diencephalic) structures were computed, as were separate volumes of anterior, posterior, and temporal limbic cortex. Detailed descriptions of the image-analytic approach used are contained in several articles (Jernigan, Archibald et al., 1991; Jernigan & Bellugi, 1990; Jernigan, Bellugi, Sowell, Doherty, & Hesselink, 1993; Jernigan, Press, & Hesselink, 1990; Jernigan, Schafer, Butters, & Cermak, 1991; Jernigan & Tallal, 1990; Jernigan, Trauner, Hesselink, & Tallal, 1991). Briefly, each pixel location within a section of the imaged brain is classified on the basis of its signal values in the two original images as most resembling cerebro-spinal fluid (CSF), gray matter, white matter, or signal hyperintensity (tissue abnormality). Consistently identifiable anatomical landmarks and structural boundaries are then designated by trained image-analysts who are unaware of any subject characteristics. The processed image data are then transformed spatially so that all locations within the brain images can be identified relative to a common anatomic coordinate system (i.e., stereotaxically). Cerebral regions are then defined either entirely manually or, when boundaries cannot be visually identified on a reliable basis, using a combination of manual and stereotaxic procedures.

The voxels designated as within the caudate, lenticular, and diencephalic regions are highlighted in black in the representative, digitally processed images shown in Fig. 3.1 A-C, respectively. The cortical gray matter voxels designated as temporal limbic region are highlighted in black in the images shown in Fig. 3.2A. All other cortical gray matter voxels were assigned either to the anterior region (Fig. 3.2B), that is, anterior to a stereotactically defined coronal plane, or to the posterior region (Fig. 3.2C). Additionally, each structure was measured separately for each hemisphere, for the purpose of examining asymmetries. Volumes of the total infratentorial and supratentorial cranial vaults were also estimated by summing over all of the imaged brain sections.

To examine pattern differences between the groups, regional gray matter volumes were expressed as proportions of the total cerebral gray matter volume (sum of all gray matter regions).

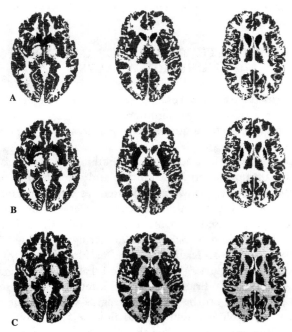

FIG. 3.1. Representative processed images illustrating definition of subcortical gray matter regions. Pixels within caudate nuclei (A), lenticular nuclei (B), and diencephalic regions (C) highlighted in black.

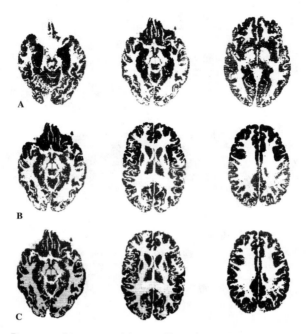

FIG. 3.2. Representative processed images illustrating definition of cortical regions. Pixels within temporal limbic (A), anterior (B), and posterior cortex (C) highlighted in black.

MORPHOLOGICAL DIFFERENCES BETWEEN WS AND DS

Nine WS subjects, ranging in age from 10 to 20 years, and six DS subjects, also ranging in age from 10 to 20 years, were studied. The groups were matched for indices of general intelligence. Diagnosis of WS was made on the basis of clinical criteria described by Jones and Smith (1975) and confirmed in most cases by Jones and by neuroendocrine markers (Bellugi, Bihrle, Marks, Jernigan, & Culler, 1987; Culler, Jones, & Deftos, 1985). Diagnosis of DS was made by a physician on the basis of distinct physical features and mental retardation and confirmed by karyotype analysis whenever possible. WS and DS subjects were enrolled in the same classes for the educable mentally retarded and drawn from similar socioeconomic backgrounds. A group of 20 normal controls was also examined. They ranged in age from 10 to 24 years. These subjects were screened for history of serious medical illness or developmental or intellectual disabilities.

Comparisons of the groups on volumes of the supratentorial and infratentorial cranial vaults yielded results virtually identical to the results of the earlier report (see Fig. 3.3). Although the cerebellum is significantly larger in WS than

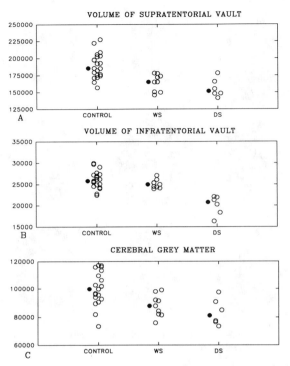

FIG. 3.3. Both WS and DS subjects show significant volume reductions of the supratentorial cranial vault and of cerebral gray matter. In contrast, the infratentorial cranial vault has normal volume in WS though it is markedly reduced in DS.

in DS (and is, in fact, normal in size), the supratentorial (cerebral) volume is equally reduced in WS. Total cerebral gray matter, like the total volume of the supratentorial vault, showed a highly significant reduction in both retarded groups, but no difference was obtained between WS and DS subjects.

Because the reduction in cerebral gray matter was approximately equal in the two groups, a pattern analysis was conducted in which each regional volume was expressed as a proportion of this total gray matter volume. The results of this regional analysis of cerebral gray matter are summarized in Fig. 3.4. When the anterior and posterior cortical regions were examined separately, a significant difference emerged between the two groups, with the DS subjects having proportionately smaller anterior regions relative to both WS and control subjects. Although the WS subjects also had anterior regions that were proportionately somewhat smaller than controls, this difference did not reach significance. The pattern observed within the limbic and brainstem regions revealed a further dissociation between DS and WS. The DS subjects had significantly greater relative volume reductions in the limbic region, whereas no difference was observed between WS and control subjects. In fact,

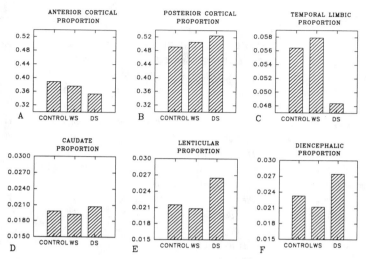

FIG. 3.4. Summary of group differences on gray matter proportions. No difference was observed for the overall cortical proportion; however, DS subjects showed relative reductions in anterior cortical structures (A), and relative increases in posterior cortical structures (B). DS subjects also showed relative decreases in temporal limbic structures (C). Among the subcortical structures, both diencephalic gray matter and lenticular nuclei were proportionately larger in DS subjects.

not only was the limbic proportion normal in WS, the absolute limbic volume was the only regional volume that did not show a significant reduction in WS relative to controls ($p > .15$).

In contrast, the diencephalic and lenticular proportions were both significantly increased in DS relative to both WS and controls. This is due to the fact that the WS subjects show reductions in these structures comparable to their overall cerebral reductions, whereas absolute diencephalic and lenticular volumes are completely normal in DS subjects ($p > .50$). The results for the caudate nuclei revealed reductions of similar magnitude for both retarded groups.

Left–right ratios of all regions were examined but only one, for the limbic region, showed a significant difference between the three groups. This was due to an aberrant right-greater-than-left (.85) ratio in the DS subjects relative to the virtually symmetrical values for controls and WS subjects (.97 and .96, respectively).

These group comparisons of the sizes of structures within the cerebrum provide further support for important distinctions between the neurodevelopmental processes associated with WS and DS. The cerebrum in WS is small; however, the frontal cortex appears to acquire a nearly normal volume relationship to the posterior cortex. In contrast, frontal cortex is disproportionately reduced in volume in DS. Limbic structures of the temporal lobe (including uncus, amygdala, hippocampus, and parahippocampal gyrus) appear to be affected in WS to approximately the same degree as are other cerebral structures, whereas in DS such structures are dramatically reduced in volume. The opposite pattern is observed in several subcortical structures, specifically in regions including thalamus, putamen, and globus pallidus. The volumes of these subcortical structures are entirely normal in DS despite dramatic overall brain size reductions.

Such distinctions, together with differences within cerebellar structures reported earlier, suggest that relatively intact linguistic-, affective-, and face-processing functions in WS may rely upon relatively normal development of some limbic, frontal cortical, and neocerebellar structures. Leiner, Leiner, and Dow (1986) recently proposed that a cerebello-frontocortical system has evolved in man to support the processing demands of fluent speech. They pointed out that large increases in the sizes of these structures occur in humans relative to apes. As reviewed earlier, WS subjects, in marked contrast to DS subjects, are sociable and affectively sensitive, and use affective linguistic devices at least as frequently as controls, perhaps excessively. It is interesting to speculate that the relative sparing of structures in the limbic system in WS is related to these observations. Perhaps a neurodevelopmental course favoring certain limbic structures over other cortical and subcortical structures results in relative prominence of affective strategies in communication. The normal symmetry observed in temporal limbic regions is further evidence for normal maturation and specialization in this system.

Our results in the DS subjects are consistent with earlier reports of the gross brain morphology of these subjects. Cerebral hypofrontality, cerebellar hypoplasia, and even relatively normal appearance of subcortical structures have been noted in autopsy studies (Benda, 1971; Coyle, Oster-Granite, & Gearhart, 1986; Schmidt-Sidor, Wisniewski, Shepard, & Sersen, 1990). Weis (1991) conducted an MRI morphometry study of seven DS adults age 30–45 years and seven matched controls. The pattern of results was similar to those reported here. DS subjects had reduced cortex, white matter, and cerebellum volumes, but no significant reductions in thalamus or basal ganglia. It is surprising, however, that the cranial cavity, which was much smaller in the DS subjects of the present study, showed no significant reduction in the study by Weis. To our knowledge, ours is the first report of normal volumes of thalamus and lenticular nuclei in DS subjects who are definitely microcephalic. The pattern of poor development of cerebellar, limbic, and neocortical (particularly frontal) systems may underlie the impoverishment of language and social-affective function in these subjects. The relatively preserved brainstem and posterior cortical structures may provide the basis for superior global form and spatial integrative functions in DS subjects relative to WS subjects. Conversely, as mentioned earlier, relatively preserved cerebellar, anterior cortical, and limbic structures may underlie the superior linguistic-, social-affective-, and local form-processing abilities of the WS subjects.

In summary, the gross morphology of the brain, as visualized with MRI, reveals little evidence for lesions to which the reduced mental capacities of children with WS and DS could be attributed. Instead, differing patterns of brain growth are observed, resulting in differing profiles of brain structural volumes. Further research will be needed to determine the nature of the neurodevelopmental processes that give rise to these differing profiles.

ACKNOWLEDGMENTS

The work described in this chapter was supported by funds from the Medical Research Service of the Department of Veterans Affairs to Dr. Terry Jernigan, by the NINDS Multidisciplinary Research Center for the Study of the Neurological Basis of Language, Learning, and Behavior Disorders in Children, Grant NS22343, and by NICHD 26022 to Dr. Ursula Bellugi.

The authors are grateful to Drs. Paul P. Wang and William C. Heindel for helpful discussions.

REFERENCES

Beery, K. E., & Buktenica, N. A. (1967). *Developmental test of visual-motor integration*. Cleveland: Modern Curriculum Press

Bellugi, U. (1991). Language and cognition: What the hands reveal about the brain. Presidential Special Lecture, Society for Neuroscience Annual Meeting. *Society for Neuroscience Abstracts, 17*(Parts 1 & 2), xii.

Bellugi, U., Bihrle, A., Jernigan, T., Trauner, D., & Doherty, S. (1990). Neuropsychological, neurological, and neuroanatomical profile of Williams syndrome. *American Journal of Medical Genetics Supplement, 6*, 115–125.

Bellugi, U., Bihrle, A. M., Marks, S., Jernigan, T., & Culler, F. (1987). Neuropsychological and neurobiological account of a disorder. *Society for Neuroscience Abstracts, 13*, 654.

Bellugi, U., Bihrle, A., Neville, H., Jernigan, T., & Doherty, S. (1992). Language, cognition and brain organization in a neurodevelopmental disorder. In M. Gunnar & C. Nelson (Eds.), *Developmental behavioral neuroscience* (pp. 201–232). Hillsdale, NJ: Lawrence Erlbaum Associates.

Bellugi, U., Sabo, H., & Vaid, J. (1988). Spatial deficits in children with Williams syndrome. In J. Stiles-Davis, M. Kritchevsky, & U. Bellugi (Eds.), *Spatial cognition: Brain bases and development* (pp. 273–298). Hillsdale, NJ: Lawrence Erlbaum Associates.

Benda, C. E. (1971). Mongolism. In J. Minckler (Ed.), *Pathology of the nervous system* (Vol. 2, pp. 1361–1371). New York: McGraw-Hill.

Bihrle, A. M. (1990). *Visuospatial processing in Williams and Down syndrome*. Unpublished doctoral dissertation, University of California and San Diego State University, San Diego.

Bihrle, A. M., Bellugi, U., Delis, D., & Marks, S. (1989). Seeing either the forest or the trees: Dissociation in visuospatial processing. *Brain and Cognition, 11*, 37–49.

Coyle, J. T., Oster-Granite, M. L., & Gearhart, J. D. (1986). The neurobiologic consequences of Down syndrome. *Brain Research Bulletin, 16*, 773–787.

Crisco, J. J., Dobbs, J. M., & Mulhern, R. K. (1988). Cognitive processing of children with Williams syndrome. *Developmental Medicine and Child Neurology, 30*, 650–656.

Culler, F. L., Jones, K. L., & Deftos, L. J. (1985). Impaired calcitonin secretion in patients with Williams Syndrome. *Journal of Pediatrics, 107*, 720–723.

Delis, D. C., & Bihrle, A. M. (1989). Fractionation of spatial cognition following focal and diffuse brain damage. In A. Ardila & F. Ostrosky (Eds.), *Brain organization of language and cognitive processes: New directions of research* (pp. 17–35). New York: Plenum.

Delis, D. C., Kiefner, M. G., & Fridlund, A. J. (1988). Visuospatial dysfunction following unilateral brain damage: Dissociations in hierarchical and hemispatial analysis. *Journal of Clinical and Experimental Neuropsychology, 10*, 421–431.

Delis, D. C., Robertson, L. C., & Efron, R. (1986). Hemispheric specialization of memory for visual hierarchical stimuli. *Neuropsychologia, 24*, 205–214.

Jernigan, T. L., Archibald, S. L., Berhow, M. T., Sowell, E. A., Foster, D. S., & Hesselink, J. R. (1991). Cerebral structure on MRI: 1. Localization of age-related changes. *Biological Psychiatry, 29*(1), 55–67.

Jernigan, T. L., & Bellugi, U. (1990). Anomalous brain morphology on magnetic resonance images in Williams syndrome and Down syndrome. *Archives of Neurology, 47*, 529–533.

Jernigan, T. L., Bellugi, U., Sowell, E., Doherty, S., & Hesselink, J. R. (1993). Cerebral morphological distinctions between Williams and Down syndromes. *Archives of Neurology, 50*, 186–191.

Jernigan, T. L., Press, G. A., & Hesselink, J. R. (1990). Methods for measuring brain morphologic features on magnetic resonance images: Validation and normal aging. *Archives of Neurology, 47*, 27–32.

Jernigan, T. L., Schafer, K., Butters, N., & Cermak, L. S. (1991). Magnetic resonance imaging of alcoholic Korsakoff patients. *Neuropsychopharmacology, 4*(3), 175–186.

Jernigan, T. L., & Tallal, P. (1990). Late childhood changes in brain morphology observable with MRI. *Developmental Medicine and Child Neurology, 32*, 379–385.

Jernigan, T. L., Trauner, D. A., Hesselink, J. R., & Tallal, P. A. (1991). Maturation of human cerebrum observed *in vivo* during adolescence. *Brain, 114*, 2037–2049.

Jones, K. L., & Smith D. W. (1975). The Williams elfin faces syndrome: A new perspective. *Journal of Pediatrics, 86*, 718–723.

Leiner, H. C., Leiner, A. L., & Dow, R. (1986). Does the cerebellum contribute to mental skills? *Behavioral Neuroscience, 100*, 443–454.

MacDonald, G. W., & Roy, D. L. (1988). Williams syndrome: A neuropsychological profile. *Journal of Clinical and Experimental Neuropsychology, 10*(2), 125–131.

Preus, M. (1984). The Williams syndrome: Objective definition and diagnosis. *Clinical Genetics, 25*, 422–428.

Reilly, J. S., Klima, E. S., & Bellugi, U. (1990). Once more with feeling: Affect and language in atypical populations. *Development and Psychopathology, 2*, 367–391.

Schmidt-Sidor, B., Wisniewski, K. E., Shepard, T. H., & Sersen, E. A. (1990). Brain growth in Down syndrome subjects 15 to 22 weeks of gestational age and birth to 60 months. *Clinical Neuropathology, 9*(4), 181–190.

Udwin, O., & Yule, W. (1991). A cognitive and behavioural phenotype in Williams syndrome. *Journal of Clinical and Experimental Neuropsychology, 13*(2), 232–244.

Von Arnim, G., & Engel, P. (1964). Mental retardation related to hypercalcaemia. *Developmental Medicine and Child Neurology, 6*, 366–377.

Weis, S. (1991). Morphometry and magnetic resonance imaging of the human brain in normal controls and Down's syndrome. *Anatomical Record, 231*, 593–598.

Williams, J. C. P., Barrett-Boyes, B. G., & Lowe, J. B. (1961). Supravalvular aortic stenosis. *Circulation, 24*, 1311–1318.

Effects of Altered Auditory Sensitivity and Age of Language Acquisition on the Development of Language-Relevant Neural Systems: Preliminary Studies of Williams Syndrome

Helen J. Neville
The Salk Institute, and
University of California, San Diego

Debra L. Mills
Ursula Bellugi
The Salk Institute

From the perspective of cognitive neuroscience, the great promise of studying populations like those with Williams syndrome is the opportunity to link the extreme degree of variability in their cognitive profiles (see chapter 2 of this volume) to concomitant and specific alterations in cerebral organization. In this endeavor, and in cognitive neurosciences generally, development can be a very powerful tool. In the adult, the brain is highly specified and behavior is optimal and so the amount of variability in both systems is typically low. In contrast the developing organism displays a high degree of change both in different neural systems and in cognition, and thus provides an important opportunity to link variability in one trajectory to variability in the other. In the case where more than one brain system and related cognitive abilities develop along a similar timecourse, populations with specific structural damage and, the topic of this volume, populations with specific patterns of deficient and spared cognitive functions, can contribute in important ways to the separation of cognitive processes and the identification of related brain systems.

Although the developmental perspective can significantly amplify the power of looking at groups with structural and functional deficits, this approach is often eschewed due to the dearth of information about developmental changes in the functional organization of the normal human brain. The massive structural, physiological, and pharmacological changes that occur until at least 15 or 20 years of age (Huttenlocher, 1990) probably influence and interact with shifts in the organization of the systems that underwrite developing cognition. Thus there is an urgent need now for studies of normal neurobehavioral development that can serve as a baseline for comparing abnormally developing groups and to assess which anomalous results are indicative of developmental arrest, and which signal the emergence of new patterns.

It is also important now to characterize the organization and operation of more than one function in these developing populations. A major goal of developmental science is to understand how the development of one domain influences the development of another. In view of the animal and human literatures documenting the role of input and competitive interactions in stabilizing the organization of particular brain systems (Kaas, 1991; Neville, 1990; Rauschecker, 1991; Sur, Pallas, & Roe 1990), it is very likely that in developmental disorders even spared cognitive functions will be mediated by brain systems that have become abnormally organized due to alterations of the systems associated with deficient cognitive processes.

In our ongoing and future research on patients with Williams syndrome we take a multitask, developmental perspective. In this chapter we address a few questions raised by the many distinctive aspects of Williams patients' cognitive profile (see chapter 2 of this volume for a complete description). These subjects display hypersensitivity to sound. Is this effect mediated by cortical or subcortical structures? Does this phenomenon impact language processing in Williams? Auditory language comprehension and production are remarkably intact in the Williams subjects, in spite of the late onset of auditory language acquisition. Are their relatively intact language skills mediated by brain systems similar to those of normal children? Reading skills are highly variable in Williams. Some individuals learn to read well, at the normal age. Others begin to learn very late, and their skills are poor. What impact does reading skill and age of acquisition of reading have on cerebral organization for language? The specific issues we begin to explore in this chapter are:

1. What is the influence of hypersensitivity to sound on the development of language-relevant brain systems? We hypothesized that alterations in the early stages of sensory processing would be likely to impact the organization of later stages of language processing.

2. Are the preserved language abilities of Williams subjects mediated by neural systems similar to those that operate in normal controls? In view of

evidence indexing the highly interactive nature of brain development, we anticipated differences in language-relevant brain systems in Williams subjects.

3. What are the effects of age of acquisition of reading on cerebral organization? In view of several lines of evidence suggesting age of acquisition of spoken language impacts the organization of neural systems in language, we anticipated that early readers would display more normally organized neural specializations than would late readers.

In these studies we have taken a combined behavioral-electrophysiological approach so that results from different levels of analysis can mutually inform and constrain each other. The event-related potential (ERP) technique enables one to monitor the timecourse of activation of different neural systems on a millisecond-by-millisecond basis. Numerous studies have shown that the ERP technique can be used to index both sensory and cognitive processes, and that it is sensitive to specific alterations in related brain systems (Hillyard & Picton, 1987; Kutas & Van Petten, 1988; Neville, 1991; Regan, 1989; see also chapters 6 and 11 of this volume).

We want to stress that the data presented in the sections that follow can only be used, at this point, to develop working hypotheses. This is because of the small number of Williams subjects within any cell (defined by age and experimental paradigm). Although we presently have data from seven patients, we know from our studies of normal development, which show large changes over short time periods (Holcomb, Coffey, & Neville, 1992; Mills, Coffey-Corina & Neville, in press-a, 1993), that we cannot group subjects who differ in age. Thus each group often has only a few subjects, precluding statistical analyses. Additional factors that have reduced our numbers of subjects are that certain subjects could not read; others systematically blinked in response to auditory stimuli (probably related to their hyperacousis) so that their ERP data were contaminated with electrooculogram (EOG) activity and could not be used. Each of these factors leads us to temper our interpretations of the patterns of results with caution. Additionally, because individual differences in ERP morphology can be large (probably related to large individual differences in anatomy), single case studies of ERPs in Williams are not feasible.

METHODS

Subjects

Due to practical constraints (as noted), and the diversity in levels of cognitive abilities among Williams subjects, the studies described in the following sections include different subsets of the Williams subjects (see Table 4.1). In general, two groups of Williams subjects were tested: children ($N = 4$), two boys and two girls, 10–14 years of age; and adults ($N = 4$), one male and three females. (One subject, #4[see Table 4.1, was tested both as a child at age 14 years and as an adult at age 18 years.)

Additionally, data are presented for several normal control children and adults for each of the paradigms. The normal subjects were volunteers recruited from local schools and colleges. For the auditory recovery cycle paradigm, the normal controls included thirty-five children, thirteen 11- to 12-year-olds and twenty-two 13- to 14-year-olds. For the auditory sentences, data are presented from 134 normal control children and adults at 5–6 years ($N = 11$), 7–8 years ($N = 19$), 9–10 years ($N = 20$), 11–12 years ($N = 16$), 13–14 years ($N = 21$), 15–16 years ($N = 14$), 17–18 years ($N = 11$), 19–20 years ($N = 12$), and 21–22 years ($N = 10$). For the visual sentences, data are presented from 94 normal children and adults at 9–10 years ($N = 17$), 11–12 years ($N = 16$), 13–14 years ($N = 22$), 15–16 years ($N = 16$), 17–18 years ($N = 11$), and 19–20 years ($N = 12$). Approximately half of the control subjects were male.

All subjects were native speakers of English and were right-handed except for one Williams adult female (19 years), who was left-handed. Subjects were paid $5 per hour for their time.

Procedure

Auditory Recovery Cycle. This paradigm was employed to study early stages of auditory sensory processing, and the neural basis for the hypersen-

TABLE 4.1
Williams Syndrome Subjects Tested in Each Experimental Paradigm

ID	Age	Sex	Age Started Talking	Age Started Reading	Reading Grade Level	Auditory Recovery	Auditory Sentences	Visual Sentences
1[a]	10	M	3 yr	7 yr	6th		X	X
1	12					X		
2	10	F	12 mo	5–6 yr	NA[b]			X
3	12	F	9 mo	—	DR	X	X	
4[a]	14	M	2–3 yr	8 yr	RNS	X	X	
4	18				5th	X	X	X
5	18	F	2–3 yr	10 yr	3rd	X	X	X
6[a]	18	F	3–4 yr	9–10	4th	X		X
6	20					X	X	
7	19	F	2–3 yr	17 yr	RNS	X	X	

Note. DR = does not read. RNS = reading level not sufficient for our task (i.e., below second-grade level). NA = reading level was not available at the time of ERP testing.
[a]Subject tested at more than one age. [b]Subject at 6 years of age was reading at second-grade level.

sitivity to sound that Williams patients display. A series of 50-msec tones were presented to the subjects through headphones. Each tone was presented in one of three spatial positions (left ear, right ear, or center). For each of the three spatial locations the rates of stimulus presentation varied. One third of the stimuli in each location were preceded by either a 200-msec, 1,000-msec, or 2,000 msec interstimulus interval (ISI). Ninety percent of the stimuli were 1,500 Hz tones (standards); the other 10% were 1,000-Hz tones (targets). The subject was instructed to press a button when he or she detected one of the targets (1,000-Hz tones).

Auditory and Visual Sentences. This study enabled an assessment of early and late neural systems important in aspects of auditory language processing in Williams syndrome and also to compare the organization of neural systems important in reading in those who learned to read early and late in development. The stimuli consisted of 160 English sentences 3 to 13 words in length. Four sets of 80 sentences were generated from a master set. Half of the sentences in each set ended in a highly probable sentence ending (e.g., "After the show they clapped their *hands*") and half in an anomalous ending (e.g., "I don't go to school on Saturday or *floor*"). Lists of sentences were counterbalanced across subjects and modalities.

The auditory sentences consisted of naturally spoken words digitized at 16KHz and presented over headphones at the rate of one per second. The visual sentences were presented word by word on a video monitor at the rate of one per second (300-msec stimulus duration with a 700-msec ISI).

For both modalities the task was self-paced; a trial was initiated only after the subject pressed a button. Three seconds after the last word of the sentence the subject was prompted to press a button labeled *Yes* or *No* to indicate whether or not the sentence made sense.

EEG Recording

Our approach to indexing the brain systems active in Williams subjects is to record ERPs from electrodes placed over different brain areas within and between the two hemispheres. The power of ERPs is that they provide information about the timing and temporal sequence of neural events (with at least a millisecond resolution) and also provide information about the location of neural activity. This information occurs well before subjects make an overt response and so, especially important in clinical populations, this approach bypasses some of the limitations associated with behavioral measures, which may reflect and be influenced by several different, relatively late response-related aspects of processing.

The electroencephelogram (EEG) was recorded from electrodes previously attached to a cap ("Electro Cap") to reduce electrode application time.

Impedances were maintained below 5 Khoms. Recordings were taken from 16 positions over the scalp including standard 10–20 system locations, Fp1, Fp2, F7, F8, Cz, Pz, 01, 02, and from six nonstandard locations including left and right anterior temporal (one half the distance between F7 [8] and T3 [4]), left and right temporal (33% of the interaural distance lateral to Cz), and left and right parietal (30% of the interaural distance lateral to a point 13% of the nasion-inion distance posterior to Cz). Additionally, we recorded the EOG from over Fp1 and under the left eye to monitor blinks and vertical eye movements and from the right outer canthus to monitor horizontal eye movements. All electrodes were referenced to linked mastoids. The EEG was amplified by Grass model 7P511 amplifiers with a bandpass of .01 to 100 Hz.

ERPs were averaged off-line. The averages include only trials that were free from artifact to which the subject responded correctly.

RESULTS AND DISCUSSION

Auditory Recovery Cycle

We have previously reported that whereas brain stem auditory evoked potentials are similar in Williams and control subjects, the early components of the cortical ERP (i.e, N100 and P200 components) to tones display abnormally high amplitudes at fast repetition rates (ISI = 200 msec) that is, they are less refractory than normal (Bellugi, Bihrle, Neville, Jernigan, & Doherty, 1991; Neville, Holcomb, & Mills, 1989). The current group of Williams subjects was tested on this paradigm, and they each displayed similar results. Whereas normal controls display markedly reduced amplitudes to tones preceded by a 200-msec ISI compared to a 1,000-msec ISI, in Williams subjects this effect is not seen. Both the N100 and P200 responses are larger in Williams than normal subjects following a 200-msec ISI. This effect is confined to the auditory modality. Refractory period effects within the visual modality are equivalent in Williams patients and normal controls.

Tone-elicited ERPs from Williams subjects and control subjects also differed from each other following a 1,000-msec ISI, the rate of presentation of the words in the sentence-processing experiments. Thus these results may be pertinent in interpreting the results for auditory sentence processing.

Figure 4.1 displays the results for the younger Williams and an age-matched normal control group. The Williams subjects display considerably positively shifted ERPs to these tone stimuli resulting in abnormally large P200 amplitudes. This is apparent for both left and right ear stimuli. The large amplitude P200 response may be shifting the N100 response positively also. Both human clinical and MEG studies report that the N100 and P200 auditory potentials are generated in different fields within the transverse gyrus

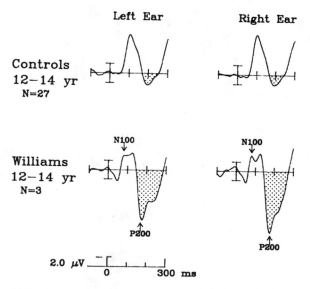

1000 ms ISI
1500 Hz tones at Cz

FIG. 4.1. ERPs elicited by 1,500 Hz tones preceded by a 1,000-ms interstimulus interval. ERPs averaged across 27 normal control subjects age 12–14 years and three Williams subjects at the same age. For both right- and left-ear stimuli the ERP is more positive in Williams subjects.

(i.e., Heschls) of the superior temporal lobe (Hari et al., 1987; Knight, Hillyard, Woods, & Neville, 1980; Pantev et al., 1990). The field that generates P200 is several centimeters anterior to the field that generates N100. Future research may find that pharmacological factors implicated in Williams (e.g., CGRP; Bellugi et al., 1991) show a distribution that differentiates these two fields. Next we consider the extent to which this abnormal early auditory response may influence auditory language-processing systems.

Auditory Sentence Processing

In Fig. 4.2 are shown the ERP responses to open class words (i.e., nouns, verbs, and adjectives that refer to specific objects and events) in the middle of spoken sentences, recorded from over the left temporal region.

Normal Subjects. On the left are ERPs from normal subjects age 5–22 years. There is a large decrease in the overall amplitude of the ERP with age,

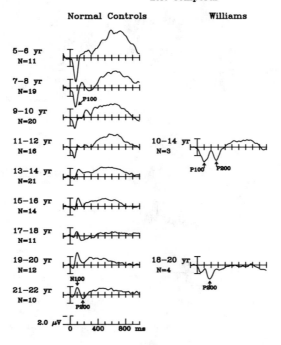

AUDITORY SENTENCES
Open Class Words
Left Temporal

FIG. 4.2. ERPs from normal control subjects age 5–22 years, and Williams subjects of two ages in response to open class words in auditory sentences. Williams subjects of both ages display P2 responses that are more positive than those of normal controls at any age.

and the morphology changes with age. For example the P100 response is large in young children, but is absent in adults. The N100 latency decreases markedly with age. However the P200 component is not prominent at any age.

Williams Subjects. The ERPs from the adult Williams subjects are of similar overall gain to the age-matched normal controls, but the morphology of the ERPs is different and is dominated by a prominent P200 response. The fact that this type of response is not evident at any age in the normal subjects suggests this effect is not indexing a developmental delay in the Williams subjects. The younger Williams subjects display a similar pattern of considerably enhanced P200 relative to age-matched controls.

These results suggest that in these Williams subjects, each very fluent in speech production and comprehension, the initial stages of auditory language processing are not conducted by the same neural systems as those that operate in normal subjects. The similarity of the abnormal ERP to that observed in the recovery cycle experiment suggests this effect may be related to the hyperexcitability of the auditory system. If this is so, we should not see a similar enhancement of P200 in Williams patients' ERPs to visually presented words. This of course assumes that, initially at least, the systems that process spoken and written language are not the same. The available evidence suggests that whereas the auditory P200 (i.e., second positive component) is generated within the transverse gyrus of the superior temporal lobe, the visual P200 is generated within extrastriate cortex.

Visual Sentence Processing

Normal Controls.   Figure 4.3 displays ERPs elicited by open class words in the middle of visual sentences recorded from over left temporal regions. On the left are responses from normal subjects age 9–20 years. Both the

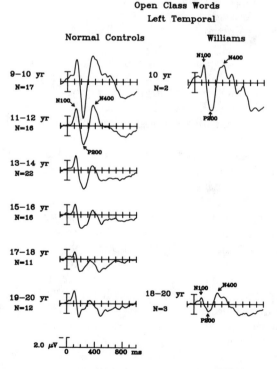

FIG. 4.3.   ERPs from normal control subjects age 9–20 years and Williams subjects of two ages in response to open class words in visual sentences. Williams subjects display an ERP morphology very similar to that of normal controls.

amplitude and latency of N100 and P200 diminish with age. Additionally, the N400 response displayed marked reductions between 9 and 13 years of age. This ERP component has been positively linked to search and/or integration of word meaning, and is negatively correlated with word frequency (Holcomb & Neville, 1990; Kutas & Van Petten, 1988; Rugg, 1990).

Williams Subjects. The N100 and P200 from the Williams subjects (right of Fig. 4.3) display ERP component amplitudes, latencies, and morphologies that are normal for their age, consistent with the hypothesis that the abnormal ERP responses to the auditorily presented words were influenced by alterations of early auditory processing. In addition, the amplitude of the N400 response in Williams adults was larger than that of age-matched controls. This less mature response is in keeping with the late onset of reading in this group. Their reduced fluency and experience with written English may require more effortful search and/or integration of words into sentence context (see Table 4.1; see also Neville, Coffey, Holcomb, & Tallal, 1993). The 10-year-old Williams subjects appear to display age-appropriate N400 amplitudes. These individuals began to read at the normal age and display reading skills close to normal for their age (Table 4.1; see also Holcomb, et al., 1992).

We have previously reported that visually presented closed class words (e.g., articles, conjunctions that are important in the grammar of English) elicit ERPs that are asymmetrical from the two hemispheres, and that the development of this asymmetry may be dependent on early exposure to English (e.g., it is absent in congenitally deaf subjects who acquire reading skills relatively late and imperfectly; Neville, Mills, & Lawson, 1992). In view of these results, Williams subjects who learned to read late should not display the normal asymmetry in response to closed class words, whereas those that begin to read at the normal age may display the pattern normal for their age.

In Fig. 4.4 are shown the ERPs to closed class words in the middle of visually presented sentences, recorded from over the left and right temporal regions. Normal subjects (left) over the age of 15 years display a marked asymmetry beginning around 200 ms whereby the left hemisphere is more negative than the right. Younger normal subjects display a reduced asymmetry in the same direction. The age-related change in asymmetry arises from the loss with age of the negative response in the right hemisphere. ERPs from Williams adults do not display any asymmetry, consistent with the hypothesis that this effect is dependent on the early acquisition of language skills. They display a normal morphology, but the negative component is apparent over both hemispheres, as in young normal children. The ERPs from the younger Williams subjects who learned to read at the normal age display an asymmetry in the normal direction. If upheld in future studies, such a pattern of results would

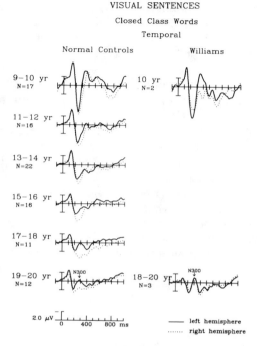

FIG. 4.4. ERPs from left and right temporal areas of normal controls and Williams subjects in response to closed class words in visual sentences. Williams adults lack the asymmetry observed in normal adults.

be in keeping with the hypothesis that early exposure to English is important in the development of this aspect of cerebral organization.

Semantic Priming

Several studies of normal adults have demonstrated that the processing of a word is facilitated when it is preceded by a semantically related word or context (Schvaneveldt, Ackerman, & Semlear, 1977; West & Stanovich, 1978). It has been proposed that these effects are mediated by the activation of connections between representations of words and that these are more numerous or stronger between related items. The threshold for activation of a particular word may be lowered by a related context or word. If neural representations of words within the auditory system are susceptible to effects of increased excitability, as are other aspects of auditory processing in Williams, it may be that more words would be more strongly interconnected and would display lower thresholds in Williams than in normal subjects. Behavioral studies (see chapter 2 of this volume) have reported that Williams subjects generate more, less frequent, and less prototypical responses to category names than IQ-matched controls. This effect could be mediated by an increased facilitation between lexical items. By this view we would predict at least normal, or greater than normal semantic priming effects in Williams subjects in the auditory but not the visual modality (i.e., in spite of their late acquisition of language).

Figure 4.5 displays ERPs from left and right temporal regions to congruous and anomalous words at the ends of auditory sentences. Responses are from normal children age 5–22 years. The early ERP components display morphological and amplitude changes with age, (as in Fig. 4.2). As fully reported in Holcomb, Coffey, and Neville (1992), at all ages anomalous words elicit a large negative response (N400) that has been linked to search or integration of word meaning. This negative response diminishes with age. Responses to congruent words display a different pattern of age-related changes. In younger children these also elicit a negative component, however with age

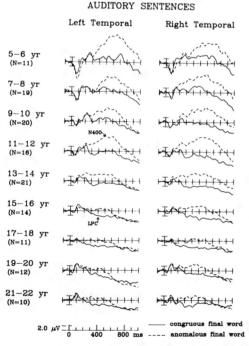

FIG. 4.5.   ERPs from normal control subjects age 5–22 years in response to semantically congruous and anomalous words at the end of auditory sentences. The N400 response to anomalous words declines with age and the LPC to congruous words increases with age.

and experience (by 15 years) this is replaced by a positive response (LPC) that indexes greater priming of the expected word.

As seen in Fig. 4.6, over the left hemisphere both Williams adults and children display a positive response (LPC) to expected words that is larger than that of normal age-matched controls. This effect is consistent with the idea that Williams subjects display normal or enhanced connections between related lexical items in the auditory modality. If this effect is related to auditory hypersensitivity, it should not be evident in the visual modality.

Figure 4.7 displays ERPs to anomalous and congruous words at the ends of visual sentences, from normal controls age 8–22 years. These results also show a gradual reduction of the amplitude of N400 to anomalous words, and a loss of N400 to congruous words by 15 years, when ERPs are characterized by a positivity (LPC).

As seen in Fig. 4.8, in contrast to the results for auditory sentences, Williams subjects display a normal (children) or less than normal (adults) degree of positivity (LPC) in ERPs elicited by contextually primed sentences. Recall that (for unknown reasons) the Williams adults learned to read late, whereas the Williams children learned to read at a relatively normal age. The reduction in priming for Williams adults in the visual modality may be

WILLIAMS SUBJECTS

AUDITORY SENTENCES

Left Temporal   Right Temporal

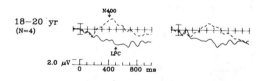

FIG. 4.6. ERPs from two groups of Williams subjects in response to semantically congruous and anomalous words at the end of auditory sentences. The positivity to congruous words is larger than that observed in normal age matched controls.

VISUAL SENTENCES

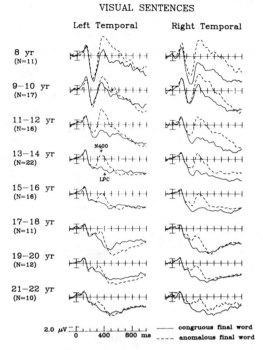

FIG. 4.7. ERPs from normal control subjects age 8–22 years in response to semantically congruous and anomalous words at the end of visual sentences. The N400 to anomalous words diminishes with age and the LPC to congruous words increases with age.

related to their late acquisition of and reduced experience with reading. The very different effects for Williams adults within the auditory modality may be, at least in part, mediated by a hyperexcitable auditory system. The normal effects for Williams children may be related to their normal age of acquisition of reading.

Finally, we note that in normal control subjects the sentence-priming effect is larger from the right than the left hemisphere for both auditory and visual sentences at virtually all ages. We have reported that this asymmetry increases with age, but we know little of other variables that may determine the development of this pattern. The Williams subjects did not show the normal pattern of asymmetry, with the exception of the Williams children when reading. As auditory language acquisition occurred later than normal in Williams children and adults, and visual reading was acquired late by the adults, but at the normal age for the children, this pattern invokes the working hypothesis that age of exposure to language is important in this aspect of cerebral development.

WILLIAMS SUBJECTS

VISUAL SENTENCES

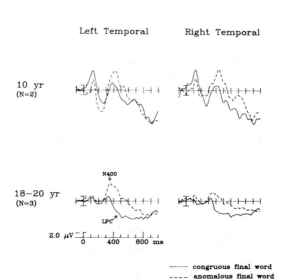

FIG. 4.8. ERPs from Williams subjects to semantically congruous and anomalous words at the end of visual sentences. The LPC to congruous words is not larger than in normal subjects, in contrast to the results for auditory sentences.

SUMMARY

Tones elicited ERPs from the Williams subjects that displayed a normal morphology but that were considerably less refractory than were those of normal subjects. This effect was not observed in the visual modality, nor at any age in normal development. These results suggest that similar neural systems are active in Williams and normal subjects, but these are hyperexcitable in Williams. By contrast, auditorily presented words elicited ERPs of highly abnormal morphology, not observed at any age in normal development. These results suggest that the identity of the systems that mediate the preserved language in Williams are not the same as those that operate in normal control subjects. By contrast, the morphology of ERPs elicited by visually presented words was normal in Williams subjects.

The priming effects for semantically congruous words at the ends of auditory sentences were larger than normal in Williams than control subjects, but within the visual modality they were normal or smaller than normal. Both of these patterns in the language studies raise the hypothesis that early sensory processing within the auditory modality influences the operation of language-relevant systems within that modality only. Finally, the abnormal pattern of hemispheric asymmetries in ERPs associated with semantic priming is difficult to interpret because very few studies have reported variation in the pattern. However, the results as a whole suggest age of acquisition of a language within a modality may be important.

Nonetheless, these patterns of results suggest that alterations in early sensory processing can impact the organization and operation of cognitive systems. The hypersensitivity of the auditory system in Williams subjects may in part underlie the sparing of and the precocious and hyperfluent nature of the Williams subjects' language, and the fact that this development occurs following abnormal delays in the acquisition of auditory language. The normal or hypernormal auditory priming effects contrast with the results for the visual modality. They also differ from the results for hemispheric differentiation, which appears to require language acquisition to occur at specific times for the normal pattern to occur.

This pattern of results taken as whole suggests that sensory development, age at testing, age of exposure, and skill level each have significant and distinct effects on different and specific aspects of the development of cerebral organization. When these variables are identified and controlled, studies on populations with specific neurocognitive deficits can inform hypotheses about brain function. The Williams population is particularly valuable in this endeavor by virtue of the several distinct sensory and cognitive functions that are affected in them. Moreover, they are one of a very few populations that provides an important testing ground for issues concerning the extent of interdependence of sensory and cognitive skills and the acquisition of language.

ACKNOWLEDGMENTS

This research was supported by grants DC00128, DC00481, NS22343, DC01289, and HD26022.

REFERENCES

Bellugi, U., Bihrle, A., Neville, H., Jernigan, T., & Doherty, S. (1991). Language, cognition, and brain organization in a neurodevelopmental disorder. In M. Gunnar & C. Nelson (Eds.), *Developmental behavioral neuroscience* (pp. 201–232). Hillsdale, NJ: Lawrence Erlbaum Associates.

Hari, R., Pelizzone, M., Makela, J. P., Hallstrom, J., Leinone, L., & Lounasmaa, O. V. (1987). Neuromagnetic responses of the human auditory cortex to on- and offsets of noise bursts. *Audiology, 26,* 31–43.

Hillyard, S. A., & Picton, T. W. (1987). Electrophysiology of cognition. In F. Plum (Ed.), *Handbook of physiology: Sec. 1. The nervous system V higher functions of the brain: Part 2* (pp. 519–584). Bethesda, MD: American Physiological Society.

Holcomb, P. J., Coffey, S. A., & Neville, H. J. (1992). Visual and auditory sentence processing: A developmental analysis using event-related brain potentials. *Developmental Neuropsychology*. *8*, 203–241.

Holcomb, P. J., & Neville, H. J. (1990). Auditory and visual semantic priming in lexical decision: A comparison using event-related brain potentials. *Language and Cognitive Processes, 5*, 281–312.

Huttenlocher, P. R. (1990). Morphometric study of human cerebral cortex development. *Neuropsychologia, 28*, 517–527.

Kaas, J. H. (1991). Plasticity of sensory and motor maps in adult mammals. *Annual Review of Neuroscience, 14*, 137–167.

Knight, R. T., Hillyard, S. A., Woods, D. L., & Neville, H. J. (1980). The effects of frontal and temporal-parietal lesions on the auditory evoked potential in man. *Electroencephalography and Clinical Neurophysiology, 50*, 112–124.

Kutas, M., & Van Petten, C. (1988). Event-related brain potential studies of language. In P. K. Ackles, J. R. Jennings, & M. G. H. Coles (Eds.), *Advances in psychophysiology* (Vol. 3, pp. 139–187). Greenwich, CT: JAI.

Mills, D. M., Coffey-Corina, S. A., & Neville, H. J., (in press-a). Changes in cerebral organization during primary language acquisition. In G. Dawson & K. Fischer (Eds.), *Human behavior and the developing brain*. New York: Guilford.

Mills, D. M., Coffey-Corina, S. A, & Neville, H. J. (1993). Language acquisition and cerebral specialization in 20-month-old infants, *Journal of Cognitive Neuroscience, 5*, 326–342.

Neville, H. J. (1990). Intermodal competition and compensation in development: Evidence from studies of the visual system in congenitally deaf adults. In A. Diamond (Ed.), *The development and neural bases of higher cognitive function* (pp. 71–91). New York: New York Academy of Sciences Press.

Neville, H. J. (1991). Neurobiology of cognitive and language processing: Effects of early experience. In K. R. Gibson & A. C. Petersen (Eds.), *Brain maturation and cognitive development: Comparative and cross-cultural perspectives* (pp. 355–380). Hawthorne, NY: Aldine de Gruyter Press.

Neville, H. J., Coffey, S. A., Holcomb, P. J., & Tallal, P. (1993). The neurobiology of sensory and language processing in language impaired children. *Journal of Cognitive Neuroscience, 5*, 235–253.

Neville, H. J., Holcomb, P. J., & Mills, D. L. (1989). Auditory sensory and language processing in Williams syndrome: An ERP study. *Journal of Clinical and Experimental Neuropsychology, 11*, 52.

Neville, H. J., Mills, D. L., & Lawson, D. S. (1992). Fractionating language: Different neural subsystems with different sensitive periods. *Cerebral Cortex, 2*, 244–258.

Pantev, C., Hoke, M., Lehnertz, K., Lutkenhoner, B., Fahrendorf, G., & Stober, U. (1990). Identification of sources of brain neuronal activity with high spatiotemporal resolution through combination of neuromagnetic source localization (NMSL) and magnetic resonance imaging (MRI). *Electroencephalography and Clinical Neurophysiology, 75*, 173–184.

Rauschecker, J. (1991). Mechanisms of visual plasticity: Hebb synapse, NMDA receptors and beyond. *Physiological Reviews, 71*, 587–615.

Regan, D. (1989). *Human brain electrophysiology*. New York: Elsevier Science.

Rugg, M. D. (1990). Event-related brain potentials dissociate repetition effects of high- and low-frequency words. *Memory & Cognition, 18*, 367–379.

Schvaneveldt, R., Ackerman, B. P., & Semlear, T. (1977). The effect of semantic context on children's word recognition. *Child Development, 48*, 612–616.

Sur, M., Pallas, S., & Roe, A. (1990). Cross-modal plasticity in cortical development: Differentiation and specification of sensory neocortex. *Trends in Neurosciences, 13*, 227–233.

West, R. F., & Stanovich, K. (1978). Automatic contextual facilitation in readers of three ages. *Child Development, 49*, 717–727.

Section 2

AUTISM

5

Neurobiologic Correlates in the Classification and Study of Autism

Eric Schopler
University of North Carolina Medical School

This volume grew out of an exciting workshop on neurocognitive deficits in children, with special emphasis on the most current methods for studying localization of cognitive functions in the brain and the stability of these patterns and their biological substrates with age and development. As an introduction to the autism section, it seems most useful to provide a historical perspective on the autism syndrome, on its official diagnostic classification, and on psychobiological research on autism. Because there have been such striking advances in the scientific methodology for studying some of the biological substrates of cognitive functions, a historical perspective may offer some guidelines for assessing which research prospects and strategies may provide better understanding and treatment in the future.

Infantile autism has had a relatively short scientific history beginning with Kanner's (1943) classic introduction of the syndrome into the mental health literature. During these last five decades, two intriguing paradoxes have been reflected and debated in the field. The first has been the question of whether autism was primarily an emotional reactive disorder, a child's social withdrawal from unconscious hostility and misguidance by the parents, or was it better understood as a biological disorder? The second paradox has to do with the official diagnosis of autism. Should the official definition of autism in the *Diagnostic and Statistical Manual of Mental Disorders* (*DSM*) of the American Psychiatric Association (APA) conform to the most precise definition available from current research knowledge or should it reflect the clinical, administrative, and legal needs for which the *Manual* is used in the United States. For the last part of this chapter, I discuss the implications of the resolution of these two paradoxes for future research strategies.

HISTORICAL PERSPECTIVE ON THE AUTISM SYNDROME

Kanner (1943) was the first to describe a series of children who shared certain abnormal characteristics from the beginning of their lives. They had difficulty in their social relationships in which they were aloof and unresponsive. Their communication skills were impaired and included a variety of language and cognitive peculiarities. These impairments were also reflected in a continuum of mental retardation, yet these children showed unusual abilities: rote memory for numbers, musical and artistic talents, and special interests in various topics and routines.

Explanation from Theory

Although Kanner (1943) was the first to describe this group of children in the mental health literature, there is evidence that similar children existed in earlier times. Strange and mysterious children have appeared throughout known history, their origins sometimes a matter of spooky rumor and wild theoretical speculation. Some were referred to as feral children, believed to be suckled and reared by wolves or other wild animals. Historically, the best known example of the wolf-reared group was probably Romulus and Remus. Legend has it they were cast into the Tiber River, mysteriously retrieved, and then reared by wolves until they rejoined the human community and founded Rome. Many other such cases have been reported (Lane, 1976; Simon, 1978). Two of the more recent cases were discovered in India in 1929. The frightened Aborigines in Reverend Singh's parish discovered two wild girls they believed to be ghosts. After investigating the ghosts, Reverend Singh reassured the natives that they were not ghosts at all, but merely two human girls who had been raised by wolves. He transferred them to his parish and kept a diary on their life with him.

After the diary was translated into English, it was studied by Gesell, at Yale University, who then published a remarkably unscientific account of the diary (Gesell, 1941). He raised no questions about the accuracy of his sources and translation. Instead he assessed the children's development according to the well-published Gesell Developmental Norms. He considered that the surviving one of the pair was probably a 17-year-old girl functioning with the language and social behavior of a normal 3-year-old child. Nevertheless, he interpreted in his developmental assessment that she was "born a normal infant" (p. 72) because he thought her developmental lag was a successful adjustment to the wolf den, an adjustment admittedly constructed by Gesell's imagination.

A parallel flight of fantasy was published by Bettelheim (1959). He believed that the girl had not been raised by wolves at all. Instead he presented clinical examples showing that she, like other feral children, behaved very much like the autistic children at his school. He argued that the so-called "feral children" were actually autistic children who had been rejected and emotionally deprived by their mothers.

The prescientific history of autism has been discussed in some detail because it nicely illustrates how intelligent and well-meaning scholars can interpret the same observational data in entirely different ways. In the instance of the Indian girls, authorities in theology, child development, and psychoanalysis each typed the child according to their own favorite and unsubstantiated theories. Singh claimed that the frightening "ghost children" were actually feral children raised by a wolf. Gesell interpreted the girls' symptoms, which might now be considered as mental deficiencies, as belonging to a normal child who had adjusted to life in a wolf den. And Bettelheim, the most vocal interpreter of autism in terms of psychoanalytic theories (Bettelheim, 1967), was convinced that the nonexistent "feral children" were actually "autistic children with feral mothers."

Shift to Empirical Explanation

Consistent with the post-World War II popularity of Freudian interpretations, Kanner (1943) tried to explain autism as a form of social withdrawal from unconscious hostility and rejections by well-to-do and highly educated parents whose controlled personalities and compulsive intellectual interests were believed to produce both professional achievements and autistic children. This explanation of autism led to counterproductive blame of parents, demoralizing their capacity to foster development in their own children.

During the 1960s, a perceptible shift occurred in the field of mental health, placing greater emphasis on the rules of evidence and empirical research than on the seductive metaphors of Freudian theory. Rimland (1964) wrote a ground-breaking review of the existing autism literature, convincingly showing the lack of evidence for psychogenesis and the greater likelihood of biological mechanisms producing the autism syndrome.

Since that time, evidence for the biological bases for autism has been accumulating at an accelerating rate. Beginning in the 1970s, a number of studies (Rutter, 1970) reported incidents of epilepsy among autistic people, which often occurred for the first time with the onset of adolescence. Epilepsy was reported in 25%–30% of the autistic population, at greater frequency in the more severely retarded population (Corbett, 1983; Olsson, Steffenberg, & Gillberg, 1988; Tuchman, Rapin, & Shinnar, 1989). When this frequency of seizures is compared with the incidence of .5% among the general population, there can be little doubt that many cases of autism involve brain abnormality. In addition to the development of seizures, other biological mechanisms have been identified with varying amounts of supporting or replicable research evidence. Some of these may be associated with other medical problems like tuberous sclerosis (Hunt & Dennis, 1987), whereas others represent more primary causal mechanisms like genetic factors identified by twin studies (Folstein & Rutter, 1977), multiple family incidence (Ritvo, Spence, Freeman, Mason-Brothers, & Marazita, 1985), and the Fragile-X phenomenon (Brown et al., 1986; Davies, 1991). Infectious diseases have been implicated such as rubella (Chess, Korn, & Fernandez, 1971), and metabolic disorders have been described as subtypes of autism (Coleman & Gillberg, 1985). Various structural abnormalities in the brain have been identified from autopsy, including temporal lobe differences (DeLong, 1978) and hydrocephalus (Coleman & Gillberg, 1985). The best replicated to date appear to be abnormalities of the cerebellum (Courchesne, Yeung-Courchesne, Press, Hesselink, & Jernigan, 1988), see Courchesne's chapter in this volume (chapter 6).

Today the paradox between the psychological and the biological causal emphasis has been resolved by an accumulation of empirical research. Where, during the early Kanner era, autism was assumed to be a single-cause disease process most likely rooted in parental psychopathology, today it is recognized that no biologic mechanism has accounted for all cases of autism. Most likely, the replicated demonstrations of biologic mechanisms may help to establish subtypes in the future. As the prevalence rate for autism has been reported as increased from 5 in 10,000 from the first epidemiological study (Wing, 1978) upward to 15 in 10,000 (Sugiyama & Tokuichiro, 1989; Wing, 1986), it is quite likely that other structures and combinations may yet be found. In the meantime, a next issue to consider is: How will the brain structures and cognitive functions discussed in the chapters of this volume be reflected in the official diagnostic classification of the autism syndrome?

Classification by Clinical or Research Criteria?

The members comprising the APA work group revising the Pervasive Developmental Disorders section of the *Diagnostic and Statistical Manual of Mental Disorders* (3rd ed., rev.) (DSM–III–R) are agreed on the general proposition that changes in the definition of psychiatric disorders should be made on the basis of scientific evidence (Rutter & Schopler, 1992). Those concerned with the latest revision of the official autism diagnostic category have been intrigued by an apparent paradox. Some members of the APA work group have argued that the *DSM–III-R* definition of autism is much broader than the one in the *Diagnostic and Statistical Manual of Mental Disorders* (3rd ed.) (*DSM–III*), whereas others have complained of the opposite. The *DSM–III–R* definition has resulted in underdiagnosis of autism because it is too complex for clinicians who then use the vaguer category of Pervasive Developmental Disorder Not Otherwise Specified (PDDNOS).

HISTORICAL PERSPECTIVE
ON THE DIAGNOSTIC CLASSIFICATION
OF AUTISM

DSM–I and –II

The paradox raised by this *DSM–III–R* revision process may be resolved by reviewing the relationship between autism research and its historically official classification. The first *DSM* was published in 1952. Most of the diagnostic labels were qualified as "reactions," and autism was not included in the *Manual*. The 16 years until *DSM–II* was published in 1968 were characterized by a preponderance of case studies, theoretical formulations, and observations based on psychoanalytic theory. Empirical research in these disorders was sparse, and editorial policies in psychiatric journals had not yet set up empirical research publication criteria. *DSM–II* also did not identify autism as a separate diagnostic category. However, biologically oriented autism research appeared during that period.

One early example of biologically oriented research during that period was my study comparing preferences in near and distance receptor usage (Schopler, 1965), showing that autistic children use more tactual than visual choices. Although this study did not offer any clue to the more important long-range finding that autistic children are relatively strong in the visual modality (Schopler, 1989), it did contribute to the explanatory concept formulated by Ornitz and Ritvo (1968) of autism as a function of perceptual inconstancy. Ornitz identified both hypersensitivity and hyposensitivity to auditory and visual stimuli as sensory disturbances specific to the autism syndrome. He interpreted these disturbances as providing sensory input through stereotypical, repetitive movement. He presented evidence that the vestibular system functions to maintain equilibrium and stabilized gaze and to modulate input from other sensory modalities and motor excitement. The spinning and rocking behaviors of autistic children were offered as evidence to support the vestibular dysfunction hypothesis. The perceptual inconstancy research was cited here as an example of an interesting research potential developed over several years without being reflected in the official diagnosis of autism.

DSM–III

In fact, it is worth noting that Kanner's (1943) autism definition did not include sensory disturbances, nor did the *DSM–III* (APA, 1980). *DSM–III* represented the four criteria, sometimes referred to as the Rutter Criteria. These were confined to the young age groups. Primary features included age of onset under 30 months along with a lack of relatedness, communications handicaps, and perseverative behavior. The research priority correlating with

DSM-III appeared to be Rutter's emphasis on autism as a cognitive disorder involving impaired language and problems with sequencing, abstraction, and coding functions (Dawson, 1983; Rutter, 1983).

Dissatisfaction with *DSM-III* was expressed to justify changes incorporated in *DSM-III-R. DSM-III* was said to be too narrow because it included only infantile autism without recognizing developmental changes in symptoms of older children. Age of onset as a defining criterion was confined to 30 months or less.

DSM-III-R

Modifications were made in *DSM-III-R* (APA, 1987). The four major criteria from *DSM-III* were reduced to three. Recent research data indicated that age of onset was sometimes 36 months or even later (Short & Schopler, 1988; Volkmar, Stier, & Cohen, 1985). Accordingly, age of onset was removed from *DSM-III-R* as one of the defining features of autism. The major syndrome components of special interests and of impairment in the social and communication functions, along with special interests, were maintained. However, the criteria for these three autism dimensions were increased to 16. The diagnosis of autism required that 8 of the 16 be present. Moreover, in *DSM-III-R* an attempt was made to include developmental changes in the several autism criteria. These changes were now said to broaden *DSM-III-R* excessively. In *DSM-III-R* the autism definition was confined to young children and did not reflect developmental changes, whereas the *DSM-III-R* covered a broader age range and tried to reflect developmental changes in the 16 criteria. On the other hand, clinicians found the *DSM-III-R* criteria too complex to apply. In order to meet the autism diagnosis criteria, the presence of the 8 of 16 had to include at least 2 under social reciprocity, 1 under communication, and 1 under special interests. The 2-1-1 pattern was cumbersome. As a result clinicians overused PDD, and many children were said to be deprived of appropriate services for autism. New pressure developed to correct this with the publication of *DSM-IV.*

Although the publication of *DSM-IV* will no doubt be a financial success, it is unlikely that it will resolve the conflict between the clinical and research requirements of a definition. For research purposes, it is important for replication and scientific communication to maximize the use of explicit characteristics and precise operational definitions. For clinical purposes, on the other hand, in the present state of the art, there are no important intervention differences between autism and pervasive developmental disorders (Campbell & Schopler, 1989). Such differences in treatment are based on individual considerations.

Relative Aspects of Classification

The proposition that the definition of a sample of autistic children should vary with the selection purpose is not new (Rutter & Schopler, 1992; Schopler & Rutter, 1978). It was based on the recognition that psychiatric disorders like the autism syndrome are composed of many complex characteristics, which often take their behavioral shape from the environmental context in which they occur. Likewise, these autism characteristics show considerable heterogeneity. It is fair to say that there is no single specific behavioral process in autism that occurs in all autistic children. Because most empirical research is focused on only a few variables, it is usually more productive to define the sample according to the research purposes. For example, in order to study self-injurious behavior, it should be recognized that most autistic children do not show this behavior. It then becomes more fruitful to study self-injurious behavior across diagnostic categories rather than just within the autistic population.

Research Emphasis on Cognition Hypothesis

A parallel situation has occurred during the past 10 years with the increased shift from research on cognitive to social deficits and the neurological underpinnings and components of social behavior in animals and humans. From a clinical perspective, it was often agreed that there was considerable overlap between cognitive and social functions. However, in developing research, the most impaired functions in autism included language and cognitive functions (Rutter, 1983; Sigman, chapter 7; Sigman & Ungerer, 1984). The dissociation between social and cognitive functions can be observed in different groups of severely retarded children who are frequently only mildly asocial, whereas there are profoundly asocial children with near normal levels of intellectual functioning, as in Asperger variations of autism (Gillberg, Steffenburg, & Jakobsson, 1987). Support for the distinction between cognitive and social deficits has also been cited because of the commonly found patterns of strengths and weaknesses in autistic children. Language and cognition have been cited among the most serious impairments for autistic children (Rutter, 1983; Sigman & Ungerer, 1984). These include the following functions not specified in *DSM* classification: problems of comprehension, verbal expression, attention, abstraction, disorganization; poor memory for nonspecial interests; deficits in auditory processing and generalization of learning; and difficulty with change. Relative patterns of cognitive strengths have been identified in the special interests and rote memory skills characteristic of the syndrome. Moreover, visual-spatial and sensory-motor processes are frequently spared or relatively well functioning

(Courchesne, Lincoln, Kilman, & Galambos, 1985; Minshew, Furman, Goldstein, & Payton, 1990). The prevalence of visual processing strengths across a heterogeneous sample of autistic children has been an especially striking clinical observation in our TEACCH Program and the basis for our developing visual teaching structures over an extended period (Schopler, 1989; Schopler, Brehm, Kinsbourne, & Reichler, 1971).

Research Emphasis on Reciprocal Social Interaction

If the cognitive deficits have received special attention in the past, the cognitive functions most directly involved in the primary impairment of reciprocal social interactions are attracting more serious research attention at present. The primary effect of the social deficit in autism has been advanced by data showing that people with autism have greater difficulty than control groups in understanding social and emotional information, even when levels of cognitive task difficulty are comparable. This sociocognitive deficit of autism has been described with heuristic eloquence by Frith and Baron-Cohen as the children's lack of a "theory of mind" (Baron-Cohen, Leslie, & Frith, 1985; Frith, 1989). This theoretical problem has been further reformulated as an impairment in shared meaning for communicative intent and reciprocal interactions. Other social and cognitive functions are being formulated and studied, including joint social attention, attention shifting, social attachment, shared understanding, taking turns, maintaining conversational topics, interpreting social cues such as tone of voice, facial expression, intonation and rhythm of speech.

It is noteworthy that many of the cognitive and social deficits named earlier and closely involved with the most interesting autism research have not been used in the official diagnosis of autism in the *DSM–III–R*, nor is it likely they will be identified in the forthcoming *DSM–IV*. These definitions have primarily a phenomenological basis, and are not conceptualized at the level of cognitive and social function cited previously.

TWO PSYCHOBIOLOGICAL RESEARCH MODELS

Thus far, I have attempted to present a brief history of two intriguing conflicts inspiring important debate and research on autism. The first revolved around casual explanations of biologic versus parental pathology. With the growing preference in the mental health field for empirical research evidence over metaphysical theory, impairment because of biological processes was established. The accumulation of empirical research data supported the inclusion of autism in the official *DSM* classification. One of the intriguing conflicts here was whether the autism definition should reflect the precision required for empirical research, or the somewhat broader criteria relevant to the administration and treatment for which individualized intervention is still needed. I have presented evidence that greater precision in the formulation of basic impairments in autism has developed, and this shift, as reflected in *DSM*, had alternately produced a research emphasis, first on cognitive deficit hypotheses, and then on the deficit in social reciprocity.

The localization model suggests that various behavioral patterns, measured by profiles of performance, reflect a single underlying pathologic process. It can affect one or more brain structures in varying combinations and severity, resulting in a syndrome classification like autism or Williams syndrome.

A multiple-systems approach, on the other hand, indicates that one or more deficits defining a syndrome involves many pathways and related structures. Impairment in a variety of these structures may produce the same syndrome. Which of these two models may be more productive in future research?

This issue is also an organizing concern for this volume. Is progress in understanding the autism syndrome and its neurobiologic substrates more likely to advance through research using the localization model, or will progress in understanding it be more rapid based on a developmental multiple-systems model, as suggested by Reichler and Lee (1987)?

Obstacles for identifying specific structures in the biologic substrata of autistic characteristics are multiple. They include: (a) heterogeneity across individuals meeting the most stringent criteria for classification, (b) variations in the semantics of defining criteria over time, (c) imperfect agreement among clinicians for the same cases, (d) variation in measures of both behavioral phenomenon and neurobiologic underpinnings, (e) multiple neurological anatomical involvement in most specific behaviors, and (f) variation in abnormal functioning during different observation periods and changes with maturation and development.

Localization Model

Given these formidable obstacles to localizing psychiatric disorders or behaviors associated with autism, it is noteworthy that a considerable body of research has been conducted or hypothesized for localized structures. I have already cited the example of Ornitz's work on the relationship between the vestibular system and autistic behaviors such as spinning and rocking. Ornitz (1983) acknowledged that other autistic characteristics such as disturbances of language and communication probably cannot be explained on the basis of vestibular dysfunction.

Damasio and Maurer (1978) attempted to extend disturbances of motility to other areas of the brain. In discussing a group of children diagnosed autistic by Rutter's criteria, they described an asymmetry of the lower part of the face noticeable when the children smiled or spoke spontaneously that did not show when they moved their facial musculature on request. This phenomenon of an emotionally determined facial asymmetry or paralysis has been interpreted as a sign of damage specifically to the thalamus or the mesial frontal lobes.

Another attempt to localize specific behavior came from DeLong's (1978) report of pneumoencephalographic (PEG) studies of a group of autistic children. He identified anatomical pathology centered on the left temporal horn of the left lateral ventricle. All of his 17 cases demonstrated failure to develop expressive speech. Language comprehension, although delayed, was less deficient, and all the cases showed profound disturbances in relationships to people. Other PEG studies showed that dilatation of the left temporal horn occurred in developmental language delay, but without autistic features. Likewise, even DeLong published such control cases. It is not necessary to criticize these studies for problems of design or methodology to see that they do not support the hypothesis that temporal lobe lesions are uniquely or uniformly associated with autism.

Subsequently, Bauman and Kemper (1985) reported a brain autopsy study of a well-documented 29-year-old man who was compared with an identically processed age- and sex-matched control. Both cerebra were well developed without gross lesions, abnormalities of myelination, or gliosis. However, cell packing was increased by 27%–58% of Purkinje cells. This reduced cell size and increased cell-packing density in the cerebellum were similar to such structures in an immature fetus and probably occurred during that phase of maturation rather than at maturity.

During the last decade, neuroimaging methodology and autopsy research have fanned new hope for finding neuroanatomic loci for autism. The most frequently identified abnormalities found in autism, regardless of the degree of mental retardation, have been the reductions of cerebellar tissue within the vermis and hemispheres (Courchesne, Hesselink, Jernigan, & Yeung-Courchesne, 1987; Courchesne et al., 1988), which with the aid of the new magnetic resonance imaging technology, has been identified in more than 10 studies demonstrating abnormalities of the cerebellum (Courchesne, 1991). It is impressive to have replicated findings of cerebellar abnormality, especially when these include autopsy studies, often considered more sensitive than neuroimaging data. Nevertheless, the question arises whether the cerebellum can be a central site in a developmental disorder involving functions of cognition and social reciprocity.

Multiple-Systems Model

The work of Courchesne and others, briefly summarized earlier, has demonstrated the involvement of the cerebellum in the autism syndrome, especially perhaps with specific cognitive functions like attention shift, an impairment involved with one of the primary features of autism—the specialized interests, causing autistic people such difficulty at times of change. Regardless of replication, brain structures implicated with a function like attention shift cannot account for the other features of the syndrome. Courchesne (1991) himself suggested indirect evidence from both animal and clinical research indicating a connection between autism and many other structures including the following: (a) cerebellar damage that has produced disturbance in smooth ocular tracking, (b) mutism, (c) problems with motor imitation, (d) projections to all levels of the reticular system are sometimes suggested as dysfunctional in autism, (e) cerebellum connections to neurotransmitter levels suggested as abnormal in autism, (f) the cerebellum modulating hippocampal activity and projecting to the hypothalamus and amygdala, both limbic regions hypothesized as dysfunctional in autism, and (g) disturbance of motivated behavior and reduction of social interaction. Even if this indirect involvement of the cerebellum with autism is supported in future research, it is evident that many different brain structures are also involved. Their contribution to the autism syndrome cannot be understood if only a specificity model is employed with a focus only on specific structure. Regardless of sophistication of imaging methodology, the specificity research model is limited by its underlying assumption of a direct relationship between the autism syndrome and specific brain structures.

It seems more likely that the important research progress in the future will have to invoke a multiple-systems model along the lines implied by Courchesne (1991) and advocated by Reichler and Lee (1987). Such a model may be derived from new models from the physical sciences admitting the coexistence of expected and unexpected events (Gleick, 1987) or using new mathematical models (Rumelhart, Hinton, & Williams, 1986). These may be adapted to study the interaction between certain cognitive functions and a network of related factors including cells and organs, biochemical processes, developmental changes, short- versus long-term environmental effects, to mention only a few. If, for example, we are studying a specific autism deficit, as in "shifting attention," rather than targeting subjects classified as autistic, it may be more fruitful to study "shifting attention" in a variety of subjects, including not only relevant brain structures, but also relevant muscle sequences, biochemical processes, and developmental factors, all shaping the function of attention shift. Such a multiple-systems approach could also use interdisciplinary research and move toward closer approximation between research and clinical phenomena.

SUMMARY

During the brief history of the autism syndrome, an important shift occurred from explaining the disorder with psychogenic theory to explaining it as the dysfunction of certain biologic processes. The change was attended by a growing acceptance of empirical research methodology for clarifying problems in the mental health domain. However, the official classification of the autism disorder serves important clinical and administrative purposes, but is not the necessary basis for biological research. Specific structures and functions identified by empirical research are not necessarily reflected in the official classification. However, it seems most likely that the newly acquired information on central nervous system structures and related functions needs to be integrated into multiple-systems, multiple-methods research strategy, if the current research momentum is to continue.

REFERENCES

American Psychiatric Association. (1980). *Diagnostic and statistical manual of mental disorders* (3rd ed.). Washington, DC: Author.

American Psychiatric Association. (1987). *Diagnostic and statistical manual of mental disorders* (3rd ed., rev.). Washington, DC: Author.

Baron-Cohen, S., Leslie, A. M., & Frith, U. (1985). Does the autistic child have a theory of mind? *Cognition, 21,* 37–46.

Bauman, M. L., & Kemper, T. L. (1985). Histoanatomic observations of the brain in early infantile autism. *Neurology, 35,* 866–874.

Bettelheim, B. (1959). Feral children and autistic children. *American Journal of Sociology, 64,* 455.

Bettelheim, B. (1967). *The empty fortress.* New York: Free Press.

Brown, W. T., Jenkins, E. C., Cohen, I. L., Fisch, G. S., Wolf-Schein, E. G., Gross, A., Waterhouse, L., Fein, D., Mason-Brothers, A., Ritvo, E., Ruttenberg, B. A., Bently, W., & Castells, S. (1986). Fragile X and autism: A multi-center survey. *American Journal of Medical Genetics, 23,* 341–352.

Campbell, M., & Schopler, E. (Eds.) (1989). Section 2: Pervasive developmental disorders. In American Psychiatric Association, *Treatment of psychiatric disorders: A task force report of the American Psychiatric Association* (pp. 179–276). Washington, DC: American Psychiatric Association.

Chess, S., Korn, S. J., & Fernandez, P. B. (1971). *Psychiatric disorders of children with congenital rubella.* New York: Brunner/Mazel.

Coleman, M., & Gillberg, C. (1985). *The biology of the autistic syndrome.* New York: Praeger.

Corbett, J. (1983). Epilepsy and mental retardation: A follow-up study. In M. Parsonage (Ed.), *Advancement of epileptology* (pp. 207–214). New York: XIV Epilepsy International Symposium.

Courchesne, E. (1991). Neuroanatomic imaging in autism. In M. B. Denckla & L. S. James (Eds.), An update on autism: A developmental disorder [Suppl.]. *Pediatrics, 85*(5, Pt. 2), 751–796.

Courchesne, E., Hesselink, J. R., Jernigan, T. L., & Yeung-Courchesne, R. (1987). Abnormal neuroanatomy in a nonretarded person with autism: Unusual findings with magnetic resonance imaging. *Archives of Neurology, 44,* 335–341

Courchesne, E., Lincoln, A. J., Kilman, B. A., & Galambos, R. (1985). Event-related brain potential correlates of the processing of novel visual and auditory information in autism. *Journal of Autism and Developmental Disorders, 15,* 55–76.

Courchesne, E., Yeung-Courchesne, R., Press, G. A., Hesselink, J. R., & Jernigan, T. C. (1988). Hypolasia of cerebellar lobules VI and VII in infantile autism. *New England Journal of Medicine, 318,* 1349–1354.

Damasio, A. R., & Maurer, R. G. (1978). A neurological model for childhood autism. *Archives of Neurology, 35*, 777–786.

Davies, K. (1991). Human genetics: Breaking the fragile X. *Nature, 351*, 439–440.

Dawson, G. (1983). Lateralized brain dysfunction in autism: Evidence from the Halstead-Reitan Neuropsychological Battery. *Journal of Autism and Developmental Disorders, 13*, 269–286.

DeLong, G. R. (1978). A neurophysiologic interpretation of infantile autism. In M. Rutter & E. Schopler (Eds.), *Autism: A reappraisal of concepts and treatment* (pp. 207–218). New York: Plenum.

Folstein, S. E., & Rutter, M. (1977). Infantile autism: A genetic study of 21 twin pairs. *Journal of Child Psychology and Psychiatry, 18*, 297–321.

Frith, U. (1989). *Autism: Explaining the enigma*. Oxford, England: Blackwell.

Gesell, A. (1941). *Wolf child and human child*. New York: Harper & Row.

Gillberg, C., Steffenburg, S., & Jakobsson, G. (1987). Neurological findings in 20 relatively gifted children with Kanner type autism or Asperger syndrome. *Developmental Medicine and Child Neurology, 29*, 641–649.

Gleick, J. (1987). *Chaos: Making a new science*. New York: Viking.

Hunt, A., & Dennis, J. (1987). Psychiatric disorder among children with tuberous sclerosis. *Developmental Medical Child Neurology, 29*, 190–198.

Kanner, L. (1943). Autistic disturbances of affective contact. *Nervous Child, 2*, 217–250.

Lane, H. (1976). *The wild boy of Aveyron*. Cambridge, MA: Harvard University Press.

Minshew, N. J., Furman, J. M., Goldstein, G., & Payton, J. B. (1990). The cerebellum in autism: A central role or an epiphenomenon? *Neurology, 40*(1), 173.

Olsson, I., Steffenberg, S., & Gillberg, C. (1988). Epilepsy in autism and autistic like conditions: A population-based study. *Archives of Neurology, 45*, 666–668.

Ornitz, E. M. (1983). The functional neuroanatomy of infantile autism. *International Journal of Neuroscience, 19*, 85–124

Ornitz, E. M., & Ritvo, E. R. (1968). Perceptual inconstancy in early infantile autism. *Archives of General Psychiatry, 18*, 76–98.

Reichler, R. J., & Lee, E. M. C. (1987). Overview of biomedical issues in autism. In E. Schopler & G. Mesibov (Eds.), *Neurobiological issues in autism* (pp. 13–41). New York: Plenum.

Rimland, B. (1964). *Infantile autism*. New York: Appleton–Century–Crofts.

Ritvo, E. R., Spence, A., Freeman, B. J., Mason-Brothers, A., & Marazita, M. L. (1985). Evidence for autosomal recessive inheritance in 46 families with multiple incidences of autism. *American Journal of Psychiatry, 142*, 187–192.

Rumelhart, D. E., Hinton, G. E., & Williams, R. J. (1986). Learning internal representations by error propagation. In D. E. Rumelhart, J. L. McClelland, & the PDP Research Group (Authors), *Parallel distributed processing: Explorations in the microstructure of cognition. Vol. 1: Foundations* (pp. 318–362). Cambridge, MA: MIT Press.

Rutter, M. (1970). Autistic children: Infancy to adulthood. *Seminars in Psychiatry, 2*, 435–450.

Rutter, M. (1983). Cognitive deficits in the pathogenesis of autism. *Journal of Child Psychology and Psychiatry, 24*, 513–531.

Rutter, M. & Schopler, E. (1992). Classification of pervasive developmental disorders: Some concepts and practical considerations. *Journal of Autism and Developmental Disorders, 22*, 459–482.

Schopler, E. (1965). Early infantile autism and receptor processes. *Archives of General Psychiatry, 13*, 327–335.

Schopler E. (1989). Principles for directing both educational treatment and research. In C. Gillberg (Ed.), *Diagnosis and treatment of autism* (pp. 167–183). New York: Plenum.

Schopler, E., Brehm, S. S., Kinsbourne, M., & Reichler, R. J. (1971). Effect of treatment structure on development in autistic children. *Archives of General Psychiatry, 24*, 415–421.

Schopler, E., & Rutter, M. (1978). Subgroups vary with selection purpose. In M. Rutter & E. Schopler (Eds.), *Autism: A reappraisal of concepts and treatment* (pp. 507–517). New York: Plenum.

Short, A., & Schopler, E. (1988). Factors relating to age of onset in autism. *Journal of Autism and Developmental Disorders, 18*, 207–216.

Sigman, M., & Ungerer, J. (1984). Cognitive and language skills in autistic, mentally retarded, and normal children. *Developmental Psychology, 20*, 293–302.

Simon, N. (1978). Kaspar Hauser's recovery and autopsy: A perspective on neuological and sociological requirements for language development. *Journal of Autism and Childhood Schizophrenia, 8*, 209–217.

Sugiyama, T., & Tokuichiro, A. (1989). The prevalence of autism in in Nagoya, Japan: A total population study. *Journal of Autism and Developmental Disorders, 19*, 87–96.

Tuchman, R. F., Rapin, I., & Shinnar, S. (1989). Epilepsy in children with developmental language and autistic spectrum disorder. *Epilepsia, 30*, 732.

Volkmar, F. R., Stier, D. M., & Cohen, D. J. (1985). Age of recognition of pervasive developmental disorders. *American Journal of Psychiatry, 142*, 1450–1452.

Wing, L. (1978). Social, behavioral, and cognitive characteristics: An epidemiological approach. In E. Schopler & M. Rutter (Eds.), *Autism: A reappraisal of concepts and treatment* (pp. 27–45). New York: Plenum.

Wing, L. (1986). *Children apart: Autistic children and their families*. Washington, DC: Historical Society for Autistic Children.

6

A New Finding: Impairment in Shifting Attention in Autistic and Cerebellar Patients

Eric Courchesne
University of California at San Diego
Children's Hospital

Jeanne P. Townsend
University of California at San Diego
Children's Hospital

Natacha A. Akshoomoff
University of California at San Diego
Children's Hospital

Rachel Yeung-Courchesne
Children's Hospital, San Diego

Gary A. Press
Kaiser Hospital of San Diego

James W. Murakami
University of Washington

Alan J. Lincoln
Children's Hospital, San Diego
California School
of Professional Psychology

Hector E. James
University of California at San Diego

Osamu Saitoh
National Center of Neurology
and Psychiatry, Tokyo

Brian Egaas
Children's Hospital, San Diego

Richard H. Haas
University of California at San Diego

Laura Schreibman
University of California at San Diego

THE THEORY

For over 200 years, the cerebellum has invariably been viewed by medical science as part of the motor control system of the human brain (Ghez & Fahn, 1991; Gilman, Bloedel, & Lechtenberg, 1981). For 50 years, infantile autism has been viewed as a disorder of the highest forms of human mental function (Kanner, 1943). Of all of the theories of infantile autism over the last

101

50 years, perhaps the oddest is the one that links the cerebellum and autism (Courchesne, 1985, 1987, 1989a, 1989b). First, it suggests that the human neocerebellum is involved in the voluntary coordination of selective, accurate, and rapid shifts of attention, a new role that is analogous to its long-established one in the coordination of smooth, accurate, and timely movements. Second, it suggests that in autism, early neocerebellar maldevelopment may interfere with the ability to shift attention in order to follow the rapidly changing events that compose reciprocal social interactions and many nonsocial situations. Much would be missed and the fragments caught would lack "context or temporal continuity." The basis for this theory and recent evidence supporting it are the topics of this chapter.

The first evidence of cerebellar abnormality in autism was a 1980 autopsy report of a single case with extensive Purkinje neuron loss (Williams, Hauser, Purpura, DeLong, & Swisher, 1980); in this individual, no abnormality was present in limbic, cerebral, basal ganglial, diencephalic, and brainstem structures. Ironically as well as erroneously, Williams et al. concluded that they were unable to discover any neural abnormality that might help explain the neural basis of autism. In 1985, a second autistic case was reported to also have extensive Purkinje neuron loss (>95%) in the posterior cerebellum, but not in the anterior cerebellum (Bauman & Kemper, 1985).

The Purkinje neuron loss results in these two cases of autism triggered the creation of the new theory linking the cerebellum to autism mentioned earlier (Courchesne, 1985, 1987, 1989a, 1989b). Specifically, this theory was prompted by facts about the cerebellum, evidence in the autism literature, and theories in the infancy and cognitive psychology literature. First, the theory predicted (Courchesne, 1985, 1987, 1989a, 1989b) that Purkinje neuron loss would prove to be a consistent finding in autism. It is a well-established fact that Purkinje neurons are the heart of cerebellar function (Courchesne, 1987, 1989b; Ghez & Fahn, 1991; Gilman et al., 1981). They provide the only path for information to leave the giant cerebellar cortex (which has as many neurons as the rest of the human brain combined) (Fig. 6.1). They also provide the only inhibitory control over the final output from the cerebellum; this final output comes from deep cerebellar nuclei and is strongly spontaneously excitatory (Fig. 6.1). Thus, the theory predicted, a substantial loss of Purkinje neurons would eliminate essential cerebellar cortical functioning and would allow the deep cerebellar nuclei to generate uncontrolled, potentially chaotic excitatory output (Courchesne, 1987, 1989b).

Second, because this excitatory output of the cerebellum connects with many brain areas believed to be involved in attentional processes, the theory also predicted that cerebellar damage would produce attentional impairments (e.g., "attentional asynergia or dysmetria"), which would be analogous to cerebellar motor impairments (Courchesne 1985, 1987, 1989a; Courchesne, Akshoomoff, Townsend, & Saitoh, in press). These cerebellar connections

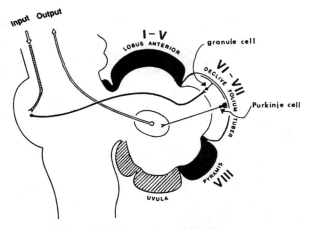

FIG. 6.1. Diagram of the midline view of the cerebellar vermis and brain stem of the human brain. Schematic representation shows the lobules of the vermis. Input from cerebral cortex, hippocampus, and other regions via mossy fibers excite granule neurons in cerebellar cortex; granule neurons excite Purkinje neurons in cerebellar cortex; Purkinje neurons are the only source of output from cerebellar and inhibit deep cerebellar nuclei; and, finally, neurons in the deep cerebellar nuclei send excitatory output, either directly or indirectly, to numerous systems including the brainstem, thalamus, hypothalamus, basal ganglia, hippocampus, and cerebral cortex. From Nieuwenhuys, Voogd, and van Huijzen, (1981). Adapted by permission.

connections include those to the reticular activating system, posterior parietal cortex, dorsolateral prefrontal cortex, superior colliculus, cingulate gyrus, and the pulvinar (Courchesne, 1987, 1989a; Courchesne et al., in press; Dow, 1988; Schmahmann & Pandya, 1989). Such connections primarily involve the neocerebellum, a region that composes the greater part of the posterior cerebellar vermis and hemispheres (Fig. 6.2). Moreover, several animal studies show that electrical stimulation of vermian neocerebellar cortex can enhance or inhibit neural activity in the brainstem, thalamus, hippocampus, and cortex in response to visual, auditory, and somatosensory stimulation (Crispino & Bullock, 1984; Newman & Reza, 1979). It is presently unknown whether such activity is employed in the selective attention and inattention to sensory stimulation. The theory predicted that future research will show that the neocerebellum can precisely regulate the enhancement and inhibition of responses to sensory stimulation.

Third, the theory argued that a severe disturbance in the dynamic control of attention could be one critical factor in producing the key cognitive and social communication abnormalities in autism (see later discussion). The first person to identify this disturbance in autism was a father of an autistic child; he wrote that his autistic son displayed "an abstraction of mind which made him perfectly oblivious to everything about him . . . and to get his attention almost requires one to break down a mental barrier between his inner

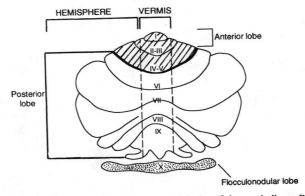

FIG. 6.2. Schematic diagram of the fissures and lobules of the cerebellum. Portions of the cerebellum caudel to the posterolateral fissure represent the flocculonodular lobe (the archicerebellum in stipples), whereas portions of the cerebellum rostral to the primary fissure constitute the anterior lobe (the paleocerebellum in stripes). The neocerebellum (the posterior) lies between these two lobes. Note that in some notational systems, vermal lobules VIII and IX are not included as part of the neocerebellum (Angevine et al., 1961). Roman numerals refer to portions of the cerebellar vermis only. From Carpenter (1980). Adapted by permission.

consciousness and the outside world" (Kanner, 1943). Since that time numerous behavioral, physiological, and metabolic studies have confirmed that autism does indeed involve some form of attention disturbance (for reviews see Courchesne, 1987; Courchesne, Akshoomoff, & Townsend, 1990; Dawson & Lewy, 1989; Frith, 1989; Martineau, Garreau, Barthelemy, & Lelord, 1984; Schreibman & Lovaas, 1973; Sigman, Ungerer, Mundy, & Sherman, 1987).

For more than a century it has been recognized that when attention is deficient, cognition suffers: William James (1890) stated that "an object once attended will remain in memory, whilst one inattentively allowed to pass will leave no trace behind" (p. 427). Therefore, an impairment in the coordination of attention could be at the root of a wide variety of commonly observed cognitive abnormalities in autism, including uneven memory, stimulus overselectivity, insistence on sameness, perseveration, repetitive and ritualistic behaviors, narrowed interests, formation of peculiar associations, and poor performance on executive function tasks requiring shifting mental sets (Kanner, 1943; Lovaas, Koegel, & Schriebman, 1979; Lovaas, Schriebman, Koegel, & Rehm, 1971; Ozonoff, Pennington, & Rogers, in press; Rumsey, 1985; Schreibman & Lovaas, 1973). For example, stimulus overselectivity or "overselective attention" (long suggested to contribute to social deficits in autism) is the tendency for the autistic child to respond only to one stimulus element of a complex array of stimuli composing an object, place or episode (Lovaas et al., 1971, 1979; Schreibman & Lovaas, 1973). The full exploration and apprehension of such complex stimulus arrays requires the ability to voluntarily shift attention from element to element smoothly, precisely, and effortlessly. A failure to attentively fully explore in a timely fashion nonsocial as well as social stimulus arrays would result in incomplete memory for events, more so for transient and variable events (e.g., social, language, acoustic) and less so for invariant or predictably repeatable events (e.g., calendars, flushing toilets). What would be retained would not necessarily be stimulus elements that had causal relationships with each other or that had spatial or temporal contiguity. For the autistic patient, the normal coherence of various elements of nonsocial and social events would be lost, as would the predictive correlations between elements. Instead, disparate fragments would often be registered. They would compose a rather impoverished picture of the actual events and the context in which they occurred; imprecise, misleading, and possibly bizarre associations and predictions about relationships between successive fragments could ensue. This condition, the theory suggested, could provoke disjointed, disorganized, and unexpected behavioral and emotional reactions by the autistic person during interactions with social partners and the nonsocial environment. Further this condition could promote a preference for repeatable, predictable, or invariant objects, events, and activities over novelty, exploration, social partners, and social settings. That is, the former would be expressed as an "insistence on sameness," repetitive behavior, and narrowed interests, and the latter situations would be avoided as confusing and distressing.

Most important, the theory recognized that a severe disturbance of the dynamic control of attention (i.e., the reorienting or shifting of attention) could have devastating consequences for social and affective development as well. Shifting attention is a key cognitive function in which the nervous system must quickly and accurately alter the pattern of neural responsiveness to sensory signals—from an enhanced neural response to certain stimuli (e.g., vocalizations) to an enhanced response to other stimuli (e.g., gestures); and from an inhibited neural response to some stimuli, to an inhibited response to others.

Consider the following vignette: Imagine a normal 18-month-old baby and his mother sitting on the floor next to a toy train. Mother moves the train and this captures the baby's attention. The baby watches closely as she moves it. She laughs and says "choo choo" and he shifts his attention to mother's face. She smiles and gestures toward the train and he shifts his attention back again. He reaches out, moves the train, and smiles, and then shifts his attention back and forth between the train and mother's face to see her reaction.

This vignette is an illustration of joint social attention, a crucial element of which is the capacity to shift attention in response to attention-directing behavioral signals such as pointing, touching, or vocalizing. This skill of coordinating attention between a social partner and objects of mutual interest is a major developmental milestone in social communication, and normally is achieved by 12–15 months of age (Bakeman & Adamson, 1984; Bruner, 1975; Trevarthen & Hubley, 1978; Werner & Kaplan, 1963). To achieve this major milestone, a baby needs to do more than simply focus his attention on a single, captivating aspect of an object or person. He needs to follow the initially unpredictable and rapid ebb and flow of human social activity: words, gestures, postures, facial expressions, and actions on objects. This activity provides signals directing the baby's attention to the varying sources of social, emotional, and situational information. The baby needs to be able to shift his attention in response to these signals so that, for example, after he regards one object or action (perhaps his own action), he can shift his attention to mother to discern her reaction and so on. By being able to smoothly, accurately, and rapidly shift his "spotlight of attention" with these signals, the baby is able to combine, as a single entity in memory, the various and separate elements of a social or nonsocial situation (see earlier quote from William James, 1890). Thus, if an infant had a deficiency in this critical cognitive operation, his affective, social, and cognitive development might be compromised.

In his book on affect, cognition, and communication in infancy, Tronick (1982) wrote that "successful regulation of joint interchanges . . . results in normal [affective and social] development (p. 1). *The critical element is that the infant and mother . . . share the same directional tendencies or focus of attention during the interaction*" (p. 4). Normal interchanges require many precise shifts of attention, and may last mere seconds. By precisely coordinating the direction and timing of attention, the baby is able to share with mother a learning experience about mother's interest in objects, his own affective reaction and interest in the same object, and his mother's reaction to his own affective and physical reactions. Tronick wrote "Failure to succeed in the regulatory process . . . derails [the] infant . . . from normal [affective and social] development" (p. 1). Presumably, then, brain damage that causes early and extreme developmental failure of this regulatory system would produce the greatest affective and communication abnormality, whereas the same damage sustained after learning is complete would have lesser consequences.

What is the evidence supporting this theory that autism involves brain damage to such a regulatory system and does this evidence lead to a fresh view of the role of the human neocerebellum? Because shifting attention is one of the key operations employed during successful joint social interchanges, we designed experiments to test this operation in autistic patients (Courchesne, Akshoomoff, & Ciesielski, 1990; Courchesne, Akshoomoff, et al., 1991) (see section entitled Impairment in Shifting Attention in Autistic and Cerebellar Patients). To determine whether damage to the neocerebellum impairs this operation, we tested nonautistic patients with acquired focal lesions of the neocerebellum (Akshoomoff & Courchesne, 1992; Townsend, Courchesne,

& Egaas, 1992) (see section entitled Impairment in Shifting Attention in Autistic and Cerebellar Patients). To determine whether impairment in shifting attention in autism may be the result of neocerebellar damage, we compared the shifting attention abilities of autistic patients to patients with acquired neocerebellar lesions as well as to patients with acquired lesions elsewhere (Courchesne et al. 1991; Townsend, 1992; Townsend et al., 1992) (see section entitled Impairment in Shifting Attention in Autistic and Cerebellar Patients). To determine whether autism involves damage to the neocerebellum, we analyzed magnetic resonance (MR) images of the cerebellum in 50 autistic patients (Courchesne, Saitoh, et al., 1993b) and evaluated the results in the light of the most recent quantitative autopsy studies of autism (Arin, Bauman & Kemper, 1991) (see section entitled Cerebellar Pathology in Autism). To determine whether damage to this hypothesized regulatory system occurred prior to the developmental acquisition of the first joint social attention skills, we review this same MR and autopsy data (see section entitled Cerebellar Pathology in Autism).

Evidence regarding the latter two issues is discussed next in order to set the stage for evidence that tests the links between the neocerebellum, shifting attention operations, and autism.

THE EVIDENCE

Cerebellar Pathology in Autism

Since 1985 when the theory that cerebellar damage would prove to be a principle feature in autism was first proposed (Courchesne, 1985, 1987, 1989a, 1989b), evidence of cerebellar abnormalities has rapidly accumulated. Specifically, cerebellar abnormalities have been found in 14 autopsy and quantitative magnetic resonance (MR) imaging reports from eight laboratories involving a total of 124 autistic cases (Table 6.1).

Autopsy Evidence

Following the initial reports of Purkinje neuron loss in two cases of autism (Bauman & Kemper, 1985; Williams et al., 1980), 10 more autistic cases have been found to have such Purkinje neuron loss (Bauman, 1991; for a review, see Courchesne, 1991). The neuron loss is not accompanied by gliosis, a finding that suggests a prenatal event (Bauman, 1991). In the only autopsy report to provide detailed quantitative and statistical information, the Purkinje neuron loss was found bilaterally throughout the posterior cerebellar vermis (lobules VI-VII and VIII-X) and hemispheres (Arin et al., 1991). Specifically, the reduction is greatest in the posterior

TABLE 6.1
Autopsy and Quantitative MR Studies of the Cerebellum in Infantile Autism

Studies Finding Abnormalities	Studies Finding No Abnormalities
Williams et al., 1980 (autopsy)	Gaffney, Kuperman et al., 1987a (MR)
Bauman & Kemper, 1985 (autopsy)	Garber et al., 1989 (MR)
Bauman & Kemper, 1986 (autopsy)	Garber et al., 1992 (MR)
Ritvo et al., 1986 (autopsy)	Holttum et al., in press (MR)
Gaffney, Tsai et al., 1987b (MR)	
Courchesne et al., 1988 (MR)	
Murakami et al., 1989 (MR)	
Bauman & Kemper, 1990 (autopsy)	
Ciesielski et al., 1990 (MR)	
Arin et al., 1991 (autopsy)	
Bauman, 1991 (autopsy)	
Piven et al., 1992 (MR)*	
Kleiman et al., 1992 (MR)*	
Courchesne, Saitoh et al., 1993b (MR)	

*Evidence based on re-analyses of study data by Courchesne, Townsend, & Saitoh (1993c).

vermis (50%–60%); slightly less in the posterior (42%–56%) and anterior (31%) hemispheres; and statistically insignificant in the anterior vermis (20%) (E. Arin, personal communication). Thus, all neocerebellar vermal and hemisphere regions (Fig. 6.2) are significantly affected in autism, as are many other cerebellar regions.

The number of granule cells may also be less than normal (Bauman, 1991), but confirmation of this impression awaits quantitative and statistical study. Neuron loss also occurs in the fastigial nucleus, which is the output pathway for the vermis; no neuron loss occurs in interpositus or dentate nuclei, which are the output pathways for the hemispheres (Bauman, 1991).

Neuroimaging Evidence

Quantitative MR studies have also found evidence of cerebellar pathology in autistic patients (Table 6.1). The first MR studies of autism found evidence of only one type of cerebellar pathology—hypoplasia. One MR study reports quantitative and statistical evidence that, relative to the cerebrum, the cerebellum was reduced in size in 14 autistic patients (Gaffney, Tsai, Kuperman, & Minchin, 1987). Another quantitative MR study shows evidence of a size reduction in the cerebellar hemispheres of 10 autistic patients, which appeared to be greatest in the posterior cerebellum (Murakami, Courchesne, Press, Yeung-Courchesne, & Hesselink, 1989). Another MR study reported a single case with extreme hypoplasia of vermal and paravermal lobules VI and VII (Courchesne, Hesselink, Jernigan, & Yeung-

Courchesne, 1987). This latter autistic patient also had parietal lobe volume loss. In a study of 18 autistic patients, still another quantitative MR analysis found an 18% reduction in the midsagittal area of neocerebellar vermal lobules VI and VII relative to normal controls (Courchesne, Yeung-Courchesne, Press, Hesselink, & Jernigan, 1988). In some of these autistic individuals, this hypoplasia included vermal lobules VIII- X (the posterior inferior vermis) as well as vermal lobules VI and VII. In that study, individual cases had reductions as large as 45%, which could therefore be detected even by routine radiologic examination.

These cerebellar size reductions were considered evidence of hypoplasia, since evidence of atrophy (i.e., increased widening of sulci) was not present (Courchesne et al., 1988; Murakami et al., 1989). Moreover, this macroscopic hypoplasia in autism occurs in the same regions where microscopic hypoplasia (reduction of Purkinje and granule neuron numbers and their associated neural elements) occurs in autism, and so, is undoubtedly the result of this microscopic cerebellar pathology.

In the most recent study, a new type of cerebellar pathology was identified by analysis of MR data from a large sample of autistic ($n = 50$; 2–39 years) and normal control ($n = 53$; 3–37 years) (Courchesne, Saitoh et al., 1993b). In this study, vermal lobules VI and VII, which are in the severely affected posterior region, were imaged using MR and measured. The autistic patients had social, language, cognitive, behavioral, and medical history characteristics that were typical of the general autistic population and included a wide age range. By using precise procedures for positioning and aligning MR slices (Fig. 6.3), comparable MR scans were obtained within and across subject groups.

Statistical analyses identified two subgroups of autistic patients. One subgroup (88% of the patients) had evidence consistent with hypoplasia as predicted by previous autopsy and quantitative MR studies. However, the other (12% of the patients) had evidence of *hyper*plasia, which has not previously been reported in autism. The hypoplasia subgroup was composed of 44 cases whose mean midsagittal area for vermal lobules VI and VII was 239.1 ± 37.7 mm^2, and the hyperplasia subgroup was composed of 6 cases whose mean was 376.8 ± 11.8 mm^2 (Figs. 6.4 & 6.5). Thus, the area of lobules VI and VII in the former subgroup was 15% smaller than the normal control mean of 282.2 ± 41.5 mm^2 (t-test, $p < 0.0001$), whereas that in the latter subgroup was 34% larger (t-test, $p < 0.0001$). Atrophy (increased sulcal width) was not present in the hypoplasia patients, and Chiari malformations were not seen in the hyperplasia patients (Fig. 6.4). Also, analyses show that these two subtypes of vermal pathology were present in the youngest autistic children as well as in older autistic children, adolescents, and adults.

Two recent quantitative MR studies were apparently unable to detect any abnormality of vermal lobules VI-VII in their autistic patients (Kleiman et al., 1992; Piven et al., 1992). A simple explanation is that if the small samples in

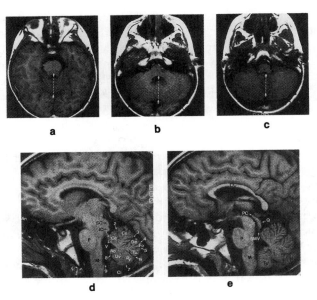

FIG. 6.3. Displays imaging procedures. Transverse (a-c) and midsagittal (d-e) T1-weighted magnetic resonance scans. (a-c): Examples of transverse scout scans (TR = 300ms; TE = 12ms) used to locate the midsagittal coordinates of the anterior, superior posterior, and inferior posterior vermis. At each level, the location of the midsagittal plane is defined by the line that connects the apex of the anterior and posterior convexities of the vermis (arrows and lines). The subject's head is positioned such that this line is parallel to the midsagittal angle of sectioning and its right/left coordinates are the same at each of the three transverse levels. (d): Midsagittal scan (TR = 600ms; TE = 12ms) through plane of section whose coordinates were determined from transverse scout scans in Panels a-c. Note that although this is a perfect midsagittal image of the vermis, it is not a midsagittal image of extra vermal structures such as the aqueduct of Sylvius, the corpora quadrigemina, the pons, and the corpus callosum. (e) Sagittal image contiguous with midsagittal vermis image in d. Shows that although several extra vermal structures (e.g., aqueduct of Sylvius, etc.) are seen at their midsagittal position, the vermis is not cut at its true midsagittal position. This demonstrates that extra-vermal structures should not be relied upon for making the determination of a slice position that will provide a midsagittal image of the vermis. Reliance upon extra-vermal structures for deciding the position of a midsagittal plane of section for the vermis could lead to vermis measurements that may be erroneous. From Courchesne, Saitoh, et al. (1993b). Reprinted by permission.

those studies were composed of 12% of the newly described hyperplasia subtype, then the autistic mean size reported by each study would have appeared to be near the normal mean size only because it was the sum of the hyperplasia and hypoplasia cases. At the time of their reports, they would not have known of the hyperplasia subtype.

Examination of data from those two MR studies confirms this explanation, and shows that in those two studies, 88% and 12% of the autistic subjects fell into the *hypo*plasia and *hyper*plasia categories, respectively. For example, in the Kleiman et al. study (1992), for 12 of their 13 autistic subjects the average

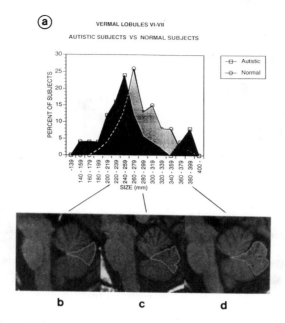

FIG. 6.4. Comparison of the midsagittal area of vermal lobules VI and VII in 50 autistic and 53 normal subjects. (a): Graph of the area of vermal lobules VI and VII versus the percentage of subjects with that size. Shows a normal, Gaussian distribution of values for the normal group, but a bimodal distribution for the autistic group. For the autistic group, a few subjects apparently have enlargement of lobules VI and VII, whereas the majority have values smaller than the normal mean size. (b-d): Examples of midsagittal T1 weighted (TR = 600ms; TE = 12ms) magnetic resonance images of small, normal average, and enlarged vermal lobules VI and VII from (b) an autistic patient (216.5 mm²); (c) a normal control subject (288.5 mm²); and (d) another autistic patient (379.3 mm²). Note that there is no evidence of atrophy (increased sulcal width) in the autistic patient with small lobules VI and VII. For anatomic landmarks specifying vermal lobules VI and VII and I–V, see Fig. 6.3. From Courchesne, Saitoh, et al. (1993b). Reprinted by permission.

area of lobules VI-VII was 214 ± 50 mm², which was significantly smaller than their smaller-than-normal pediatric patients controls (258 mm²) and smaller than any group of autistic or normal subjects reported by anyone else. In contrast, for their 13th autistic subject, the midsagittal area of vermal lobules VI-VII was 403 mm², which was 88% and 3.8 standard deviations larger than the average of their other 12 autistic patients and 56% larger than that of their controls.

Figure 6.5 is a scatterplot showing the midsagittal size of vermal lobules VI-VII from 78 individual autistic patients from three separate studies. The replication of results across MR studies is quite clear and provides further confidence that there is cerebellar pathology in the majority of these autistic patients (Courchesne, Townsend, & Saitoh, 1993c).

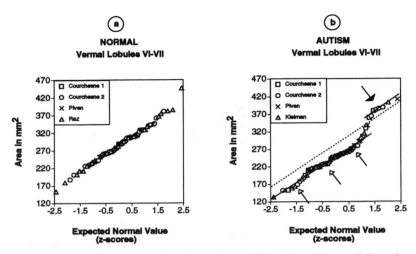

FIG. 6.5. Comparison of data from four separate MR studies of the vermis in autism (Courchesne et al., 1988, Courchesne, Saitoh, et al., 1993b; Kleiman et al., 1992; Piven et al., 1992). Graphs show the degree to which the size distributions of vermal lobules VI-VII approximate a unimodal Gaussian curve of normal distribution. Note: A perfectly normal unimodal distribution of data always forms a straight line when plotted against expected values on a Gaussian curve. (a) Data from normal subjects closely approximated a straight line for vermal lobules VI-VII. The line from this normal data is graphed for comparison against the autism data in panel (b). (b) Data from autistic patients shows that the size distribution of lobules VI-VII deviates significantly (p < 0.001) from a normal distribution. Instead, the distribution is bimodal. Specifically, there are two separate clusters of autistic patients: one (open arrows) with smaller-than-normal lobules VI-VII and the second (closed arrow) with enlarged lobules VI-VII. From Raz-Raz et al., 1992; Courchesne, Townsend, and Saitoh, 1993c. Adapted by permission.

Thus, the apparent failure of two recent MR studies to find statistical evidence of *hypo*plasia of vermal lobules VI-VII in groups of autistic patients appears to be due to this type of abnormality being masked by the presence in these samples of a quite different type of abnormality—*hyper*plasia of vermal lobules VI-VII. Nonetheless, because of the apparently low frequency of the *hyper*plasia subtype, not all studies will have both types; for example, the Ciesielski et al. (1990) MR study also replicates the finding of hypoplasia of vermal lobules VI-VII in autism, but apparently none of the 10 autistic subjects in their study had excessively large vermal size.

Although the majority of quantitative MR studies have found cerebellar abnormalities in autistic groups (Table 6.1), not all MR studies have been able to detect cerebellar abnormalities in autistic patients. However, scrutiny of the design, analyses, and results of these negative studies raise several questions about their validity.

First, a flaw common to nearly all of these studies was the use of suboptimal methods for establishing the midsagittal position of the vermis. The method often followed in each study involved a dependence on extra-cerebellar structures when establishing midsagittal MR positions. Garber et al. (1989, Garber & Ritvo, 1992) depended on the third ventricle and apex of the fourth ventricle,and Holttum et al. (in press) depended on the anterior commissure, fornix, and aqueduct of Sylvius, as well as the primary and prepyramidal cerebellar fissures. Unfortunately, an MR section aligned with these extra-cerebellar structures may be **misaligned** with respect to a true midsagittal section of the vermis, as exemplified in 2D and in vivo 3D brain images (see Fig. 6.6). Such misalignment can result in an MR section that is essentially a diagonal one through the vermis, and so, could produce erroneous vermis measures. Misalignment can also result in a section that is a partial volume of the vermis and adjacent hemispheres, and so, could also produce erroneous "vermis" measures. Far more accurate **intravermal** landmarks should be used. A second and related technical flaw was the use of 10 mm thick MR sections by another group (Gaffney, Kuperman et al., 1987). Because the vermis can be as thin as 5 or 6 mm, such a thick section could similarly result in partial voluming of the vermis and hemispheres, and so, produce erroneous vermis measures.

Second, some negative studies (Garber et al., 1989; Garber & Ritvo, 1992) used older, less accurate measurement routines available at the clinical MR console, rather than the newer, more sensitive and precise special purpose algorithms that are now in common use.

Third, subject selection procedures may be a concern in some studies. For example, in one study autistic patients had measures of language abilities that were average normal (Holttum et al., in press), which is very atypical of the autistic population. In two other studies, brain scan data were selected retrospectively, and control and contrast subjects were not normal volunteers (Kjos et al., 1990; Nowell et al., 1990); the nonautistic pediatric patient controls used in those studies may very well have been abnormal and so would not be a suitable standard against which to judge whether autistic patients have a normal cerebellum. Also, retrospective MR studies run the risk of subject and scan selection bias. In addition, in retrospective studies, MR slice location is not likely to be comparable across patients. One study (Kjos et al., 1990) failed to quantify and statistically analyze the size of the vermis in the autistic subjects; failed to report selection and diagnostic procedures; and failed to provide any information about the patients' characteristics and histories (e.g., medical, psychological, etc).

Fourth, most studies have included 18 or fewer autistic patients. However, in developmental disorders, macroscopic anatomic differences from normal are often rather small. In autism, measures of the cerebellum differ from normal by, at the most, only 15% to 17% or 1 standard deviation. When true group anatomical differences are only 1 standard deviation, then at least 27 subjects per group are needed in order to have a 95% chance of obtaining a

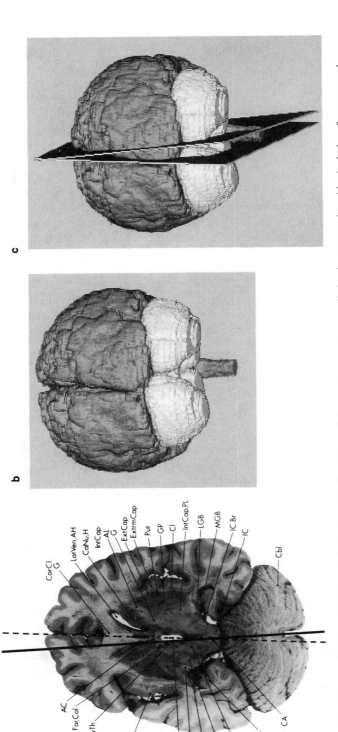

FIG. 6.6. Shows in 2D (a) and 3D (b and c) that the midsagittal plane of the vermis may *not* necessarily be the same as the midsagittal plane for nonvermal structures such as the fornix, anterior commissure, third ventricle, or aqueduct of Sylvius. The midsagittal plane of the vermis is frequently not naturally aligned with the midsagittal plane of nonvermis structures. Nonetheless, several recent MR studies of the vermis in autism have oriented MR sections based on one or more of these nonvermal structures. Alignment based on such nonvermal midsagittal planes can in some cases result in a *misalignment* relative to the midsagittal position of the vermis. Any MR study that uses such nonvermal midsagittal planes will report erroneous measures of the vermis. Because the differences from normal in vermal structures may be small (many neural structures in disorders with severe maldevelopment such as Rett syndrome may differ from normal by 15% or less), such errors could mask real differences and may cause negative findings to be reported. Panel (a): Transverse brain section reproduced from the *Structure of the Human Brain: A Photographic Atlas*, Fig. 11 (Haines, 1987). Dotted line = midsagittal alignment based on noncerebellar structures including the columns of the fornix (For,Col), anterior commissure (AC), third ventricle (Third Ven), and aqueduct of Sylvius (CA). Solid line = midsagittal alignment based on vermal landmarks. Panels (b and c): Two in vivo 3D images of the brain of an autistic child. Shows that in the living brain, the midsagittal plane of the vermis can sometimes differ from the midsagittal plane of nonvermal structures such as those just listed. From Courchesne et al., 1993b. Reprinted by permission.

significant difference at the $p < 0.05$ level. Any factor that reduces this difference—such as the use of atypical high verbal IQ autistic patients, diagnostic imprecision or heterogeneity (e.g., the inclusion of PDD nonautistic or Asperger patients with autistic patients), imprecision in selecting the anatomical position of MR sections, or imprecise measurement algorithms and devices—will correspondingly greatly increase the number of subjects needed in each study sample in order to detect a true difference. Clearly, exclusive reliance on the radiologic eye (Ekman et al., 1991) to detect such small differences is not likely to be an accurate approach. Thus, even in cases where small but real differences do exist between patients and normals, a variety of methodological design difficulties could easily lead to false negative findings.

Summary: Evidence of Cerebellar Pathology in Autism

The results of quantitative MR and autopsy studies together provide neurobiological evidence of two autistic subgroups with distinctly different etiologies. They also provide evidence that cerebellar pathology is present at the earliest stages of autism and remains persistent feature at all ages. Whereas environmental factors (e.g., toxins, infections, hypoxia, etc., which commonly cause a reduction in neural tissue), and/or genetic factors may underlie the hypoplasia subtype, it would seem likely that genetic factors, but not environmental ones, underlie the hyperplasia (increased formation of structural elements) subtype. Hyperplasia may therefore mark autistic patients in whom genetic analyses could prove to be most fruitful. We speculate that underlying autism in this new subtype is a genetic disorder causing abnormal regulation of proliferation, growth, or regressive developmental events, with the latter being most likely.

At present, 14 autopsy and quantitative MR reports from eight independent research groups involving 124 autistic cases support the finding of cerebellar pathology in infantile autism (Table 6.1). Infantile autism appears to be among the first developmental neuropsychiatric disorders for which substantial concordance exists among several independent microscopic and macroscopic studies as to the location and type of neuroanatomical maldevelopment. Discovery of the etiologies of these cerebellar pathologies may be the key to uncovering the causes of infantile autism.

Impairment in Shifting Attention in Autistic and Cerebellar Patients

Behavioral Evidence: The First Shifting Attention Studies in Autism

The second central component of the theory herein under consideration links the neocerebellum to attention. To test this hypothesis, we conducted behavioral and neurophysiological studies of shifting attention between auditory and visual modalities, between color and form, and between two visual spatial locations. Study groups were autistic patients with parietal MR abnormalities; autistic patients without parietal MR abnormalities; patients with acquired neocerebellar lesions; patients with acquired cerebral lesions; and normal controls (Akshoomoff, 1992; Akshoomoff & Courchesne, 1992; Courchesne et al., 1990b; Courchesne, Press, & Yeung-Courchesne, 1993, 1991; Townsend, 1992; Townsend et al., 1992).

In one study (Courchesne et al., 1991), we compared the shifting attention abilities of autistic, neocerebellar, and normal subjects in a task that was a distillation of the social world in which cues presented at unpredictable time intervals directed them to voluntarily initiate shifts of attention between auditory and visual stimuli. Because our shift attention task is new, the procedures and findings are presented in detail as follows:

All of the autistic patients passed the criteria for infantile autism defined by the *Diagnostic and Statistical Manual of Mental Disorders* (3rd ed.) (*DSM–III*; APA, 1980), *The Diagnostic and Statistical Manual of Mental Disorders* (3rd ed., rev.) (*DSM–III–R;* APA, 1987), the Autism Diagnostic Interview (LeCouteur et al., 1989) and the Autism Diagnostic Observation Schedule (Lord et al., 1989). In these patients, autism was not complicated by severe mental retardation, cerebral palsy, epilepsy, Fragile X, or other neurologic disease. Also, all had normal auditory brainstem event-related potentials (ERPs; Courchesne, Courchesne, Hicks, & Lincoln, 1985; Lincoln, Allen, & Piacentini, in press), and showed no evidence of visual or auditory sensory malfunction during neurologic examination. Color vision was normal in all patients as assessed by the Ishihara Test for Color Blindness (Ishihara, 1985). The pattern of relative ability and inability on IQ and other neuropsychological tests is shown in Table 6.2, and is similar to that of other samples of autistic patients (e.g., Bartak, Rutter, & Cox, 1975; Lincoln, Courchesne, Kilman, Elmasian, & Allen, 1988; Lockyer & Rutter, 1970; Ohta, 1987; Rumsey, 1985; Rumsey & Hamburger, 1988). Normal control subjects had no history of substance abuse, special education, major medical illness, psychiatric illness, or developmental disorder. The normal adults were matched with autistic adults on gender, chronological age, and performance on subtests of the Wechsler Adult Intelligence Scale–Revised (WAIS–R) that reflect nonverbal cognitive strengths in autism (Table 6.2) (Bartak et al., 1975; Lincoln et al., 1988). The normal adolescents were matched with autistic adolescents on gender, chronological age, and performance on subtests of the Wechsler Intelligence Scale for Children–Revised (WISC–R) that reflect nonverbal cognitive strengths in autism (Table 6.2) (Bartak et al., 1975; Lincoln et al., 1988). The normal children were matched with the adolescent autistic patients on mental age, which was based on the WISC–R Verbal IQ; this IQ index reflects areas of verbal and cognitive weaknesses

TABLE 6.2
Matching Characteristics of Normal and Autistic Subjects

			Wechsler IQ Subtests	
Group	Gender	Age	Block Design	Object Assembly
Normal				
Adult	7M	23.0(4.1)	13.3(0.8)	11.8(3.5)
Adolescent	6M,2F	13.8(0.8)	11.0(1.7)	10.5(2.6)
Child	7M,3F	8.6(1.7)	10.5(2.8)	12.0(3.2)
Autistic				
Adult	5M	28.8(4.1)	12.8(2.6)	10.5(1.0)
Adolescent	6M,2F	13.9(1.6)	11.8(3.9)	12.1(3.1)

Note. The WISC–R was administered to child and young adolescent subjects and the WAIS–R was administered to adult subjects. Average Wechsler subtest scores for the normal population are 10.0 with ± 3.0 as the standard deviation.

typical of autism (Table 6.2) (Bartak et al., 1975; Lincoln et al., 1988). Specifically, the mean mental age of the normal children was 9.3 years (chronologic age times VIQ/100) and that of the autistic adolescents was 8.2 years. Additional subject characteristics are listed in Table 6.3.

The data from these autistic and normal subjects were compared to that from six patients with acquired neocerebellar lesions from Akshoomoff and Courchesne (1992). The damage was substantial in five of these six patients. Five of the six patients were children who had undergone surgical resection of cerebellar astrocytomas, and, as in Akshoomoff and Courchesne, they were age- and IQ-matched to the 10 normal children described earlier (Table 6.3). The mean age at the time of diagnosis was 5.2 years (SD = 1.2) and the mean age at the time of testing was 8.6 years (SD = 1.8). Neurological symptoms associated with cerebellar damage had improved since the time of surgery, but persisted in all patients (e.g., dysmetria, gait difficulty). Two received focal irradiation of the posterior fossa, but three did not; none of the patients received chemotherapy. Three patients had unilateral neocerebellar hemisphere lesions (including the ventral dentate nucleus in one case) and one patient had damaged superior cerebellar peduncles bilaterally, thus eliminating the principal output pathways of the neocerebellum. The fifth patient had a small focal unilateral lesion and no indication of extensive damage to neocerebellar structures or input and output pathways. The adult patient was a 21-year-old man with a normal developmental history who exhibited signs of an idiopathic cerebellar degenerative disorder at 16 years of age (Akshoomoff, Courchesne, Press, & Iragui, 1992). He had extensive parenchymal volume loss in the cerebellum but relatively little cerebral cortical atrophy. Prior to his disability, this patient was an honors student in high school.

The autistic, neocerebellar, and normal subjects participated in two tasks,

TABLE 6.3
Additional Characteristics of Subjects

Group	PPVT–R	Wechsler Verbal IQ	Wechsler Performance IQ	Clinical Seizure Activity	Medications
Normal					
Adult	105(9.2)	108(8.8)	115(8.8)	—	—
Adolescent	118(11.5)	114(10.5)	107(8.6)	—	—
Child	111(12.1)	108(6.6)	111(12.2)	—	—
Autistic					
Adult	65(5.6)	82(11.2)	95(10.3)	5/5: neg	4/5: none
Adolescent	54(13.4)	59(13.7)	89(10.4)	8/8: neg	7/8: none
					1:Haldol
					1:Trilafon and Cogentin
Cerebellar	97(14.8)	97(15.5)	96(23.2)	—	—

Note. PPVT–R (Peabody Picture Vocabulary Test–Revised) is a test of receptive language ability. Average PPVT–R and Wechsler IQ scores in the normal population = 100 ± 15.0. The large discrepancy between verbal and performance Wechsler IQ scores in this sample of autistic subjects is principally due to two very low Verbal subtest scores (Vocabulary and Comprehension), and two relatively normal Performance subtest scores (Block Design and Object Assembly), (e.g., in the adolescent autistic patients, these four subtest scores were 2.8, 1.4, 11.8, and 12.1, respectively). Such an extreme discrepancy has been suggested to be typical of patients with infantile autism (Bartak et al., 1985; Lincoln et al., 1988, in press; Ohta, 1987), and stands in contrast to the normally expected pattern of comparable scores across all subtests (e.g., in the adolescent normals, these four subtest scores were 11.6, 11.9, 11.0, and 10.5).

which are schematically diagrammed in Fig. 6.7. The shift attention task (Fig. 6.7a), section a required them to rapidly shift their attention back and forth between visual and auditory stimuli as signaled by the appearance of the rare target stimuli. Correct detection of a visual target (a "Hit") served as a signal to shift attention to the auditory stimuli. When the next auditory target occurred, correct detection of it (another "Hit") served as a signal to shift attention back to the visual stimuli. Thus, correct detection of targets ("Hit") in the attended modality served to signal subjects to inhibit or disengage their attention from the current modality and activate or reengage their focus of attention as rapidly as possible to the other modality in order to detect the very next target appearing in that modality (Fig. 6.7a).

The focus attention task (Fig. 6.7b) required subjects to continuously maintain their attention on stimuli in only one modality for minutes at a time, and to detect and press a button to each target signal in that modality. All stimuli in the other modality were continuously ignored. There

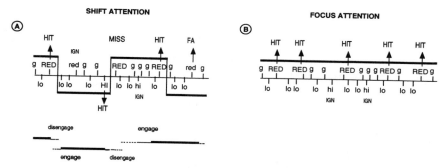

FIG. 6.7. Schematic drawing of the shift (a) and focus attention (b) tasks. Visual stimuli were red ("red") and green ("g") flashes; auditory stimuli were 2,000 Hz ("hi") and 1,000 Hz ("lo") tone pips. "HIT" = correctly detected target; "MISS" = a failure to respond to a target; "FA" = an erroneous response to a rare stimulus that was in a modality to be ignored; "IGN" = a rare stimulus that was correctly ignored. In the example of the shift experiment, the subject pressed a button (arrow) to the first rare visual target stimulus ("RED"). This served as a cue to shift attention to the auditory stimuli, ignore ("IGN") the rare visual stimuli, and respond to the next auditory target ("HI"). The auditory target in turn served as a cue to shift attention back to the visual stimuli. From Courchesne et al., 1991. Reprinted by permission.

was a focus visual attention condition and a focus auditory attention condition. To assess the ability to rapidly make two detections and responses in a row while continuously maintaining a focus of attention, the hit and false alarm data in the focus attention task were analyzed at five intervals of elapsed time immediately following the onset of the last correctly detected target, as was done for the shift attention task.

The focus attention task was a control for the shift attention task. In both, subjects were required to be selectively attentive, to make an identical target discrimination, to organize a motor response to correctly detect targets, and to make such discriminations and responses rapidly and at unpredictable intervals. The only difference between the two tasks was the requirement to shift the focus of selective attention.

Deficits in Disengaging Attention. In our experimental design, a failure to fully disengage and inhibit attention to stimuli in the same modality following a signal to do so would register as a false alarm. For instance, after a signal to shift attention away from the visual modality, a false alarm was registered if a subject continued to press the button to rare visual stimuli (see example in Fig. 6.7a). Analyses showed that, compared to chronological age-matched and mental age-matched normal controls, the autistic patients had a statistically significantly elevated false alarm rate in the shift attention task (13.7% vs. 4.6%), but not in the focus attention tasks (1% vs. 0.2%).

This result suggests that the autistic patients have a deficit in fully disengaging attention following a signal to shift attention. Among the six neocerebellar patients, the one with bilateral lesions of output pathways also had a very high false alarm rate (50%); the one whose lesion was smallest and spared input and output pathways did not have elevated false alarm rates (Akshoomoff & Courchesne, 1992).

Extra Time Needed To Reengage Attention.   A failure to rapidly reengage attention in the opposite modality would register as a miss, and would result in a reduced percentage of correct target detections in the time period immediately following a signal to shift attention (Fig. 6.7 section a). Therefore, to assess the time course of attention shifts, hit data in the shift attention task were analyzed at five intervals of elapsed time immediately following the onset of each correctly detected target: 0.5–2.5 sec, 2.5–4.5 sec, 4.5–6.5 sec, 6.5–10.5 sec, and 10.5–30.0 sec.

Following signals to shift attention, autistic and neocerebellar patients failed to reengage attention as rapidly as the chronological age-matched and mental age-matched normal controls, as indexed by their reduced hit rate within the first 2.5 sec following cues to shift attention (Fig. 6.8a). Specifically, in this short time interval, the shift performance of autistic and cerebellar patients was 6.1 and 3.8 standard deviations, respectively, below the age-matched normal mean; this difference is plotted for individual subjects in Fig. 6.8b. With longer intervals following a cue to shift, autistic and neocerebellar patients performed more like normal subjects and scored hits on a greater percentage of all possible targets (Fig. 6.8a).

Both the shift task and the baseline focus task required making equally rapid detections and responses to successive targets, but as compared to the baseline task, the shift task had the additional requirement to shift attention between modalities to make such successive correct detections. By subtracting the performance in the baseline focus task from that in the shift task, deficits due to this additional shift of attention requirement were revealed and are graphed in Fig. 6.9. This figure shows that whereas normal subjects experienced only a small drop in performance from the baseline focus task even when shifts of attention had to occur very rapidly, autistic and neocerebellar patients experienced huge drops in performance ability. This figure also shows that given sufficient time to shift attention (roughly more than five times the time needed by normals), these patients were able to accurately detect successive targets. Thus, in the baseline focus attention task at all intervals and in the shift attention task with more than 2.5 sec between targets, there were no statistically significant differences in the performance of autistic patients, neocerebellar patients, and normal control groups (Figs. 6.8a & 6.9).

In another study (Akshoomoff, 1992), neocerebellar patients, normal controls, and patients with cerebral cortical lesions performed in a shift attention task that was analogous to the Courchesne et al. (1991) visual-auditory shift attention task just described. However, in this version, the subjects shifted attention between color and form information (instead of between visual and auditory information as in Fig. 6.7). In this visual-visual shift task, the neocerebellar patients with substantial unilateral or bilateral damage were poorer than normals and cerebral lesioned patients at making accurate and rapid shifts of attention. Also, the neocerebellar patients made more false alarms than normals and cerebral lesioned patients, which suggests that they had difficulty disengaging attention as well as difficulty in rapidly reengaging it.

In a third study (Townsend, 1992; Townsend et al., 1992), autistic, neocerebellar, and normal subjects performed in six tasks involving shifts of attention between different visual-spatial locations. The tasks were derived from the well-known Posner paradigm (Posner, Walker, Friedrich, & Rafal, 1984). In this paradigm, there were two spatial locations where a small target light could appear; subjects pressed a button as soon as they detected the target. At the beginning of each trial, subjects did not know where the target was likely to occur. Either a short time (100 ms) or a longer time (800 msec) before the target appeared, a cue signaled subjects as to which of the two spatial locations was much more likely to have the target. Thus, this task involved two cognitive stages. The first was an attention-orienting stage, and the second was a detection stage. That is, in the first, the cue alerted the subject as to where to set up an enhanced "attentional map" (i.e., where to orient their "spotlight of attention"), and in the second cognitive stage, the target was detected using the "map" or "spotlight." The performance of our autistic and neocerebellar patients was compared to our normals as well as to the performance of patients with acquired brainstem, diencephalic, or cerebral lesions and to that of normal children and aged subjects whose data have been published by others (e.g., Petersen, Robinson, & Currie, 1989; Posner et al., 1984; Swanson et al., 1991) (see Fig. 6.10).

There were two important findings in the Townsend study (1992; Townsend et al., 1992). First, autistic and neocerebellar patients had significantly delayed responses to targets presented shortly after the attentional cue, but with longer cue-to-target delays these patients produced responses to targets at the cued location that were as fast as those of normals (Fig. 6.10). This time-related delay has not been reported for other patient groups (e.g., those with acquired lesions of either parietal, frontal, temporal, thalamic, or mid-brain regions). It is however, an abnormality consistent with the time-related delays that these autistic and neocerebellar patients showed in the visual-auditory and color-form attention-shifting tasks described previously.

Second, some autistic patients also showed a specific type of target detection deficit that has been shown by Posner et al. (1984) and Peterson et

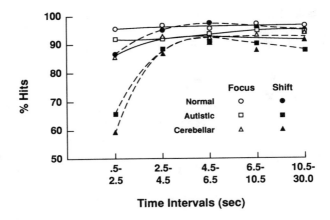

a

Focus vs Shift Attention

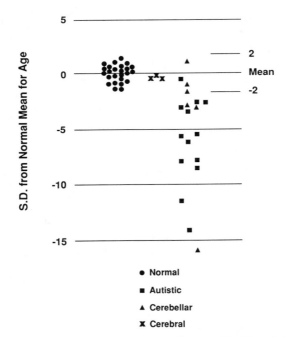

b   **% Hits (5 - 2.5 sec)**

- ● Normal
- ■ Autistic
- ▲ Cerebellar
- ✕ Cerebral

FIG. 6.8. (a) Shows mean percentage hits for normal control (circles), autistic (squares), and cerebellar (triangles) groups in the baseline focus attention tasks (all open symbols) and shift attention task (all closed symbols). All data were analyzed at five intervals of time (in seconds) elapsed since the onset of every immediately preceding target that had been correctly detected. Shows that with less than 2.5 sec between visual and auditory targets in the shift attention task, autistic and cerebellar patients were significantly impaired relative to normal subjects. In the baseline focus task when autistic and cerebellar patients

al. (1989) to be characteristic of adult patients with acquired parietal lesions. Bilateral parietal lobe abnormalities have been detected by MR analysis in 43% of a sample of 21 autistic patients (Courchesne et al., 1993a) (Fig. 6.11). In the Townsend study (Townsend, 1992; Townsend et al., 1992), there were two subgroups of autistic patients drawn from this MR study: those with MR evidence of parietal lobe abnormality and those without. As compared to normals and autistic patients without MR parietal lobe abnormality, the autistic subgroup with parietal lobe MR abnormalities were extremely slow to respond to targets that appeared in the uncued and location (rather than in the cued location). This performance deficit was statistically significantly correlated with quantitative measures of parietal abnormality in the autistic group (Fig. 6.12). This deficit is also similar to that seen in adult patients with acquired parietal injury when they must respond to a target in a visual field contralateral to their lesion after their attention had been directed to the opposite side (Fig. 6.13). This specific type of performance deficit has been likened to the sensory inattention seen in the parietal neglect syndrome. One possible explanation for the successful performance of parietal patients and autistic patients with parietal MR abnormalities to targets that occur where cued but slowed performance when targets occur in uncued locations is that parietal damage may lead to the creation of an abnormally narrowed focus or spotlight of attention; stimuli that unexpectedly appear outside that abnormally narrowed beam would receive little sensory processing. Using the visual P1 evoked brain response as a marker of sensory processing, Townsend (1992) reported evidence in autistic patients with parietal MR abnormalities that was consistent with this explanation (Fig. 6.14).

FIG. 6.8. (*Continued*)

did not have to shift attention, their performance was similar to normal subjects even when little time had elapsed (5–2.5 sec) between two targets in the same modality. (b) Shows that in the shift task there was little overlap in performance levels at the shortest time interval between autistic and cerebellar patients, on the one hand, and normal control subjects and cerebral cortex lesioned patients, on the other. With less than 2.5 sec to shift attention from one modality to the other in order to detect two successive targets, nearly all autistic and cerebellar individuals performed worse than all 25 individual normal controls. "Mean" equals the mean hit rate in this shortest time interval for each of the three normal age groups. The hit rate for each individual is plotted in standard deviations from the normal group mean for that person's chronological age (e.g., all normal and autistic adolescent individuals were plotted based on the mean and standard deviation for the normal adolescent group). The one autistic individual who overlapped with the normal individuals in the shift task was the highest functioning adult autistic person. Although he had a high hit rate in the shift task, he simultaneously also had a false alarm rate five times worse than normals. It took him an average of more than 6.5 sec to achieve the normal pattern of high levels of hits plus low levels of false alarms. Thus, he was substantially deviant in his ability to selectively and accurately control attention. The one cerebellar individual who overlapped with normal individuals was the case with the small focal lesion largely sparing neocerebellar cortex and cerebellar input and output pathways. From Courchesne, et al., 1991. Reprinted by permission.

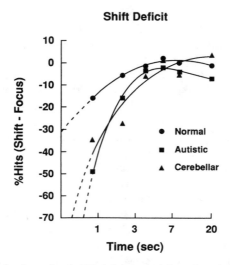

FIG. 6.9. Shows the time-related shift deficit in autistic and cerebellar patients. This shift deficit is revealed by subtracting the mean percentage of hits in the baseline focus task (Fig. 6.8 open symbols) from the mean percentage of hits in the shift task (Fig. 6.8 closed symbols). This difference in the mean percentage of hits is graphed as a function of elapsed time since the occurrence of the immediately preceding target. Natural log time scale in seconds. From Courchesne et al., 1991. Reprinted by permission.

Neurophysiological Evidence: Abnormal Responses to signals to Shift Attention

Neurophysiological responses, ERPs, were recorded while each subject performed the shift and focus attention tasks (Akshoomoff, 1992; Courchesne, Akshoomoff, & Ciesielski, 1990; Courchesne et al., 1991) (described in Fig. 6.7). To isolate the neural response triggered by the signal to shift attention, the ERPs elicited by the target signals in the shift task and in the focus task were subtracted from each other. In this way the neural responses common to both tasks (e.g., activity elicited by detection and response mechanisms) were subtracted out, and the additional neural activity elicited by the requirement to execute a shift of attention remained. This additional response, termed *Sd* (for shift difference response), had a positive polarity and a latency of 700 to 900 ms following visual and auditory target shift signals. This Sd response evoked by visual cues in normal children and adults and in children with cerebral cortical lesions is shown in Fig. 6.15. In the normal and cerebral lesioned groups, maps of the magnitudes of the Sd evoked by visual target cues showed that it was localized to parieto-occipital recording sites. In the autistic and neocerebellar patients, the Sd was greatly diminished in response to visual signals to shift (Fig. 6.15).

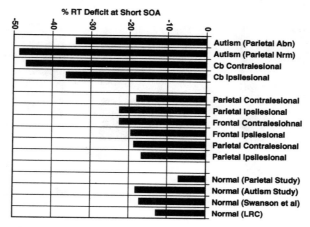

FIG. 6.10. Orienting deficits are seen in autistic and cerebellar patients. "% RT Deficit" is the percent increase in reaction time seen at short cue-to-target intervals (100–150 ms) relative to that seen at long intervals (800–900 ms). Adult data are from autistic patients with and without parietal abnormalities, and their normal controls (Townsend, 1992) and from patients with either parietal or frontal lesions (age 16–54 years) and their controls (age 29–42 years Posner et al., 1984 Petersen, Robinson & Currie 1989;). Child data are from two children with cerebellar lesions in posterior hemispheres (Townsend, 1992) responding to targets presented contralateral and ipsilateral to lesion sites, and comparison data from similar peripheral cueing tasks for 33 control children, mean age 9 years (Swanson et al., 1991), and 12 control children age 7–12 years (from the Language Research Center, San Diego). Greater negativity indicates greater slowness in response to target at cued location when there is little time (100–150 ms) between cue and target onset (cb = cerebellar patients). From Townsend (1992). Reprinted by permission.

CONCLUSIONS

Autism and Neocerebellar Pathology

Anatomic evidence strongly supports the first central component of the theory linking autism to the neocerebellum: The great majority of autistic patients have specific neural abnormalities of the neocerebellum: (See Table 6.1; Figs. 6.4 and 6.5); the flocculonodular lobe and nonneocerebellar regions of the posterior lobe are also affected, but the anterior lobe appears to be much less affected. In the majority of cases, the key loss is the Purkinje neuron without which the neocerebellar cortex cannot control deep cerebellar nuclei and influence distant brain activity (Fig. 6.1). This reduction in Purkinje neurons may begin as early as the second trimester but not later than the first few months of postnatal life. The anatomic evidence also shows that this reduction seen in the majority of cases and the hyperplasia seen in the minority of cases, is in the portion of the cerebellum that has connections with

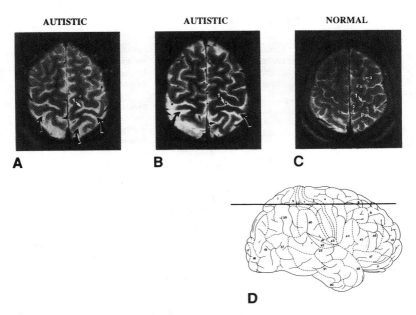

FIG. 6.11. Examples of abnormalities of parietal cortex in autistic patients seen on MR images. Transverse MR images (SE 2000/80, TR ms/RE ms), from a young adult normal control, and two autistic young adults with increased sulcal width in superior parietal lobe. Numbers and letters on images identify the following anatomical landmarks; central sulcus (1), marginal ramus of cingulate sulcus (2), superior frontal sulcus (3), superior frontal regions (FS), and superior parietal regions (PS). The arrows at base of the images from the autistic patients mark regions of abnormal sulcal width. The line through the tracing at the bottom shows the approximate position for the MR slices, and from which quantitative estimates of parietal damage in autistic patients were computed. Brain schematic from Nieuwenhuys et al. (1988, p. 10), with numbers corresponding to Brodmann's cytoarchitectonic areas. From Courchesne et al. (1993a). Adapted by permission.

many brain areas believed to be involved in attentional processes (see section entitled The Theory).

Thus, it appears that infantile autism can serve as a unique model for investigating the theory that neocerebellar cortex plays a role in attentional operations, because in autism (a) Purkinje neuron loss effectively disconnects and isolates this specific neocerebellar cortical system from the rest of the brain, and (b) autopsy studies (Bauman, 1991; Williams et al., 1980) report that other neural systems thought to be involved in attention typically appear normal in autistic patients.

The Neocerebellum and Shifts of Attention

Behavioral and neurophysiological evidence also support the second central component of this theory: The mental (i.e., nonmotor) control of attention is severely impaired in autistic patients and in patients with acquired neo-

Autistic Patients

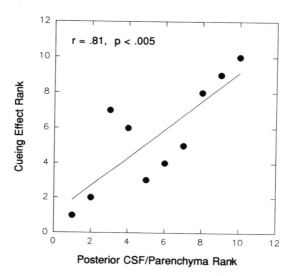

FIG. 6.12. Scattergram with regression line showing the relationship in autistic patients between the rank for a subject of the ratio of cerebrospinal fluid (CSF) to parenchyma and that subject's rank for the overall cueing effect in the Posner paradigm (i.e., difference between response time to correctly and incorrectly cued targets). Cueing effects were averaged across six designs and across short- and long-time cue-to-target delay intervals. From Townsend (1992). Adapted by permission. Also from Townsend, Courchesne, and Egaas (1992).

cerebellar damage (Akshoomoff & Courchesne, 1992) (Figs. 6.8, 6.9 & 6.10). Most importantly, the results to date appear to show that the neural pathology in autistic and neocerebellar patients did not prevent the execution of shifts of attention, but instead produced *suboptimal* performance of such shifts. That is, performance appeared to be more variable, inaccurate, poorly timed, and effortful. In these two types of patients, such deficits were found in tasks requiring voluntary, nonmotor shifts of attention between sensory modalities (Akshoomoff & Courchesne, 1992) as well as between perceptual domains within a single sensory modality (Akshoomoff, 1992), and in tasks requiring rapid mental attentional orienting between visual spatial locations (Townsend, 1992; Townsend et al., 1992). Because Purkinje neuron loss in the neocerebellum is a consistent feature in autopsy studies of autism, it is reasonable to conclude that neocerebellar damage underlies the similar attentional impairments present in autistic patients and patients with acquired neocerebellar lesions. These specific types of attentional impairments were not seen in patients with cerebral cortical, thalamic, or midbrain lesions

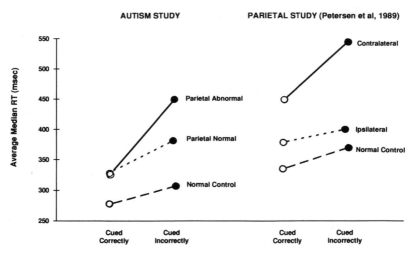

FIG. 6.13. Effects after long (800–900 ms) cue-to-target delay intervals for autistic patients with and without parietal abnormalities and control subjects. Data were averaged across three designs that used peripheral (box-brightening) attentional cues. Comparison data were from five patients age 16–54 years with unilateral parietal lesions, and seven normal controls age 29–42 years (Petersen, Robinson, and Currie, 1989). Average median response times to targets that were correctly cued (open circles) and incorrectly cued (filled circles) are presented. Solid lines represent autistic patients with parietal abnormalities and contralesional targets for parietal patients. Short dashed lines represent autistic patients with no parietal abnormalities and ipsilesional targets for parietal patients. Long dashed lines represent normal control subjects from both studies. From Townsend (1992). Adapted by permission. Also from Townsend, Courchesne, and Egaas (1992). Adapted by permission.

(Akshoomoff, 1992; Akshoomoff & Courchesne, 1992; Townsend, 1992; Townsend et al., 1992) (e.g., see Fig. 6.10).

Although our autistic patients were severely impaired in their performance on our shift attention tasks, we speculate that this evidence greatly underestimates the severity of their attention problem and that of autistic patients in general. The shift attention deficit is likely to be far worse in the very young autistic patient who will have developed few neurocognitive compensatory strategies and skills, and whose nervous system is still maturing. The deficit is also likely to be far worse in those who are more mentally impaired than in the subjects of our current studies. Also, the consequences of this attention problem for the autistic patient, especially the autistic infant and very young autistic child, will be far worse in natural settings than in our controlled testing situation where the stimulus and rule context is highly simplified and structured for the patient, and where specific training is provided for this single specific task. In his everyday world, the autistic child encounters a far more complex and demanding social, language, and environmental context in

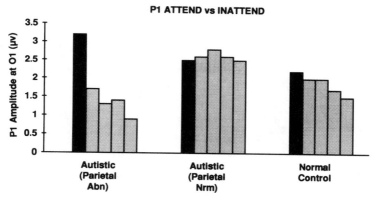

FIG. 6.14. Bar graphs for three groups (autistic patients with parietal MR abnormalities; autistic patients with normal parietal MR findings; and normal controls), collapsed across the five locations, showing P1 peak amplitude at O1 to an attended spatial location (dark bar), compared to when attention was focused one, two, three, and four locations away (light bars). From Townsend (1992). Adapted by permission.

which information continuously, rapidly, and unpredictably changes. This may help explain why the autistic child has a preference for repeatable, predictable, or invariant objects, rules, events, and activities, and avoids novelty, exploration, and social partners and social settings. Such preferences may lead the autistic child to develop an insistence on sameness, repetitive behavior, and narrowed interests, whereas the situations they avoid are avoided because they are experienced as confusing and distressing.

Cerebellar pathology can lead to other deficits in addition to the attentional deficits found in our studies. In his treatise on signs of human cerebellar dysfunction, Holmes (1939) quoted a cerebellar patient as saying, "The movements of my left [unaffected] arm are done subconsciously, but I have to think out each movement of the right [affected] arm. I come to a dead stop in turning and have to think before I start again." So, cerebellar pathology does not eliminate voluntary motor action, but instead makes motor action slow, inaccurate, and effortful; the patient has to consciously "think" through each step in preparation for action and during the execution of each action. In a parallel fashion, the evidence just cited suggests that cerebellar pathology does not eliminate voluntary shifts of attention, but instead makes such shifts slow and inaccurate. Similarly, cerebellar pathology apparently does not prevent relatively good gross judgements of time intervals between any two stimuli, but instead makes such judgements more variable (Ivry & Keele, 1989). Likewise, cerebellar pathology apparently does not eliminate the classically conditioned nictitating membrane response or its engram, but instead does produce variability in response onset and amplitude (e.g., Fig. 16.13 from Welsh & Harvey, 1992). So, it appears that in motor, attentional,

SHIFT - FOCUS DIFFERENCE WAVES

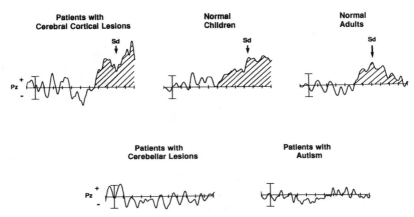

FIG. 6.15. For normal children, adults, and three children with cortical lesions, the figure shows a large *Sd*, the shifting attention related difference ERP response, at Pz (parietal scalp site) evoked by visual stimuli; the Sd may reflect neural activity elicited by the requirement to execute a shift of attention (see text). In autistic adults and in children with cerebellar lesions, the Sd was greatly reduced in response to these visual cues to shift attention. The horizontal scale is time; tick marks are at 100-ms intervals; time of stimulus delivery at large vertical bar, and the large vertical bar is amplitude and its size represents ± 5 uV.

perceptual, and learning domains, cerebellar damage does not eliminate function, but does increase variability in response thresholds, times, amplitudes, and effort.

A parsimonious suggestion would be that the cerebellum provides an analogous function for all of the systems with which it is interconnected, including motor, attention, arousal, sensory, memory, limbic, hypothalamic, serotonergic, dopaminergic, noradrenergic, and so on (For reviews, see Courchesne, 1989a, 1991). That is, without the aid of the cerebellum, each system continues to perform its prescribed specific function, but suboptimally. Interestingly, in autism, disorder in each of these systems has been identified and suggested to be the developmental result of abnormal cerebellar influences (Courchesne, 1985, 1987, 1989b, 1991).

The contempory concept that the cerebellum ensures "the optimal performance of the voluntary motor act" can be traced back as far as the work of Rolando (1809–1823) and Flourens (1824–1842), according to Welsh and Harvey (1992). This concept can now be extended to include the idea that the cerebellum ensures the optimal performance (i.e., timely and error-free) of all neural systems (motor, sensory, attentional, etc.) to which it has functional interconnections (Akshoomoff & Courchesne, 1992; Botez, Gravel, Attig, & Vezina, 1985; Courchesne, 1987; Courchesne et al., 1991;

Courchesne, Akshoomoff, Townsend, & Saitoh, in press; Leiner, Leiner, & Dow, 1986;). Elsewhere (Courchesne et al., in press), we have speculated that perhaps it does so by "adjusting responsiveness in whatever neural array or network is *anticipated* to be needed to attain a prescribed goal (the goal perhaps being prescribed by cerebral cortical or other subcortical systems). The cerebellum is no more an "attentional" structure or a "timing module" than it is a motor one. Rather it is a master computational system for providing the optimal context for the smooth interdigitated, coordinated neural action of whatever systems are needed from moment-to-moment to achieve a specified goal within the context of continuously fluctuating internal and external contexts.

Shifts of Attention and Social and Cognitive Deficits

Behavioral and neurophysiological evidence also lends indirect support to the third central component of the "autism-cerebellum-attention" theory: Because shifting attention is a cognitive operation commonly utilized in social and nonsocial situations, its impairment could, to paraphrase Tronick (1982; see earlier discussion), derail the autistic infant from normal social, affective, and cognitive development.

According to Tronick's (1982) model, the "critical element" for such normal development is that during joint social attention, the mother and baby coordinate their focus of attention on each other and an object of mutual interest. In this process, behavioral signals, such as pointing, touching, or vocalizing, direct shifts in the focus of attention, much as the visual and auditory cues in our experiments (aforementioned) directed shifts in the focus of attention in our patients and control subjects. It is through the process of attending and reacting to these behavioral signals that babies normally learn joint social attention skills, and social and affective knowledge. It is axiomatic that joint social attention requires shifts of attention (Bakeman & Adamson, 1984).

Autistic patients, who are impaired in shifting attention, have been consistently found to be extremely poor in utilizing such behavioral signals to coordinate their focus of attention in joint social attention situations (Curcio, 1978; Landry & Loveland, 1988; Loveland & Landry, 1986; Mundy, Sigman, & Kasari, 1990; Mundy, Sigman, Ungerer, & Sherman, 1986; Sigman et al., 1987; Wetherby & Prutting, 1984). This impairment could interfere with their ability to continuously follow the rapidly and unpredictably changing events that direct and compose reciprocal social interactions. Because the neocerebellar abnormality in autism apparently begins in prenatal or early postnatal life, from the earliest months the autistic infant would miss much, and the fragments caught would lack "context or temporal continuity" and his "knowledge of the [social] world would be made up of disconnected

fragments of [gestural, facial, vocal, and emotional] information" (Courchesne, 1987, p. 314). In sum, the autistic infant is indeed missing Tronick's
(1982) "critical element."

For the autistic baby, the lack of the ability to make use of such signals and
engage in joint attention precludes the development of more complex social
communication skills—such as imitation, turn taking, representational play,
and the ability to exchange experiences and emotions with others about
topics of mutual interest. Such complex skills normally follow the development of joint social attention skills (Bakeman & Adamson, 1984; Bruner,
1975; Trevarthen & Hubley, 1978; Tronick, 1982; Werner & Kaplan,
1963).

Summary

Much like the principles that govern neural development, normal social and
cognitive development is a self-organizing phenomenon wherein emergent
properties and processes at any given point enable the construction of new
properties and processes and the further elaboration of those that had
previously emerged. By contrast, abnormal development is a self-
mis-organizing phenomenon wherein damage at one stage disables the construction of some new normal properties and processes, distorts the form of
other later emerging ones, enables the construction of ones that normally
never appear, and limits the elaboration and usage of previously emerged
ones.

In autism, we suggest, Purkinje neuron loss marks the beginning of such a
misorganizing path. Its occurrence in prenatal or early postnatal life precludes
the emergence of normal processes that underlie the regulation of attention
shifting and orienting. Thus, in the autistic baby, the derailment of regulatory
mechanisms occurs before he or she can take even the first cognitive and
affective steps toward learning from joint social interchanges. The autistic
baby is unable to follow the rapid and unpredictable ebb and flow of human
social activity, such as words, gestures, postures, facial expressions, and
actions on objects. Such activity normally provides signals that direct a baby's
attention to the varying sources of social, emotional, and situational information, but the autistic baby is unable to coordinate his or her attention and
arousal systems to apprehend this important information. The baby is unable
to smoothly and selectively shift his or her spotlight of attention in a timely
fashion with these signals, and so, he is unable to combine, as a single entity
in memory, the various and separate affective and sensory (gestures, words,
facial expressions, etc.) elements of a social situation. The baby also is unable
to express in a timely fashion his or her own affective and cognitive reactions
to information. Brain damage sustained after the normal development and

elaboration of affective and communicative reactions and knowledge would not necessarily lead to their regression or loss.

Structures other than the cerebellum (e.g., limbic, cerebral) and neural functions other than attentional are undoubtedly involved in the social, language, and cognitive deficits seen in autism. These considerations are the topic of future discussions (e.g., Townsend, 1992).

ACKNOWLEDGMENTS

Supported by funds from National Institute of Mental Health Grant 1-RO1-MH36840 and National Institute or Neurological Disorders and Stroke Grant 5-RO1-NS19855 awarded to Eric Courchesne. We thank Lynne Lord for her technical assistance with magnetic resonance imaging, and Robert Elmasian and Kristina Ciesielski for assistance with ERP studies preliminary to those presented herein. Portions of this work and the theory described were presented at the National Conference of the Autism Society of America (1989, 1990, & 1991) and at the National Institute of Mental Health (1985).

REFERENCES

Akshoomoff, N. (1992). *Neuropsychological studies of attention and the role of the cerebellum.* Unpublished doctoral dissertation, University of California, San Diego, and San Diego State University.

Akshoomoff, N., & Courchesne, E. (1992). A new role of the cerebellum in cognitive operations. *Behavioral Neuroscience, 106,* 731–738.

Akshoomoff, N., Courchesne, E., Press, G., & Iraqui, V. (1992). Contribution of the cerebellum to neuropsychological functioning: Evidence from a case of cerebellar degeneration disorder. *Neuropsychologia, 30,* 315–328.

American Psychiatric Association. (1980). *Diagnostic and statistical manual of mental disorders* (3rd ed.). Washington, DC: Author.

American Psychiatric Association. (1987). *Diagnostic and statistical manual of mental disorders* (3rd ed., rev.). Washington, DC: Author.

Angevine, J. B. Jr., Mancall, E. L., & Yakovlev, P. I. (1961). *The human cerebellum: An atlas of gross topography in serial section.* Boston: Little, Brown.

Arin, D. M., Bauman, M. I., & Kemper, T. L. (1991). The distribution of Purkinje cell loss in the cerebellum in autism. *Neurology, 41* (Suppl. 1), 307.

Bakeman, R., & Adamson, L. B. (1984). Coordinating attention to people and objects in mother-infant and peer-infant interaction. *Child Development, 55,* 1278–1289.

Bartak, L., Rutter, M. & Cox, A. (1975). A comparative study of infantile autism and specific developmental receptive language disorder: 1. The children. *British Journal of Psychiatry, 126,* 127–145.

Bauman, M. L. (1991). Microscopic neuroanatomic abnormalities in autism. *Pediatrics, 87,* 791–796.

Bauman, M. L., & Kemper, T. (1985). Histoanatomic observations of the brain in early infantile autism. *Neurology, 35,* 866–874.

Bauman, M. L., & Kemper, T. L. (1986). Developmental cerebellar abnormalities: A consistent finding in early infantile autism. *Neurology, 36* (Suppl. 1), 190.

Bauman, M. L., & Kemper, T. L. (1990). Limbic and cerebellar abnormalities are also present in an autistic child of normal intelligence. *Neurology, 40* (Suppl. 1), 359.

Botez, M. I., Gravel, J., Attig, E., & Vezina, J. L. (1985). Reversible chronic cerebellar ataxia after phenytoin intoxication: Possible role of cerebellum in cognitive thought. *Neurology, 35,* 1152–1157.

Bruner, J. (1975). The ontogenesis of speech acts. *Journal of Child Language, 2,* 1–19.

Carpenter, M. B. (1976). *Human neuroanatomy.* Baltimore: Williams & Wilkins.

Ciesielski, K. T., Allen, P. S., Sinclair, B. D., Pabst, H. F., Yanossky, R., & Ludwig, R. (1990). Hypoplasia of cerebellar vermis in autism and childhood leukemia. In *Proceedings of the 5th International Child Neurology Congress* (p. 650). Tokyo: Karger.

Courchesne, E. (1985, May). *The missing ingredients in autism.* Paper presented at the Conference on Brain and Behavioral Development: Biosocial Dimension, Eldridge, MD.

Courchesne, E. (1987). A neurophysiological view of autism. In E. Schopler & G. B. Mesibov (Eds.), *Neurobiological issues in autism* (pp. 285–324). New York: Plenum.

Courchesne, E. (1989a, July). *The control of attention: A key cognitive deficit in autism.* Paper presented at the 1989 National Conference of the Autism Society of America, Seattle.

Courchesne, E. (1989b). Neuroanatomical systems involved in infantile autism: The implications of cerebellar abnormalities. In G. Dawson (Ed.), *Autism: New perspectives on diagnosis, nature and treatment* (pp. 119–143). New York: Guilford.

Courchesne, E. (1991). Neuroanatomic imaging in autism. *Pediatrics, 87,* 781–790.

Courchesne, E., Akshoomoff, N. A., & Ciesielski, K. T. (1990). *Shifting attention abnormalities in autism: ERP and performance evidence.* Poster presented at the meeting of the International Neurpsychological Society, Orlando, FL.

Courchesne, E., Akshoomoff, N. A., & Townsend, J., & Saitoh, O. (in press). A model system for the study of attention and the cerebellum: Infantile autism. *Electroencephalography and Clinical Neurophysiology.*

Courchesne, E., Akshoomoff, N. A., Townsend, J., Yeung-Courchesne, R., Lincoln, A. J., James, H. E., Haas, R. H., Schreibman, L., & Lau, L. (1991). *Impairment in shifting attention in autistic and cerebellar patients.* Manuscript submitted for publication.

Courchesne, E., Courchesne, R. Y., Hicks, G., & Lincoln, A. (1985). Functioning of the brainstem auditory pathway in non-retarded autistic individuals. *Electroencephalography and Clinical Neurophysiology, 61,* 491–501.

Courchesne, E., Hesselink, J. R., Jernigan, T. L., & Yeung-Courchesne, R. (1987). Abnormal neuroanatomy in a nonretarded person with autism: Unusual findings with magnetic resonance imaging. *Archives of Neurology, 44,* 335–341.

Courchesne, E., Press, G. A., & Yeung-Courchesne, R. (1993a). Parietal lobe abnormalities detected on magnetic resonance images of patients with infantile autism. *American Journal of Roentgenology, 160,* 387–393.

Courchesne, E., Saitoh, O., Yeung-Courchesne, R., Press, G. A., Lincoln, A. J., Haas, R. H., & Schreibman, L. (1993b). Two subtypes of cerebellar pathology detected with MR in patients with autism: Hyperplasia and hypoplasia of vermal lobules VI and VII. Manuscript submitted for publication.

Courchesne, E., Townsend, J. P., & Saitoh, O. (1933c). The brain in infantile autism: Posterior structures are abnormal. Manuscript submitted for publication.

Courchesne, E., Yeung-Courchesne, R., Press, G. A., Hesselink, J. R., & Jernigan, T. L. (1988). Hypoplasia of cerebellar vermal lobules VI and VII in autism. *The New England Journal of Medicine, 318,* 1349–1354.

Crispino, L., & Bullock, T. H. (1984). Cerebellum mediates modality-specific modulation of sensory responses of the midbrain and forebrain in rat. *Proceedings of the National Academy of Sciences of the United States of America, 81,* 2917–2920.

Curcio, F. (1978). Sensorimotor functioning and communication in mute autistic children. *Journal of Autism and Childhood Schizophrenia, 8*, 281–292.

Dawson, G., & Lewy, A. (1989). Arousal, attention, and the socioemotional impairments of individuals with autism. In G. Dawson (Ed.), *Autism: New perspectives on diagnosis, nature and treatment* (pp. 49–74). New York: Guilford.

Dow, R. A. (1988). Contributions of electrophysiological studies to cerebellar physiology. *Journal of Clinical Neurophysiology, 5*, 307–323.

Ekman, G., De Chateau, P., Marions, O., Sellden, H., Wahlund, L. O., & Wetterberg. L. (1991). Low field magnetic resonance imaging of the central nervous system in 15 children with autistic disorder. *Acta Piediatr Scand, 80*, 243–247.

Frith, U. (1989). A new look at language and communication in autism. *British Journal of Disorders of Communications, 24*, 123–150

Gaffney, G. R., Kuperman, S., Tsai, L. Y., Minchin, S., & Hassanein, K. M. (1987a). Midsagittal magnetic resonance imaging of autism. *British Journal of Psychiatry, 151*, 831–833.

Gaffney, G. R., Tsai, L. Y., Kuperman, S., & Minchin, S. (1987b). Cerebellar structure in autism. *American Journal of Diseases in Children, 141*, 1330–1332.

Garber, H. J., & Ritvo. E. R. (1992). Magnetic resonance imaging of the posterior fossa in autistic adults. *American Journal of Psychiatry, 149*, 245–247.

Garber, H. J., Ritvo, E. R., Chui, L. C., Griswold, V. J., Kashanian, A., & Oldendorf, W. H. (1989). A magnetic resonance imaging study of autism: Normal fourth ventricle size and absence of pathology. *American Journal of Psychiatry, 146*, 532–535.

Ghez, D., & Fahn, S. (1991). The cerebellum. In E. R. Kandel, J. H. Schwartz, & T. M. Jessell (Eds.), *Principals of neural sciences* (3rd ed., pp. 626–646). New York: Elsevier Science.

Gilman, S., Bloedel, J. R., & Lechtenberg, R. (1981). *Disorders of the cerebellum*. Philadelphia: Davis.

Haines, D. E. (1987). *Nueroanatomy: An Atlas of Structures, Sections and Systems*. (p. 61). Urban and Schwarzenberg: Baltimore-Munich.

Holmes, C. (1939). The cerebellum of man. *Brain, 7*, 121–172.

Holttum, J. R., Minshew, N. J., Sanders, R. S., & Phillips, N. E. (in press). Magnetic resonance imaging of the posterior fossa in autism. *Biological Psychiatry*.

Ishihara, D. (1985). *Ishihara's tests for colour-blindness*. Tokyo: Kenehara.

Ivry, R., & Keeele, S. W. (1989). Timing functions of the cerebellum. *Journal of Cognitive Neuroscience, 1*, 136–152.

James, W. (1890). *The principles of psychology* (Vol. 1, p. 427). New York: Dover Publication.

Kanner, L. (1943). Autistic disturbances of affective contact. *Nervous Child, 2*, 217–250.

Kjos, B. O., Umansky, R., & Barkovich, A. J. (1990). Brain MR imaging in children with developmental retardation of unknown cause: Results in 76 cases. *American Journal of Neuroradiology, 11*, 1035–1040.

Kleiman, M. D., Neff, S., & Rosman, N. P. (1992). The brain in infantile autism: Are posterior fossa structures abnormal? *Neurology, 42*, 753–760.

Landry, S. H., & Loveland, K. A. (1988). Communication behaviors in autism and developmen- tal language delay. *Journal of Child Psychology and Psychiatry and Allied Disciplines, 29*, 621–634.

LeCouteur, A., Rutter, M., Lord, C., Rios, P., Robertson, S., Holdgrafer, M., & McLennan, J. (1989). Autism diagnostic interview: A standardized investigator-based instrument. *Journal of Autism and Developmental Disorders, 3*, 363–387.

Leiner, H. C., Leiner, A. L., & Dow, R. S. (1986). Does the cerebellum contribute to mental skills? *Behavioral Neurscience, 100*, 443–454.

Lincoln, A. J., Allen, M., & Piacentini, A. (in press). Assessment and interpretation of intellectual abilities in people with autism. In: E. Schopler & G. Mesibov (Eds.), *Learning and cognition in autism*. New York: Plenum.

Lincoln, A. J., Courchesne, E., Kilman, B. A., Elmasian, R., & Allen, M. (1988). A study of intellectual abilities in high-functioning people with autism. *Journal of Autism and Developmental Disorders, 18*, 505–524.

Lockyer, L., & Rutter, M. (1970). A five to fifteen year follow-up study of infantile autism: Patterns of cognitive ability. *British Journal of Social and Clinical Psychology, 9*, 152–163.

Lord, C., Rutter, M., Goode, S., Heemsbergen, J., Jordan, H., Mawhood, L., & Schopler, E. (1989). Autism diagnostic observation schedule: A standardized observation of communicative and social behavior. *Journal of Autism and Developmental Disorders, 2*, 185–212.

Lovaas, O. I., Koegel, R. L., & Schreibman, L. (1979). Stimulus overselectivity in autism: A review of research. *Psychological Bulletin, 86*, 1236–1254.

Lovaas, O. I., Schreibman, L., Koegel, R. L., & Rehm, R. (1971). Selective responding by autistic children to multiple sensory input. *Journal of Abnormal Psychology, 77*, 211–222.

Loveland, K., & Landry, S. (1986). Joint attention and language in autism and developmental language delay. *Journal of Autism and Developmental Disorders, 16*, 335–349.

Martineau, J., Garreau, B., Barthelemy, C., & Lelord, G. (1984). Evoked potentials and P300 during sensory conditioning in autistic children. In R. Karrer, J. Cohen, & P. Tueting (Eds), *Brain and information: Event-related potentials* (pp. 362–369). New York: New York Academy of Sciencies.

Mundy, P., Sigman, M., & Kasari, C. (1990). A longitudinal study of joint attention and language development in autistic children. *Journal of Autism and Developmental Disorders, 20*, 115–128.

Mundy, P., Sigman, M., Ungerer, J., & Sherman, T. (1986). Defining the social deficits of autism: The contribution of non-verbal communication measures. *Journal of Child Psychology and Psychiatry and Allied Disciplines, 27*, 657–669.

Murakami, J. W., Courchesne, E., Press, G. A., Yeung-Courchesne, R., & Hesselink, J. R. (1989). Reduced cerebellar hemisphere size and its relationship to vermal hypoplasia in autism. *Archives of Neurology, 46*, 689–694.

Newman, P. P., & Reza, H. (1979). Functional relationships between the hippocampus and the cerebellum: An electrophysiological study of the cat. *Journal of Physiology* (London), *287*, 405–426.

Nieuwenhuys, R., Voogd, J., & van Huijzen, C. (1988). *The human central nervous system: A synopsis and atlas* (3rd ed.). New York: Springer-Verlag.

Nowell, M. A., Hackney, D. B., Murski, A., & Coleman, M. (1990). Varied MR appearance of autism: Report on fifty pediatric patients having full autistic syndrome. In *Proceedings of the 8th Annual Meeting of the Society of Magnetic Resonance Imaging* (p. 84). Washington, DC: Pergammon Press.

Ohta, M. (1987). Cognitive disorders of infantile autism: A study employing the WISC, spatial relationship conceptualization, and gesture imitations. *Journal of Autism and Developmental Disorders, 17*, 45–62.

Ozonoff, S., Pennington, B., & Rogers, S. J. (in press). Executive function deficits in high functioning autistic children: Relationship to theory of mind. *Journal of Child Psychology and Psychiatric and Allied Disorders.*

Petersen, S. E., Robinson, D. L., & Currie, J. N. (1989). Influences of lesions of parietal cortex on visual spatial attention in humans. *Experimental Brain Research, 76*, 267–280.

Piven, J., Nehme, E., Simon, J., Barta, P., Pearlson, G., & Folstein, S. E. (1992). Magnetic resonance imaging in autism: Measurement of the cerebellum, pons, and fourth ventricle. *Biological Psychiatry, 31*, 491–504.

Posner, M. I., Walker, J. A., Friedrich, F. J., & Rafal, R. D. (1984). Effects of parietal injury on covert orienting of attention. *Journal of Neuroscience, 4*, 1863–1874.

Ritvo, E. R., Freeman, B. J., & Scheibel, A. B., et al. (1986). Lower Purkinje cell counts in the cerebella of four autistic subjects: initial findings of the UCLA-NSAC autopsy research report.

American Journal of Psychiatry, 143, 862–866.

Rumsey, J. M. (1985). Conceptual problem-solving in highly verbal, nonretarded autistic men. *Journal of Autism and Developmental Disorders, 15,* 23–36.

Rumsey, J. M., & Hamburger, S. D. (1988). Neuropsychological findings in high-functioning men with infantile autism, residual state. *Clinical Experimental Neuropsychology, 10,* 201–221.

Schmahmann, J., & Pandya, D. N. (1989). Anatomical investigation of projections to the basis pontis from posterior parietal association in rhesus monkey. *Journal of Comparative Neurology, 289,* 53–73.

Schreibman, L., & Lovaas, O. I. (1973). Overselective response to social stimuli by autistic children. *Journal of Abnormal Child Psychology, 1,* 152–168.

Sigman, M., Ungerer, J. A., Mundy, P., & Sherman, T. (1987). Cognition in autistic children. In D. J. Cohen & A. M. Donnellan (Eds.), *Handbook of autism and pervasive developmental disorders* (pp. 103–120). New York: Wiley.

Swanson, J. M., Posner, M., Potkin, S., Bonforte, S., Youpa, D., Fiore, C., Cantwell, D., & Crinella, F. (1991). Activating tasks for the study of visual-spatial attention in ADHD children: A cognitive anatomic approach. *Journal of Child Neurology, 6,* 119–127.

Townsend, J. (1992). *Abnormalities of brain structure and function underlying the distribution of visual attention in autism.* Unpublished doctoral dissertation, University of California, San Diego, and San Diego State University.

Townsend, J., Courchesne, E., & Egaas, B. (1992, October). *Visual attention deficits in autistic adults with cerebellar and parietal abnormalities.* Abstracts vol. 18, Part 1, p. 64. Paper presented at the Society for Neuroscience 1992 annual meeting, Anaheim, CA.

Trevarthen, C., & Hubley, P. (1978). Secondary intersubjectivity. In A. Lock (Ed.), *Confidence, confiding and acts of meaning in the first year: Action, gesture, and symbol.* London: Academic.

Tronick, E. Z. (1982). Affectivity and sharing. In E. Z. Tronick (Ed.), *Social interchange in infancy: Affect, cognition and communication* (pp. 1–6). Baltimore: University Park Press.

Welsh, J. P., & Harvey, J. A. (1992). The role of the cerebellum in voluntary and reflexive movements: history and current status. In R. Llinas & C. Sotelo (Eds.), *The Cerebellum Revisited* (pp. 301–334). New York: Springer-Verlag.

Werner, H., & Kaplan, B. (1963). *Symbol formation.* New York: Wiley.

Wetherby, A., & Prutting, C. (1984). Profiles of communicative and cognitive-social abilities in autistic children. *Journal of Speech and Hearing Research, 27,* 264–377.

Williams, R. S., Hauser, S. L., Purpura, D. P., DeLong, R., & Swisher, C. N. (1980). Autism and mental retardation: Neuropathological studies performed in four retarded persons with autistic behavior. *Archives of Neurology, 37,* 749–753.

7

What are the Core Deficits
in Autism?

Marian Sigman
University of California, Los Angeles

The purpose of this chapter is to review a program of research aimed at identifying the central areas of disorder in autistic individuals. The identification of the disabilities specific to autism is important for several reasons. First, we need to understand the strengths and limitations of people with autism if we are to plan effective interventions. Although some intervention programs claim to have brought about nearly total remediation, most autistic individuals remain severely disturbed even with fairly intensive educational intervention. If core deficits are identified, these deficits can become the targets of intervention programs. Moreover, treatment programs are most effective that make use of the strengths of the participants so that the identification of intact abilities and interests in autistic people is important.

The study of autism also provides a perspective on normal development. The normal child develops abilities in various domains in an integrated fashion with one stage building upon the next. Although there is some variation across domains even in normal children, various abilities and interests emerge together so that development appears seamless. The domains of development are not so tightly interwoven in children with autism so that we can begin to see how much development in one domain depends on development in other domains. As an example, the deft handling of a sensorimotor task (such as using the end of a rake to obtain a candy placed in a long tube) by a child who has no verbal skills is convincing evidence that sensorimotor skills may be necessary but are certainly not sufficient for language acquisition.

The third source of significance of the identification of core behavioral deficits is the possibility that brain-behavior relations would be elucidated if

139

a specific neurological site was found to be disordered in the brains of autistic individuals. Although one of the aims of this volume is to encourage this line of inquiry, neurophysiological investigations in autism have only just begun (see chapter 6 of this volume) so progress in this direction has been minimal.

THE DEFINITION OF CORE BEHAVIORAL DEFICITS

Before we attempt to identify core behavioral deficits, we need to have some criteria for defining what constitutes a behavioral deficit and what would make it central to the disorder. If autistic children are unable to perform certain tasks successfully, the abilities required by these tasks would seem to be deficient. However, there are a number of difficulties involved in ascertaining what is truly a deficit. First, children have to be willing to perform the task if one is to measure abilities. Second, children may choose to perform a task in a particular way even though higher level abilities are available. Third, many of the problems that we use with children require a variety of abilities so that it is not clear what is lacking if a group of children cannot perform the task.

In order to circumvent these difficulties, investigators attempt to design tasks that children are willing to perform. If the children seem involved and interested but do not show a behavior or skill across settings, there is some justification for considering this an area of deficit. In order to make the specification of abilities clearer, most investigators use sets of problems or situations that overlap in some ways and are divergent in other ways. An example is the administration of both social and nonsocial cognitive tasks to determine whether a deficit is specific to the social realm. However, the catch in this approach is the problem of ensuring that tasks are of equivalent difficulty across domains.

Even when a deficit is identified, there is always the question as to whether the deficit represents delayed development as opposed to deficient development. It is rare to find abilities that children can never achieve if their overall intellectual development continues. Of course, many autistic and mentally retarded children do seem to reach a plateau in their cognitive and language development that would limit their skills in diverse areas.

The issue as to what makes a deficit core or central to the disorder needs to be discussed. Specificity and universality are often considered criteria for the centrality of a deficit. In terms of specificity, the deficit should not be shared by children with disorders other than autism. However, there are limits to specificity as a criterion. Any syndrome probably involves a constellation of deficits so that a particular deficit may show up in a number of syndromes. Furthermore, there are limits in the way that development can occur. For this reason, children with a variety of syndromes may show a similar deficit even though the deficit is more central to one syndrome than the others.

Universality, the other criterion, is equally problematic. It seems obvious that a truly core deficit should appear in all children with the same syndrome. However, as we discuss later, the manifestations of the deficit are likely to change with development.

A third criterion that can be considered is primacy, that is that central disorders should emerge early in development. If we are to take a developmental viewpoint, then we cannot overlook the point in development where disorders become apparent. Psychological development after this point is likely to be influenced by what the child can and cannot learn. On the other hand, some disorders do not become apparent or even emerge until the child has reached certain stages of physical or psychological development. Thus, there are deficits that are difficult to identify until the child has language, and disorders that do not appear until certain maturational points such as puberty.

DEVELOPMENTAL CONSIDERATIONS

Developmental change is taken for granted in studies of normal individuals. A similar appreciation for developmental change has only slowly been emerging in the study of autism. In the last 10–15 years, the search for core deficits in autism has been conducted as if these deficits would be manifested in the same way at all ages and developmental levels. However, the physical and psychological changes in children as a function of age mandate that disorders differ in form at different periods of development. In line with this notion is the evidence that continuity in development seems to be manifested much more in a "continuity of underlying processes" than a "continuity of identical behaviors" in normal children (Bornstein & Sigman, 1986, p. 260).

The investigation of the effects of developmental change is complicated in autism by the co-occurrence of autism and mental retardation in about 75% of autistic individuals. This requires the investigator to consider both the chronological and mental age of the autistic individual. For a deficit to be considered central to the disorder, the deficit should be manifested in some way in autistic individuals of all developmental levels. However, the form in which the deficit is manifested is likely to change with psychological and physical development.

Another complication is that autistic children are not only mentally retarded but also language delayed. If the autistic children are matched to a control group on performance abilities rather than language abilities, the autistic group is likely to have inferior receptive and expressive language skills. If the autistic group is matched on language skills to the control group, then they are likely to be superior to the control group on performance abilities. Matching on a general intelligence test may equate the groups or may not, depending on overall characteristics. The choice of control groups and matching procedures should depend on the nature of the question asked. Most investigators find themselves using a variety of control groups. One reason for this is that any single control group itself may have particular characteristics, strengths, or weaknesses that influence the comparison with the autistic group.

In our own research program, which is the focus of this chapter, we have concentrated our efforts on the study of young autistic children, most of whom are also mentally retarded. As a group, the 70 autistic children we have studied were about 3–5 years of age with overall mental functioning similar to those of 2-year-olds at the time they were subjects. We have used two control groups. The first control group was composed of mentally retarded children, half of whom have Down syndrome, who were matched on a general developmental or intelligence test to the autistic group and are of equivalent chronological age. The second group was composed of normal children matched similarly to the other two groups on mental age. Depending on the study, either part of or the whole control group has had language abilities equivalent to those of the autistic children.

Recently, we have conducted a study of 18 older, nonretarded autistic children whose mean chronological and mental age at the time of testing was about 12 years. The control group of normal children was matched on mental age and verbal abilities to the autistic group. This leaves a large gap in our information, which can partly be filled in by the studies of other investigators, most of whom have examined retarded and nonretarded autistic children who were older than our 4-year-old sample. What is missing almost entirely from the literature is information about young, nonretarded autistic children. It may be necessary to examine both retarded and nonretarded autistic individuals at all age levels because the effects of the two disabilities combined may be more severe than those of only one disability. Put another way, nonretarded autistic individuals may be able to ameliorate some of their difficulties by making use of their intellectual skills, an hypothesis for which we have some evidence.

COGNITIVE ABILITIES

We began our research with studies of the early object concepts of young autistic children. This line of research showed that autistic children had equivalent sensorimotor abilities to nonautistic retarded children and normal children matched on mental age. The autistic children seemed to understand object permanence, could use tools, and were as likely to categorize objects by color, form, and function as were the control children (Morgan, Cutrer, Coplin, & Rodrigue, 1989; Sigman & Ungerer, 1981, 1984b; Ungerer & Sigman, 1987).

Cognitive Deficits in Young Autistic Children. Although sensorimotor skills and elementary knowledge of object categories did not seem impaired in autistic children relative to controls, two areas did show specific deficits. First, the autistic children were much less likely to imitate gestures or vocalizations made by an adult than were the control children, an observation made by other investigators as well (Dawson & Adams, 1984; DeMyer et al., 1972). Second, the autistic children showed much less sophisticated play with objects in both an unstructured situation and in a situation structured by the experimenter (Sigman & Ungerer, 1984b; Ungerer & Sigman, 1981). Limitations in play skills have been described by many experimenters in a variety of situations and with children of varying developmental and chronological ages (Baron-Cohen, 1987; Riquet, Taylor, Benroya, & Klein, 1981; Wing, Gould, Yeates, & Brierly, 1977).

The deficits in representational play could be explained in two ways. First, the cognitive demands made by play could be more advanced than those required for sensorimotor and categorization tasks. Wolf and Gardener (1981) suggested that representational thought may be manifested in two different systems. One system, reflected in the development of sensorimotor skills, may involve the capacity to recall information that is then accessible for problem solving. The capacity to translate experience into language and play symbols may reflect a second system. Other theorists have also recognized that pretend play requires the child to go beyond the knowledge of reality (something that he or she has only recently achieved) to temporarily make one object stand for another. Thus, it has been suggested that children of this age are able to make use of secondary representational systems that allow them to posit hypothetical situations (Perner, 1991). Leslie (1987) proposed that pretend play is an early form of metarepresentation in which a decoupling device is used to separate primary from secondary representations. For this theory, metarepresentational ability consists of the capacity to understand that other people can hold propositional attitudes toward events or objects and is particularly necessary for the child to engage in social pretend play. As an example, if the child pretends that a banana is a telephone in play with a parent, the child has to be able to have some notion that the parent knows the banana is a banana and also can let the banana stand for a telephone for the purposes of play. In this conceptualization, the core deficit in autism is considered to be metarepresentational and manifested not only in pretend play but also in the understanding of theory of mind, an issue that I discuss later in this chapter.

Cognitive Deficits in Older Autistic Children. In accordance with hypotheses that deficits may be apparent in more advanced cognitive functions, our recent work with older autistic children does show cognitive deficits in these children (Yirmiya, Sigman, Kasari, & Mundy, 1992). Six conservation tasks were administered to the autistic and control groups of children. The autistic children ranged in age from 9 to 16 years 10 months, whereas the normal children ranged in age from 9 to 14 years 10 months. The mean IQ on the Wechsler Intelligence Scale for Children–Revised (WISC–R) was 102 for the autistic group and 104 for the normal group.

The following conservation tasks were administered: two-dimensional space, number, substance, continuous quantity, weight, and discontinuous quantity. After the child had agreed that two substances were equivalent, one substance was transformed in shape and the child was asked if they were the same and why. Only half the children in the sample of 12-year-old, nonretarded autistic children solved all the conservation tasks whereas very few normal children made any errors. The autistic children were not just wrong on their explanations; they tended to claim that the substance had been changed in the attribute on which it had been equivalent to the matched substance. Thus, half the group did not seem to understand the principle of conservation.

It is true that the autistic children who failed the conservation tasks were the less intelligent autistic children. However, none of the autistic children had a mental age below 10 years, and normal 10-year-olds do understand conservation. It is also true that children with schizophrenia and other psychological disorders seem to have some difficulty in understanding conservation (Caplan, Foy, Sigman, & Perdue, 1990; Sigman, Ungerer, & Russell, 1983). However, the deficiencies of the autistic children seem greater and the lack of understanding seems more prevalent among the autistic children than among schizophrenic children or children with other emotional disorders.

The nonretarded autistic children were also less able to take the spatial perspective of the experimenter (Yirmiya, Sigman, & Zacks, in prep.). Several objects were placed on a wooden turntable and the experimenter stood across from the child or at the child's right or left. The child was asked to rotate the turntable by the experimenter so that "you see the toys in the same way that I now see them from where I am standing." The autistic children were correct on only 75% of the trials whereas the normal children were correct on 96% of the trials. Seven autistic children made 30 errors, 21 of these consisting of turning the turntable to its original position. Three normal children each made one error.

In line with this evidence for cognitive dysfunction are the findings that nonretarded autistic children, including children with Asperger's syndrome, show deficits in executive functions (Ozonoff, Pennington, & Rogers, 1991; Ozonoff, Rogers, & Pennington, 1991). Tasks measuring executive functioning require that individuals use internally formulated plans and set aside more habitual actions evoked by the external context. Autistic individuals have been shown to have difficulty in guiding their behavior in terms of forseeable consequences, especially when more direct approaches are available. Evidence for this is that high-functioning autistic children made more perseverative errors and failed to maintain set more on the Wisconsin Card Sort and scored lower on the Tower of Hanoi than matched controls. Rumsey and collaborators (Rumsey, 1985; Rumsey & Hamburger, 1988, 1990) have had similar findings with high functioning, autistic adult men. Thus, there is increasing evidence for difficulties with planning cognitive strategies in older, nonretarded autistic children and adults.

SOCIAL INTERACTION AND SOCIAL UNDERSTANDING

In the previous section, I have explored the possibility that autistic children perform little pretend play because play requires more advanced cognitive abilities and have presented evidence that tasks requiring more advanced abilities are challenging for autistic adolescents and adults. An alternative line of explanation for the limited use of pretend play and imitation may be that both require social observation and interaction. Almost all play involves social acts and play is often carried out with dolls or other imaginary actors. Even functional play with objects usually involves acts that are performed within a social context in most children's lives. Imitation clearly involves social interaction. Therefore, the deficits in representational play and imitation could be linked to disorders in social interaction or social understanding.

Social Interactions. Clinical descriptions of autistic children often paint a picture of individuals who are extremely aloof and socially unresponsive. However, more extensive experience with autistic children reveals that this picture is far too global and undifferentiated. Observational studies of autistic children show that they will engage in eye contact with other people depending on the circumstances. In several observations of structured play between parent and children, we have found no differences among groups of autistic, mentally retarded, and normal children in the frequency with which the children look at their parents (Sigman & Mundy, 1989; Sigman, Mundy, Sherman, & Ungerer, 1986). Moreover, when parents interrupted their children's play with objects and attempted to elicit social interaction, the autistic children, like the other children, increased their eye contact with the parents and did not show avoidance. In a structured play interaction with an experimenter, the autistic children initiated and responded to social bids as much as the control children. Although there were differences in the amount of time that the children looked at the experimenter, these differences were attributable to the behavior of the mentally retarded group of children. Mentally retarded children, particularly those with Down syndrome, appear to be more interested in social interaction than do other children (Kasari,

Mundy, Yirmiya, & Sigman, 1990; Ruskin, Mundy, Kasari, & Sigman, in press).

Social Attachments. Autistic children also appear to form social attachments to their caregivers. In studies with two different samples, we have identified changes in the children's behaviors when the parent left and increased social behavior when the parent returned to the room where the child was playing (Sigman & Mundy, 1989; Sigman & Ungerer, 1984a). Moreover, autistic children did not differ from mental and chronological age-matched mentally retarded children in their patterns of behavior in response to separation from the reunion with their caregivers. These finding have been corroborated by a number of other investigations (Rogers, Ozonoff, & Maslin-Cole, 1991; Shapiro, Sherman, Calamari, & Koch, 1987).

Joint Attention and Social Understanding. Although autistic children are not as socially unresponsive as originally thought, they universally show disordered social behavior. In young children, this is most apparent in terms of bids for joint attention. At the end of the first year of life, the young normal child begins to look at other people in order to share experiences. This social referencing is particularly frequent in ambiguous situations when the child looks to the adult as if searching for guidance. By the second year of life, infants frequently engage in protodeclarative gestures of pointing to objects and showing objects to familiar adults. Autistic children engage in social referencing and protodeclarative gestures far less than normal and mentally retarded children of similar developmental level (Baron-Cohen, 1989; Loveland & Landry, 1986; Mundy, Sigman, Ungerer, & Sherman, 1986; Sigman et al., 1986). In a study of social interaction between children and a parent, 17 of the 18 children in the normal and mentally retarded groups pointed to, showed, or shared an object with their parent at least once, whereas only 6 of the 18 autistic children ever engaged in one of these behaviors.

Several explanations can be suggested for the lack of social referencing and protodeclarative gestures. First, it may be that autistic children do not see other people as having views, ideas, or emotions that can be shared. This hypothesis is congruent with the idea that the central deficit in autism is in *theory of mind* and the evidence that autistic children cannot identify accurately the information possessed by others (Baron-Cohen, Leslie, & Frith, 1985).

Theory of Mind. Theory of mind refers to the commonsense notion that adults use in everyday life that attributes desires, beliefs, intentions, and emotions to other people. The issue for research investigation is when and how children develop the understanding that they and others have minds and that mental states guide human actions. Normal children understand that others can have ideas that are different from theirs by age 4 years if not earlier. However, autistic children even with the language abilities of 4-year-olds do not seem able to attribute information to other people that differs from the information that they possess. In joint attention, the normal infant acknowledges that the adult can share attention to the same object with him or her. It would seem unlikely that the autistic child could easily understand the differences in the information possessed by another when this child has had such difficulty early on in sharing similar experiences or information with another person.

A second possible reason why autistic children may not engage in joint attention is that they may be unable to read emotional signals on the faces of others. Without this ability, even if the child was interested in the reactions of others, their facial expressions would be incomprehensible. Finally, autistic children may be able to understand the faces and minds of others, but they may either lack some basic interest in the reactions of others or these reactions may be threatening or aversive to them. The last two explanations bring us to a consideration of emotional reactions in autistic children.

EMOTIONAL EXPRESSIVENESS AND RESPONSIVENESS

Autistic children and adults are frequently characterized as being affectively flat. These descriptions vary from the extreme statements of Bettelheim in "Joey, the Mechanical Boy" (Bettelheim, 1987) to more restrained portrayals in the recent literature. The current diagnostic system, outlined in the *Diagnostic and Statistical Manual of Mental Disorders* (3rd ed., rev.) (*DSM–III–R*; APA, 1987), describes autistic children as having an "apparent absence of emotional reaction" (p. 35).

Emotional Expressions. Our current research has focused on the emotional reactions of autistic children in structured social interactions, in situations where another individual shows affective responses, and situations designed to elicit affect in the child. In order to characterize the affective reactions of the children in social situations, we have coded their facial affect second by second using the microanalytic system designed by Izard (1979). With this system, muscle changes in each section of the face were coded and then the simultaneous codings of the three sections were translated into specific affects. The coding system allowed the identification of even fleeting emotions as well as the marking of incongruous affects, which are ambiguous facial expressions where different sections of the face appear to show different expressions.

Using this system on seven representative segments of the structured interaction between the child and the experimenter, the affective reactions of autistic children were compared to those of mentally retarded and normal controls (Yirmiya, Kasari, Sigman, & Mundy, 1989). There were surprisingly few differences between the groups. Although the autistic children showed somewhat less positive affect, the differences between groups were not significant. Very little negative affect was shown in this playful social interaction, which was not unexpected because the situation was planned to be pleasant for the child. The autistic children did show somewhat more neutral affect than the normal and mentally retarded children. Perhaps most important, one third of the autistic children showed incongruous blends of affect whereas only one mentally retarded child and none of the normal children showed incongruous blends. As mentioned earlier, an incongruous blend occurs when one portion of the face shows one affect, such as the mouth smiling, whereas another portion shows a different affect, such as the eyes showing fear.

Although the affective displays of the three groups of children were not very different in other regards, the question remained whether the integration of affect with attention and behavior might differ. In a study by Dawson, Hill, Spencer, Galpert, and Watson (1990), autistic children did not differ from normal controls in the amount or frequency of smiles or frowns. However, they smiled less during sustained eye contact and in response to their mothers' smiles. Similarly, autistic children in another study showed much of their positive affect while playing alone (Snow, Hertzig, & Shapiro, 1987).

In order to examine the integration, affect and attention were coded during the first 8 min. of the structured interaction between child and experimenter (Kasari et al., 1990). All three groups of children showed more affect when looking at the experimenter's face than at the objects, and there were no significant group differences. However, there were group differences when communicative context was taken into account.

Normal children displayed significantly more positive affect to the adult during joint attention than when requesting an object or some help. The autistic children displayed less positive affect to the adult during their infrequent joint attention acts than the normal children but did not differ from the normal children in terms of affect displayed during requesting behaviors. The mentally retarded children showed uniformly high levels of positive affect in both communicative contexts. They showed more positive affect than the autistic children when indicating or requesting objects and more positive affect than the normal children only during requesting.

Thus, the autistic children seem able to express emotion but do not carry out communicative acts with appropriate emotions. This suggests that autistic children are able to express emotions and are only affectively flat in certain contexts. Maternal reports corroborate these findings from observations of structured interactions (Capps, Kasari, Yirmiya, & Sigman, 1993). When asked to report on the affects shown by their children over the course of the last week, mothers of children in the younger autistic group and the older, nonretarded autistic group described more frequent displays of negative affect than did the mothers of the control children. Normal children were reported to show more happiness and interest than the autistic children. Although one can question the validity of maternal reports, it can be asserted that these parents did not experience their autistic children as emotionally unresponsive.

Responses to the Emotions of Others. Studies of the reactions of the children to strong emotions shown by others give one hint as to why the children are often described clinically as emotionally unresponsive (Sigman, Kasari, Kwon, & Yirmiya, 1992). In situations where adults modeled pain, fear, or discomfort, normal and mentally retarded children showed considerable attention to the face of the adult actor. Autistic children looked only fleetingly at the adult showing distress. In contrast to the control children who appeared to be inhibited in their play, the autistic children played continuously with a toy. The difference in reaction was shown dramatically when the adult pretended to feel unwell and lay down on a coach following a period of social interaction. Half the autistic children did not appear to notice their parent's discomfort whereas this was true for only six mentally retarded and four normal children.

We cannot know whether the autistic children have an emotional reaction to this situation that is not shown in their behavior. In fact, autistic children may be aware of the emotional displays of others but be entirely unable to understand these emotional displays. The lack of attention to the distressed adult may be active avoidance rather than simply unawareness or lack of interest. When these same autistic children were praised for having completed a puzzle successfully, they tended to look away or walk away more than the control children (Kasari, Sigman, Baumgartner, & Stipek, 1993). This observation suggests that the display of strong emotion by another individual is confusing or disturbing to the autistic child and, therefore, may elicit affective distress even when the emotion is positive in tone. One way to answer these questions about responsiveness would be to measure the autonomic reaction of autistic individuals to such stimuli. As far as I know, this has not been done as yet.

Emotional Understanding. The study of older autistic children and adults often allows the investigation of social understanding because these individuals frequently have sufficient verbal abilities to respond to questions. A number of studies have investigated simple recognition of emotions shown by adults on photographs, slides, or videotapes (Braverman, Fein, Lucci, &

Waterhouse, 1989; Hobson, 1986; Ozonoff, Pennington, & Rogers, 1990; Prior, Dahlstrom, & Squires, 1990). Although autistic individuals do less well than control subjects on such tasks, differences between groups are smaller and often not significant when the groups are matched on verbal abilities. However, nonretarded autistic individuals perform less well than normal controls on emotion recognition tasks so this does seem to be an area of difficulty (MacDonald et al., 1989; Ozonoff, Pennington, & Rogers, 1991).

We have found that nonretarded autistic children are less able than normal children to identify affects correctly in videotaped vignettes designed to show children in an emotion-arousing situation (Yirmiya et al., 1992). Although the autistic children could appropriately identify many of the affects portrayed, they were significantly less accurate than the normal children. Moreover, they were less likely to claim that they felt a similar emotion to the one they described for the protagonist. Thus, they demonstrated less social comprehension and less empathy in response to these videotaped portrayals.

Surprisingly, the autistic children showed a great deal of positive affect and concentration while watching the videotapes (Capps et al., 1993). In fact, they showed more affect than the normal children who may have been following emotion display rules that prohibit the expression of strong emotion in public. In general, the affect shown by the autistic children was appropriate to the situation in that they demonstrated positive affect to happy situations (such as a boy getting a new bicycle) and concentration to unhappy situations. Moreover, those autistic children who showed the most positive facial affect were also the most empathetic.

As part of this study, the children were asked to tell the experimenter about a time that they had felt each of the following emotions: happiness, sadness, pride, and embarrassment (Capps, Yirmiya, & Sigman, 1992). The children were able to come up with fairly appropriate responses for the simple emotions of happiness and sadness. However, the autistic children manifested some difficulty in talking about socially derived emotions of pride and embarrassment. They required more time and more prompts, their responses were more tentative and "scripted," and they displayed limited appreciation for the salience of others in embarrassing situations. The autistic children described embarrassing situations that were external ("My uncle got married") rather than internal ("I'm too tall"), whereas the normal children tended to describe internal events. The autistic children may have described external events more and made less mention of an audience because of an inability to refer to other people. On the other hand, autistic children may have many more experiences in which they are embarrassed because of external, uncontrollable events, and they may refer less to an audience because they experience most audiences as critical of their behavior.

The advantage of studying older autistic children is that they are often verbal and can express their reactions to social and emotionally arousing situations. The children we have studied do not describe themselves as lacking in feelings. They are aware of the reactions of others although their understanding is less subtle and seems to require more effort than is true for normal children. Their parents do not describe them as flat but do see them as more distressed than is generally true for normal children.

There are certain disadvantages or ambiguities that arise in studying an older group of children rather than a younger group. First, it is not clear how much the difficulties of the children at older ages are continued manifestations of earlier difficulties and/or the cumulation of experiences or lack of experiences over years of development. An analogy can be drawn to the study of children with learning disabilities in junior high school. The children may show academic difficulties because of the problems that interfered with their learning earlier in life and/or their academic difficulties may result from their lack of skill development during the elementary school years.

A second ambiguity resulting from the use of an intelligent group of older autistic children is that they may have been able to compensate for some of their difficulties in social and emotional responsiveness. There is evidence in our studies that this is true. There was a significant positive correlation between the empathy scores and intelligence among the autistic children but not among the normal children. Thus, the more intelligent autistic children may make use of their intelligence to solve problems intellectually that do not require cognitive strategies for normal children. In other words, normal children have direct access to their emotional reactions, so even children with limited intelligence can answer questions about their own emotional experiences. In contrast, autistic children may not have this kind of access to their own emotions but the more intelligent autistic adolescents may have been able to learn the "correct" responses to questions about the emotions of themselves and others.

If the children have learned the appropriate responses to the emotions of themselves and others, this learning is only partly effective. The labeling of the emotions of others as well as the recounting of their own socially mediated emotional experiences appeared to require concentrated effort, much hesitation, and great uncertainty on the part of these autistic children. The normal child is easily able to describe a time when he or she was angry and does so with little hesitation and concentrated effort. In contrast, autistic children answer questions about their own emotional experiences like normal children answer difficult arithmetic questions. It is not surprising, then, that autistic adolescents continue to have severe difficulties in social adjustment.

DISCUSSION

In order to integrate these findings, I propose a model of the precursors required for the understanding of others and attempt to pinpoint areas of function that are impaired in autistic children. This model presupposes that basic to the understanding of others are four processes that normally develop over the first 12–15 months of life (see Fig. 7.1). First, the child must have emotional reactions to social and nonsocial events. Second, the child must have some perception of his or her own emotional reactions. Third, the child must attend to and perceive the vocal, facial, and behavioral displays of others. Fourth, there must be some matching of the child's sense of his or her own reactions to those of the other person, which ultimately develops into an awareness of the emotional responses of the other person. The understanding that other people have perceptions, desires, and beliefs that may differ from one's own must develop from this early matrix.

It is difficult to conclude that the autistic child is either impaired or unimpaired in the development of any of these precursors. Much of the research described in this chapter shows that autistic children do have emotional reactions that are similar in some regards to the emotional reactions of normal children. For example, they are not markedly different in affective expressions during pleasant social interactions nor do their parents describe them as emotionally unfeeling. At older ages, they attribute emotional reactions to themselves as do their parents and they show emotional responses to the videotaped depictions of other children in emotionally arousing situations. On the other hand, one cannot know about the nature of their emotional experience. There is evidence from physiological studies that autistic children are hyperresponsive to simple visual and auditory stimuli (James & Barry, 1984). If this is so, then they may be flooded with feelings in certain social situations that make it difficult for them to distinguish their own emotional experiences.

Autistic children seem to have primitive awareness of their own simple emotional responses. Perhaps, the first developmental evidence we have that the infant has some awareness of knowing what she or he wants is manifested by attempts to obtain objects or regulate the behavior of others. At this very basic level, autistic children are as likely to attempt to manipulate others to

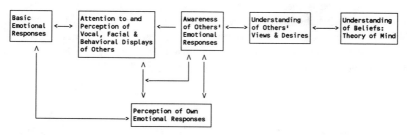

FIG. 7.1.   Model proposed for the normal development of social understanding.

get what they want when it is inaccessible to them. At older ages, they can describe events that make them happy, sad, or angry. Thus, they seem to react emotionally and to be at least somewhat aware of these reactions.

Attention to the vocal, facial, and behavioral displays of others is clearly lacking in 3 to 5-year-old autistic children when emotion is expressed strongly and explicitly. However, autistic children will attend to others in some situations. In two structured interactions with their caregivers, autistic children were as attentive and showed as much face-to-face interaction as normal children matched on mental age. Moreover, when the caregiver initiated social games, the children in all groups increased their attention to the caregiver's face and there were no group differences. Similarly, Dawson and her collaborators (Dawson et al., 1990) videotaped children and their mothers during a free- play period, a more structured period, and a face-to-face interaction. In all three situations, autistic and normal children matched on mental age did not differ in the frequency or duration of gaze at their mothers' faces. Thus, autistic children do not look less at the faces of others in all settings.

The capacity for contrasting the emotional reactions of others with those of the self would seem to be necessary for social referencing. If this is so, the 3 to 5-year-old autistic children observed by us did not seem able to carry out this kind of comparison. It would seem impossible to develop an appreciation for the emotional responses of others if one does not contrast these to emotional reactions of one's own.

In summary, autistic children could be deficient in any or all of these precursors of emotional understanding. Moreover, the deficiency could stem from a lack of emotional responsiveness, a difference in emotional reaction pattern, or a limited awareness of the emotional reactions of oneself and/or others. In other words, the basic deficit could be either affective or cognitive or, what is most likely, in the integration of affect and cognition. Another possibility is that there are subgroups of autistic individuals that vary in the extent to which the cognitive or affective deficit is primary.

My conviction is that it is premature to attempt to identify subgroups of autistic individuals. First, even with the differences in intelligence and severity of symptoms, an identifiable group sharing core social, communicative, and imaginative impairments can be identified and these children are remarkably similar in many locales (see Frith, 1989, for discussion). Second, the disorders identified across research groups are often very similar even when the groups study individuals of different ages and levels of ability. Third and most important, a proper appreciation of heterotypic continuity in development allows one to see that the differences that have been found are often developmentally different manifestations of the same impairment. Just as we would not expect intelligence to be manifested in the same behaviors by a normal infant and a normal teenager, so we cannot expect that disorders will appear in exactly the same way in children who vary in developmental level. We may find that there truly are subgroups but we need first to look for similar processes across individuals. Developmental understanding can make its greatest contribution to the study of disorder by preventing the splintering of disordered groups into subgroups so that research becomes fragmented and aconceptual.

To return to the three sources of significance discussed in the opening paragraphs of this chapter, the implications of these findings for intervention seem fairly obvious. Autistic children have problems with social interaction that are rooted in their lack of emotional understanding. To the extent that it is possible, intervention programs need to help these children perceive and differentiate the facial and gestural language of others. Just as the high-functioning children use their cognitive skills to understand (however incompletely) the feelings and thoughts of others, so intervention programs need to teach emotional and social understanding didactically. In line with the findings of this research and that of other investigators, some intervention programs in the United States and Europe are designing and using techniques to encourage autistic children to share attention and affect with others.

The implications of this research for understanding normal development are also straightforward. Social understanding cannot occur without the child being able to read the emotional messages of others. The evidence from autistic children has already convinced some investigators of normal development that the normal infant must possess these abilities at some point in the second year of life (see Wellman, in press, for further discussion). Furthermore, this capacity must depend to some extent on basic perceptions of the child's own emotional reactions. Theories of the development of social understanding that fail to include reactions to the attention and emotions of others must be flawed. The only individuals who develop social understanding in a logical, conscious manner are high-functioning autistic children, and their understanding is hard-won and incomplete.

The application of these findings to the identification of brain-behavior associations is not so evident. One might expect that there would be limbic system involvement given the problems in the reactions to emotional cues. If a disorder in executive function is also substantiated, the prefrontal area would seem to be implicated because patients with prefrontal damage show similar deficits (Damasio & Damasio, 1990). For parallels to be drawn between structural and functional deficits in autism, we will need still clearer delineation of the deficits in both structures and functions of autistic individuals.

ACKNOWLEDGMENTS

The research described in this chapter was supported by Grants NS25243 from the National Institute of Neurological Disorders and Stroke, HD17662 from the National

Institute of Child Health and Human Development, and MH33815 from the National Institute of Mental Health. I am indebted to the following individuals for their contributions to this research: Lisa Capps, Connie Kasari, Jung-Hye Kwon, Peter Mundy, Judy Ungerer, and Nurit Yirmiya. Portions of this chapter were written while the author was in residence at the MRC Cognitive Development Unit in London, England.

REFERENCES

American Psychiatric Association. (1987). *Diagnostic and statistical manual of mental disorders* (3rd ed., rev.). Washington, DC: Author.

Baron-Cohen, S. (1987). Autism and symbolic play. *British Journal of Developmental Psychology, 5,* 139–148.

Baron-Cohen, S. (1989). Perceptual role-taking and protodeclarative pointing in autism. *British Journal of Development Psychology, 7,* 113–127.

Baron-Cohen, S., Leslie, A., & Frith, U. (1985). Does the autistic child have a "theory of mind." *Cognition, 21,* 37–46.

Bettelheim, B. (1987). *The empty fortress-infantile autism and the birth of the self.* New York: Free Press, Collier–Macmillan.

Bornstein, M. H., & Sigman, M. D. (1986). Continuity in mental development from infancy. *Child Development, 57,* 251–274.

Braverman, M., Fein, D., Lucci, D., & Waterhouse, L. (1989). Affect comprehension in children with pervasive developmental disorders. *Journal of Autism and Developmental Disorders, 19,* 301–315.

Caplan, R., Foy, J. G., Sigman, M., & Perdue, S. (1990). Conversation and formal thought disorder in schizophrenic and schizotypal children. *Development and Psychopathology, 2,* 183–192.

Capps, L., Kasari, C., Yirmiya, N., & Sigman, M. (1993). Parental perception of emotional expressiveness in children with autism. *Journal of Consulting and Clinical Psychology, 61.*

Capps, L., Yirmiya, N., & Sigman, M. (1992). Understanding of simple and complex emotions in non-retarded children with autism. *Journal of Child Psychology and Psychiatry, 33,* 1169–1182.

Damasio, H., & Damasio, A. R. (1990). The neural basis of memory, language, and behavioral guidance. *Seminars in The Neurosciences, 2,* 27–286.

Dawson, G., & Adams, A. (1984). Imitation and social responsiveness in autistic children. *Journal of Abnormal Child Psychology, 12,* 209–226.

Dawson, G., Hill, D., Spencer, A., Galpert, L., & Watson, L. (1990). Affective exchanges between young autistic children and their mothers. *Journal of Abnormal Child Psychology, 18,* 335–345.

DeMyer, M. D., Alpern, G. D., Barton, S., DeMyer, W. E., Churchill, D. W., Hingtgen, J. N., Bryson, C. Q., Pontius, W., & Kimberlin, C. (1972). Imitation in autistic, early schizophrenic, and non-psychotic subnormal children. *Journal of Autism and Childhood Schizophrenia, 2,* 264–287.

Frith, U. (1989). *Autism, explaining the enigma.* Oxford, England: Blackwell.

Hobson, R. P. (1986). The autistic child's appraisal of expressions of emotion. *Journal of Child Psychology and Psychiatry, 27,* 321–342.

Izard, C. E. (1979). *The maximally discriminative facial movement coding system (MAX).* Newark: University of Delaware.

James, A. L., & Barry, R. J. (1984). Cardiovascular and electrodermal responses to simple stimuli in autistic, retarded and normal children. *International Journal of Psychophysiology, 1,* 179–193.

Kasari, C., Mundy, P., Yirmiya, N., & Sigman, M. (1990). Affect and attention on children with Down syndrome. *American Journal on Mental Retardation, 95*, 55–67.

Kasari, C., Sigman, M., Baumgartner, P., & Stipek, D. J. (1993). Pride and mastery in children with autism. *Journal of Child Psychology and Psychiatry, 34*, 353–362.

Leslie, A. M. (1987). Pretense and representation: The origins of "theory of mind." *Psychological Review, 94* (4), 412–426.

Loveland, K., & Landry, S. (1986). Joint attention and language in autism and development language delay. *Journal of Autism and Developmental Disorders, 16*, 335–349.

MacDonald, H., Rutter, M., Howlin, P., Rios, P., Le Conteur, A., Evered, C., & Folstein, S. (1989). Recognition and expression of emotional cues by autistic and normal adults. *Journal of Child Psychology and Psychiatry, 30*, 865–877.

Morgan, S. B., Cutrer, P. S., Coplin, J. W., & Rodrigue, J. R. (1989). Do autistic children differ from retarded and normal children in Piagetian sensorimotor functioning? *Journal of Child Psychology and Psychiatry, 30*, 857–864.

Mundy, P., Sigman, M., Ungerer, J., & Sherman, T. (1986). Defining the social deficits of autism: The contribution of nonverbal communication measures. *Journal of Child Psychology and Psychiatry, 27*, 657–669.

Ozonoff, S., Pennington, B. F., & Rogers, S. J. (1990). Are there emotion perception deficits in young autistic children? *Journal of Child Psychology and Psychiatry, 31*, 343–361.

Ozonoff, S., Pennington, B. F., & Rogers, S. J., (1991). Executive function deficits in high-functioning autistic children: Relationship to theory of mind. *Journal of Child Psychology and Psychiatry, 32*, 1081–1105.

Ozonoff, S., Rogers, S. J., & Pennington, B. F. (1991). Asperger's syndrome: Evidence of an empirical distinction from high-functioning autism. *Journal of Child Psychology and Psychiatry, 32*, 1107–1122.

Perner, J. (1991). *Understanding the representational mind.* Cambridge, MA: MIT Press.

Prior, M., Dahlstrom, D., & Squires, T. (1990). Autistic children's knowledge of thinking and feeling states in other people. *Journal of Child Psychology and Psychiatry, 31*(4), 587–601.

Riquet, C. B., Taylor, N. D., Benroya, S., & Klein, L. S. (1981). Symbolic play in autistic, Down's, and normal children of equivalent mental age. *Journal of Autism and Developmental Disorders, 11*, 439–448.

Rogers, S. J., Ozonoff, S., & Maslin-Cole, C. (1991). A comparative study of attachment behavior in young children with autism or other psychiatric disorders. *Journal of the American Academy of Child and Adolescent Psychiatry, 30*, 483–488.

Rumsey, J. M. (1985). Conceptual problem-solving in highly verbal, nonretarded autistic men. *Journal of Autism and Developmental Disorders, 15*, 23–36.

Rumsey, J. M., & Hamburger, S. D. (1988). Neuropsychological findings in high-functioning men with infantile autism, residual state. *Journal of Clinical and Experimental Neuropsychology, 10*, 201–221.

Rumsey, J. M., & Hamburger, S. D. (1990). Neuropsychological divergence of high-level autism and severe dyslexia. *Journal of Autism and Developmental Disorders, 20*, 155–168.

Ruskin, E., Mundy, P., Kasari, C., & Sigman, M. (in press). Attention to people and toys during social and object mastery in children with Down syndrome. *American Journal on Mental Retardation.*

Shapiro, T., Sherman, M., Calamari, G., & Koch, D. (1987). Attachment in autism and other developmental disorders. *Journal of the American Academy of Child and Adolescent Psychiatry, 226*, 485–590.

Sigman, M., Kasari, C., Kwon, J. H., & Yirmiya, N. (1992). Responses to the negative emotions of others by autistic, mentally retarded, and normal children. *Child Development, 63*, 796–807.

Sigman, M., & Mundy, P. (1989). Social attachments in autistic children. *Journal of the American Academy of Child and Adolescent Psychiatry, 28*, 74–81.

Sigman, M., Mundy, P., Sherman, T., & Ungerer, J. A. (1986). Social interactions of autistic, mentally retarded, and normal children with their caregivers. *Journal of Child Psychology and Psychiatry, 27,* 647–669.

Sigman, M., & Ungerer, J. A. (1981). Sensorimotor skills and language comprehension in autistic children. *Journal of Abnormal Child Psychology, 9,* 149–165.

Sigman, M., & Ungerer, J. A. (1984a). Attachment behaviors in autistic children. *Journal of Autism and Developmental Disorders, 14,* 231–244.

Sigman, M., & Ungerer, J. A. (1984b). Cognitive and language skills in autistic, mentally retarded, and normal children. *Developmental Psychology, 20,* 293–302.

Sigman, M., Ungerer, J. A., & Russell, A. (1983). Moral judgment in relation to behavioral and cognitive disorders in adolescents. *Journal of Abnormal Child Psychology, 11,* 503–512.

Snow, M. E., Hertzig, M. E., & Shapiro, T. (1987). Expressions of emotion in young autistic children. *Journal of the American Academy of Child and Adolescent Psychiatry, 26,* 836–838.

Ungerer, J. A., & Sigman, M. (1981). Symbolic play and language comprehension in autistic children. *Journal of the American Academy of Child Psychiatry, 20,* 318–338.

Ungerer, J. A., & Sigman, M. (1987). Categorization skills and language development in autistic children. *Journal of Autism and Developmental Disorders, 17,* 3–16.

Wellman, H. (1993). Early understanding of mind: The normal case. In S. Baron-Cohen, H. Tager-Flusberg, & D. Cohen (Eds.), *Understanding other minds: Perspective from autism.* Oxford England: Oxford University Press.

Wing, L., Gould, L., Yeates, S. R., & Brierly, L. M. (1977). Symbolic play in severly mentally retarded and autistic children. *Journal of Child Psychology and Psychiatry, 18,* 167–178.

Wolf, D., & Gardner, H. (1981). On the structure of early symbolism. In R. L. Schiefelbusch & D. O. Bricker (Eds.), *Early language: Acquistion and intervention* (pp. 287–329). Baltimore: University Park Press.

Yirmiya, N., Kasari, C., Sigman, M., & Mundy, P. (1989). Facial expressions of affect in autistic, mentally retarded and normal children. *Journal of Child Psychology and Psychiatry, 30,* 725–735.

Yirmiya, N., Sigman, M., Kasari, C., & Mundy, P. (1992). Empathy and cognition in high-functioning children with autism. *Child Development, 63,* 150–160.

Yirmiya, N., Sigman, M., & Zacks, D. (in prep.). *Perceptual perspective taking and seriation abilities in high-functioning children with autism.*

8

Severity of Impairment in Autism

Lynn Waterhouse
Trenton State College

Autism is a puzzling disorder. It is considered a severe psychopathology of development, but consensus on the characterization of that severity has eluded researchers (Gillberg, 1990; Waterhouse, Wing, & Fein, 1989). Current models define autism as a behavioral syndrome of multiple genetic and nongenetic etiology, determined by a neurological deficit or deficits whose locus is uncertain (Rapin, 1991). The severity of impairment lies in aberrant social affect, aberrant social cognition, aberrant social communication, and impairment in associated intellectual, motor, and vegetative functions (APA, 1987).

The goal of this chapter is to explore the significance of the severity of diagnostic and nondiagnostic behaviors in understanding the nature of the syndrome. The chapter has four sections. The first section presents definitions and indices of severity in autism. The second section explores the question of a developmental shift in the severity of symptoms. The third section considers the implications of variation in symptom severity for constructing brain-behavior inferences. The fourth section suggests a methodological change for exploring patterns of severity in autistic symptomatology, and proposes a new theoretical model as a framework for interpreting neural deficits associated with autism.

DEFINITIONS AND INDICES OF SEVERITY

There are at least seven ways in which clinicians and researchers document the severity of individual cases of autism. One way is by measuring the degree of developmental lag on normative scales of behaviors within a specific domain, such as language or play (Fein et al., 1991; Sigman, Mundy, Ungerer, &

Sherman, 1987; Stone & Caro-Martinez, 1990; Waterhouse & Fein, 1982; Wetherby, Yonclas, & Bryan, 1989). A second way is by measuring degree of mental retardation (Gillberg, 1990). A third way is to confirm the presence of a known neurological disorder (Coleman & Gillberg, 1985; Rapin, 1987). A fourth way is to assess the number of criterial symptoms expressed by an individual (APA, 1987). A fifth way is to note the disruptive salience of those symptoms deemed to represent the key causal features of the syndrome (Baron-Cohen, 1991; Folstein & Piven, 1991). A sixth way is to show degree of conformity to a diagnostic standard for the syndrome (Rutter & Schopler, 1988; Waterhouse et al., 1989). A seventh way is to demonstrate developmental "lag" within the framework of a series of pathognomonic states thought to reflect the possible maturational course of diagnostic behaviors (Wing, 1988).

The first three indices (specific developmental lag on normative scales, mental retardation, and presence of a known neurological disorder) may mark a severe handicap in an autistic individual, but do not necessarily mean that the criterial features of the syndrome are expressed in a severe form. The remaining four indices (number of criterial symptoms, disruptive salience of criterial symptoms, degree of conformity to a diagnostic standard, or a "lag" in pathognomonic developmental course), however, are likely to mark an individual as severely autistic.

Thus, in clinical practice when an autistic individual is identified as a severe case, the use of the term *severe* may mean one of three things. First, it may mean that the autistic individual is severely handicapped in domains of behavior that are not criterial to the diagnosis. Second, it may mean that the autistic individual has shown severity in diagnostic behaviors in one or more ways: (a) has expressed a very wide range of the criterial behaviors, or (b) has expressed one or more criterial behaviors in a disruptively salient way, or (c) has expressed a pattern of diagnostic behaviors that appear to exactly fit a diagnostic standard (e.g., a "true Kanner's case"), or, finally, (d) has expressed behaviors that indicate that the individual is at an early stage in what is hypothesized to be a linear course of successive pathognomonic features. Third, the use of the term severe may mean that a positively diagnosed individual's behavior profile fits the patterns of severe handicap for both diagnostic and nondiagnostic features of autism.

TWO APPROACHES TO SEVERITY

Though the significance of the severity of criterial and noncriterial features in autism, and in the wider spectrum of autistic disorders, has not been addressed in a consolidated fashion, there have been two lines of activity concerned with severity of symptomatology in autism. One line is the methods by which researchers and clinicians have attempted to document developmental states by creating scales for behaviors within discrete domains. To this end, two types of scales have been developed that outline states of social development. In one type of scale each developmental level describes a diagnostic social impairment (Wing, 1988; Wing & Gould, 1979). In another type of scale, autistic children are tested for the development of normal skills. Scales have been developed to document deviation from normal development in language (Stone & Caro-Martinez, 1990; Wetherby et al., 1989), and deviation from normal development in play (Fein et al., 1991; Sigman et al., 1987).

The second line of activity that considers severity of symptomatology is work done to develop subgroups within the autistic spectrum of disorders. Clinical consensus committees and individual clinicians have generated sets of diagnostic subgroups that tacitly incorporate notions of relative severity in order to create distinct subgroup boundaries (Gillberg, 1990; Waterhouse, Spitzer, Wing, & Siegel, 1992).

There are two standard psychiatric diagnostic systems in use at present: the *DSM–III–R* and the *ICD–10*. The *DSM–III–R* is the revised third edition of the *Diagnostic and Statistical Manual of Mental Disorders* published by the the American Psychiatric Association (1987). The *ICD–10* (1990) is the 10th International Classification of Diseases to be developed by the World Health Organization. The *DSM–III–R* is nosology of the psychiatric disorders of children and adults. It defines and describes disorders, and offers diagnostic algorithms based on specific sets of criteria that have been identified by committees of clinicians. In the diagnostic system of *DSM–III–R*, there are two general subgroups of the autistic spectrum (which is defined as Pervasive Developmental Disorders). These two subgroups are Autistic Disorder (AD) and a remainder group, Pervasive Developmental Disorders—Not Otherwise Specified (PDDNOS). In *DSM–III–R*, the boundary between AD and PDDNOS is created by a diagnostic feature requirement involving both absolute number and range of expressed criterial features. This feature requirement means that the diagnosis of AD represents a more severe disorder than does PDDNOS. Thus, the diagnostic contrast between AD and PDDNOS involves a formally interpreted difference in severity—in quantity, or range, or both quantity and range, of expressed criterial symptoms.

Like *DSM–III–R*, the *ICD–10* is a nosology. It describes and defines human diseases, both physical and mental. As in *DSM–III–R*, in *ICD–10* the autistic spectrum is identified as Pervasive Developmental Disorders. Unlike *DSM–III–R*, there are six subgroups: Childhood Autism (CA), Atypical Autism (AA), Rett Syndrome (RS), Other Childhood Disintegrative Disorder (OCDD), Overactive Disorder associated with Mental Retardation and Stereotyped Movements (OD), and Asperger's Syndrome (AS). The boundaries between the six groups in *ICD–10* are constructed by diagnostic formulations that focus on aggregate patterns of features, some of which include differential salience of many of the same diagnostic features. For example, stereotyped movements may occur in association with CA, AA, RS, and OCDD, but such movements are diagnostically salient only for OD.

Although *ICD-10* and *DSM-III-R* both employ aspects of differential severity of symptoms to draw boundaries between subgroups within Pervasive Developmental Disorders, measurement scales rely on an underlying conceptualization of immaturity or delay to index level of severity of impairment to functioning. Understanding severity in scales, and severity in subgroup formation, requires answers to two as-yet-unanswered questions: (a) What is the meaning of developmental change in severity of symptoms? and (b) to what extent can severity in behavioral expression be understood to represent severity of the implied neurofunctional deficit?

The next two sections of this chapter consider each of these two questions in turn. Although definitive answers await future research, exploration of the issues these questions raise may help shape specific problems for such future research.

THE MEANING OF DEVELOPMENTAL CHANGE

In order to be able to consider the meaning of maturational change in severity of symptoms, we need to establish which behaviors do change in autism, and how they change. Many different normative skills and aberrant behaviors have been codified and scaled in order to index the severity of impairment in autism. As with other systems of psychiatric diagnosis, in schemes of diagnosis for autism there are two sets of behaviors: criterial behaviors, used for making the diagnosis, and associated, noncriterial behaviors, often found in conjunction with the syndrome, but not used in making a diagnosis. For either a *DSM-III-R* or *ICD-10* diagnosis of autism, there are three domains of criterial behaviors: (a) qualitative impairment in reciprocal social behaviors, (b) qualitative impairment in verbal and nonverbal interaction and imaginative activity, and (c) markedly restricted repertoire of activities and interest. In both *DSM-III-R* and *ICD-10* the associated symptoms/behaviors for autism include deficits or deviations in a variety of cognitive functions (other than language), vegetative functions, and motor behaviors.

Most of the criterial behaviors for autism, and many associated behaviors, have been scaled for relative severity of deficit. The key criterial behavior in autism—under any diagnostic formulation—is social impairment. Exploration of the severity of social impairment has led to a variety of scales. The single most important scales of social impairment developed to date are that of Wing and Gould (1979). These scales became the basis for both *DSM-III-R* and *ICD-10* criteria for a diagnosis of autism. More recently, working with the findings from an epidemiological study, Wing and Attwood (1988) defined Wing's three scales of severity of impairment for different aspects of sociability. In Wing's system there are three scales: social recognition, social communication, and social imagination. Wing's scale of severity for impairment to social recognition has four descriptive levels: (a) is aloof and indifferent to other people, (b) is passive and controllable but lacks any social initiative, (c) actively makes odd or bizarre social approaches to others, and (d) lacks the ability to use subtle social rules.

The scale of severity for impairment to social communication has four levels as well: (a) shows an absence of any desire to communicate, (b) expresses needs but has no other form of communication, (c) makes only irrelevant factual comments that are generated outside the usual rules of interactive conversation, and (d) talks a great deal in somewhat obsessive monologues and is insensitive to social cues from the other interactant(s).

The third of Wing's (Wing & Atwood, 1988) proposed domains of impaired social skills is that of social imagination and activity. In this domain Wing proposed five levels of impairment: (a) exhibits no imitation and pretend play whatsoever, (b) has mechanical imitation but no pretend play, (c) can engage in stereotyped enacting of a role without variation or empathy, (d) recognizes that others have different ideas but has no ability to infer the intentions of others, and (e) expresses evidence of the ability to imagine the minds of others but without any empathic sharing of emotions.

Wing's (Wing & Atwood, 1988) three scales are implicitly developmental, but are not based on notions of the unfolding stages of normal social development. The three scales each represent a range of behaviors wherein the first behavior pattern described is assumed to be more severely aberrant than the second, and so on. Wing made no argument for a linear path of development through these states for individuals diagnosed as autistic. In fact, some individuals may stay at the same level of functioning throughout their lives, whereas others may pass through the stages of impairment sequentially. Still other individuals may express one level of aberrant behavior at school and another at home. Although each level of each of the three scales reflects significant impairment, nonetheless it is Wing's assumption that the impairments described for each scale are in an order of decreasing dysfunction.

Other researchers have developed scales that index severity of deficit against a model of normal developmental stages. Wetherby et al. (1989) constructed a scale of three levels of social communicative intent. In this scale the three levels are: (a) An individual generates communications that are designed to regulate the behavior of others to achieve nonsocial goals, (b) an individual produces communications that focus attention on the communicator with the general goal of gaining attention, and (c) an individual produces communications that involve the direction of another's attention to some tangible present object, or directs attention to an idea, plan, or bit of information.

In the realm of play behavior, Sigman et al. (1987) outlined four normative levels of play: (a) stereotypic play—including mouthing, banging, or waving an object; (b) relational play—using two or more objects in a nonfunctional manner; (c) functional play—using a realistic toy in a conventional manner; and (d) symbolic play—engaging in acts that involve imagining present objects to be transformed, or imagining and acting out activities with objects or people who are not present.

The scales for play, communicative intent, and social impairments are presented here as examples of the many varied types of scales that have been developed to explore both sequences of normal developmental stages, and the sequences of the unfolding of aberrant behaviors. All such scales, however, share the same underlying conceptualization of the meaning of *severity*. Severity is immaturity. For Wing, Wetherby et al., and Sigman et al., the lowest levels in their descriptive sets can be construed as describing the earliest developmental stage—whether for young normal children or young autistic children. When these scales are used to ascertain the severity of deficit in autistic individuals, greater immaturity is assumed to be greater severity of deficit.

Therefore, in general, scalar systems of documenting deficit carry the implicit assumption that maturation means a movement toward a milder version of symptoms, as well as a movement toward normal functioning. In fact, in the natural history of autistic spectrum disorders, development often does bring positive changes. Young children who were mute can develop speech. Many cognitive and perceptual school skills can be learned. Basic self-care can become a consistent habit. Many children diagnosed as autistic do develop a greater interest in and awareness of others after puberty (Coleman & Gillberg, 1985; Volkmar, 1987).

Development, however, may also bring negative changes as well. Aggressive behavior may appear peri-pubertally. Seizures may occur. Self-injurious behaviors may emerge or increase in intensity. Adolescents and young adults often reach a plateau in the development of cognitive skills beyond which little additional cognitive growth seems to take place (Coleman & Gillberg, 1985; Waterhouse & Fein, 1984).

Although no large sample, long-term longitudinal study of the development of autistic individuals has been done, data from case studies, cross-sectional studies, and follow-up studies converge on the general finding that behavioral impairment seems the most severe at two points. The first point is in early childhood, immediately after diagnosis. The second point is later, during and immediately after puberty (Wing, 1988).

At the first point—3–5 years of age—the severity is often defined by absence of speech, lack of self-care in daily living, and, most important, a salient absence of normal interest in social interaction. At the second point—14–17 years—the severity is often indexed by a flattening of cognitive skills, a rise in aggressive behavior, and general decrease in self-control of behavior.

These two time points of severity in the continuum of autistic disorders suggest a distinction between the criterial and noncriterial symptoms of autism. Criterial features of autism (lack of speech, bizarre features of speech, absence of social interest) are often noted to be most severe in early childhood. Conversely, noncriterial features are often noted to be most severe at or after puberty. Cognitive development may plateau or decline, and patterns of aggression may appear at puberty. These are associated behaviors that do not determine diagnosis. If a 17-year-old autistic boy shows increasing interest in others but at the same time becomes more aggressive, he will be less severely autistic, but his day-to-day functioning will nonetheless give the picture of severe disturbance. Although many vegetative and motor dysfunctions may be expressed throughout development, the most severe expression of diagnostic features often does ameliorate throughout life course.

Do measured maturational shifts signify amelioration of "autism"? Yes and no. Yes, in that normal adult functioning in social, cognitive, motor, and vegetative behaviors is assumed as the target for all development. Any movement toward that goal does represent amelioration of a specific deficit, lag, or deviance. However, the answer can be no in that development may progress in some domains, but different problems may emerge in other domains of behavior. The net result may be that the individual's global functioning in daily living may remain severely impaired. More important, even the emergence of milder more normative variants of diagnostic behavior may not really mean that the mechanism generating the syndrome is operating in a more benign form.

In the *Diagnostic and Statistical Manual of Mental Disorders* (3rd ed.) (APA, 1980) and several other earlier diagnostic systems, the symptom behavior shift during the course of development has been marked by use of the term *residual state*. In present diagnostic formulations (e.g., *DSM–III–R* and *ICD–10*) the term residual state is eschewed. The term residual implies that the syndrome's central effects are now over, or are diminished, leaving only a residuum of behavioral impairment. As we do not know whether or not this is true, the notion of there being a residual state of autism remains a hypothesis.

It may be that the shift in severity of symptomatology actually means that the syndrome hits different developmental targets according to the times of onset of "active maturation" of those behaviors. In other words, it is particularly when a behavior emerges in the individual's developmental repertoire that the effects of the syndrome are made manifest. For an extreme example, many autistic young adults develop paraphilias—sexual interest in inappropriate objects. Such aberrant interest can only become manifest at the time of the development of secondary sex characteristics, that is, at a point of emergent sexual maturation. Language impairment is manifest when language development is expected, and social interest is manifest when social interest is expected.

If this is the case, then the implied causal mechanism(s) generating the syndrome should not be viewed as being in a residual state or "turned off" at a later point in development. In fact, it may be precisely because sociability, language, and social communicative behaviors appear early in the normal human developmental repertoire and thus are shown to be affected early in development, that they have become "hallmarks" of the syndrome of autism. As it is likely that the syndrome's causal mechanism(s) continue to operate throughout life course—affecting both the neurofunctional systems in a state of onset of maturation, and those in ongoing development but compromised earlier—we should consider later life symptoms as significant for understanding the disorder as earlier life course impairments. At present, this is not done.

A related question is whether autistic individuals can "learn their way out" of social dysfunction. As stated earlier, the core criterial domain of autistic symptomatology is social impairment, and impairment in this domain appears most florid when our expectation for the active maturation of social behavior is highest (c. 18–48 months). If an autistic child becomes more social with time, this improved sociability may be internally generated through the process of central nervous system (CNS) maturation of the presumably multiple neurobiological bases of social behavior. But an autistic child's social skills may also be in part the product of behavioral training. This latter, however, often leads to hollow or "as-if" social behavior. Hollow social skills indicate that the child can learn new behaviors, but also imply that the learned skills are not incorporated into a network of internally meaningful social motivations.

Clinical evaluation and testing of autistic individuals in the teen years and in adulthood suggests that in a majority of cases maturation does not significantly alleviate social and cognitive impairments (Rumsey, Rapoport, & Sceery, 1985; Volkmar, 1987; Waterhouse & Fein, 1984). Teens and adults continue to have fairly severe social difficulties including withdrawal, absence of friends, antisocial behavior (including aggression), inappropriate behavior, and the like. They also often fail to progress in cognitive development and show problems in planful thinking. Thus, the syndrome may be judged as "severe" throughout the lifespan, even though the severity of the early childhood diagnostic behaviors may abate to some degree.

BEHAVIORAL SEVERITY AND NEUROFUNCTIONAL DEFICITS

The implications of behavioral severity for possible neurofunctional deficit permit no easy inferences because autism is not a unitary disease with a single etiology. It is a heterogeneous behavioral syndrome found in association with many etiologies. A variety of genetic disorders (Folstein & Piven, 1991), infectious diseases, birth injuries, metabolic diseases, and a variety of structural abnormalities of the brain all have been found for individuals diagnosed as autistic (Bauman, 1991; Coleman, 1987).

Although it has been argued that "true" autism is a genetic disorder conferring vulnerability to cognitive and social impairment (Folstein & Rutter, 1977), and although there is evidence for possible social and cognitive impairment in "form fruste" or low-dose genetic effects in family members (Piven, et al., 1990), nonetheless, the wide range of etiologies seen in conjunction with an equally wide array of behavioral variation within groups of individuals diagnosed as autistic has led most researchers and clinicians to conclude that autism is best viewed as a behavioral syndrome only (Reichler & Lee, 1987). It has also led to the view that autism as currently diagnosed is a spectrum of disorders that in turn is part of a larger behavioral continuum of disorders of social impairment (Gillberg, 1990; Waterhouse et al., 1992; Wing Attwood, 1988).

If autism were found only in association with a single etiology, and if autism were found only in association with a narrowly definable behavioral pattern, it would be reasonable to search for a unique neural causal mechanism. However, given that there exists great heterogeneity in both behavior and etiology, it does not seem likely that a single or simple neural mechanism will be found to account for the autistic spectrum. The question then becomes, how can we search for the possible multiple or complex mechanisms that may give rise to the autistic spectrum?

In the spectrum view of autism, it is the relative degree of behavioral severity that determines the range and extent of the spectrum. The "severe" end of the spectrum will include individuals who evince complete social withdrawal, are mute or have very immature language development, show bizarre features of speech, are mentally retarded, have vegetative dysfunctions, and engage in aberrant motor behaviors. The "mild" end of the spectrum will include individuals who evince social impairment but without extreme withdrawal, have milder communication dysfunctions, show little impairment to cognitive functions, have no vegetative dysfunctions, and engage in few, if any, aberrant motor behaviors.

If we attempt to model the simplest possible inferential equation between a hypothesized neural mechanism and autistic spectrum behaviors, the severe end of the behavioral spectrum could be argued to correspond to the greatest neurological insult, and the mild end should thus correspond to the least neurological insult. Accordingly, the various genetic and nongenetic etiologies associated with the autistic spectrum might be presumed to have individual differential effects, thus generating a range of functional lesions from severe to mild. Alternatively, the hypothesized causal neural mechanism(s) could be modeled as the functional amalgam of a set of negative effects arising from an individually varying set of etiologic agents. In this notion, individuals diagnosed as autistic might be hypothesized to have been subject to one or more than one etiologic agent. The resultant functional nexus of neural deficit(s) could be hypothesized to generate a wide spectrum of behavioral impairment.

A more specific model used to conceptualize brain behavior relationships is domain localization: For every defined domain of behavioral impairment there will be a causal and distinct isolable functional brain "lesion." Although this localization view of brain deficit is a reasonable way to organize empirical research (Rumsey & Denckla, 1987), a one-to-one mapping of behavioral domain to brain location is unlikely to be a productive approach. Damage to minute neuroanatomical sites and impairment to single neurotransmitters can have effects on a wide range of behaviors. Conversely, widespread neural damage may leave little mark on the expression of behavior. This, of course, adds to the difficulty of drawing brain-behavior inferences in regards to autistic spectrum disorders.

Still more important is the fact that our maps of locations in the brain and our conceptualizations of domains of behavior are limited by current knowledge. Reviews of research and theoretical speculation reveal that many possible pathognomonic brain deficits in autism have been explored, and many possible links between deviant behaviors and systems that might be damaged have been proposed (Fein, Pennington, & Waterhouse, 1987; Gillberg, 1990; Reichler & Lee, 1987; Rumsey & Denckla, 1987). Although neuroanatomical research to date has suggested that there may be specific lesions associated with autism (Bauman 1991; Courchesne, 1991; Reichler & Lee, 1987; Rumsey & Denckla, 1987), none of the studies include sufficient data on severity of behavioral expression of the syndrome to attempt to associate location and extent of lesions with domain-specific severity of behavioral impairment. More important, even though lesions and abnormalities have been found in association with autism, it has been very difficult to frame these neural deficits as causal to the behaviors criterial to the syndrome (Rapin, 1987; Rumsey & Denckla, 1987; Waterhouse et al. 1989).

There are other reasons that using simple models (severity of functional lesions = severity of behavioral impairment, and, location of functional lesions = type and severity of behavioral impairment) may be problematic. First, it is difficult to interpret the meaning of developmental delay, deviance, and deficit for brain-behavior relationships. Second, we are limited in generalizing about brain-behavior relationships because there are very sharp differences in the individual profiles of differential severity of impairments across diagnosed individuals. Third, our present theoretical net of inference must allow unproductively wide spaces because our current conceptualizations of social versus cognitive behaviors are inherently false aggregations:

Dividing observed behaviors this way can permit us—at best—to capture only large brain-behavior associations. It is quite possible that concepts of social and cognitive bear no inferentially useful relation to brain-behavior associations at all. In fact, the reality is likely to be more fine-grained and complex. A fourth problem is that our knowledge of brain systems that subserve social and cognitive behavior development is just now developing, and we have only first-wave speculative models of neurofunctional deficit. All of these problems can only be addressed by further research—research in which the biological basis of social behavior is explored with a reconceptualized understanding of the nature of social behavior. The following discussion considers background concerns for such reconceptualization.

DELAY AND DEVIANCE

In most evaluations of the impairments associated with autism, three terms are used to describe impaired behaviors: *deficit*, *delay*, and *deviance*. The term deficit has been used most loosely—to index the absence of an expected behavior, to label evidence for delay, or to mark deviance. The term deviance has been used to label a behavior that does not occur in the repertoire of normal children or adults. The term delay has been used as a label for behavior that is essentially normal but should appear earlier in the life course of the individual. Deviance is indexed against the set of normal behaviors. Delay is indexed against a known chronological schedule of development.

In models of autism it has been assumed that delayed functions cannot be uniquely causal or pathognomonic to the syndrome. The belief behind this assumption, presumably, is that if a behavior does eventually come "on-line" in a near normal fashion, it cannot represent a uniquely impaired neural function. For example, research in the field currently defines language skills as delayed, with some deviant features: echolalia, neologisms, aberrant prosody, unusual pronoun use. (Volden & Lord, 1991; Waterhouse & Fein, 1982). Research efforts are focused on exploring the deviant features as pathognomonic, and the character and variable extent of the delay is studied but not modeled as pathognomonic (Volden & Lord, 1991; Waterhouse & Fein, 1982).

Delay and deviance are difficult to distinguish. At present, in studies of autistic spectrum disorders, the development of social skills and social interest is generally defined as deviant—not delayed. It is argued that very young normal infants show social interest that is often missing in autistic children and adults (Fein et al., 1987), and that there is a special deficit in social cognition—absence of a theory of mind—that only autistic individuals experience (Baron-Cohen, 1991). However, social development, in fact, may be severely delayed in autism. A reasonable subset of autistic individuals do show increasing interest in other people, especially after puberty. The course of this increase in interest in others may be so extremely slow that it appears as deviant. Furthermore, one key form of social interest—attachment to mother—is found to be present in many autistic children (Sigman & Mundy, 1989).

Another important developmental issue concerning deficit and delay is that many behaviors defined as deviant in autism actually appear in the repertoires of normal children and adults. Dysprosody, echolalia, social withdrawal, lack of social interest, self-injury, perseverative behaviors, and many other behaviors do appear in the context of normal adult and child behavior. Such behaviors may be of short duration, may be rare, and may be noted consciously by the individual, but they do appear within the context of normal behavior. The presence of deviant behaviors in normal individuals defines some limits to the inference that such deviant behaviors appearing in autism can be uniquely pathognomonic. One limit suggested is that, if normal individuals can produce such deviant behavior, then that behavior must be a permissable function of a normally organized CNS. This, in turn, must limit inference on "neural deficit" as directly causal to the specific behavior.

If normal individuals exhibit—though rarely or fleetingly—behaviors deemed deviant in autism, it may be argued that the difference lies in the amount of deviant behavior produced, and the inability to generate normal behavior per se. This, however, suggest still another important consideration. Context—broadly defined—may be more of a determinant of each individual's behavior than is currently appreciated. Unique internal (to the individual) and external (environmental) life-course factors may drive patterns of deviant behavior in ways that are not definable as a specific function of the syndrome of autism. If we make the assumption that normal adults and children produce abnormal or deviant behaviors depending on the context, we need to include context as a variable in understanding deviant behavior in autism.

Given these complexities, it would be helpful if the impairments to social skills and the impairments to cognitive skills in autism are interpreted more openly, that is without the division-making labels of delayed and deviant. Another important step is that we develop a better conceptualization of the relationship between social and cognitive functions. At present, much research seems to be based on a very simple additive notion of labeled definitions: social = people and emotions; cognitive = perception, memory, judgment, and reasoning; therefore social cognition = perception, memory, judgment, and reasoning in relation to people and emotions. This sort of additive model is too simple to capture the phenomenon of interest.

It has been argued that cognition for social events is the core deficit in autism (Rutter, 1983), and currently the "theory of mind" school argues for a particular component of social cognition as being impaired (Baron-Cohen,

1991). Neither of these models is garnering clear support in empirical investigations. It may be that the idea of isolating social cognition as a behavior is itself misguided. It may be that in aggregating behaviors in conceptual categories like social interest and social cognition, we may be incorrectly lumping patterns of subcomponents of these defined domains.

For example, it has been argued that impairment to attentional systems may affect aspects of sociability and cognition (Dawson, 1987; Kinsbourne, 1987). If measured attentional skills cross the boundaries of defined behavioral domains such as social interest and social cognition, then it is difficult to infer the natural coherence of these domains as pathognomonic. The same sort of argument applies to hypotheses claiming deficits in other systems—such as pain and reward (Panksepp & Sahley, 1987), and memory (Bauman, 1991; Boucher & Warrington, 1976)—where such systems also must be modeled to subserve social behaviors.

Despite all the complexities involved in modeling possible brain-behavior links in autism, nonetheless, the tendency of the field has been to follow a standard empirical line of isolating a key symptom, or limited symptom cluster, as deviantly pathognomonic, and then look for a single neurofunctional lesion that will explain the presence of that single deviant behavior (Reichler & Lee, 1987). Implicit to such research is the inference that the mechanism conferring the deviant behavior is itself directly damaged.

A still more complex brain-behavior issue concerning the severity of impairment associated with delay and deviance is the reorganizing effect that behavior itself has on brain mechanisms. From a series of studies of the early motor development of normal infants, McGraw (1946) argued that underlying brain structure determining a given piece of behavior was actively being modified by the ongoing expression of the behavior. Current work on learning and memory in development has suggested that brain mechanisms for the control of behavior are restructured continuously as the individual engages in the behavior (Hinde, 1991). This means, as an individual expresses a disordered behavior (whether labeled deviant or delayed) the ongoing functioning of the underlying mechanism will interactively provide feedback that determines an ongoing reconfiguration of the underlying mechanism itself: That is, expressed behavior changes neural structure. Therefore, even though it may be inferred that delayed and deviant behaviors arise from fettered or damaged brain mechanisms, those impaired mechanisms may not remain stable in the parameters of their dysfunctional state. Depending on the character of the environment, specifically the external feedback received, and the nature of the impairment to the neurofunctional mechanism, it may be that the expression of impaired behavior could lead to some beneficent reorganization of the underlying mechanism, or, conversely, could drive the mechanism into further dysfunction.

Taken together all these complexities for drawing brain-behavior inferences argue that models generated to outline a causal neural mechanism for autism will have to be designed to accommodate (a) behavioral and etiological variability, (b) differences in delay and deficits in the repertoire of impairments, and (c) the reorganizing effects of behavior on neural mechanisms.

A NEW METHOD AND A NEW THEORETICAL MODEL

In samples of autistic individuals studied, researchers have discovered considerable differential severity of impairment in different domains of behavior (Gillberg, 1990). One autistic individual may have a full-scale Stanford Binet IQ of 140, have no eye contact, no spontaneous expressive language, but have complex rituals. Another autistic individual may have an IQ of 40 but be passively social, and have minimal language. The differential severity of symptoms expressed by each diagnosed individual, and the syndrome heterogeneity generated by the variability have led to efforts to create subgroups of autistic individuals. These efforts, however, have not led to the creation of empirically validated subgroups (Gillberg, 1990; Reichler & Lee, 1987; Waterhouse et al., 1989).

As noted earlier, this unresolved heterogeneity also imposes limitations on inferences concerning brain-behavior relationships in the syndrome.

A variety of solutions to the problem of heterogeneity have been proposed. One is to abandon the syndrome entirely (Reichler & Lee, 1987). However, this does not make sense to clinicians who "see" the syndrome, and there are clear salient and disruptive deficits in all positively diagnosed individuals (Waterhouse et al., 1989). Another way is to shift the perception of the syndrome to a continuum rather than a strictly defined disorder (Waterhouse et al., 1992). Still another way is to change research strategies. Reichler and Lee recommended an exploration of autistic symptoms rather than study of the syndrome as a whole. They also suggested a shift in research emphasis to an interactive model of the CNS away from the current equivalence model (i.e., one behavior—one neurofunctional lesion). They further recommended that more research be done to explore patterns of development in the autistic spectrum.

Another possible methodological strategy for dealing with current limitations to inference concerning autism is the systematic exploration of current data sets for the possibility of very small subgroups. If subgroups within the autistic spectrum are created whose membership is determined by matching symptom patterns, skills, behaviors, etiology, age, and sex, then the exploration of possible associated neural deficits may yield helpful insights.

Much current research attempts to assemble samples of autistic individuals into hypothetically "pure" homogeneous groups. This is done by excluding all autistic individuals who have low IQ or known etiology, such as Fragile X or Rett syndrome. This formula for group selection does not ensure purity of the sample, however, as many etiologies will remain untested for, and using low IQ as an exclusion criteria will still leave a sample with an extremely wide range of IQ, as well as an extremely wide range of behavioral abnormalities (Waterhouse et al., 1989). The belief that underpins this form of research is that there is one reasonably large subgroup of individuals within the autistic spectrum who are the "true" syndrome. This is the historic basis of the syndrome. This same belief has determined the form of diagnostic systems, whether *DSM–III–R* or *ICD–10*. The clinical belief is that true, "classic" or Kanner's autism is a "real disorder," and individuals who do not meet diagnostic criteria for the real disorder are diagnostically relegated to constructed categories without clinical basis such as *ICD–10* Overactive Disorder with Mental Retardation and Stereotyped Movements, or to remainder categories such as *DSM–III–R* Pervasive Developmental Disorder—Not Otherwise Specified.

Exploration of the notion that there might be very small subgroups depends on pro tem acceptance of the spectrum notion of autistic disorders, and on pro tem acceptance of the very simple inference that shared behavioral characteristics in association with shared etiology may index some shared functional deficit. Searching for very small subgroups also is likely to mean abandoning traditional statistical means of inference. It is difficult to prove that a set of very small groups is a more valid grouping than is a larger group of the same individuals. Cross-comparisons of tiny groups are unlikely to reach statistical significance on standard tests, and a small subset of shared symptoms across individuals may make larger groups function as a meaningful unit for subsets of measured behaviors. Despite these difficulties, such a methodological approach may help disambiguate the complexity of the autistic spectrum.

APPLICATION OF A NEW THEORETICAL MODEL

Another direction for research is to explore models of functional neural systems, in which systems a variety of deficits could be hypothesized to yield a range of impairments to behavior. Although it is certainly premature to endorse any single particular model, nonetheless, at this stage of exploration, models of this sort can function as heuristics to guide brain-behavior inferences regarding autism to become more clearly grounded and more explicit.

Examples of potentially relevant models include Black's (1991) model of the transduction of information in the CNS, Insell's (1992) model of oxytocin as the basis for human social bonding, Le Doux's (1989) model of the emotional system of the brain as a mechanism to compute the biological significance of the environment, and Damasio's (1990) model of cross-modal association and behavioral seriation as "convergence zones." Each of these models has a different level of specificity and a different explanatory focus. Black and Insell modeled aspects of the relationship between brain-active molecules and behavior; they were concerned to explain the fact that "while the environment endows the regulated molecules with meaning, the physical structure of the molecule, and the locus of the molecule in the structure of cell and system, determine the manner in which environmental stimulus is translated into neural function" (Black, 1991, p. 47). Le Doux and Damasio modeled systems at a more macro level, without specific attention to the molecular level of information transmission. Le Doux was concerned to explain how neural interactions between large tissue areas—amygdala, neocortex, and hippocampus—determine the links between affect and cognition. Damasio was concerned to explain the link between complex cross-modal learning, and seriation of behaviors.

Each of these models has the potential to provide an explanation that will circumscribe some construal of the social/cognitive deficits of autism. I have chosen to spell out implications of Damasio's (1990) model because his model is focused on determining the form of a mechanism that will explain the nature of the complex contextualization of human memory, a function I believe is lacking or impaired in many autistic individuals.

In this model—the convergence zone theory—Damasio (1990) argued for the existence of two types of convergence zones, each of which functions to organize ongoing memory. In this model, the hypothesized zones do not hold a final representation of the information derived from sensory or motor cortical activity; instead the convergence zones are modeled to contain no specific information. They are hypothesized as amodal and time locking— "freezing" information together. Damasio defined neural convergence zones as "knowing about" cortical activity by being fed information from the major cortical sensory-analytic and motor areas, and as being able to promote further cortical activity through feedback to those same cortical sensory-analytic and motor areas.

Damasio (1990) claimed that the "role of the convergence zones is to enact formulas for the reconstitution of fragment-based momentary representations of entities or events in sensory or motor cortices" (p. 46). He hypothesized two types of convergence zones. Type I zones arise in sensory cortex, are dependent on hippocampal function, and account for the development of associations in memory as they etch time-bound coincidences of activations. Type II zones arise in motor-related cortices, are dependent on functions of cerebellum and basal ganglia, and account for the development of linear patterns as they etch time-bound temporal sequences.

In Damasio's (1990) model, damage to the hippocampus and the cerebellum would lead to impaired zones of convergence. If Type I zones of convergence depend on functions of the hippocampus, and Type II zones depend on functions of the basal ganglia and cerebellum, then both types of convergence zones must be hypothesized to be negatively affected in autism, because both hippocampal and cerebellar deficits have been found in the brains of autistic individuals (Bauman, 1991; Courchesne, 1991).

Bauman (1991) argued that anatomic findings of her autopsy research suggest that there has been a "curtailment of the normal development of portions of the limbic system and cerebellar circuits" (p. 794), and that "the anatomic defects noted in the autistic brain appear to have been acquired early in development, and are areas that are critical to normal behavioral, cognitive, and memory function" (pp. 794–795). Courchesne (1991) claimed that "autistic subjects and patients with acquired cerebellar damage are unable to rapidly shift their mental focus of attention" (p. 788).

In the Damasio (1990) model, albeit damage to the hippocampal complex, cerebellar circuits, and the cerebellum itself would lead to impairment in both the establishment of convergence zones, and the ongoing function of whatever convergence zones were established, nonetheless specific site sensory analysis and specific site motor programs could be functional. Impairment would be found for the organization of the analysis of sensory information at each point in time (complex associations), and the organization of sequences of behavior across time periods (complex temporal sequences).

The resultant behavioral picture would seem to be consistent with the findings for autism in general. Autistic individuals without other additional neural damage—that is damage to brain systems in addition to the defects found for the hippocampal complex, cerebellar circuits, and limited portions of the cerebellar cortex—would be able to function satisfactorily in those activities of daily life that depend more on "feature-based records" of "primary and early association cortices, both sensory and motor" (Damasio, 1990, p. 27). Such autistic individuals would be more impaired in those behavioral activities that depend on the ongoing shifting of attention from one complex context to another, or awareness or recall of complex associations, or the constant selection of different motor programs to enact.

In terms of Damasio's (1990) model, ongoing shifting of attention away from external stimuli to internal information processing could be hypothesized to depend on the emergence of an internally salient complex association that functions to interpret the ongoing stream of stimuli. This complex association might presumably arise from the hypothesized constant process of the generation of Type I convergence zones. If such zones are formed in an aberrant way, or not formed at all, it can be hypothesized that complex associations might not appear in working memory. If such is the case, then normal (presumably cycling) patterns of shifting of attention from external stimuli to internal processing might be altered, and attention (to features of the external world) could be aberrantly stimulus-bound in the autistic individual. Similarly, if the generation or activation of a constant stream of Type II convergence zones is impaired, then the process of selection of behaviors to enact will be impaired.

Consequently, if the interactive process involved in human social behavior is construed as an activity requiring both (a) ceaseless ongoing shifts of attention, and (b) ceaseless serial selection of behaviors to enact, then it is human social behavior, more than reading printed text or calculating solutions to mathematical problems, that will tax the neural processes modeled by Damasio (1990). It is these processes that can be presumed to be affected by the specific neural damage found in anatomic studies (Bauman, 1991; Courchesne, 1991).

Although the Damasio (1990) model does appear to provide a framework in which to understand the implications of the several key neuroanatomical deficits found for autism in prior studies, this model does not, however, clearly provide a framework to understand the implications of the various neurochemical deficits found in association with autism (Coleman, 1987; Panksepp & Sahley, 1987). One speculative means to integrate the findings for neurochemical deficits with the Bauman (1991) and Courchesne (1991) findings and the Damasio model constraints is to hypothesize that oxytocin receptor sites in the hippocampus are crucial to the formation of contextual memories of acts of affiliative behavior, as well as crucial to the formation of memories of internal states temporally associated with such affiliative behavior.

The convergence zones model as applied to autism does, in fact, suggest the exploration of a different way of understanding human social behavior. In much theoretical modeling of social behavior (e.g., Hinde, 1991), a distinction is made between sociability, which would include social interest or social motivation, and social cognition, which includes the ability to make productive and functional judgments about others within the framework of social (interactive) situations. In the simplest possible terms, these components of social behavior may be seen to reflect a distinction between a drivelike disposition (whether called social interest, social motivation, or sociability), and a set of cortical, interpretive skills that permit the fluid processes of social interaction (social cognition). Both of these aspects of social behavior are thought to be impaired in autism.

If social interest or motivation depends on an individual's being able to contextualize basic life needs in relation to other human beings, then social cognition (at this rather basic level of definition) is crucial for social interest. We will not be interested in other human beings if we cannot establish what they mean in terms of our own needs. The nursing infant is "rewarded" by its mother without establishing a meaningful understanding of her or the context, and the infant cannot be said to be interested in its mother. The infant's adaptive special attention to mother's voice and smell, and the infant's regulation of emotional expression in imitation of mother or caretaker's face are adaptive elements of sociability, which appear to be built-in mechanisms that underpin the emergence of social interest. Unlike an infant, a toddler at the stage of attachment has, however, constructed a meaning for "mother-in-context." Hard-wired elements of early behavior do not appear to require the contextual construction of "meaning" for their enactment, but later learning does require such construction.

> Damasio (1990) posited that in his model: . . . meaning is reached by widespread multiregional activation of fragmentary records pertinent to a stimulus, wherever such records may be stored within a large array of sensory and motor structures, according to a combinatorial arrangement specific to the entity. A display of the meaning of an entity does not exist in a permanent fashion. It is recreated for each new instantiation. The same stimulus does not provoke the same evocations at every instantiation. (p. 28)

Therefore, if there is neural damage that impairs the generation and function of the hypothesized Type I and Type II convergence zones, then the nature of presently perceived experience will be impaired, and will be divorced from a productive connection with prior similar experience. At every instantiation, an individual with such neural damage will be impaired in the ability to generate a clear contextual meaning for human beings or any other complex or changing aspects or elements of their environment. Baron-Cohen (1991) and Frith (1989) argued that autistic individuals fail to develop a theory of the minds of others. Applying the Damasio (1990) model, as it fits the neural damage found for autism, it is not necessary to invoke such a "down-stream" concept as *theory of mind*. Human beings and the abstraction of their minds would have no contextual meaning for autistic individuals, but neither would other complex, changing systems.

Frith (1989) argued that autism may result from a "weak drive for coherence" (p. 163). In terms of the Damasio (1990) model, however, there would be no "drive" that could be "weak" but rather that neural damage impairing the establishment of convergence zones would mean that the individual could not generate either a time-point or time-series coherence of experience or could not integrate the two. This failure would lead to disordered understanding of ongoing and past events, and would limit the integration of past and ongoing events. An autistic child's mother would not be significant to that child, not because the child failed to develop a theory of the mind of the mother, but because the child had an impaired ability to repeatedly generate a meaning for the mother in contexts.

In summary, the Damasio (1990) convergence zone model, when coupled with a different understanding of the information processing required for social behavior, appears to have productive possibilities for understanding the nature of autism.

CONCLUSION

The behavioral syndrome of autism remains a puzzle. In the last section of the present chapter I have argued for new thinking in two opposing directions. In one direction is the recommendation for a methodological shift to the detailed exploration of the possibility of very small groups within the autistic spectrum. In the other direction is the application of a new neurofunctional model that may provide an explanation for some of the behavioral heterogeneity and neural deficits found in association with the spectrum. Although these are opposing stances, nonetheless both may be helpful in working to solve the puzzle of autism.

REFERENCES

American Psychiatric Association. (1980). *Diagnostic and statistical manual of mental disorders* (3rd ed.). Washington, DC: Author.

American Psychiatric Association. (1987). *Diagnostic and statistical manual of mental disorders* (3rd ed., rev.). Washington, DC: Author.

Baron-Cohen, S. (1991). Do people with autism understand what causes emotion? *Child Development, 62*, 385–395.

Bauman, M. L. (1991). Microscopic neuroanatomic abnormalities in autism. *Pediatrics, 87*, (Suppl. 5), 791–796.

Black, I. B. (1991). *Information in the brain: A molecular perspective*. Cambridge, MA: MIT Press.

Boucher, J., & Warrington, E. K. (1976). Memory deficits in early infantile autism. *British Journal of Psychology, 67*, 73–87.

Coleman, M. (1976). *The autistic syndromes*. Dordrecht, Netherlands: Elsevier.

Coleman, M. (1987). The search for neurological subgroups in autism. In E. Schopler & G. Mesibov (Eds.), *Neurobiological issues in autism* (pp. –). New York: Plenum.

Coleman, M. & Gillberg, C. (1985). *The biology of the autistic syndrome*. New York: Praeger.

Courchesne, E. (1991). Neuroanatomic imaging in autism. *Pediatrics, 87* (Suppl. 5), 781–790.

Damasio, A. (1990). Time-locked multiregional retroactivation: A systems-level proposal for the neural substrates of recall and recognition. In P. Eimas & A. Galaburda (Eds.), *Neurobiology of cognition* (pp. 25–62). Cambridge, MA: MIT Press.

Dawson, G. (1987). The role of abnormal hemispheric specialization in autism. In E. Schopler & G. Mesibov (Eds.), *Neurobiological issues in autism*. (pp. 213–228). New York: Plenum.

Fein, D., Pennington, B., & Waterhouse, L. (1987). Implications of social deficits in autism for neurological dysfunction. In E. Schopler & G. Mesibov (Eds.), *Neurobiological issues in autism* (pp. 127–144). New York: Plenum.

Fein, D., Wainwright, L., Morris, R., Waterhouse, L., Allen, D., Aram, D., Wilson, B., & Rapin, I. (1991, February). *Symbolic play development in autistic and language disordered children*. Paper presented at the meeting of the International Neurological Society, San Antonio.

Folstein, S., & Piven, J. (1991). The etiology of autism: Genetic influences. *Pediatrics, 87* (Suppl. 5). 767–775.

Folstein, S. & Rutter, M. (1977). Genetic influences and infantile autism. *Nature, 265,* 726–728.

Frith, U. (1989) *Autism: Explaining the enigma.* London: Basil Blackwell.

Gillberg, C. (1990). Autism and pervasive developmental disorders. *Journal of Child Psychology and Psychiatry, 31,* 91–119.

Hinde, R. (1991). When is a fundamental evolutionary approach useful? *Child Development, 62,* 671–675.

Insell, T. (1992). Oxytocin—A neuropeptide for affiliation: Evidence from behavioral, receptor autoradiographic, and comparative studies. *Psychoneuroendocrinology, 17,* 3–35.

International classification of diseases (1990). 5. Diagnostic criteria for research (10th ed.) Geneva: World Health Organization.

Kinsbourne, M. (1987). Cerebral-brainstem relations in infantile autism. In E. Schopler & G. Mesibov (Eds.), *Neurobiological issues in autism* (pp. 107–126). New York: Plenum.

Le Doux, J. E. (1989). Cognitive-emotion interactions in the brain. *Cognition and Emotion, 3,* 267–289.

McGraw, M. B. (1946). Maturation of behavior. In L. Carmichel (Ed.), *Manual of child psychology* (pp.332–369). New York: Wiley.

Panksepp, J., & Sahley, T. L. (1987). Possible brain opioid involvement in disrupted social intent and language development of autism. In E. Schopler & G. Mesibov (Eds.), *Neurobiological issues in autism* (pp. 357–373). New York: Plenum.

Piven, J., Gayle, J., Chase, G., Fink, B., Landa, R., Wzorek, M., & Folstein, S. (1990). A family history study of neuropsychiatric disorders in the adult siblings of autistic children. *Journal of the Academy of Child and Adolescent Psychiatry, 29*(2), 177–183.

Rapin, I. (1987). Searching for the cause of autism: A Neurologic perspective. In D. Cohen, A. Donellan, & R. Paul (Eds.), *Handbook of autism and pervasive developmental disorders* (pp. 710–717). New York: Wiley.

Rapin, I. (1991). Autistic children: Diagnosis and clinical features. *Pediatrics, 87* (Suppl. 5), 751–760.

Reichler, R. J., & Lee, E. M. C. (1987). Overview of biomedical issues in autism. In E. Schopler & G. Mesibov (Eds.), *Neurobiological issues in autism* (pp. 14–43). New York: Plenum. pp. 14–43

Rumsey, J., & Denckla, M. (1987). Neurobiological research priorities in autism. In E. Schopler & G. Mesibov (Eds.), *Neurobiological issues in autism* (pp. 44–62). New York: Plenum.

Rumsey, J., Rapoport, J., & Sceery, W. R. (1985). Autistic children as adults: Psychiatric, social and behavioral outcomes. *Journal of the Academy of Child Psychiatry, 24,* 465–473.

Rutter, M. (1983). Cognitive deficits in the pathogenesis of autism. *Journal of Child Psychology and Psychiatry, 24,* 513–531.

Rutter, M., & Schopler, E. (1988). Autism and pervasive developmental disorders. In E. Schopler & G. Mesibov (Eds.), *Diagnosis and assessment of autism* (pp. 15–36). New York: Plenum.

Sigman, M., & Mundy, P. (1989). Social attachment in autistic children. *Journal of the American Academy of Child and Adolescent Psychiatry, 28,* 74–81.

Sigman, M., Mundy, T., Ungerer, J., & Sherman, T. (1987). Cognition in autistic children. In D. Cohen, A. Donellan, & R. Paul (Eds.), *Handbook of autism and pervasive developmental disorders* (pp. 103–120). New York: Wiley.

Stone, W., & Caro-Martinez (1990). Naturalistic observations of spontaneous communication in autistic children. *Journal of Autism and Developmental Disorders, 20,* 437–454.

Volden, J., & Lord, C. (1991). Neologisms and idiosyncratic language in autistic speakers. *Journal of Autism and Developmental Disorders, 21,* 109–130.

Volkmar, F. R. (1987). Social development. In D. Cohen, A. Donellan, & R. Paul (Eds.), *Handbook of autism and pervasive developmental disorders.* New York: Wiley, 41–60.

Waterhouse, L., & Fein, D. (1982). Language skills in developmentally disabled children. *Brain and Language, 15,* 307–333.

Waterhouse, L., & Fein, D. (1984). Developmental trends in cognitive skills for children diagnosed as autistic and schizophrenic, *Child Development, 55,* 312–326.

Waterhouse, L., Spitzer, R., Wing, L., & Siegel, B. (1992). PDD: From *DSM–III* to *DSM–III–R. Journal of Autism and Developmental Disorders* (Special Issue).

Waterhouse, L., Wing, L., & Fein, D. (1989). Reevaluating the syndrome of autism in the light of empirical research. In G. Dawson & S. Segalowitz (Eds.), *Autism: Perspectives on diagnosis, nature and treatment* (pp. 263–281). New York: Guilford.

Wetherby, A. M., Yonclas, D. G., & Bryan, A. A. (1989). Communication profiles of preschool children with handicaps: Implications for early identification. *Journal of Speech and Hearing Disorders, 54,* 148–158.

Wing, L. (1988). The continuum of autistic characteristics. In E. Schopler & G. Mesibov (Eds.), *Diagnosis and assessment in autism* (pp. 3–19). New York: Plenum.

Wing, L., & Attwood, A. (1988). Syndromes of autism and atypical development. In D. Cohen & A. Donellan (Eds.), *Handbook of autism and pervasive developmental disorders.* New York: Wiley.

Wing, L., & Gould, J. (1979). Severe impairments of social interaction and associated abnormalities in children: Epidemiology and classification. *Journal of Autism and Developmental Disorders, 9,* 11–29.

Section 3

TURNER SYNDROME

The Turner Syndrome: Origin, Cytogenetic Variants, and Factors Influencing the Phenotype

Beverly J. White
National Institute of Diabetes, Digestive,
and Kidney Diseases, National Institutes of Health

Since its recognition as a clinically distinct disorder (Turner, 1938), and discovery of an association with monosomy X (Ford, Jones, Polani, de Almeida, & Briggs, 1959), the Turner syndrome has become one of the most widely recognized and investigated syndromes. It is less common at birth than other conditions with sex chromosomal abnormalities, occurring in approximately 1:2,000 to 1:5,000 live female births. This has been attributed to a much greater prenatal mortality rate than cytogenetically normal embryos, or those with additional X or Y chromosomes (47,XXX, 47,XXY, and 47,XYY) (Hook & Warburton, 1983). Half of first-trimester spontaneous abortuses have abnormal karyotypes, and nearly 20% of those are 45, X or have other cytogenetic variants found in individuals with the Turner phenotype. The reduction in viability of 45,X is thought to result from vascular abnormalities and gross fluid imbalance (Canki, Warburton, & Byrne, 1988), as well as generalized growth retardation, rather than to the effects of specific malformations. It has therefore been difficult for individual investigators to accumulate enough patients with the Turner syndrome for systematic, controlled studies of its postnatal manifestations.

CLINICAL FINDINGS

The classical features of the syndrome include short stature, webbed neck, a broad chest, cubitus valgus, and failure of gonadal development (De la

Chapelle, 1990; Turner, 1938; Vogel & Motulsky, 1986). Germ cells are present in the gonads of 45,X embryos, but begin to deteriorate in late fetal life. By early childhood, there are usually no oocytes remaining, and the gonads consist of fibrous streaks. In the normal fetal ovary, all 46 oocyte chromosomes become associated during prophase of the first meiotic division to form 22 homologous autosomal pairs and 1 additional pair consisting of two X chromosomes. This pairing is maintained until the meiotic division is actually completed postnatally in the mature oocyte at ovulation. The corresponding phases of germ cell development occur postnatally in men. In the Turner syndrome, it has been proposed that absence or structural abnormality of one X chromosome precludes or disrupts the normal X pairing process in the fetal ovary, which eventually leads to premature germ cell loss (Therman, Laxova, & Susman, 1990).

Some of the other clinical findings of the syndrome are described in Table 9.1. In addition to a generalized effect upon growth and development, abnormalities are found in multiple systems and include skeletal, craniofacial, cardiovascular, renal, lymphatic, and epidermal defects (Cohen, 1989; De la Chapelle, 1990; Lippe, Geffner, Dietrich, Boechat, & Kangarloo, 1988; Noonan, 1990; Rosenfeld, 1989; Sybert, 1990). The lymphatic defects may be the most critical primary problem leading to other phenotypic abnormalities, because it has been suggested that they result in altered thoracic pressure and the characteristic cardiac defects (Lacro, Jones, & Benirshke, 1988; Noonan, 1990). Also, the webbed neck and hypoplastic nails typical of 45,X occurs in areas of the body with prominent fetal or neonatal lymphedema, which is presumably secondary to defective lymphatics. Gross structural abnormalities of the central nervous ststem are not usually found, although agenesis of the corpus callosum has been reported in several patients (Kimura, Nakajima, & Yoshino, 1990).

Effects upon function of the central nervous system (CNS) have also been observed, including delayed psychological development, visual-spatial and visual-motor deficits, delayed gross and fine motor development, and sensory-motor integration dysfunction (Ratcliffe & Paul, 1986; Salbenlatt, Meyers, Bender, Linden, & Robinson, 1989; Vogel & Motulsky, 1986). However, interpretation of studies of the CNS manifestations of the Turner syndrome is complicated by karyotypic heterogeneity, including mosaicism. Some patients with the Turner phenotype have a mixture of normal 46,XX and abnormal 45,X cells in their peripheral blood and other tissues, or may have a mixture of cells with different X structural abnormalities and no normal cells. Although reduced performance and full-scale IQ have been reported in controlled studies of nonmosaic patients with complete and partial monosomy X, IQ measurements of mosaic patients with 45,X and a normal 46,XX cell line were not significantly different than those of controls (Ratcliffe & Paul, 1986).

Some affected individuals may develop complications of hypertension,

TABLE 9.1
Clinical Findings of the Turner Syndrome

Type	Characteristics
Classical:	Short stature
	Short webbed neck
	Broad chest
	Cubitus valgus
	Gonadal dysgenesis
Growth:	Decreased mean birth weight
	Lack of pubertal growth spurt
Skeletal:	Scoliosis
	Madelung wrist deformity
	Genu valgum
	Exostosis medial tibial condyle
	Short metacarpals, metatarsals
Craniofacial:	Craniosynostosis
	Narrow palate
	Micrognathia
	Strabismus
	Malrotation of ears
	Inner ear defects
Cardiovascular:	Aortic coarctation
	Biscuspid aortic valve
	Mitral valve prolapse
	Septal defect
	Partial anomalous venous return
Renal:	Horseshoe or pelvic kidney
	Unilateral aplasia or hypoplasia
	Unilateral double ureter
Lymphatic:	Intestinal lymphangiectases
	Congenital lymphedema hands, feet
Hair and Skin:	Low posterior hairline
	Increased pigmented nevi
	Hypoplastic nails
	Dermatoglyphic variations
Nervous System:	Delayed psychological development
	Visual-spatial, visual-motor deficit
	Delayed gross and fine motor development
	Sensory-motor integration dysfunction
	Agenesis of corpus callosum

carbohydrate intolerance, or autoimmune disorders such as Hashimoto's thyroiditis as they grow older (Rosenfeld, 1989), although there is no known increase in frequency of presenile dementia of the Alzheimer type in older Turner syndrome patients. Therefore, the abnormal decline in cognition and memory observed in many middle-age Down syndrome adults with trisomy 21 is not characteristic of individuals with the Turner syndrome or other sex chromosomal abnormalities.

ORIGIN OF MONOSOMY X

The mean maternal age of Turner syndrome patients is not increased, and a paternal age effect has also not been consistently demonstrated (Mathur et al., 1991). There is also no association with birth order. In order to determine whether a maternal or paternal sex chromosome was missing, variation in expression of the X-linked blood group antigen XG was utilized. This was not informative in many cases, and more recently, X-linked polymorphic molecular markers have been used for family studies. These were consistent with XG analyses and indicated absence of a paternal sex chromosome in over 70% of 45,X liveborn and spontaneous abortuses (Harbison, Hassold, Kobryn, & Jacobs, 1988; Hassold, Benham, & Leppert, 1988; Mathur et al., 1991).

Two mechanisms have been proposed to explain the absence of a sex chromosome in 45,X individuals. The first is meiotic nondisjunction of the sex chromosomes of the oocyte or spermatocyte, resulting in a gamete with no sex chromosome, and the second involves the loss of one sex chromosome from the zygote after fertilization has occurred.

During meiotic pairing, crossing over and recombination of genetic material occurs along both arms of the homologous autosomes and X chromosomes of women. However, in the XY pair during normal spermatogenesis, only their terminal short arms (pseudoautosomal regions) are paired and undergo recombination. Failure of recombination in the latter regions was suggested as a mechanism predisposing to XY meiotic nondisjunction and the 47,XXY Klinefelter syndrome. Because every XY nondisjunction event that produces an XY gamete also results in one without a sex chromosome, this could also be an important mechanism of origin of paternally derived Turner syndrome. DNA studies of the 47,XXY syndrome that support this theory were recently reported (Hassold, Sherman, Pettay, Page, & Jacobs, 1991). There are no definitive studies establishing the alternative hypothesis, that monosomy X may also originate from loss of a sex chromosome from the zygote after fertilization.

CYTOGENETIC VARIANTS

There is considerable variation in the clinical abnormalities of individual patients, and attempts have been made to determine whether these phenotypic differences are related to the cytogenetic variants that have been observed (De la Chapelle, 1990; Vogel & Motulsky, 1986). These variants include mosaicism and structurally abnormal X chromosomes. Some of these and their postulated mechanism of origin are shown in Table 9.2. Loss or nondisjunction of a sex chromosome at or after the first mitosis of the zygote is thought to explain most cases of mosaicism. Some mosaics with Turner

TABLE 9.2
Origin of Karyotypic Variants in Turner Syndrome: Mosaics and
X Structural Abnormalities

Variant Karyotype	Zygote	Possible Mechanism
Mosaic		
45,X/46,XX	46,XX	Loss of X at or after first mitosis
45,X/46,XY	46,XY	Loss of Y at or after first mitosis
45,X/47,XXX	46,XX	X nondisjunction at first mitosis
45,X/46,XX/47,XXX	46,XX	X nondisjunction after first mitosis
Nonmosaic[a]		
46,X,r(X)	46,X,r(X)	Breakage within Xp and Xq, rejoining, in germ cell
	46,XX	X breakage, rejoining, in zygote
46,X,del(Xp)	46,X,del(Xp)	Deletion of Xp in germ cell
	46,XX	Deletion of Xp in zygote
46,X,del(Xq)	46,X,del(Xq)	Deletion of Xq in germ cell
	46,XX	Deletion of Xq in zygote
46,X,i(Xq)	46,X,i(Xq)	Breakage of both chromatids of single X near centromere, chromatid exchange, in germ cell
	46,XX	X breakage and exchange in zygote

[a]Mosaic with 45,X cell line may arise due to mitotic instability of abnormal X.

syndrome have a cell line with a normal or atypical Y chromosome. These patients are at risk for gonadal tumors and may have ambiguous genitalia or even a nearly normal male phenotype.

Structural changes of the X chromosome include deletion of the short or long arm, breakage of both arms to form a ring chromosome, or breakage and exchange in the X centromere region to form an isochromosome. Examples of these aberrations are shown in Fig. 9.1. Deletions or other structural aberrations may arise in a parental germ cell, zygote, or in embryonic or fetal tissues. The deleted portion, which does not contain a centromere, is usually lost during subsequent mitotic divisions.

Mosaicism, with some cells having a normal 46,XX karyotype and others one normal and one structurally abnormal X, may be found if the deletion or other breakage is postzygotic. Alternatively, an atypical X may be present in all cells if the breakage occurs in a parental germ cell or in the zygote. However, when a structurally abnormal X is present in a zygote with 46 chromosomes, mosaicism with a 45,X cell line may eventually arise. The mechanism postulated to explain this is that mitotic instability of aberrant sex chromosomes may predispose to anaphase lag or nondisjunction. For example, anaphase lag of an i(Xq) in a 46,X,i(Xq) zygote or embryo could lead to 45,X/46X,i(Xq) mosaicism.

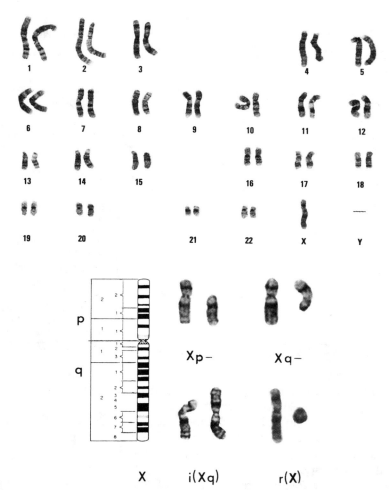

FIG. 9.1. Above: The complete giemsa-trypsin in banded karyotype of a nonmosaic 45,X Turner syndrome NIH patient. Below: Four types of X structural abnormalities found in other NIH Turner syndrome patients: Xp- (X short-arm deletion), Xq- (X long-arm deletion at band Xq22), i(Xq) (isochromosome for the X long arm), and r(X) (ring X chromosome). In each case, the normal X from the same cell is to the left. The banding pattern of a normal X is also illustrated. Both the short (p) and long (q) arms are divided into two regions and each region into several bands. Smaller subbands are present within each band, but their numerical designations are not shown.

In different studies, the frequency of mosaicism was 15%–20% and X structural abnormalities 20%–25%. Of 80 Turner syndrome patients enrolled in the National Institutes of Health (NIH) Clinical Center Study of Turner Syndrome (Developmental Endocrinology Branch, NICHD, Drs. Gordon Cutler and Judith Levine-Ross, and Lauren Long, R.N.), 25.1% were mosaics. Most of the remaining nonmosaics were 45,X except for several patients with a 46,X,i(Xq) karyotype (see Table 9.3). Most of the NIH mosaics had a cell line with an X structural abnormality, usually an i(Xq). Recent molecular studies indicate that the breakage and exchange between two X long arms leading to i(Xq) formation can be either maternal or paternal, and that this exchange occurs between the two identical copies of the long arm of a single X chromosome (Harbison et al., 1988; Phelan et al., 1988).

CORRELATION OF PHENOTYPE AND KARYOTYPE

In a recent review, Sybert (1990) emphasized the extreme variation in clinical abnormalities between individual Turner syndrome patients and the difficulty in correlating the clinical findings with specific karyotypic variations. Although some have concluded that mosaic patients with 45,X and a normal cell line (mos45,X/46,XX) are less severely affected than nonmosaic 45,X individuals (De Paepe & Matton, 1985), this effect could not be clearly demonstrated in their series of patients. The origin of the single X of nonmosaic 45,X individuals does not appear to affect their phenotype, according to Mathur et al. (1991). They compared patients with maternal versus paternal X origin for six clinical traits and observed no difference in these between the two groups.

TABLE 9.3
Karyotypes of 80 NIH Turner Syndrome Patients

Karyotype	No. cases	Percentages of all cases
Nonmosaic		
45,X	57	71.2
46,X,i(Xq)	3	3.7
Total nonmosaic	60	74.9
Mosaic		
45,X/46,X,i(Xq)	11	13.7
45,X/46,X,del(X)(p11.2)	3	3.7
45,X/46,X,del(X)(q21)	1	1.3
45,X/46,X,r(X)	2	2.5
45,X/46,X,ter rea(Xp;Xp)	1	1.3
45,X/46,XX	1	1.3
45,X/47,XXX	1	1.3
Total mosaic	20	25.1
Total all cases	80[a]	100.0

[a]Includes 21 with structurally abnormal X: 3 nonmosaic with i(Xq) and 18 mosaic with i(Xq) or other abnormal X.

It has been observed that the phenotype of many patients with X structural abnormalities resembles that of 45,X patients. However, individuals with a structurally altered X frequently have an additional 45,X cell line, presumably because of postzygotic loss of the atypical X during mitosis. For example, in the NIH study, 18 of 21 individuals with X structural abnormalities were mosaics with a second 45,X cell line (Table 9.3). In such mosaics, clinical abnormalities could be either the result of monosomy X, or the consequences of imbalance of a particular region of the patient's structurally abnormal X. Because of this, in clinical studies of the Turner syndrome, observations should be grouped so that data from mosaic and nonmosaic subjects can be analyzed separately.

The most accurate phenotype-karyotype comparisons should then come from studies of 45,X patients and nonmosaic individuals with X structural abnormalities. In the NIH survey, this would include nearly 75% of all individuals studied; 57 were 45,X and 3 were nonmosaic 46,X,i(Xq) patients. In most laboratories, screening of at least 50 peripheral blood metaphases is considered sufficient to exclude mosaicism, and studies of additional tissues such as skin fibroblasts have generally not revealed results different than that of the peripheral blood study (Sybert, 1990; also unpublished observations, Laboratory of Chemical Biology, National Institute of Diabetes, Digestive and Kidney Diseases).

From previous studies of Turner syndrome patients with different X abnormalities, the typical phenotype has been correlated with short-arm deletions, with the region between the centromere and band p11 on the short arm considered most critical (Therman et al., 1990); it has been postulated that X long-arm abnormalities may result in the same phenotype by exerting some influence on the critical short-arm region, possibly via a specific locus on the long arm (Therman & Susman, 1990).

Although the individual Turner traits could be determined by loci along both arms of the X, the presence of gonadal dysgenesis is correlated more with X abnormalities that have breakpoints in the Xq13-q26 region. According to a survey of Therman et al. (1990), ovarian dysgenesis occurs in 93% of individuals with long-arm deletions and in 65% of those with short-arm deletions. On the other hand, short stature is invariably present in 45,X patients and in most of those with short-arm deletions (88%), but is less frequent in long-arm deletions (43%).

INFLUENCE OF X INACTIVATION

Correlation of clinical with cytogenetic studies of X chromosomal disorders is complicated by the phenomenon of Lyonization, or X inactivation. In normal females only one of the two X chromosomes remains active in somatic cells; all copies in excess of one are inactivated in individuals with two or more X chromosomes. This occurs early in embryonic life and initially is a random process that becomes fixed or clonal in the descendants of the original cells. One important consequence of this is that genes from only one X chromosome are expressed at the cellular level in both men and women (dosage compensation). Another result is that different women carrying the same X-linked mutation on only one of their two X chromosomes may differ both at the cellular level and clinically, because each may have different proportions of cells with an active mutant X following the inactivation process (heterozygote variability). Also, women are mosaic for X-linked genes, because their cells consist of a mixture, some with an active maternally derived X and others in which the paternally derived X remains active (cellular mosaicism) (Vogel & Motulsky, 1986).

At least three loci near the terminal end of the X short arm in the pseudoautosomal region are not included in the inactivation process (for details, see Chang et al., 1990; Johnson et al., 1991). More recent studies indicate that additional loci elsewhere on the X short arm and on the long arm also escape inactivation (Brown & Ballabio et al., 1991; Davies, 1991). There is evidence from studies of XY women with gonadal dysgenesis that two of the latter loci contain the genes ZFX and RPS4X that may play a role in sex determination and development of the Turner phenotype (Fisher et al., 1990; Scherer et al., 1989). Both genes are thought to have corresponding sequences on the Y chromosome (Palmer, Berta, Sinclair, Pym, & Goodfellow, 1990).

RPS4X coincides with the X region thought to contain the X inactivation center (XIC). It has been suggested that hemizygosity for genes in the XIC region in monosomy X may lead to the Turner phenotype and that XIC gene defects could lead to inactivation of the same X in all cells. The latter phenomenon could then account for some instances of expression of X-linked recessive diseases in 46,XX women.

Structural abnormalities of the X are known to affect the X inactivation process. Generally, the normal X is active and abnormal X inactive in patients whose second X has a short- or long-arm deletion, or is in the form of a ring or isochromosome. In these types of X abnormalities, retention in the abnormal X of the long-arm region containing the X-inactivation center appears to be a requirement for late replication and inactivation (Brown & LaFreniere et al., 1991). Although isochromosomes for the X long arm are relatively common among Turner syndrome patients with X structural abnormalities, isochromosomes for the short arm, i(Xp), have not been convincingly documented.

The Turner phenotyope may result from the effects of the X abnormality or imbalance during the period of embryogenesis prior to X inactivation, and is probably influenced by multiple loci. It has also been suggested that recessive genes important for normal viability and development are located within the pseudoautosomal region of both the X and Y, and that hemizygosity for such loci or expression of recessive lethal mutations in this region in 45,X hemizygotes could explain the Turner phenotype and its high prenatal mortality (Canki et al., 1988).

The various sex-linked loci thought to be critical in determining the Turner phenotype are summarized in Table 9.4. Other sex-linked and autosomal genes are known to be important in the complex process of sex determination and development, including those necessary for expression of male-associated (H-Y) antigen and for binding of androgens; a review of these is not attempted in the present report.

TABLE 9.4
X- and Y-linked Loci and the Turner Phenotype

Locus[a] (Gene Symbol)	Location	Role in Determining Phenotype
Pseudoautosomal Regions	Xpter and Ypter	Hemizygosity for genes in regions may result in Turner phenotype or reduce viability
Ribosomal Protein S4, Y-Linked (RPS4Y)	Yp	Deleted, some XY female gonadal dysgenesis patients with Turner phenotype
Testis Determining Factor, Y-Linked Zinc-Finger Protein (TDF, ZFY)	Yp11.2	Deleted, some XY female gonadal dysgenesis patients
X-Linked Zinc-Finger Protein (ZFX)	Xp21.3-22.2	Escapes inactivation, duplicated in some XY female gonadal dysgenesis patients
X-Inactivating Center (XIC)	Xq13	Required for inactivation, cis-acting, mutation may lead to inactivation same X, all cells
Inactive X-Specific Transcript (XIST)	Xq13 at XIC	Expressed by inactive X, cis-acting, may block X transcription, hemizygosity may lead to Turner phenotype
Ribosomal Protein S4, X-Linked (RPS4X)	Xq13 at or near XIC	Escapes inactivation, hemizygosity may lead to Turner phenotype

[a]Autosomal and sex-linked loci for expression of male-specific antigen (H-Y) and for androgen receptors (AR, DHTR) not included.

CENTRAL NERVOUS SYSTEM ABNORMALITIES

Most studies correlating the phenotype with karyotypic variants have focused on the physical stigmata of Turner syndrome rather than the more subtle functional CNS abnormalities. Although genes distributed along both arms of the X appear to determine the somatic anomalies, the localization of X-linked genes affecting development and function of the CNS in the Turner syndrome is uncertain. Therefore, in order to correlate CNS deficits with specific cytogenetic variations, evaluation of patients should include an accurate determination of cytogenetic status. At least 25–50 peripheral blood cells should be screened microscopically for sex chromosomal abnormalities. Karyotyping of another tissue such as skin fibroblasts may be needed in some individuals who have the Turner phenotype but a normal peripheral blood study, or a low percentage of karyotypically abnormal peripheral blood cells. In some cases, fluorescent in-situ hybridization with X- and Y-specific DNA probes may be used with metaphase chromosome preparations to determine origin of atypical sex chromosomes that cannot be identified with routine banding methods. This is particularly important in patients with small atypical marker chromosomes that could be derived from a Y. If Y-specific sequences are present, evaluation for gonadal tumors is indicated because of the known increased risk of gonadoblastoma in Turner syndrome patients with a Y chromosome (Gemmill, Pearce-Birge, Bixenman, Hecht, & Allanson, 1987).

Data from nonmosaic Turner syndrome patients should be the most reliable in determining the effects of the 45,X karyotype, specific X structural abnormalities, and normal or atypical Y chromosomes. Ideally, data could be grouped according to the specific type of karyotypic variant. If numbers permit, mosaic 45,X patients with specific X structural abnormalities or Y chromosomes could be compared with nonmosaic individuals with the same aberrations. Because the Turner syndrome is relatively rare at birth, it may not be possible to compare large numbers of patients with the different variants, and observations of different investigators may have to be combined for analysis.

Correlation of cytogenetic, molecular, and clinical evaluations should ultimately reveal more about the influence of sex-linked loci, particularly those excluded from X inactivation, or in the pseudoautosomal regions and X-inactivation center, in determining any structural and functional abnormalities of the CNS found in the Turner syndrome. This disorder may then prove to be an important model for identifying the relationship between specific neurocognitive deficits and sex-linked genetic sequences.

REFERENCES

Brown, C. J., Ballabio, A., Rupert, J. L., Lafreniere, R. G., Grompe, M., Tonlorenzi, R., & Willard, H. F. (1991). A gene from the region of the human X inactivation centre is expressed exclusively from the inactive X chromosome. *Nature, 349,* 38–44.

Brown, C. J., Lafreniere, R. G., Powers, V. E., Sebastio, G., Ballabio, A., Pettigrew, A. L., Ledbetter, D. H., Levy, E., Craig, I. W., & Willard, H. F. (1991). Localization of the X inactivation centre on the human X chromosome in Xq13. *Nature, 349*, 82–84.

Canki, N., Warburton, D., & Byrne, J. (1988). Morphological characteristics of monosomy X in spontaneous abortions. *Annals of Genetics, 31*, 4–13.

Chang, P. L., Mueller, O. T., Lafrenie, R. M., Varey, P. A., Rosa, N. E., Davidson, R. G., Henry, W. M., & Shows, T. B., (1990). The human arylsulfatase C isoenzymes: Two distinct genes that escape from X inactivation. *The American Journal of Human Genetics, 46*, 729–737.

Cohen, M. M. (1989). Craniosynostosis in the Ullrich–Turner syndrome. *The American Journal of Medical Genetics, 35*, 289–290.

Davies, K. (1991). The essence of inactivity. *Nature, 349*, 15–16.

De la Chapelle, A. (1990). Sex chromosome abnormalities. In A. E. H. Emery & D. L. Rimoin (Eds.), *Principles and practice of medical genetics* (Vol. 1, pp. 273–299). New York: Livingstone.

De Paepe, A., & Matton, M. (1985). Turner's syndrome: Updating on diagnosis and therapy. In C. J. Papadatos & C. S. Bartsocas (Eds.), *Endocrine genetics and genetics of growth* (pp. 283–300). New York: Liss.

Fisher, E. M. C., Beer-Romero, P., Brown, L. G., Ridley, A., McNeil, J. A., Lawrence, J. B., Willard, H. F., Bieber, F. R., & Page, D. (1990). Homologous ribosomal protein genes on the human X and Y chromosomes: Escape from X inactivation and possible implications for Turner syndrome. *Cell, 63*, 1205–1218.

Ford, C. E., Jones, K. W., Polani, P. E., de Almeida, J. C., & Briggs, J. H. (1959). A sex chromosome anomaly in a case of gonadal dysgenesis (Turner's syndrome). *Lancet, 1*, 711–713.

Gemmill, R. M., Pearce-Birge, L., Bixenman, H., Hecht, B. K., & Allanson, J. E. (1987). Y chromosome-specific DNA sequences in Turner-syndrome mosaicism. *The American Journal of Human Genetics, 41*, 157–167.

Harbison, M., Hassold, T., Kobryn, C., & Jacobs, P. A. (1988). Molecular studies of the parental origin and nature of human X isochromosomes. *Cytogenetics and Cell Genetics, 47*, 217–222.

Hassold, T., Benham, F., & Leppert, M. (1988). Cytogenetic and molecular analysis of sex-chromosome monosomy. *The American Journal of Human Genetics, 42*, 534–541.

Hassold, T. J., Sherman, S. L., Pettay, D., Page, D. C., & Jacobs, P. A. (1991). XY chromosome nondisjunction in man is associated with diminished recombination in the pseudoautosomal region. *The American Journal of Human Genetics, 49*, 253–260.

Hook, E. B., & Warburton, D. (1983). The distribution of chromosomal genotypes associated with Turner's syndrome: Livebirth prevalence rates and evidence for diminished fetal mortality and severity in genotypes associated with structural X abnormalities or mosaicism. *Human Genetics, 64*, 24–27.

Johnson, C. L., Charmley, P., Yen, P. H., & Shapiro, L. J. (1991). A Multipoint linkage map of the distal short arm of the human X chromosome. *The American Journal of Human Genetics, 49*, 261–266.

Kimura, M., Nakajima, M., & Yoshino, K. (1990). Ullrich–Turner syndrome with agenesis of the corpus callosum. *The American Journal of Medical Genetics, 37*, 227–228.

Lacro, R. V., Jones, K. L., & Benirshke, K. (1988). Coarctation of the aorta in Turner syndrome: A pathologic study of fetuses with nuchal cystic hygromas, hydrops fetalis, and female genitalia. *Pediatrics, 81*, 445–451.

Lippe, B., Geffner, M. E., Dietrich, R. B., Boechat, M. I., & Kangarloo, H. (1988). Renal malformations in patients with Turner syndrome: Imaging in 141 patients. *Pediatrics, 82*, 852–856.

Mathur, A., Stekol, L., Schatz, D., MacLaren, N. K., Scott, M. L., & Lippe, B. (1991). The parental origin of the single X chromosome in Turner syndrome: Lack of correlation with parental age or clinical phenotype. *The American Journal of Human Genetics, 48*, 682–686.

Noonan, J. A. (1990). Chromosomal abnormalities. In W. A. Long (Ed.), *Fetal and neonatal cardiology* (p. 590). Philadelphia: Saunders.

Palmer, M. S., Berta, P., Sinclair, A. H., Pym, B., & Goodfellow, P. N. (1990). Comparison of human ZFY and ZFX transcripts. *Proceedings of the National Academy of Sciences, 87,* 1681–1685.

Phelan, M. C., Prouty, L. A., Stevenson, R. E., Howard-Peebles, P. N., Page, D. C., & Schwartz, C. E. (1988). The parental origin and mechanism of formation of three dicentric X chromosomes. *Human Genetics, 80,* 81–84.

Ratcliffe, S. G., & Paul, N. (Eds.). (1986). *Prospective studies on children with sex chromosome aneuploidy* (Birth Defects Original Article Series 22[3]). New York: Liss.

Rosenfeld, R. G. (1989). *Turner syndrome: A guide for physicians.* Greenwich, CT: The Turner Syndrome Society.

Salbenblatt, J. A., Meyers, D. C., Bender, B. G., Linden, M. G., & Robinson, A. (1989). Gross and fine motor development in 45,X and 47,XXX girls. *Pediatrics, 84,* 678–682.

Scherer, G., Schempp, W., Baccichetti, C., Lenzini, E., Bricarelli, F. D., Carbone, L. D. L., & Wolf, U. (1989). Duplication of an Xp segment that includes the ZFX locus causes sex inversion in man. *Human Genetics, 81,* 291–294.

Sybert, V. P. (1990). Mosaicism in Turner syndrome. *Growth Genetics and Hormones, 6*(4), 4–8.

Therman, E., Laxova, R., & Susman, B. (1990). The critical region on the human Xq. *Human Genetics, 85,* 455–461.

Therman, E., & Susman, B. (1990). The similarity of phenotypic effects caused by Xp and Xq deletions in the human female: A hypothesis. *Human Genetics, 85,* 175–183.

Turner, H. H. (1983). A syndrome of infantilism, congenital webbed neck, and cubitus valgus. *Endocrinology, 23,* 566–574.

Vogel, F., & Motulsky, A. G. (1986). Sex chromosomes. Chromosome aberrations and psychological abnormalities. In F. Vogel & A. G. Motulsky (Eds.), *Human genetics* (pp. 69–79, 575–584). New York: Springer-Verlag.

Neurocognitive and Psychosocial Phenotypes Associated with Turner Syndrome

Bruce G. Bender
Mary G. Linden
Arthur Robinson
National Jewish Center for Immunology and Respiratory Medicine
University of Colorado School of Medicine

Turner syndrome (TS) occurs in about 1 of 2,500 live female births. The incidence of TS is markedly higher at conception, as only about 1% survive to birth (Hook & Warburton, 1983). The karyotype of TS females can be either a pure 45,X cell line or partial monosomy X, including a variety of sex chromosome abnormality (SCA) mosaics involving monosomy X. The physical phenotype typically includes short stature and ovarian dysgenesis, and may include cardiovascular malformations, renal malformations, webbing of the neck, low posterior hairline, increased carrying angle, shieldlike chest, triangular facies, high-arched palate, short fourth metacarpal, hyperconvexity of the fingernails, and multiple nevi. Some of these TS complications, such as cardiovascular and renal malformations, require close medical scrutiny and occasional intervention. TS patients are increasingly being offered human growth hormone therapy aimed at increasing stature. Secondary sex characteristics are sometimes achieved and maintained through supplemental estrogen therapy. For more extensive discussion of the TS physical phenotype, see chapter 9 in this volume.

Attempts to define the psychological phenotype of TS have inspired a considerable number of investigations, hypotheses, and speculations over the past 30 years. It is the purpose of this chapter to examine the evolution of these definitions. The first descriptions of psychological characteristics have undergone repeated modifications as investigations have become more sophisticated and our understanding of these individuals more comprehensive. The examination of a psychological phenotype can be divided into two major categories in order to define both the neurocognitive and psychosocial parameters. The following section addresses the neurocognitive characteristics of TS, describing early disagreements as to whether TS was accompanied by general or specific cognitive impairment, and addressing attempts to identify etiology at the level of the cerebral hemispheres that were sometimes based upon theoretical and methodological misconceptions. The second section of this chapter addresses broader attempts to describe the behavioral/psychological characteristics of TS, including the incidence of psychiatric disturbance and patterns of psychosocial adaptation. The final section addresses investigators' attempts to integrate the relationships between the neurocognitive and psychosocial TS phenotypes, attempting to develop a causal relationship between cognitive impairments and difficulties with social adaptation in some TS patients. Efforts have also been directed at integrating the medical and psychological experiences of TS patients to determine potential associations between hormones, growth patterns, brain development, and neuropsychological or behavioral characteristics. A complete and definitive psychological description cannot be produced from the information available to date. Nonetheless, enough has been learned to begin to bring these phenotypes into focus.

NEUROCOGNITIVE PHENOTYPE

It has been well documented that individuals with TS are at increased risk for intellectual and neuropsychological impairment. Attempts to define a neurocognitive TS phenotype have been impeded by misunderstandings about the severity, specificity, and homogeneity of neurocognitive characteristics found in these individuals. Earlier reports indicated that TS was associated with mental retardation (Grumbach, Van Wyck, & Wilkins, 1955; Haddad & Wilkins, 1959). Polani (1961) corrected this picture in his conclusion that TS is likely to be accompanied by "slight intellectual impairment" (p. 202), and concluded that this impairment frequently co-occurs with the presence of webbing of the neck. Indeed, the bulk of evidence following these early reports failed to support the contention that mental deficiency is common among TS patients or that it may be accompanied by increased physical stigmata (Money & Granoff, 1965). Investigators soon began to describe a specific nonverbal, visual-spatial deficit among TS patients with otherwise normal intelligence (Cohen, 1962; Shaffer, 1962). Verbal skills were found to be relatively unaffected, and were believed by some to be above average (Money & Alexander, 1966).

Identification of Specific Deficits. The identification of a specific cognitive impairment in TS women was greeted with considerable interest and spawned a large number of investigations. This interest stemmed in part from the realization that this linkage between chromosomal constitution and neuro-cognitive phenotype provided evidence of a genetically mediated learning disability, and produced an opportunity to advance neuropsychological models explaining sex differences in brain development and hemispheric specialization. Money and Alexander (1966) coined the term *space-form blindness*, and were joined by numerous other investigators in describing an assembly of related deficits that included difficulty identifying positions in space (Money & Alexander, 1966), mentally rotating geometric shapes (Rovet & Netley, 1980, 1982), orienting to left–right directions (Alexander, Walker, & Money, 1964; Waber, 1979), drawing human figures or copying geometric shapes (Alexander, Ehrhardt, & Money, 1966; Silbert, Wolff, & Lilienthal, 1977), handwriting (Pennington, Bender, Puck, Salbenblatt, & Robinson, 1982), and solving arithmetic problems (Garron, 1977; Money & Alexander, 1966; Shaffer, 1962). Because these deficits largely involve visual-spatial functioning, the inference was made that the source of this deficit was an abnormality of brain function (Money & Granoff, 1965), most likely localized in the brain's right hemisphere (Alexander & Money, 1966).

Due to the widespread use of Wechsler intelligence scales, and the popular notion that the resulting verbal IQ largely reflected left-hemisphere func-tioning whereas performance IQ reflected right-hemisphere functioning, many studies of TS patients included this instrument. Rovet (1990) reviewed 19 of these IQ studies, concluding that on average TS women scored 7 to 15 IQ points below average on the performance scales of these standardized intelligence tests. A total sample of 226 TS women produced a mean verbal IQ of 101 and performance IQ of 89, indicating an average discrepancy of 12 points. Rovet concluded that these results were consistent across varying countries, and that the size of the verbal-performance IQ discrepancy was not related to age or genetic karyotype.

Garron (1977) concluded that earlier interpretations of increased mental deficiency in TS patients were the product of failure to recognize the verbal-performance IQ discrepancy. It is Garron's argument that investiga-tions that look only at full-scale IQ, or that focus upon the areas of greatest deficiency for TS women, including spatial problem solving, provide a misleading picture of the overall cognitive abilities of these patients. Because their verbal IQ scores are frequently in the average range, he concluded that the intellectual abilities of TS women are basically normal, and that their impairment is quite specific to spatial and perceptual thinking and not particularly relevant to the majority of their intellectual skills. This argument errs on several points. First, the conclusions from early reports of increased mental deficiency occurred not because of failure to take into account the verbal-performance IQ discrepancy, but because these reports were based primarily upon a severely affected subgroup of TS patients who had come to medical attention. The verbal-performance IQ discrepancy, as demonstrated in Rovet's (1990) review, averages 12 points; thus, the impact on full-scale IQ is a reduction of only about 6 points, a drop that would certainly not lead any individual to fall from the normal range to the mentally deficient range of intelligence. An additional error in this focus upon the verbal-performance IQ discrepancy occurs with the assumption that performance IQ best captures the cognitive impairment of TS patients. In fact, performance IQ is only a rough index of right-hemisphere function and dysfunction (Todd, Coolidge, & Satz, 1977). Finally, the focus on mean IQ scores propagates the misconception that a singular profile can be drawn into which most TS patients conform.

A number of investigators have moved beyond the verbal-performance IQ question to use more specific measures of right-hemisphere functioning in order to more clearly define the neuropsychological deficits present in TS. Two of the methodologically stronger studies in this area have utilized a mental rotation paradigm developed by Shepard and Metzler (1971) to identify the components of cognitive processing that might account for the TS spatial deficit. Using this task, subjects were required to compare pairs of three-dimensional figures resembling stacks of cubes, determining whether the two members of the pair, each represented in different spatial orientations, had identical three-dimensional configurations. Both the method and speed of task approach were analyzed. Rovet and Netley (1982), using this task with 31 TS subjects and 31 age- and verbal IQ-matched chromosomally normal female controls, concluded that the TS subjects used the same mental rotation strategy as controls, but that they were far less efficient at completing the rotational process. Interestingly, these investigators repeated the same procedure with a pair of twin sisters, one with and one without TS, obtaining the same result. The TS twin was significantly less efficient at processing the spatial information, but equalled her non-TS twin in the completion of a verbally loaded sentence verification task. Using another version of this task, Berch and Kirkendall (1986) found that a group of TS girls performed the mental rotation task more slowly, demonstrating slower encoding proficiency and poorer transformational abilities than did a group of female control children. Both studies concluded that TS individuals appear to have difficulty in coding and transforming visual-spatial information, although they can remember spatial information accurately.

Right-Hemisphere Impairment. Interest in identifying neurocognitive specificity in TS patients has included not only attempts to define specific intellectual deficits, but also attempts to differentiate right- and left-hemisphere capacities for information processing. Rovet (1990) assessed hemispheric lateralization in 15 TS subjects and 118 normal female controls with four tasks presumed to measure left- and right-hemispheric functioning. The two measures of left-hemisphere specialization included the dichotic presentation of stop consonants and a tachistoscopically presented letter recognition task. Right-hemispheric specialization was assessed with a musical dichotic listening task and a tachistoscopically presented dot enumeration task. Results indicated that the TS subjects were using their left hemispheres to a greater degree than were normal subjects when processing nonverbal information although showing less left-hemisphere involvement than controls while processing verbal information. Rovet concluded that the left hemisphere of TS individuals may be compensating for underdeveloped right-hemisphere functions for spatial information processing, with the result that its potential for processing verbal information is compromised. Other studies of TS patients featuring dichotic listening to evaluate hemispheric specialization have similarly indicated that TS individuals demonstrate weaker left-hemisphere involvement, sometimes accompanied by increased right-hemisphere involvement, during verbal information processing (Gordon & Galatzer, 1980; Lewandowski, Costenbader, & Richman, 1985; Netley, 1977).

Other studies have attempted to make more specific inferences as to the location of brain impairments. Christensen and Nielsen (1981) employed Luria's neuropsychological procedures to evaluate 17 TS women. These subjects demonstrated greatest difficulty on visual tasks requiring sequencing and on complex motor tasks, particularly on the left side of the body. The authors concluded that the results were suggestive of cerebral impairment in the right posterior area of the brain, especially the temporo–parieto–occipital junction. As early as 1973, Money concluded that space-form dysgnosia, directional-sense dysgnosia, and impaired numerical ability implicated right parietal lobe involvement. Kolb and Heaton (1975) administered the Halstead–Reitan Neuropsychological Battery to a single adult TS patient, concluding that her average impairment index fell in the impaired range, and that the pattern of test scores was indicative of cerebral dysfunction lateralized to the right hemisphere. Others have identified the right postcentral and adjacent parietal cortex (McGlone, 1985), right cerebral cortex (Silbert et al., 1977), and the right and left parietal and frontal (Waber, 1979) as the defective areas of TS brains.

Misconceptions. Attempts to precisely define the neurocognitive phenotype of TS, including descriptions of the exact cognitive processes that are impaired and the precise area of the brain that is impeded, have failed for two reasons. First, there appears to be an underlying assumption that the identification of an exact genetic etiology, in this case an aberration involving the sex chromosomes, should result in a narrowly defined psychological phenotype. In other words, if a group of individuals demonstrate the same genetic syndrome, including signs of neurocognitive impairment, then a series of psychological studies will naturally become increasingly refined until investigators hone in on the precise genetically targeted cognitive process. Furthermore, this impaired skill should be matched to a highly localized area of the brain, because the origin of this deficit is initially a genetic/physiological aberration. Unfortunately, the assumptions here are incorrect. Genetic homogeneity does not necessarily result in phenotypic homogeneity. Genetic influences are multifactorial, and individuals with the same chromosomal lesion may have quite different phenotypes. The "reaction range" may be large because the effects of a detrimental gene or genes are being modified by other genes and by the interaction of the genotype with the environment. Although available evidence firmly establishes that Turner syndrome is associated with an increased risk for deficits involving spatial thinking, it does not necessarily follow that an exact intellectual deficit is shared by all individuals with this condition. Different TS patients may express different forms of this spatial impairment, whereas others demonstrate no spatial impairment at all. For example, we have been impressed by the observation that many parents of TS girls have been told by health professionals that their child is likely to have difficulty with mathematics. In our study of academic skills of nine TS girls, only one demonstrated a specific arithmetic problem (Bender, Puck, Salbenblatt, & Robinson, 1984). In fact, we have encountered TS girls who described math as their best subject in school. Clearly, familial tendencies and experience account for some of this variability (Bender, Linden, & Robinson, 1987). The fact that most studies examine group means, usually including a TS and control group, reflects a desire to reduce the phenotype to a single profile that can be conveniently summarized along with a few additional brief descriptors and placed in a compendium of genetic disorders as a quick and easy reference for those who wish to know what to expect of a TS patient, or how to advise parents about the prognosis of their prenatally diagnosed TS fetus. It is accurate to describe risks and tendencies encompassed in the TS phenotype, but individual differences must not be overlooked to satisfy the convenience of using group means and simple profiles.

Two well-controlled studies employing comprehensive neuropsychological batteries provide an appreciation for variability in the neurocognitive phenotype of TS. Waber (1979) evaluated 11 TS patients (13–23 years of age) along with 11 age-and verbal IQ-matched, chromosomally normal female controls. Results from the 3-h neuropsychological battery failed to identify a clear spatial ability deficit. Rather, this group of TS patients was found to have impaired visual memory, motor coordination, word fluency, and right–left discrimination, leading to the conclusion that the group as a whole was impaired in both right- and left-hemisphere functions. Pennington et al.

(1985) evaluated 10 TS subjects, all of whom had a 45,X karyotype. Controls included 20 normal age-matched controls, 12 neurological patients with right-hemisphere damage, 10 with left-hemisphere damage, and 10 with diffuse lesions. Results of the expanded Halstead–Reitan battery indicated that the TS group was more impaired than the normal controls. Only half of the TS patients demonstrated a verbal-performance discrepancy of 10 points or greater. Further, results for the TS group were not similar to the right-hemisphere damaged patients. Rather, they were most similar to the diffuse damaged neurological patients, demonstrating moderate impairment in memory, auditory processing, language fluency, attention, and concept development. In our study of nine TS girls, we have reported a large impairment in perceptual organization and fine motor skills but also some difficulty with auditory processing and memory. We concluded that TS is associated with spatial and perceptual deficits, but that other impairments may be present, and that interindividual variations are significant (Bender et al., 1984).

A second important misconception in attempts to define the neuropsychological characteristics of TS is found in the belief inherent in many of the earlier studies that a right-hemisphere-based cognitive impairment in TS subjects reflects a process comparable to patients with known right-hemisphere damage or lesion. Autopsies performed on TS patients have revealed no consistent neuroanatomic finding (Brun & Skold, 1968; Reske-Nielsen, Christensen, & Nielsen, 1982). Both Waber (1979) and Rovet and Netley (1982) argued that neurocognitive impairment in TS patients may be best understood as an alteration in normal brain development rather than a localized area of damage waiting to be discovered. The neurodevelopmental explanation of Rovet and Netley argues that the verbal functioning, primarily located in the left hemisphere in normal women, is more diffusely distributed between the right and left hemispheres in women with TS. As a result, the right hemispheres do not develop a specialized capacity to process nonverbal information. Thus, although most TS individuals may experience a disruption in maturation and specialization of the cerebral hemispheres, individual expression of that disrupted process in the from of cognitive ability patterns can vary across individual subjects. This neurodevelopmental view is consistent with the laterality studies, reviewed previously, which show disruption of the relationship of left- and right-hemispheric specialization in TS subjects.

The Neurodevelopmental Model. The neurodevelopmental approach accounts for both the tendency toward spatial impairment/right-hemisphere involvement as well as individual variability observed in most studies. In addition, it allows for speculation as to the biological processes responsible for interruption of the maturational process. Two different theories have emerged to explain how the developing nervous system is affected by TS.

Polani (1977) and Barlow (1973) promoted the hypothesis that the absence of an X chromosome in the cell shortens the cell cycle thus accelerating the rate of cell division. This increased rate of cell division subsequently alters the rate of brain growth. Netley (1977) advanced this theory to explain that disruption of normal critical periods during which the hemispheres develop their specialized capacities for information processing accounts for the atypical lateral specialization and cognitive impairments found among TS patients. In other words, despite short stature, the brains of TS girls may be developing faster than those of chromosomally normal girls. Early maturing, normal adolescents demonstrate less cerebral lateralization than do late maturers (Waber, 1976). Rovet and Netley (1982) noted additionally that children with delayed growth have verbal but not spatial deficits, concluding that the rate of brain growth affects the development of normal cerebral lateralization for cognitive processing, and that alterations of this process in TS girls may account for their atypical lateralization and relatively poor performance on spatial thinking tasks.

The Role of Sex Hormones. An alternative underlying biological mechanism that may account for atypical brain and ability development in Turner syndrome patients recognizes that abnormal hormone levels in TS patients may play a significant role. The hormone-behavior relationship begins during prenatal development and infancy, when early exposure to gonadal steroids can alter behavior and ability (Williams, Barnet, & Meck, 1990). Thus, in the case of TS, the presence of atypical hormone levels, pre- and postnatally, may significantly impact hemispheric specialization. Although the hormonal etiology theory is an alternative to the cell growth-rate theory, both share the presumption that the search for mechanisms underlying the cognitive impairments of TS patients will result not in the discovery of marked structural brain abnormalities, but rather a less anatomically distinct alteration in neurodevelopment with the possible result that the right cerebral hemisphere is less specialized for spatial thinking and shares with the left hemisphere more responsibility for language processing than found in eukaryotic individuals.

In conclusion, neurocognitive studies of TS individuals have identified a tendency toward difficulty with spatial thinking. However, the neurocognitive phenotype is much more heterogeneous than was once assumed. Some TS patients have been found to have difficulty with memory and language processing, whereas others demonstrate no deficits and may excel at intellectual tasks, including mathematics. It must be concluded that, although TS brings a neurologically mediated risk for neurocognitive impairment, a host of other factors, both genetic and environmental, dictate the degree to which this neurocognitive phenotype will be expressed. Although no consensus has been reached as to the biological mechanisms by which the neurocognitive phenotype is expressed, most investigators now agree that the neurological impact of TS is best viewed as a process subtly affecting neurological development and hemispheric specialization, rather than an anatomically identifiable abnormality similar to a brain lesion. Altered cell growth rate and atypical hormone levels are two biological mechanisms that have been theorized to deliver the impact of TS on the developing brain. Limited evidence is yet available to adequately evaluate the validity of either theory.

TS and the Normal Development of Cognitive Skills.   Turner syndrome, as with other disorders altering the individual's neurodevelopment, can add understanding to development of cognition, particularly spatial thinking, in chromosomally normal children. As information becomes available, it may be possible to more specifically identify the biological mediators responsible for below-average development of spatial thinking skills in TS girls and, in turn, the development of these skills in other children. Because spatial thinking is different in boys and girls (Semrud-Clikeman & Hynd, 1990), the unraveling of spatial thinking impairment in TS subjects also offers the promise of clarifying the source of these sex differences. As has already been noted, the possibility that impaired spatial thinking results from altered cell-division rates supports a limited literature suggesting that normal sex differences in the development of spatial and verbal abilities are the result of different rates of brain growth and cerebral organization in boys and girls (Waber, 1976). Insufficient information is available to determine whether decreased levels of sex hormones in TS girls are associated with defects in spatial information processing. However, several studies in progress are evaluating the effectiveness of hormone therapies to increase growth in TS girls; a secondary benefit of these investigations is the opportunity to assess whether such therapies change patterns of cognitive abilities in TS girls. The identification of decreasing cognitive deficits following hormone treatments may provide additional evidence of the roles of various sex hormones in brain development and function. Finally, as is seen in the next section, attempts to establish a relationship between deficits in social cognition and impeded social interaction in TS girls adds to a growing literature demonstrating an important relationship between cognition and social behavior in both normal and atypical populations.

Methodological Problems.   McCauley (1990) noted several methodological problems that impede our ability to draw clear conclusions from the TS literature. First, the manner in which TS samples are recruited for research studies varies greatly. Selection bias is particularly a problem where TS samples include patients obtained from medical centers and endocrinology clinics, as the most accessible research patients may also be those having a history of greatest physical and psychological complications related to their condition. Sampling problems also occur as a result of the utilization of TS patients with varying karyotypes, including partial deletions of the X chromosome as well as mosaicism. Thus, although patients with varying karyotypes may be grouped with the observation that they have similar physical stigmata, it is not so clear that they share homogeneous alterations in their neurological system. Second, McCauley emphasized that the presence of physical anomalies associated with TS can significantly impact on psychological, and perhaps neurocognitive, development. To the degree that TS patients are treated differently, and see themselves as different from other individuals, their developmental psychological experience may influence their self-perceptions, confidence, and drive toward particular tasks and challenges. A third methodological criticism was offered by Rovet (1990) who noted an inadequacy of controls for age, verbal IQ, socioeconomic status, race, ethnicity, growth retardation, or family membership. Each control group was accompanied by various advantages and disadvantages, leading in some cases to quite varied conclusions. In short, the variety of conclusions, sometimes conflicting, gathered throughout the TS literature may reflect methodological variations in these studies, including distinctly different TS patient samples as well as distinctly different control groups. As is seen in the next section, these methodological issues are significant to psychosocial as well as neurocognitive studies.

PSYCHOSOCIAL PHENOTYPE

Attempts to characterize the psychological development and features associated with TS have been as varied as attempts to study neurocognitive characteristics. Interest in the psychological phenotype of TS, as with other conditions involving sex chromosome abnormalities, grew rapidly as advances in laboratory technology made possible the inspection of the human chromosomes under a microscope. Although the more sophisticated and precise banding techniques allowing for clear inspection of chromosome structure did not evolve until 1970, the early buccal smear followed by confirming karyotype permitted the identification of an abnormal number of X chromosomes. Furthermore, this quick and simple technique could be employed with large numbers of individuals in a relatively short amount of time. Therefore, investigators began to apply this technique to screen the chromosomes of deviant populations in order to determine whether sex chromosome abnormalities were associated with aberrant human behavior. As a result of chromosome screening in penal and mental institutions in the United States and Europe in the early 1960s, it was determined that the incidence of 45,XXY men and 47,XXX women among mentally retarded or psychotic populations was four to five times increased relative to the general population of chromosomally normal individuals. For 47,XYY men a 4-fold increase was found in penal institutions, jumping dramatically to a 20-fold increase in combined mental-penal populations (Hook, 1979). These studies failed to allow an appreciation for the large number of sex chromosome aneuploidy individuals with relatively normal behavior and led to a series of stereotypes of extreme aberration among men and women with an additional X or Y chromosome. At the same time, the relative absence of TS women in these screening studies led to the stereotype that psychiatric problems and aberrant behavior were not a problem for TS women (Polani, 1977).

McCauley (1990) identified 21 investigations of social and emotional development in TS women, aside from individual case reports. More such studies have been conducted among TS individuals than other groups with sex chromosome abnormalities (SCAs) largely because Turner syndrome is associated with a distinct physical phenotype, whereas the remaining SCA conditions include much more subtle physical features. It follows that TS propositae are generally identified early in life, and hence are more available to study than the remaining SCA propositi, many of whom are never diagnosed.

Psychiatric Disturbance in TS.   Aside from the psychiatric- and the penal institution-screening studies, a number of investigations have attempted to determine whether an increased incidence of psychiatric disturbance can be found in the TS population. A number of case reports have described anorexia nervosa, depression, and schizophrenia in TS women (Darby, Garfinkel, Vale, Kirwan, & Brown, 1981; Halmi & DeBault, 1974; Raft, Spencer & Toomey, 1976; Sabbath, Morris, Menzer-Benaron, Sturgis, 1961). Berch and McCauley (1990) reviewed 11 cases of anorexia nervosa in Turner syndrome women. Although the unusual physical appearance of some TS women may place them at risk for anorexia nervosa, reflecting extreme concerns about body image, both Berch and McCauley and Darby et al. concluded that anorexia nervosa remains relatively uncommon in the TS population.

Four large-scale studies have examined the incidence and specificity of psychopathology among TS women. Money and Mittenthal (1970) reviewed interviews with 68 TS patients, finding only 3 with "severe" psychopathology and an additional 6 with evidence of "mild" psychopathology. They concluded that psychopathology was most likely to occur in the presence of distinct parental psychopathology, and inappropriate relationships between parents and their daughters including rejection or overprotectiveness of the proposita. Nielsen, Nyborg, and Dahl (1977) conducted a study in Denmark of 45 TS patients ranging in age from 7 to 39 years. They identified five TS patients and one control with significant psychopathology, again concluding that stressful family environments had contributed significantly to the psychopathology in these patients. In a study of 49 TS patients in Finland, ranging in age from 9 to 22 years, Taipale (1979) found evidence of "severe" psychopathology in 4 patients. These investigators concluded that the presence of psychopathology in all four was associated with the lack of pubertal development and absence of hormonal replacement treatment. In another and larger Danish study, Nielsen and Sillesen (1981) reviewed interviews and records of 103 TS patients, 7 to 24 years of age. None of the 103 propositae had histories that included psychiatric treatment.

Evidence from multiple studies supports the conclusion that significant psychopathology is not increased among TS girls and women. A few psychological studies have even described strengths in the TS group that exceed those in the control group. For example, Money and Mittenthal (1970) and Baekgaard, Nyborg, and Nielsen (1978) each evaluated groups of TS women and found them to have unusually high stress tolerance. McCauley (1990) reviewed nine studies in which TS women demonstrated clear and unambiguous female gender identification, strong heterosexual orientation, and a tendency to follow "traditional" patterns of female goals and behavior. Results from these selected studies provide an optimistic picture of the psychological development of TS girls and women that is unsupported by most available data. Growing up with TS certainly brings psychological stress and impacts significantly on self-perceptions and inter-personal relationships. Although the conclusion that TS women are not prone to severe psychiatric disturbance appears to have general agreement (Berch & McCauley, 1990; McCauley, 1990), these individuals are clearly at risk for problems in their psychosocial adaptation.

Psychosocial Adaptation.   As noted in the preceding section, many TS women have been found to have a strong and sometimes stereotyped female gender identification. Although sexual drive is also of a heterosexual orien-tation (Garron & Vander Stoep, 1969), problems around sexual functioning have been observed. Thus, "normal" sexual and romantic fantasies are common among TS women (Hampson, Hampson, & Money, 1955; Money & Mittenthal, 1970), but TS girls tend to date later than peers (Senzer et al., 1973), have lower sex drive (Garron & Vander Stoep, 1969), have sex later and less often than chromosomally normal controls (Nielsen et al., 1977), and are less likely to have significant heterosexual relationships or to become married (Hampson et al., 1955; Nielsen et al., 1977). In short, although TS women generally have a clear heterosexual orientation, they are less likely than chromosomally normal controls to date, to develop significant romantic relationships, or to enjoy satisfactory sexual relationships.

There is evidence of other difficulties in the psychosocial adaptation of TS women. In their interviews with 86 TS women, Nielsen and Sillesen (1981) described the majority of their sample as having fairly adequate psychological functioning but some evidence of immaturity. Twenty-three of the girls (just under a third of the sample) had behavioral difficulties that indicated insecurity, shyness, and excessive sensitivity. Shaffer (1962) utilized the Minnesota Multiphasic Personality Inventory and the Guilford–Zimmerman Temperament Survey to evaluate 13 TS subjects, 13–23 years of age. Tests results indicated low energy, nonreactive personality style, and somewhat overcooperative behavior. Money and Mittenthal (1970) similarly documented unassertive and overcompliant behavior in 73 TS patients. McCauley, Sybert, and Ehrhardt (1986) evaluated 27 TS women but no controls. Results from the psychiatric interviews indicated decreased self-esteem and increased symptoms of anxiety and depression.

Several investigators have described age-related difficulties in the psychosocial adaptation of TS. Rothchild and Owens (1972) studied TS patients in two age groupings (9–14 years old and 17–29 years old). The younger subjects demonstrated immaturity and muting of affect, whereas the older subjects, who had received hormone treatments, were described as somewhat more mature but with diminished heterosexual activity and a limited capacity to understand nuances in social interactions. Studying 16 TS girls, 6–16 years of age, Sonis et al. (1983) found increased activity level and difficulty with concentration in 6-to 11-year-old TS girls, in contrast to more anxious, depressed, and social withdrawal behavior in the older girls. Similarly, Rovet (1986) evaluated 29 girls, age 7–16 years, with a series of psychological questionnaires. She concluded that the younger girls (age 11 years and younger) tended to be more distracted and hyperactive, whereas the older girls tended to be more anxious.

In summary, although TS propositae demonstrate a relatively low incidence of psychopathology, problems in their psychosocial adaptation have been identified, which include social immaturity and overcompliance. The etiology of their psychosocial problems is less clear. Reluctance, overcompliance, and social immaturity can be attributed either to the direct effect of the missing chromosome upon developing behavior and personality, or to the secondary effects of appearing different physically and feeling inferior to other girls and women. Recognizing the difficulty of making this discrimination, several investigators have attempted to utilize control groups other than physically and chromosomally normal women. For instance, Nielsen et al. (1977) utilized 15 short-stature, amenorrheic women as one control group, with a second control group consisting of 46 chromosomally normal sisters of TS women. They found that both the short-stature controls and the TS women were less likely to live independently from parents than were the unaffected sister control group, leading to the conclusion that short stature and delayed sexual development may have been major contributing factors impeding the psychosocial development of TS women. Holmes, Karlsson, and Thompson (1985) similarly found social withdrawal in all three groups of short girls studied, including 9 girls with TS, 17 short-stature girls with growth hormone deficiency, and 21 short-stature girls with constitutional delay. The TS group differed from the other two only in their tendency to have greater academic difficulty. In contrast to these two investigations, other studies have reported differences between TS women and short-stature controls. Baekgaard et al. (1978) employed three control groups, one consisting of sisters of the TS propositae, 9 women with short stature and amenorrhea but no chromosomal anomaly, and 19 nurses. The TS women were found to have lower scores on the neuroticism scale of the Maudsley Personality Inventory and elevated scores on the extroversion scale. Furthermore, there were karyotype-related differences among the TS women. Those with a pure 45,X karyotype were found to have limited emotional arousal, and as noted earlier, unusually high stress tolerance. In another study with short-stature controls conducted by McCauley, Ito, and Kay (1986), 17 Turner syndrome and 16 short-stature female controls completed a detailed psychological evaluation that included clinical interviews and a series of self-report instruments. The investigators reported that the Turner syndrome subjects, all of whom were 17 years of age or younger, had fewer friends, were more immature and socially isolated, and had more difficulty completing tasks than did the short-stature controls. In a study of 23 TS women, Downey, Ehrhardt, Morishima, Bell, and Gruen (1987) included 23 controls with constitutional short stature matched with the TS group for age, socioeconomic status, IQ, and marital status, along with a second control group consisting of 10 normal sisters of the TS women. Results from the psychological interviews indicated greater stereotypic feminine behavior, and a tendency to express less anger in the TS group relative to the two control groups.

Taken together, the studies utilizing short-stature controls present a varied picture of TS women and do not allow an easy interpretation of the degree to which the difficulties with psychosocial adaptation are attributable to the short stature of TS girls and women. Our review of the evidence suggests that short stature does indeed hamper psychosocial adaptation in this group, but we cannot conclude that short stature alone accounts for emotional and behavioral problems in these propositae. The employment of short-stature controls is a methodological innovation that provides some insight into the origin of psychosocial difficulties. However, it must be recognized that TS girls and women experience psychological burdens related to their physical phenotype aside from short stature. Other dysmorphology, including unusual facies and webbing of the neck, certainly impede the development of self-esteem. Furthermore, the threat of ongoing medical problems, some of which may require surgical intervention, along with knowledge of one's own infertility, increase the developmental burden in this group.

Social Cognition.   Evidence from a large number of studies reviewed earlier has indicated an increased difficulty in psychosocial adaptation among TS women that can be globally characterized as social immaturity. Two potential sources of difficulty in the behavioral adaptation of TS women have been identified and include the direct influence of the missing chromosome or the secondary influence of short stature and related physical and medical anomalies. Recently, a third possible explanation for the social shortcomings of TS women has been proffered. Specifically, investigators have begun to question whether a relationship exists between the neurocognitive impairments and the social impairments experienced by this group.

The hypothesis that cognitive deficits may underlie the social immaturity of TS women begins with the recognition of the role of right-hemisphere functions in social interactions. Semrud-Clikeman and Hynd (1990) recently reviewed studies of nonverbal learning disabilities and right-hemisphere dysfunction, concluding that there is considerable evidence that the right hemisphere plays an important role in social behavior. Individuals with right-hemisphere dysfunction and nonverbal learning disabilities frequently have difficulty perceiving and understanding subtle social cues, with the result that they fail to appreciate nuances of facial expression and gestures, and often cannot anticipate and respond appropriately to the many small behavioral signals around which social relationships are organized. As a result, these individuals often have difficulty developing and maintaining a network of mutually satisfying social relationships. In the case of TS, we have seen evidence of both diminished social adaptation and impairment of nonverbal skills, but is there any direct evidence that the two are linked?

A study by McCauley and colleagues (McCauley, Kay, Ito, & Treder, 1987) was designed to address directly the question of social cognition in TS. Seventeen TS girls, ages 9–17 years, participated in this study along with 17 short-stature control girls comparable in age, height, weight, verbal IQ, and family socioeconomic status. Intellectual skills of all subjects were evaluated, and parents completed a number of questionnaires evaluating social behavior and psychological adaptation. The focal dependent measure was the Affective Discrimination Task, consisting of a series of 40 videotaped facial expressions. After viewing each facial vignette, the subject was required to determine whether the facial message was to "come closer" (positive affective intent) or to "go away" (negative affective intent). The segments were dichotimized and balanced such that half the facial expressions were positive and half negative, half male and half female, and half clear (low ambiguity) and half somewhat vague (high ambiguity).

When the results of these evaluations were analyzed, the Turner syndrome girls were found to have performed more poorly than the short-stature controls on measures of nonverbal and visual motor skills. Parent questionnaires revealed immature, inadequate social relationships among propositae. On the Affective Discrimination Task, the TS group was significantly less accurate at reading facial affect, although mean differences were not large. Level of ambiguity, type of affect, or gender of video subject produced no group differences. Secondary analyses indicated that completion of the Affect Discrimination Task did not significantly covary with spatial, attention, or memory skills, although it was associated with parents' ratings of social skills. The authors concluded that impaired ability to discriminate facial affect among TS girls is not simply secondary to weak perceptual problem-solving or attention/memory skills, but represents yet another area of diminished cognition that may underlie their psychosocial difficulties.

SUMMARY

Neurocognitive and psychosocial phenotypes of TS are identifiable but not homogeneous. Girls and women with TS are at increased risk for diminished intellectual ability, often involving specific deficits of spatial thinking and related skills. Neurocognitive deficits in TS are not exclusive to nonverbal abilities, and at times have been reported to include memory, verbal, and conceptual skills. In general, the pattern of neurocognitive deficits suggests difficulty with information processing usually occurring in the right hemisphere. Models of neurodevelopment and atypical hemispheric specialization are more compatible with the available data than those presuming that specific sites of damage can be found in the brains of these propositae. The biological mechanisms that underlie this neurological development are not known, but may include inadequate exposure of the developing brain to sex hormones or alteration in the brain's rate of growth caused by alteration in rate of cell division.

Psychopathology is not a defining component of the psychosocial phenotype. Female gender identity appears well established in the majority of TS women, to the point at times of stereotypic pursuit of feminine roles. Although psychiatric disturbance is not common, problems in psychosocial adaptation are increased and characterized by social immaturity and insecurity. Young TS girls may demonstrate hyperactivity, whereas in adolescence mood problems including symptoms of anxiety and depression may emerge. Whether the absence of all or part of an X chromosome dictate personality patterns and behavior changes is unknown. Most likely, some portion of the psychosocial difficulty of TS women may be attributable to the burden of growing up with this syndrome. TS individuals have been found to experience emotional and social problems not shared by short-stature controls. Beyond the effect of short stature, difficulties in their physical and sexual development, along with their variably abnormal appearance, likely impacts significantly on self-perception and confidence. Recent evidence from one study indicates that the social and cognitive problems of TS women may be linked. Diminished ability to "read" facial affect, and perhaps other subtle social cues, may contribute to impaired social competence.

Finally, we note that the TS neurocognitive and psychosocial phenotypes include considerable variability. Not every proposita fits the mold suggested by group means and a search for "typical" or "classical" characteristics. Further investigations of this syndrome will likely help clarify the nature of TS development and the biological mechanisms altering developmental outcome, but are unlikely to uncover homogeneous characteristics of the psychological phenotype. Some women with TS will demonstrate strong math skills, easily develop friendships, and enjoy a satisfying heterosexual relationship. Sensitivity to psychological risks as well as individual variability are essential to counseling of TS girls and their parents, as well as to parents with a prenatally diagnosed fetus with X or partial X monosomy.

ACKNOWLEDGMENTS

This study was supported, in part, by United States Public Health Services Grant 5R01-HD10032; Grant RR-69 from the General Clinical Research Centers Program of the Division of Research Resources, National Institutes of Health; and The Genetic Foundation.

REFERENCES

Alexander, D., Ehrhardt, A., & Money, J. (1966). Defective figure drawing, geometric and human, in Turner's syndrome. *Journal of Nervous and Mental Disease, 142*, 161.

Alexander, D., & Money, J. (1966). Turner's syndrome and Gerstmann's syndrome: Neuropsychologic comparisons. *Neuropsychologia, 4*, 165–273.

Alexander, D., Walker, H. T., & Money, J. (1964). Studies in direction sense. *Archives of General Psychiatry, 10*, 337–339.

Baekgaard, W., Nyborg, H., & Nielsen, J. (1978). Neuroticism and extroversion in Turner's syndrome. *Journal of Abnormal Psychology, 87*, 583–586.

Barlow, D. (1973). The influence of inactive chromosomes on human development. *Humangenetik, 17*, 105–136.

Bender, B., Linden, M., & Robinson, A. (1987). Environment and developmental risk in children with sex chromosome abnormalities. *Journal of the American Academy of Child Psychiatry, 26*, 499–503.

Bender, B., Puck, M., Salbenblatt, J., & Robinson, A. (1984). Cognitive development of unselected girls with complete and partial X monosomy. *Pediatrics, 73*, 175–182.

Berch, D. B., & Kirkendall, K. L. (1986, May). *Spatial information processing in 45,X children*. Paper presented at the meeting of the American Association for the Advancement of Science, Philadelphia.

Berch, D., & McCauley, E. (1990). Psychosocial functioning of individuals with sex chromosome abnormalities. In C. S. Holmes (Ed.), *Psychoneuroendocrinology: Brain, behavior, and hormonal interactions* (pp. 164–183). New York: Springer-Verlag.

Brun, A., & Skold, G. (1968). CNS malformations in Turner's syndrome: An integral part of the syndrome? *Acta Neuropathologica, 10*, 159–161.

Christensen, A. L., & Nielsen, J. (1981). Neuropsychological investigation in 17 women with

Turner's syndrome. In W. Schmid & J. Nielsen (Eds.), *Human behavior and genetics* (pp. 151–166). Amsterdam, Netherlands: Elsevier/North Holland Biomedical Press.

Cohen, H. (1962). Psychological test findings in adolescents having ovarian dysgenesis. *Psychosomatic Medicine, 24*, 249–256.

Darby, P. L., Garfinkel, P. E., Vale, J. M., Kirwan, P. J., & Brown, G. M. (1981). Anorexia nervosa and Turner syndrome: Cause or coincidence? *Psychological Medicine, 11*, 141–145.

Downey, J., Ehrhardt, A. A., Morishima, A., Bell, J. J., & Gruen, R. (1987). Gender role development in two clinical syndromes: Turner syndrome versus constitutional short stature. *Journal of the American Academy of Child and Adolescent Psychiatry, 26*(4), 566–573.

Garron, D. C. (1977). Intelligence among persons with Turner's syndrome. *Behavior Genetics, 7*, 105–127.

Garron, D. C., & Vander Stoep, L. R. (1969). Personality and intelligence in Turner's syndrome. *Archives of General Psychiatry, 21*, 339–346.

Gordon, H., & Galatzer, A. (1980). Cerebral organization in patients with gonadal dysgenesis. *Psychoneuroendocrinology, 5*, 235–244.

Grumbach, M. M., Van Wyck, J. J., & Wilkins, L. (1955). Chromosomal sex in gonadal dysgenesis relationship to male pseudohermaphroditism and theories of human sex differentiation. *Journal of Clinical Endocrinology, 15*, 1161–1193.

Haddad, H. M., & Wilkins, L. (1959). Congenital anomalies associated with gonadal aplasia: Review of 55 cases. *Pediatrics, 23*, 885–902.

Halmi, K. A., & DeBault, L. E. (1974). Gonosomal aneuploidy in anorexia nervosa. *American Journal of Genetics, 26*, 195–198.

Hampson, J. L., Hampson, J. C., & Money, J. (1955). The syndrome of gonadal agenesis (ovarian agenesis) and male chromosomal pattern in girls and women: Psychologic studies. *Bulletin of Johns Hopkins Hospital, 97*, 207–226.

Holmes, C. S., Karlsson, J. A., & Thompson, R. G. (1985). Social and school competencies in children with short stature: Longitudinal patterns. *Developmental and Behavioral Pediatrics, 6*, 263–267.

Hook, E. B. (1979). Extra sex chromosomes and human behavior: The nature of the evidence regarding XYY, XXY, XXYY, and XXX genotypes. In H. L. Vallet & I. Y. Porter (Eds.), *Genetic aspects of sexual differentiation* (pp. 437–463). New York: Academic.

Hook, E. B., & Warburton, D. (1983). The distribution of chromosomal genotypes associated with Turner's syndrome: Livebirth prevalence rates and evidence for diminished fetal mortality and severity in genotypes associated with structural X abnormalities or mosaicism. *Human Genetics, 64*, 24–27.

Kolb, J. E., & Heaton, R. K. (1975). Lateralized neurological deficits and psychopathology in a Turner syndrome patient. *Archives of General Psychiatry, 32*, 1198–1200.

Lewandowski, L., Costenbader, V., & Richman, R. (1985). Neuropsychological aspects of Turner's syndrome. *International Journal of Clinical Neuropsychology, 7*, 144–149.

McCauley, E. (1990). Psychosocial and emotional aspects of Turner syndrome. In D. Berch & B. Bender (Eds.), *Sex chromosome abnormalities and human behavior: Psychological studies* (pp. 78–99). Boulder, CO: Western Press & the American Association for the Advancement of Science.

McCauley, E., Ito, J., & Kay, T. (1986). Psychosocial functioning in girls with the Turner syndrome and short stature. *Journal of the American Academy of Child Psychiatry, 25*, 105–112.

McCauley, E., Kay, T., Ito, J., & Treder, R. (1987). The Turner syndrome: Cognitive deficits, affective discrimination, and behavior problems. *Child Development, 58*, 464–473.

McCauley, E., Sybert, V., & Ehrhardt, A. A. (1986). Psychosocial adjustment of adult women with Turner syndrome. *Clinical Genetics, 29*, 284–290.

McGlone, J. (1985). Can spatial deficits in Turner's syndrome be explained by focal CNS dysfunction or atypical speech lateralization? *Journal of Clinical and Experimental Neuropsychology, 7*, 375–394.

Money, J. (1973). Turner's syndrome and parietal lobe functions. *Cortex, 9*, 385–393.

Money, J., & Alexander, D. (1966). Turner's syndrome: Further demonstration of the presence of specific cognitional deficiencies. *Journal of Medical Genetics, 3*, 47–48.

Money, J., & Granoff, D. (1965). IQ and the somatic stigmata of Turner's syndrome. *American Journal of Mental Deficiency, 70*, 69–77.

Money, J., & Mittenthal, S. (1970). Lack of personality pathology in Turner syndrome: Relations to cytogenetics, hormones and physique. *Behavior Genetics, 1*, 43–56.

Netley, C. (1977). Dichotic listening of callosal agenesis and Turner's syndrome. *Language Development and Neurological Theory, 11*, 133–143.

Nielsen, J., Nyborg, H., & Dahl, G. (1977). Turner's syndrome. *Acta Jutlandica, XLV, 1*, 190.

Nielsen, J., & Sillesen, I. (1981). Turner's syndrome in 115 Danish girls born between 1955 and 1966. *Acta Jutlandica, LIV*, Medicine Series 22, Arhus.

Pennington, B. F., Bender, B., Puck, M., Salbenblatt, J., & Robinson, A. (1982). Learning disabilities in children with sex chromosome anomalies. *Child Development, 53*, 1182–1192.

Pennington, B. F., Heaton, R. K., Karzmark, P., Pendleton, M. G., Lehman, R., & Shucard, D. W. (1985). The neuropsychological phenotype in Turner syndrome. *Cortex, 21*, 391–404.

Polani, P. E. (1961). Turner's syndrome and allied conditions. *British Medical Bulletin, 17*, 200–205.

Polani, P. E. (1977). Abnormal sex chromosomes, behavior and mental disorder. In J. Tanner (Ed.), *Developments in psychiatric research* (pp. 89–128). London: Hodder & Stoughton.

Raft, D., Spencer, R. F., & Toomey, T. C. (1976). Ambiguity of gender identity fantasies and aspects of normality and pathology in hypopituitary dwarfism and Turner's syndrome: Three cases. *Journal of Sex Research, 12*, 161–172.

Reske-Nielsen, E., Christensen, A. L., & Nielsen, J. (1982). A neuropathological and neuropsychological study of Turner's syndrome. *Cortex, 18*, 181–190.

Rothchild, E., & Owens, R. P. (1972). Adolescent girls who lack functioning ovaries. *Journal of the American Academy of Child Psychiatry, 11*, 88–113.

Rovet, J. (1986, May). *Processing deficits in 45,X females.* Paper presented at the annual meeting of the American Association for the Advancement of Science, Philadelphia.

Rovet, J. (1990). The cognitive and neuropsychological characteristics of females with Turner syndrome. In D. Berch & B. Bender (Eds.), *Sex chromosome abnormalities and human behavior: Psychological studies* (pp. 38–77). Boulder, CO: Western Press & the American Association for the Advancement of Science.

Rovet, J., & Netley, C. (1980). The mental rotation task performance of Turner syndrome subjects. *Behavior Genetics, 10*, 437–443.

Rovet, J., & Netley, C. (1982). Processing deficits in Turner's syndrome. *Developmental Psychology, 18*, 77–94.

Sabbath, J. C., Morris, T. A., Menzer-Benaron, D., & Sturgis, S. H. (1961). Psychiatric observation in the adolescent girls lacking ovarian function. *Psychosomatic Medicine, 23*, 224–231.

Semrud-Clikeman, M., & Hynd, G. W. (1990). Right hemispheric dysfunction in nonverbal learning disabilities: Social, academic, and adaptive functioning in adults and children. *Psychological Bulletin, 107*, 196–209.

Senzer, N., Aceto, T., Cohen, M. M., Ehrhardt, A. A., Abbassi, V., & Capraro, V. J. (1973). Isochromosome X. *American Journal of Diseases of Children, 126*, 312–316.

Shaffer, J. (1962). A specific cognitive deficit observed on gonadol aplasia (Turner's syndrome). *Journal of Clinical Psychology, 18*, 403–406.

Shepard, R. N., & Metzler, J. (1971). Mental rotation of three-dimensional objects. *Science, 171*, 701–702.

Silbert, A., Wolff, P., & Lilienthal, J. (1977). Spatial and temporal processing in patients with Turner's syndrome. *Behavior Genetics, 7*, 11–21.

Sonis, W. A., Levine-Ross, J., Blue, J., Cutler, G. B., Loriaux, P. L., & Klein, R. P. (1983,

October). *Hyperactivity of Turner's syndrome*. Paper presented at the meeting of the American Academy of Child Psychiatry, San Francisco.

Taipale, V. (1979). *Adolescence in Turner's syndrome*. Monograph from Children's Hospital, University of Helsinki, Helsinki.

Todd, J., Coolidge, F., & Satz, P. (1977). The Wechsler Adult Intelligence Scale discrepancy index: A neuropsychological evaluation. *Journal of Consulting and Clinical Psychology, 45,* 450–454.

Waber, D. P. (1976). Sex differences in cognition: A function of maturation rate? *Science, 192,* 572–574.

Waber, D. P. (1979). Neuropsychological aspects of Turner syndrome. *Developmental Medicine and Child Neurology, 21,* 58–70.

Williams, C. L., Barnett, A. M., & Meck, W. H. (1990). Organizational effects of early gonadal secretions on sexual differentiation in spatial memory. *Behavioral Neuroscience, 104,* 84–97.

Event-Related Potential Indications of Altered Brain Development in Turner Syndrome

Ray Johnson, Jr.
National Institute of Neurological Disorders and Stroke,
National Institutes of Health

Judith L. Ross
The Medical College of Pennsylvania

The role of sex hormones in normal brain development, including hemispheric specialization, remains largely undetermined. Studies of subjects with Turner syndrome (TS) can provide unique information on this question because one distinguishing characteristic of TS females is that they are hypogonadal and therefore lack the capability to produce estrogen. Not surprisingly, given the potential for demonstrating a link between genetic, sex-linked characteristics and cognition, researchers have shown considerable interest in studying TS subjects. Nevertheless, it is still unknown whether the cognitive deficits seen in TS are due to functional differences induced by the absence of circulating hormones, to congenital differences, or to some combination of both these factors.

Turner syndrome is a genetic disorder that is characterized by a variety of somatic (e.g., short stature, webbing of the neck, congenital heart defects, lack of secondary sex characteristics) and cognitive deficiencies (chapters 9 & 10 of this volume). Although females with TS typically have normal verbal IQs, they consistently show selective impairments in the types of tasks that are included in tests of performance IQ (for reviews, see Rovet, 1990, and Chapter 10 of this volume). Although the descriptions of the specific deficits in TS have varied somewhat across studies, possibly due to the small numbers of subjects in each, some deficits have been found consistently. For example, most reports present clear evidence of impairments in TS females' performance in spatial rotation (e.g., Rovet & Netley, 1980, 1982) and left–right discrimination tasks (e.g., Alexander & Money, 1966; Alexander, Walker, & Money, 1964; Waber, 1979). Other studies have described processing deficits in visuospatial memory, visual-motor coordination, and motor learning (Lewandowski, Costenbader, & Richman, 1985; Silbert, Wolff, & Lilienthal, 1977; Waber, 1979). Females with TS also have been shown to have significantly slower motor responses than matched controls (Lewandowski et al., 1985; Rovet & Netley, 1980, 1982), a finding that is probably responsible for at least part of the reduced performance IQ scores in this group. It should be noted that virtually all researchers agree that the cognitive deficits observed in TS subjects are selective in nature and not part of some more generalized mental deficiency. For example, scores on tests of verbal ability fall into the normal range in TS females.

Based on their deficient spatial abilities, Money (1973) suggested that TS females have a parietal lobe anomaly related to their chromosomal defect. Although the findings from some subsequent studies have supported the notion of a right-hemisphere-based deficit (Silbert et al., 1977), others have argued for left-hemisphere involvement (Lewandowski et al., 1985; McGlone, 1985; Waber, 1979). The available histological data provide little additional information (Reske-Nielsen, Christensen, & Nielsen, 1982), so the neurological basis of the processing impairments documented in TS remains unknown.

Despite this neuropsychological characterization of TS, it has been difficult in practice to identify the source and/or the relative contributions of different sources to the cognitive deficits (e.g., perceptual vs. cognitive). The slowed motor responses of TS females further complicates the picture by adding another layer of altered processing that must be differentiated from possible deficits in earlier stages. The fact that the event-related brain potential (ERP) can provide simultaneously information on the timing and activation of processing stages at a variety of levels makes it an ideal measure for disentangling the relative contributions of different processing stages to the overall deficit. In this chapter, we present results from a study using both ERP and behavioral measures that was intended to shed light on the nature of the processing deficits in TS females.

BACKGROUND

It is now well established that the ERP can be used to index changes in the extent and timing of information processing activities (see Johnson 1986, 1988, for reviews). This has led to its use in, among other cases, characterizing information-processing activities across the entire lifespan, both in normal subjects and in patients with neurobehavioral disorders (see Bashore, 1990, & Friedman, 1991 for reviews). In addition to those described in this volume (chapters 4 & 6), numerous studies have documented the changes in ERP component amplitudes and/or latencies during the course of normal development (e.g., Johnson, 1989b) and in developmental disorders such as dyslexia (e.g., Taylor & Keenan, 1990), hyperactivity (e.g., Satterfield, Schell, Nicholas, & Backs, 1988), and others (see Johnson, Rohrbaugh, & Parasuraman, 1987).

The majority of these studies have focused on changes to the cognitive, P300, component of the ERP. However, by quantifying a larger number of ERP components, it is possible to determine the approximate stage in the series of steps between sense organ and consciousness that the processing deficits actually occur (see Johnson, 1992, e.g.). By combining information on ERP component's amplitude and scalp distribution, the functional and anatomical divisions of the underlying cognitive processes can be characterized. When component latency information, with its millisecond resolution, is added to the functional and anatomical characterization of the component, it is possible to infer the processes that occur serially and those that occur in parallel. ERP activity in subjects with any kind of motor slowing can be particularly informative because the timing and occurrence of most ERP components, including the P300, is almost entirely independent of response selection and execution processes. Using ERP component latencies in combination with response times (RTs) can, therefore, provide a detailed picture of the relative contributions of encoding processes, stimulus evaluation processes, and response selection and execution processes to overall cognitive slowing. Hence, the combination of different types of simultaneously available information (i.e., amplitude, latency, and scalp distribution) about a succession of processing stages makes the ERP a unique tool for elucidating the nature of cognitive deficits.

We tested 20 untreated TS females and matched controls between the ages of 9 and 20 years. All subjects performed in two different psychological paradigms, each with multiple conditions, while their ERP activity was recorded from a montage of nine scalp electrodes. The first paradigm required the subjects to make a relatively simple auditory discrimination (i.e., *Oddball* paradigm) in a way that provides a sensitive measure of the intactness of sensory and cognitive processes at a number of different stages. This paradigm has been used across a wide variety of normal and patient populations with varying degrees of sensory and cognitive deficits, so the results from the TS group can be understood in a larger context. To assess the relative magnitude of sensory, cognitive, and motor deficits, this paradigm was performed both with and without the requirement for a speedy discriminative RT after every stimulus.

As discussed previously, a variety of neuropsychological investigations have demonstrated that most TS females have at least some difficulty with spatial rotation of objects and left–right discriminations. The issue of whether TS females have stimulus encoding deficits that contribute to their object rotation deficits remains unresolved. Experiments by Rovet and Netley (1980, 1982), however, have supported the position that the locus of this deficit in TS subjects lies in their impaired ability to perform the rotational operations, rather than in their encoding operations. Because the ERP provides a convenient way to quantify the relative magnitudes of possible deficits in these two stages, we recorded the ERP activity elicited in a paradigm that required the subjects to make a left–right discrimination at varying levels of difficulty.

The aim of our study was to assess the relative roles of the presence of congenital brain alterations versus the maturational differences caused by an absence of estrogen as possible bases of the cognitive deficits seen in TS females. We hypothesized that, if the cognitive changes in TS are due to congenital brain changes, then the magnitude of the cognitive changes in TS females, relative to controls, should be relatively constant across all ages. If, on the other hand, the cognitive changes in TS were due mainly to maturational factors, then, in comparison to normal controls, any differences should be greater in older TS females than in younger, pre-, and peripubertal TS females. Thus, we divided our subjects into two groups on the basis of age (9–14 years and 15–20 years) and compared the ERP activity in these two TS groups, prior to any hormone replacement treatments, with each other and with age-matched normal controls.

METHODS

Subjects

Twenty females with TS between the ages of 9 and 20 years and 20 age- and education-matched normal controls from the local school systems were tested. In the TS group, 14 had a 45 XO chromosomal makeup on lymphocyte karyotype (N at each age: 9 = 3, 10 = 2, 11 = 3, 12 = 1, 14 = 1, 15 = 1, 16 = 1, and 20 = 2). An additional six TS females with a mosaic (mixed) chromosomal makeup (age 9, 10, 11, 12, 13, and 18 years) were also tested. The mosaic karyotypes included 45XO/46XX, 45XO/46XXi(Xq), and 45XO/46XX/47XXX. Blood tests confirmed the presence of normal pubertal stage-appropriate estrogen levels in all control subjects and undetectable levels of estrogen in all TS females except for one who had a low level. In every case, the TS females demonstrated no evidence of significant breast development and all were tested prior to any hormone replacement treatments.

In addition, one 17-year-old TS female with a history of spontaneous breast development was tested and her data were kept separate. Moreover, two TS subjects (one 15- and one 20-year-old) were retested after being treated with Ethinyl Estradiol (20–30 μgrams daily) for 6 months. The retest data were also handled separately.

Oddball Paradigm

All subjects performed the standard Oddball paradigm under two instructional conditions: *Count* and *Reaction Time* (RT). In this paradigm, the subject was presented with a random (Bernoulli) series of two readily discriminable tones (1,000 and 1,500 Hz) of moderate intensity. In the count task, the subjects were instructed to keep a mental count of the number of occurrences of one of the two tones and to report their count at the end of the series. In the RT task, the subjects were instructed to make a choice RT response as quickly as possible following every stimulus. In both tasks, the low-pitched tones (1,000 Hz) were presented at different probability levels (i.e., .10, .30, .50) in separate series. High-pitched tones (1,500 Hz) were presented at the complementary probabilities (i.e., .90, .70., .50). The tones were presented for 50 ms (10-ms rise/fall time) binaurally through earphones over a background of white noise. To compensate for possible hearing losses in the TS females, auditory thresholds were determined individually for all subjects and the tones were set to an intensity of 50 dB SL. Subjects counted silently the 1,000 Hz tones. In the RT task, subjects responded to every tone by pressing one of two buttons as quickly as possible. The interstimulus interval was 1,605 ms. There was a 1-sec limit for making a response and the pairing of responding hand with the two stimuli was counterbalanced across subjects. Prior to the Count conditions, subjects received 30 practice trials whereas prior to the RT conditions, subjects received 100 practice trials. In the RT conditions, only trials with correct responses were included in the averages. Further details on the results from the Oddball paradigm can be found in Johnson, Rohrbaugh, and Ross (1993).

Hand Identification Paradigm

To evaluate the TS females' ability to make left–right discriminations, all subjects received a random series of stimuli consisting of the outlines of left and right hands (i.e., the back of the hand). In different series, task difficulty was varied by presenting the hands in different orientations. In one condition the left- and right-hand stimuli were seen with the fingers pointing up (Fixed-Up) and in another, the same stimuli were seen with the fingers pointing down (Fixed-Down). The third, Mixed, condition consisted of a random series of left and right hands in both the Up and Down orientations. In all conditions, the different stimuli had equal probabilities (.50 in the Fixed conditions and .25 in the Mixed condition). The subjects' task was always to identify which hand was presented and press the appropriate button (left or right) as quickly as possible. The probabilities of the response categories (i.e., left, right) were always .50. The stimuli were delivered on a computer terminal CRT for 350 msec with an interstimulus interval of 4.54 sec and a response deadline of 3 sec.

Recording and Data Analysis Procedures

The electroencephelogram (EEG) was recorded with chlorided silver disk electrodes from midline and bilateral placements over frontal (F3, Fz, F4), central (C3, Cz, C4), and parietal (P3, Pz, P4) scalp, all referred to linked mastoid electrodes (bandpass = .01–35 Hz, 3 dB/octave roll-off). Trials contaminated with electrooculogram artifacts were excluded from the averages.

To evaluate the experimental hypotheses, the TS females and controls were divided into two groups: Young ($N = 15$, ages 9–14 years, mean age = 11.1 years) and Old ($N = 5$, ages 15–20 years, mean age = 18.4 years). This division was designed to permit a comparison of subjects at pre- and peripubertal ages with those who were clearly at postpubertal ages. For both the Young and Old groups, separate repeated-measures analyses of variance (ANOVAs), with Greenhouse–Geisser epsilon corrections, were used to assess the significance of group and experimental (stimulus probability, task, electrode site) effects on component amplitudes. Additional repeated-measures ANOVAs were done using the same design, without the electrode factor, to assess the significance of possible differences in component latencies and RT as a function of group and the experimental manipulations. The .05 probability level was used to determine significance. Because there were no differences between the 45 XO and mosaic females on any of the dependent measures, all TS females were included together for statistical purposes.

RESULTS

Oddball Paradigm

Young Subjects (Ages 9–14 Years). Counting performance was generally quite accurate in both the TS and normal groups with only a few cases in which the counts were wrong by more than two. Counts were always within five of being correct with the greatest errors occurring in the youngest subjects in both groups.

The grand-averaged ERPs for the Young TS females and controls elicited at all five levels of stimulus probability during the Counting task are shown in Fig. 11.1. These waveforms reveal a complex pattern of activity. First, at the midline parietal electrode site (Pz), it is obvious that the large positive wave that peaked between 300 and 400 ms (i.e., the P300) showed the usual significant inverse relation with stimulus probability in both groups. In both groups, larger P300s were elicited by the counted (i.e., the .10, .30, and .50) stimuli than by the uncounted stimuli (i.e., the "target" effect). In addition, mean P300 latencies were the same in both groups. There was no evidence of any group differences in the distribution of P300 activity over the scalp or of any differential hemispheric symmetries.

The morphology of the ERP waveform changed substantially in both groups over more anterior scalp sites. The early negative components (N1 at about 100 msec and N2 with a latency at almost 300 msec) were, as usual,

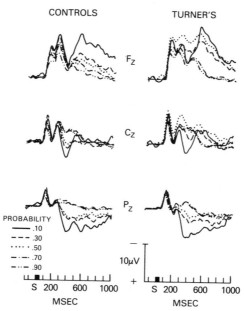

FIG. 11.1. Grand-averaged waveforms for the Young control (left column) and Turner syndrome subjects (right column) from the Count task. The waveforms elicited by the uncounted .50 stimuli are not shown. In this and subsequent figures, stimulus onset is denoted by the "S" on the time scale and stimulus duration by the filled rectangle. Positive voltages are plotted as downward deflections. From Johnson, Rohrbaugh, and Ross (1993). Reprinted by permission.

considerably larger at the central and frontal electrode sites than over posterior scalp. Moreover, in place of a large positive P300, there was a large and prolonged negativity at all frontal electrode sites (F3, Fz, F4) that spanned the interval from 400 to 900 msec and peaked between 500 and 600 msec after stimulus onset. The timing, scalp topography, and graded response to stimulus probability indicates that this late frontal negativity corresponds to the *O-wave*.[1] The O-wave component has been reported to reflect attentional shifts or orienting, with increased amplitude indicative of an increased orienting response (Rohrbaugh, 1984). There was a nonsignificant trend in which O-wave amplitude tended to be larger in the young TS subjects than in their matched controls, particularly at higher levels of stimulus probability. This trend appeared to be due largely to the fact that the counted stimuli at all three probability levels elicited large O-waves in the TS females. The reasons why the TS females would show such similar responses for all target stimuli are not clear. There were no significant group differences in O-wave scalp distribution or hemispheric symmetry.

Despite showing larger N1 amplitudes, there were no significant amplitude differences between the two groups for either the P2 (positive peak with a latency around 200 ms) or N2 components. In addition, there were no significant group differences in the latencies, scalp distributions, or hemispheric symmetries of the N1, P2, or N2 components. Further, all of these components showed the expected significant relations with stimulus probability in both groups.

The grand-averaged ERPs from the Oddball paradigm with the RT task for the Young subjects in both groups are shown in Fig. 11.2 These waveforms demonstrate that the same pattern of results was obtained when a motor response was required after every tone as when the subjects simply had to count the low-pitched tones. There were no significant group differences in the amplitudes, latencies, scalp distributions, or hemispheric symmetries of the N1, P2, N2, P300, or O-wave. As expected, significantly larger P300 amplitudes were elicited in this task compared to those elicited in the Count task (Johnson, 1989a, 1989b). The same inverse relation between the amplitudes of the N1, P2, N2, P300, and O-wave and stimulus probability were obtained in both groups indicating that the sensory and psychological responses to these stimuli were the same in both groups. Note that, because the subjects responded to all stimuli, there were no target effects in the RT task in the amplitudes of either the P300 or O-wave. Taken together, the amplitude, latency, and scalp distribution results for the early (N1, P2) and late components (N2, P300, O-wave) of the ERP in these two tasks suggest that, in general, the TS females processed the stimuli in the same manner and at the same speed as the normal controls.

---

[1]We are particularly grateful to John W. Rohrbaugh for pointing out to us the similarity between the properties of the late frontal negativity and the O-wave.

REACTION TIME (Ave Age = 11.1)

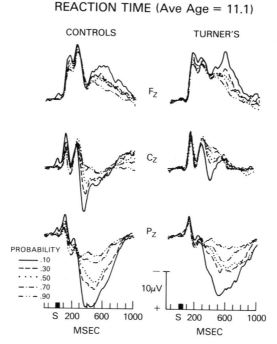

FIG. 11.2. Grand-averaged waveforms for the Young control (left column) and Turner syndrome subjects (right column) from the RT task. From Johnson et al. (1993). Reprinted by permission.

In contrast to the ERP results, the TS subjects had significantly slower RTs than their controls at all probability levels (Table 11.1). Moreover, although both groups made essentially the same number of error responses at each probability level, their longer RTs meant that the Young TS subjects had more responses that exceeded the 1-sec response deadline than their controls (11.0%, 9.1%, and 7.9% vs 3.0%, 2.0%, and 1.8% for the 10/90, 30/70, and 50/50 series). Nevertheless, RTs in both groups showed the expected inverse relation with stimulus probability. This fact, coupled with the lack of any significant delays in the latencies of any of their ERP components, suggests that the slowed responses evidenced by the TS females were most likely due to slowing in response-related processing stages (i.e., response selection and preparation, response execution). One interesting finding was that, whereas the controls' RTs were negatively correlated with age ($-.28 < r < -.61$ across probability levels), there was a general lack of any correlation between age and RT for the TS subjects ($-.16 < r < +.25$).

Old Subjects (Ages 15–20 Years).   The grand-averaged ERP waveforms for the Count task for the stimuli at all five probability levels for the Old controls

TABLE 11.1
Mean and (Standard Deviation) Reaction Times (in Milliseconds) for Turner Syndrome
and Normal Subjects

	Stimulus Probability				
Group	.10	.30	.50	.70	.90
Young (N = 15)					
Controls	441 (64)	431 (72)	405 (72)	382 (66)	337 (57)
Turner	543 (83)	535 (73)	538 (81)	488 (82)	445 (67)
Old (N = 5)[a]					
Controls	361 (86)	360 (94)	362 (110)	345 (83)	303 (69)
Turner	496 (116)	402 (60)	465 (124)	394 (78)	437 (119)

[a]*n* = 4 for TS group.
Note. From Johnson et al. (1993). Reprinted by permission.

and TS females are presented in Fig. 11.3. As in the Young subjects, the ERP activity elicited over posterior scalp in both Old groups was strikingly similar. P300 amplitude again showed a significant inverse relation with stimulus probability in both groups and there were no group differences in P300 amplitude, latency, scalp distribution, or hemispheric symmetry.

Unlike the Young subjects, however, significantly larger O-wave amplitudes were elicited in the Old TS subjects compared to their age-matched controls. Clearly, O-wave amplitude in the Old TS subjects failed to decrease with age in same way as it did in the controls. In fact, the waveforms of these Old TS females appeared to resemble more closely those of the Young controls and TS females than those of the Old controls. Also, the finding in the Young TS females that there was little distinction between the amplitudes of the O-waves elicited by the counted (target) stimuli at the different stimulus probabilities was even more exaggerated in the Old TS females. Nevertheless, the significant inverse relation between stimulus probability and O-wave amplitude still obtained in both groups.

There were no other group differences except for a nonsignificant tendency for the Old TS females to have larger N1s than their controls. Otherwise, the amplitudes of the P2 and N2 were not significantly different across groups and there were no significant group differences in the latencies, scalp distributions, or hemispheric symmetries of any of these components.

The grand-averaged ERPs elicited in the two Old groups in the RT task are shown in Fig. 11.4. As in the younger subjects, the results from the RT version of the Oddball paradigm closely matched those obtained in the Count task in all respects. There were no significant group differences in amplitude, latency, scalp distribution, or hemispheric symmetry of the N1, P2, N2, or P300 components. Furthermore, the amplitude and latency activity of all these components showed the same pattern of significant and nonsignificant

COUNT (Ave Age =18.4)

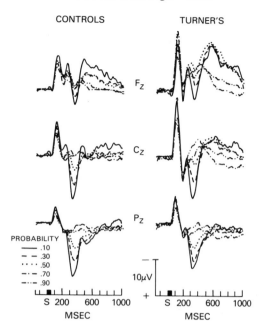

FIG. 11.3. The grand-averaged waveforms for the Old control (left column) and Turner syndrome subjects (right column) from the Count task. The waveforms elicited by the uncounted .50 stimuli are not shown. From Johnson et al. (1993). Reprinted by permission.

results in both groups in response to the probability and task manipulations. For example, P300 amplitude was inversely related to stimulus probability in both groups and significantly larger P300s were elicited under the RT instructions than under the count instructions in both groups. Note also that, compared to the Count task, the group differences in N1 amplitude were smaller.

As in the Count task, the Old TS subjects showed significantly larger O-wave amplitudes than did their controls. Note that, when the subjects responded to both stimuli, there was a more continuous inverse relation between stimulus probability and O-wave amplitude than was present in the Count task due to the absence of any target effect.

The normal developmental course of the O-wave, in which it decreases in both amplitude and duration with increasing age, is readily apparent in comparisons of the grand-averaged waveforms elicited in the Young and Old control groups (Figs. 11.1–11.4). It is equally evident from these figures that the amplitude and duration of the O-wave failed to decrease in the same manner in the older TS subjects either in the grand-averages or in individual

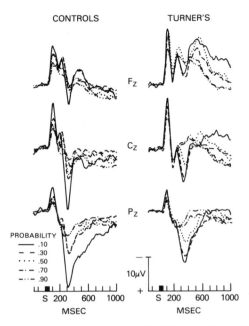

FIG. 11.4.   The grand-averaged waveforms for the Old control (left column) and Turner syndrome subjects (right column) from the RT task. From Johnson et al. (1993). Reprinted by permission.

subjects (e.g., see the waveforms from two subjects in Fig. 11.7). The absence of the normal maturational pattern of O-wave activity in the Old TS subjects was, however, accompanied by an absence of significant group differences in the amplitude or latency of any of the other components (i.e., N1, P2, N2, P300). This combination of results suggests that their deficit in this task was quite specific and not due to some generalized sensory or cognitive dysfunction.

The O-wave results from all four groups are summarized in Fig. 11.5 where the quantified amplitudes are shown for both conditions and all probability levels. the inverse relation between O-wave amplitude and stimulus probability in all groups and both tasks is readily apparent. The finding that O-wave amplitude was inversely related to age in the controls but not in the TS group is clear in comparisons across columns in both age groups. Note how the overall amount of O-wave activity did not diminish with age in the 15- to 20-year-old TS females. The uniqueness of this pattern of O-wave amplitude differences between the TS females and controls can be seen in the absence of

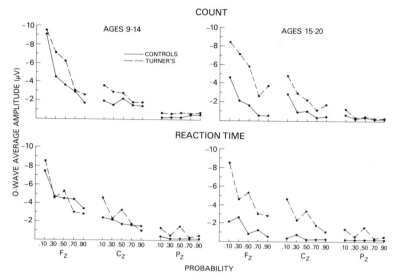

FIG. 11.5. The grand-averaged average O-wave amplitude elicited by the stimuli at all five levels of probability in both the Count and RT versions of the Oddball paradigm for the Young (left column) and Old (right column) control (solid lines) and Turner syndrome subjects (dashed lines). From Johnson et al. (1993). Reprinted by permission.

the same pattern of results for the N1, the only other ERP component for which there were any significant group differences (Fig. 11.6). As shown in Fig. 11.6, N1 amplitudes tended to be larger in TS subjects of all ages compared to their controls rather than showing a differential, age-related difference. In fact, the largest amplitude changes exhibited by the N1 component were those related to stimulus probability, which were the same for both groups.

Reliable RTs could only be obtained from four subjects in the Old TS group because the left arm of one TS woman was immobilized for the purposes of another experimental procedure. Thus, although the RTs obtained from the Old TS females were more than 80 msec slower on average (across probability levels) than those of their controls, this difference was not sufficient to reach statistical significance with this small number of subjects (Table 11.1). However, the error rates and number of late responses were not significantly different across groups and the RTs in both Old groups were significantly inversely related to stimulus probability. In addition, the correlations between age and RT in the Old controls showed the same negative relation as in the Young controls and the Old TS subjects showed the same lack of any relation as was found in the Young TS subjects. However, none of the RT correlations for the Old controls was significant.

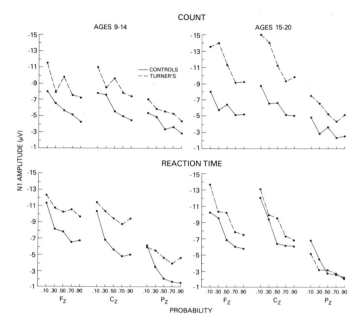

FIG. 11.6. The grand-averaged N1 amplitude elicited by the stimuli at all five levels of probability in both the Count and RT versions of the Oddball paradigm for the Young (left column) and Old (right column) control (solid lines) and Turner syndrome subjects (dashed lines). From Johnson et al. (1993). Reprinted by permission.

Posttreatment Results. After the initial ERP testing session, two TS females from the Old group were given estrogen replacement for 6 months. To determine whether estrogen replacement treatments would reverse or diminish the magnitude of the group differences in their ERP activity, we retested these two 45 XO TS females (ages 15 and 20 years) after 6 months. As evident from the waveforms in Fig. 11.7, there were no apparent changes in any aspect of the ERP activity in these two TS subjects as a consequence of the hormone treatments. In both cases, the abnormally large amounts of O-wave activity were undiminished from the initial recording session. These findings indicate that the estrogen replacement treatments had no effect on the ERP activity in these two subjects.

Endogenous Estrogen: A Case Study. The results described thus far point to a relation between the absence of endogenous estrogen and the presence of abnormally large amounts of O-wave activity in Old TS females. If this hypothesis is correct, then the O-wave activity in TS females with histories of spontaneous ovarian function should more closely resemble that observed in normal controls of the same age than that in other TS females. To evaluate this hypothesis, we tested one 17-year-old TS subject (AV) who had

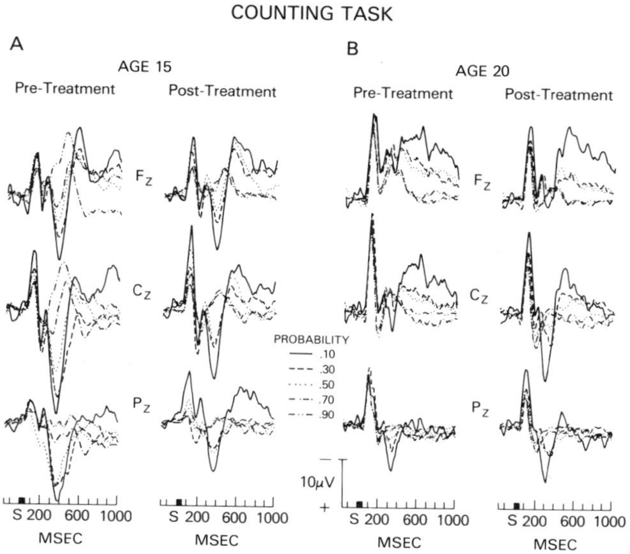

COUNTING TASK

FIG. 11.7.   The ERP waveforms elicited in the Counting task for two TS subjects age 15 years (left panel) and 20 years (right panel) from before (left column) and after (right column) receiving 6 months of estrogen treatments.

a history of spontaneous pubertal development (marked breast development and spontaneous onset of menses).

The ERP waveforms recorded from AV during the Counting task are shown in Fig. 11.8. Despite the presence of a large amount of 10-Hz "noise" in these waveforms, it is clear from the ERP activity at both the frontal (Fz) and central (Cz) electrode sites that AV did not show the same exaggerated amounts of O-wave activity as the other postpubertal TS females who had had no early exposure to estrogen (compare these waveforms with those in the right column of Fig. 11.3 or the two subjects in Fig. 11.7). It should be noted that none of the other females in the Old TS group failed to show the pattern of enlarged O-wave activity. In fact, AV's waveforms more closely resemble those of the normal controls (left column of Fig. 11.3) than those of the other TS females. Also, other than containing less 10-Hz noise, there were no other qualitative or quantitative differences between AV's ERP activity recorded before and after receiving estrogen replacement treatments for 6 months. The same absence of any unusual amounts of O-wave activity was replicated in AV's waveforms elicited during the RT task. The data from this TS female, therefore, provide converging evidence in support of the hypothesis that the presence of exaggerated O-wave amplitudes observed in the Old TS females is caused, or at least influenced, by the absence of circulating estrogen at some point prior to the end of puberty.

ENDOGENOUS ESTROGEN

COUNTING TASK

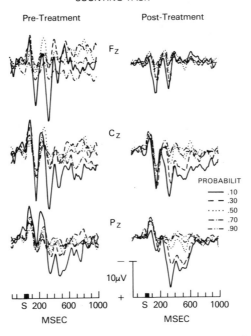

FIG. 11.8. The ERP waveforms elicited in the Counting task from one Turner syndrome subject (age 17 years) who had a history of spontaneous breast development. This subject was tested before (left column) and after (right column) receiving estrogen treatments.

Left–Right Discrimination Paradigm

In the two Fixed conditions, the Hand Identification paradigm consisted of a straightforward left–right discrimination. In fact, the Fixed-Up and Fixed-Down conditions provide close approximations of the left–right discriminations required by the Road-map test of direction sense (Money, Alexander, & Walker, 1965) that has been used previously to test TS subjects (Alexander & Money, 1966; Alexander et al., 1964; Waber, 1979). In our paradigm, the Fixed-Up condition corresponds to the "away" direction and the Fixed-Down condition corresponds to the "toward" direction of the Road-map test.

In contrast to the two Fixed conditions, the Mixed condition is considerably more difficult and subjects can use more than one performance strategy. In a previous study using the same stimuli, Johnson, Cox, and Fedio (1987) found that subjects performing the different variations of this task showed one of two very different patterns of ERP activity. These two patterns of ERP activity were linked to the particular strategy that the subjects used to identify the hands (i.e., either with verbal rules or by mentally rotating the stimulus). Thus, we hoped that the Mixed condition might provide some insights into whether the TS subjects used the same strategies during mental rotation operations as controls (cf., Rovet & Netley, 1980, 1982).

In accord with the results of previous studies, the TS females at all ages were considerably less proficient at performing all variations of this task than were their matched controls. Figure 11.9 shows the percentage of TS subjects at each age able to identify the hand stimuli in each condition at a level greater than chance. For comparison, the equivalent data are shown for their matched controls, plus those from an additional 30 normal females including 4 7- and 4 8-year-old girls. These data clearly show that, although the same percentage of subjects in both groups were proficient at identifying the hands in the Fixed-Up task, the development of the ability to make accurate left–right discriminations in the Fixed-Down and Mixed conditions was delayed considerably in the TS subjects. For example, in the Fixed-Down condition, the age at which the same percentage of TS females and controls could make this discrimination was delayed by 2 years in the TS subjects. Similarly, in the more difficult Mixed condition, the ability of the TS females

HAND IDENTIFICATION TASK

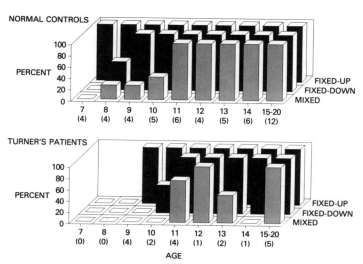

FIG. 11.9. Histograms showing the percentage of the normal controls and Turner syndrome subjects at each age who could successfully perform the Fixed-Up, Fixed-Down, and Mixed conditions of the Hand Identification paradigm. The number of subjects is shown in parentheses. For this comparison only, the performance data from an extra 30 normal controls were combined with those for the 20 age-matched controls.

to perform this task appeared to lag that of the controls by at least 3 years. In the case of our single 14-year-old TS subject, she was completely unable to make reliably accurate discriminations in the Mixed condition. Note that, with the ages in our sample, it was not possible to determine whether the TS subjects' ability to perform the Hands-Up condition was also delayed relative to the controls.

Even when the TS females successfully made the different left–right discriminations, their RTs were considerably slower than those of the controls. In the Young group, the TS subjects' RTs were an average of 230 msec, 160 msec, and 154 msec slower in the Fixed-Up, Fixed-Down, and Mixed conditions, respectively. Similarly, the Old TS subjects' RTs were an average of 240 msec, 229 msec, and 174 msec slower in the Fixed-Up, Fixed-Down, and Mixed conditions, respectively. However, even this degree of slowness understates the true magnitude of the Young TS females' difficulty with this task because these mean RTs were calculated only on the basis of the subjects who could perform each task. Thus, given the delayed ability of TS subjects to perform the Fixed-Down and Mixed conditions, there were fewer Young TS females included in the grand means and they were, on average, older than the controls. Because RT in these tasks decreased with age, the Young TS groups' RTs were faster than they would have been if these means were based on age-matched groups. This fact explains why the magnitude of the Young TS subjects' RT delays, relative to the controls, decreased with increasing task difficulty (i.e., as fewer young subjects' data were included in the grand means).

Subjects can, and frequently do, use verbal strategies to identify the hand stimuli in the two Fixed conditions. One way in which this is manifested is that the RTs to the Fixed-Down stimuli are faster than those to the Fixed-Up stimuli. This seemingly paradoxical result is due to the configuration of the thumbs: The thumb points in the direction opposite to the correct button press when the hands (the backs) are Up whereas the thumbs point in the same direction as the correct button press when the hands are Down. Thus, it becomes obvious when people use this strategy to identify the hands because faster RTs are obtained in the Fixed-Down condition than in the Fixed-Up condition.

Two observations can be made on the basis of performance data from the Fixed-Down condition. First, even normal 7-year-olds and half of our 8-year-olds were unable to discover this simple "rule of thumb" (see Fig.11.9). Second, this capability was delayed by an additional 2 years in the TS females compared to their controls. Nevertheless, once they were able to perform this task successfully, the subjects in both groups appeared to use thumb position as an aid to stimulus identification because the RTs in both the TS females and controls were fastest in the Fixed-Down condition.

Preliminary analyses of the ERP data from the Mixed condition suggest that the TS groups, particularly those in the 15–20 year age range, do not use the same strategy as the majority of the normal controls. Although acknowledging that averaging across subjects of such diverse ages may result in some distortions, we did this analysis to obtain a overview of these data. The ERP waveforms elicited in all four groups in all three conditions are shown in Fig. 11.10. These waveforms suggest that, although the frontal negative activity that has been associated with mental rotation of hand stimuli (cf., Johnson et al., 1987) was present in their ERPs, its onset was delayed considerably in both the Young and Old TS subjects. This may be an indication that the TS subjects of all ages were relying more on verbal strategies to identify the hands than did their controls. In addition, the posterior P300 activity (peaking here between 500 and 600 msec after stimulus onset) was more similar across groups for the Young subjects than for the Old subjects (peaking between 400 and 500 ms) because the considerable amplitude and duration reductions in the Old normal controls were not matched by the Old TS subjects. Nevertheless, final conclusions on the results from the Mixed condition must await more detailed analysis.

As evident from the data in Fig. 11.9, averaging across all Young and Old subjects in the Hand Identification task in the same way as for the Oddball paradigm could obscure important group differences. To reduce such potential confounds, we compared the ERP and RT data from the TS subjects and controls in the simplest, Fixed-Up, task at two different ages. The Fixed-Up

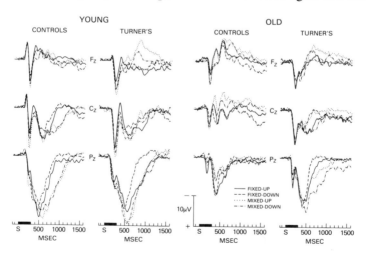

FIG. 11.10.   Grand-averaged waveforms elicited at the three midline electrode sites by the stimuli in all three conditions of the Hand Identification paradigm. The waveforms for the different conditions are superimposed separately for the Young and Old control and Turner syndrome subjects. These averages are based only on subjects who could perform the task at better than chance levels so the number and ages of subjects contributing to the averages was different for the two Young groups.

condition was picked because all subjects in both groups were able to perform the task. Note that, in the Fixed-Up condition, the task is equivalent to looking at the backs of one's own hands and identifying which is left and which is right.

The grand-averaged ERPs for the 9- and 11-year-old TS females and controls ($N = 4$ in each average) for the Fixed-Up condition are compared in Fig. 11.11. Although a number of differences are apparent between the ERPs elicited in these two groups, the most important is the delay in the P300 elicited at the Pz electrode site. These data indicate that, at age 9 years, even in this comparatively simple task of discriminating their left hand from their right, the P300 component was delayed in the TS females by more than 100 msec compared to their age-matched controls. Later, at age 11 years, the TS females P300 activity was still delayed by more than 50 msec relative to their controls. In the same comparisons, the TS subjects' RTs showed even greater delays: RTs for the 9-year-old TS subjects were more than 200 msec slower than their controls whereas the 11-year-old TS subjects were about 270 msec slower. Nevertheless, the fact that the latency of the sensory, P2, component (the large positive component at Cz at about 300 msec) was the same in both groups suggests that sensory processes were not the source of the altered task performance in the TS females. In summary, the ERP and RT data from the

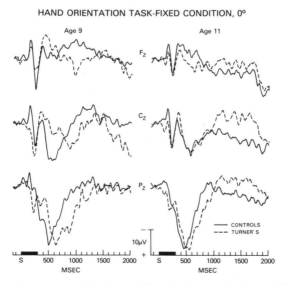

FIG. 11.11. Grand-averaged waveforms ($N = 4$) elicited at the three midline electrode sites by the left-hand stimuli in the Fixed-Up condition of the Hand Identification paradigm. The waveforms from the normal controls (solid lines) are superimposed on those from the Turner syndrome subjects (dashed lines) at age 9 years (left column) and 11 years (right column).

Hands-Up task demonstrate that the TS females at all ages showed a clear deficit in their ability to make left–right discriminations and that at least a portion of this deficit has a central origin.

DISCUSSION

Taken together, the ERP and behavioral results from these two paradigms point to the existence of two different kinds of cognitive deficits in untreated TS females, each of which appears to arise from a different mechanism. In the Oddball paradigm, only TS subjects past the age of puberty were affected, suggesting a maturational defect. In the Left–Right discrimination paradigm, task performance in TS subjects of all ages was reduced, consistent with the existence of a congenital defect. Moreover, TS subjects at all ages showed a considerable degree of motor slowing in both paradigms, suggesting an additional congenital difference. Thus, variations in the relative extent of the congenital and maturational deficits, in combination with motor deficits, in each individual TS subject may explain some of the variability in results across paradigms and across studies in previous reports on cognitive activity in TS.

The results from the Oddball paradigm indicated that, whereas the ERPs recorded from the Young TS females were essentially the same as those of their age-matched controls, the ERP activity recorded from the Old TS females more closely resembled those of both Young groups than those of their own age-matched controls. Specifically, the late frontal O-wave activity in the Old TS subjects failed to show the normal maturational course in which the amplitude and duration of this component steadily decreases with age. The persistent, exaggerated appearance of the O-waves in the Old TS subjects may underly some difficulty in regulating the orienting response in these subjects. These data suggest that Old TS females show a hyperorientation response, at least to auditory stimuli of moderate intensity, that can be interpreted as an inability to habituate normally or to place events in their proper context. It is possible to speculate that this "immature" response to events may be related to (or the basis for) the reported inability of TS females to discern properly a variety of social clues and contexts (McCauley, Kay, Ito, & Treder, 1987).

Given the absence of estrogen in the TS females, the results from the Oddball paradigm suggest that sex hormones play a role in the development of at least some cognitive processes. Further support for this hypothesis was provided by the near-normal O-wave amplitudes in the one older TS subject who had endogenous estrogen. In addition, the fact that O-wave amplitudes remained at abnormally high levels even after 6 months of estrogen treatments suggests that the normal development of the O-wave may rely on the presence of estrogen during some critical period. It would not be inconsistent with these results, then, to postulate that if levels of circulating estrogen do not reach normal levels within some critical period, then the brain's response to auditory stimuli presented under these conditions will remain abnormal. The possible existence of a critical period in brain development in which womens' brains require exposure to estrogen warrants further investigation because current treatment strategies of TS females favor delaying estrogen treatments to maximize growth. If the results from these three cases are replicated and extended, then it would support the idea that circulating estrogen must be present at some point prior to age 15 years or brain development may be permanently altered. It would be important then to determine the timing of this critical period and the significance of these ERP changes for general cognitive functioning.

With the exception of somewhat larger N1 amplitudes in the Young TS subjects, the amplitudes, latencies, scalp distributions, and response to the psychological variables included in the Oddball paradigm were indistinguishable for all the other ERP components (P2, N2, P300) between our untreated TS subjects and their controls. The absence of any alterations in the latency of the early, sensory components (i.e., N1, P2) indicated that the TS subjects showed no signs of delayed perceptual processing. The lack of any significant alterations in the amplitude, latency, or scalp distributions of the late components (i.e., N2, P300) indicates that there were no gross signs of any cognitive problems in this paradigm. The fact that there were no group differences in the scalp distributions of any of these ERP components is further evidence that the same brain areas were activated during task performance and there were no signs of differential hemispheric activation.

Overall, the slowed RTs in our TS subjects replicate those reported previously (Lewandowski et al., 1985; Rovet & Netley, 1980, 1982). Given the normal ERP component latencies, it appears that the motor slowing exhibited by our TS subjects was not due to deficiencies in their sensory or stimulus evaluation stages. In fact, despite their general slowness, the TS subjects did not make more errors and their RTs showed the usual inverse relation with stimulus probability. These behavioral data provide additional evidence that the TS subjects correctly processed the auditory stimuli at all stages leading up to and including those concerned with stimulus evaluation. Thus, the slowed responses in the TS subjects were most likely due to slowing in response-related processing stages (i.e., response selection, preparation, and execution).

The absence of altered N1, P2, N2, and P300 latencies in the TS subjects in the Oddball paradigm is in clear contrast to the commonly found changes in other patient groups with cognitive dysfunction. For example, significant latency delays as small as 10–20 ms have been found routinely for the N1 and P2 components in patients with subcortical dementias (i.e., Huntington's, Parkinson's disease; see Johnson, 1992, for a review). The lack of ERP changes in the TS subjects also differs from recent findings in patients with early stage human immunodeficiency virus (HIV) disease. Under the same conditions used here (i.e.,Oddball paradigm—RT task), clear changes in both early and late ERP component latencies were found, along with increased RTs, in HIV+ patients who were asymptomatic and who all scored within normal limits on a battery of neuropsychological tests (Ollo, Johnson, & Grafman, 1991). Such results indicate that the lack of ERP changes in our TS subjects is not likely to be due to a lack of sensitivity of the ERP to alterations in sensory and cognitive processing.

The timing and scalp distribution of our late frontal O-wave activity appears to correspond to the late, frontal negative Nc component that was discovered to occur in children during normal development (Courchesne, 1977, 1983). Because the Nc component was recorded in response to very low-probability, novel visual stimuli, Courchesne suggested that it reflected the activity of a novelty detector. Courchesne (1990) also reported that rare auditory stimuli can elicit an Nc component, although the nature and developmental parameters of the auditory Nc are much less well studied. Further, Courchesne demonstrated that both the amplitude and latency (i.e., duration) of the Nc had protracted developmental courses that could be linked to maturational changes in the brain (i.e., cortical synaptogenesis and metabolic activity). However, because of Courchesne's limited experimental manipulations, it is not known whether the Nc is elicited exclusively by unrepeated stimuli or, like the O-wave, it has a graded relation with stimulus probability for stimuli in all modalities. Some evidence of such a graded relation with stimulus probability was provided by Karrer and Ackles (1987), who found an inverse relation between the amplitude of the Nc-like activity elicited by visual stimuli with probabilities of .20 and .80, results that are more similar to ours. In addition, the cognitive processes associated with the O-wave (i.e., attentional shift, orienting) require the assessment of stimulus probability or context and are therefore quite similar to Courchesne's (1977) notion of the Nc as a novelty detector. Thus, given the similarities between the timing, scalp distribution, maturational courses, and psychological correlates of our O-waves for auditory stimuli and the Nc, it is possible that these are the same activity.

The maturational data from the Hand Identification task replicated those of previous studies showing that TS subjects have difficulties making left–right discriminations and performing mental rotation tasks (Alexander & Money, 1966; Alexander et al., 1964; Rovet & Netley, 1980, 1982 Waber, 1979;). In contrast to the maturational deficits revealed by the Oddball paradigm, the ERP and RT results from this paradigm were more consistent with a congenital deficit. That is, when faced with making simple left–right discriminations, TS subjects at all ages showed considerable cognitive and motor deficits. For example, the development of the ability of the TS subjects to make these discriminations in at least two of the three conditions was delayed by 2–3 years compared to their age-and education-matched controls. Furthermore, TS subjects showed clear delays in P300 latency and slowed RTs even for the simplest discrimination, even at ages well past that at which they could perform the task. Thus, 11-year-old TS females showed considerable delays in both P300 latency and RT when they had to perform a task equivalent to discriminating their left hand from their right hand. Because these delays occurred even in the youngest subjects (age 9 years), well before the onset of puberty, these left–right discrimination deficits appear to be the result of congenital brain changes rather than to maturational factors. The fact that normal latencies were found at the next earlier (i.e., P2) component suggests that visual sensory processing was normal in the TS patients in this task and hence that the P300 latency delays reflected delays at a later, stimulus identification stage. These results therefore replicate those found by Rovet and Netley (1980, 1982) in a similar task. Finally, although the data analyses are incomplete, the ERPs elicited in this paradigm suggest that the TS subjects did not use the same strategies to rotate and/or identify the hand stimuli in the Mixed condition as the controls.

In summary, the ERP and behavioral data from these two paradigms suggest that the cognitive and motor deficits in TS result from a combination of factors. It appears that both congenital and maturational abnormalities contribute differentially and to varying degrees to the overall pattern of cognitive deficits in TS. The ERP data also clearly indicate that, for the auditory and visual stimuli used in these two paradigms, sensory processes did not appear to contribute to the overall pattern of deficits in the TS subjects. The largest deficits in our TS subjects were found in their response-processing and execution operations. In this regard, the ERP has proven especially valuable in disambiguating the relative contributions of different sources of the sensory, cognitive, and motor deficits in TS subjects and in identifying more precisely the temporal characteristics of these deficits.

REFERENCES

Alexander, D., & Money, J. (1966). Turner's syndrome and Gerstmann's syndrome: Neuropsychologic comparisons. *Neuropsychologia, 4,* 265–273.

Alexander, D., Walker, H. T., Jr., & Money, J. (1964). Studies in direction sense: I. Turner's syndrome. *Archives of General Psychiatry, 10,* 337–339.

Bashore, T. R., Jr. (1990). Age-related changes in mental processing revealed by analyses of event-related potentials. In J. W. Rohrbaugh, R. Parasuraman, & R. Johnson, Jr. (Eds.), *Issues in event-related potential research: Tutorials and interdisciplinary vantages* (pp. 242–275). New York: Oxford University Press.

Courchesne, E. (1977). Event-related brain potentials: Comparison between children and adults. *Science, 197,* 598–592.

Courchesne, E. (1983). Cognitive components of the event-related brain potential: Changes associated with development. In A. W. K. Gaillard & W. Ritter (Eds.), *Tutorials in ERP research: Endogenous components* (pp. 329–444). Amsterdam, Netherlands: North Holland.

Courchesne, E. (1990). Chronology of postnatal human brain development: Event-related potential, positron emission tomography, myelinogenesis, and synaptogenesis studies. In J. W. Rohrbaugh, R. Parasuraman, & R. Johnson, Jr. (Eds.), *Issues in event-related potential research: Tutorials and Interdisciplinary vantages* (pp. 210–241). New York: Oxford University Press.

Friedman, D. (1991). The endogenous scalp-recorded brain potentials and their relationship to cognitive development. In J. R. Jennings & M. G. H. Coles (Eds.), *Handbook of cognitive psychophysiology: Central and autonomic nervous system approaches* (pp. 621–683). Chichester, England: Wiley.

Johnson, R., Jr. (1986). A triarchic model of P300 amplitude. *Psychophysiology, 23,* 367–384.

Johnson, R., Jr. (1988). The amplitude of the P300 component of the event-related potential: Review and synthesis. In P. K. Ackles, J. R. Jennings, & M. G. H. Coles (Eds.), *Advances in psychophysiology* (Vol. 3, pp. 69–137). Greenwich, CT: JAI.

Johnson, R., Jr. (1989a). Auditory and visual P300s in temporal lobectomy patients: Evidence for modality dependent generators. *Psychophysiology, 26,* 367–384.

Johnson, R., Jr. (1989b). Developmental evidence for modality-dependent P300 generators: A normative study. *Psychophysiology, 26,* 651–667.

Johnson, R., Jr. (1992). Event-related potential insights into progressive supranuclear palsy. In I. Litvan & Y. Agid (Eds.), *Progressive supranuclear palsy: Clinical and research approaches* (pp. 122–154). New York: Oxford University Press.

Johnson, R., Jr., Cox, C., & Fedio, P. (1987). Event-related potential evidence for individual differences in a mental rotation task. In R. Johnson, Jr., J. W., Rohrbaugh, & R. Parasuraman (Eds.), *Current trends in event-related potential research. Electroencephalography and clinical neurophysiology* (Suppl. 40, pp. 191–197). Amsterdam, Netherlands: Elsevier.

Johnson, R., Jr., Rohrbaugh, J., & Parasuraman, R. (Eds.). (1987). *Current trends in event-related potential research. Electroencephalography and clinical neurophysiology* (Suppl. 40). Amsterdam, Netherlands: Elsevier.

Johnson, R., Jr., Rohrbaugh, J. W., and Ross, J. L. (1993). Altered brain development in Turner's Syndrome: An event-related potential study. *Neurology, 43,* 801–808.

Karrer, R., & Ackles, P. K. (1987). Visual event-related potentials of infants using a modified oddball procedure. In R. Johnson, Jr., J. W. Rohrbaugh, & R. Parasuraman (Eds.), *Current trends in event-related potential research. Electroencephalography and clinical neurophysiology* (Suppl. 40, pp. 603–608). Amsterdam, Netherlands: Elsevier.

Lewandowski, L., Costenbader, V., & Richman, R. (1985). Neuropsychological aspects of Turner syndrome. *The International Journal of Clinical Neuropsychology, 7,* 144–147.

McCauley, E., Kay, T., Ito, J., & Treder, R. (1987). The Turner syndrome: Cognitive deficits, affective discrimination, and behavior problems. *Child Development, 58,* 464–473.

McGlone, J. (1985). Can spatial deficits in Turner's syndrome be explained by focal CNS dysfunction or atypical speech lateralization? *Journal of Clinical and Experimental Neuropsychology, 7* 375–394.

Money, J. (1973). Turner's syndrome and parietal lobe functions. *Cortex, 9,* 385–393.

Money, J., Alexander, D., & Walker, H. T., Jr. (1965). *A standardized road-map test of direction sense.* Baltimore: Johns Hopkins University Press.

Ollo, C., Johnson, R., Jr., & Grafman, J. (1991). Signs of cognitive change in HIV disease: An event-related brain potential study. *Neurology, 41,* 209–215.

Reske-Nielsen, E., Christensen, A. -L., & Nielsen, J. (1982). A neuropathological and neuropsychological study of Turner's syndrome. *Cortex, 18,* 181–190.

Rohrbaugh, J. W. (1984). The orienting reflex: Performance and central nervous system manifestations. In R. Parasuraman & D. R. Davies (Eds.), *Varieties of attention* (pp. 323–373). Orlando: Academic.

Rovet, J. F. (1990). The cognitive and neuropsychological characteristics of females with Turner syndrome. In D. Berch & B. Bender (Eds.), *Sex chromosome abnormalities and human behavior* (pp. 38–77). Boulder, CO: Western Press & the American Association for the Advancement of Science.

Rovet, J. F., & Netley, C. (1980). The mental rotation task performance of Turner syndrome subjects. *Behavior Genetics, 10,* 437–443.

Rovet, J. F., & Netley, C. (1982). Processing deficits in Turner's syndrome. *Developmental Psychology, 18,* 77–94.

Satterfield, J. H., Schell, A. M., Nicholas, T., & Backs, R. W. (1988). Topographic study of auditory event-related potentials in normal boys and boys with attention deficit disorder with hyperactivity. *Psychophysiology, 25,* 591–611.

Silbert, A., Wolff, P. H., & Lilienthal, J. (1977). Spatial and temporal processing in patients with Turner's syndrome. *Behavior Genetics, 7,* 11–21.

Taylor, M. J., & Keenan, N. K. (1990). Event-related potentials to visual and language stimuli in normal and dyslexic children. *Psychophysiology, 27,* 318–327.

Waber, D. P. (1979). Neuropsychological aspects of Turner's syndrome. *Developmental Medicine and Child Neurology, 21,* 58–70.

Part III

RESEARCH METHODS

12

Methods of Studying Small Samples: Issues and Examples

Elizabeth Bates
University of California, San Diego

Mark Appelbaum
Vanderbilt University

Developmental cognitive neuroscience is devoted to the study of brain-behavior relationships, and the way that those relationships develop over time. One of the most important methodologies within this growing field is the study of rare clinical populations that present unusual profiles of language, cognition and/or social-emotional development. For example, older children and adolescents with Williams syndrome display remarkable sparing of language and social interaction, despite severe deficits in many other aspects of cognition and perception (Bellugi, Bihrle, Trauner, Jernigan, & Doherty, 1990; Bellugi, Marks, Bihrle, & Sabo, 1988). Many autistic children display what appears to be a contrasting and perhaps complementary pattern: particularly severe deficits in language and avoidance of social interaction, despite islands of normal or (in some cases) supranormal ability in some domains of spatial cognition (Rutter, 1978). If these complementaries at the behavioral level could be mapped onto contrasting and complementary patterns of brain morphology, we could learn a great deal about the brain systems responsible for the behaviors in question. Indeed, recent neuroanatomical studies of Williams syndrome (Jernigan & Bellugi, 1990; Jernigan, Bellugi, & Hesselink, 1989) and autism (Courchesne, 1991) do provide evidence for contrasting forms of brain organization, including contrasts in areas that were traditionally excluded from consideration in speculations about the brain bases of higher-order cognitive functions (e.g., the cerebellum).

These are dramatic findings, the kind of result that could inspire whole new

245

theories of mind-brain relations. However, because the clinical populations of interest are so rare, studies of this kind are invariably based on relatively small (and often heterogeneous) samples of children, averaging somewhere between 3 and 10 subjects in most studies. This unavoidable fact raises classical questions about the reliability and validity of our results. But that is not the only problem. Research with small groups has to pass through a methodological Scylla and Charybdis. On one side, we face all the well-known problems associated with groups that are too small. On the other side, we have to face a growing movement in cognitive neuropsychology against the use of clinical groups (of any size). According to the proponents of this small but influential movement, any group larger than one is too big!

How can we navigate these dangerous methodological waters? The populations of children described in this volume are a precious resource, experiments of nature that provide invaluable information about the architecture of mind and brain. We owe it to them and to ourselves to put their information to use in the most valid, reliable, and credible way that we can. There are no easy answers, but the situation is not hopeless. In this chapter, we begin by addressing some of the methodological problems inherent in research with small groups. For the reasons just described, this discussion is divided into two parts: Scylla (the dangers of research that combines subjects into clinical groups) and Charybdis (the dangers of research with single cases and/or with groups that are quite small). Then we provide some positive recommendations for the analysis of small samples, with particular emphasis on two related methods: randomization tests (which make no assumptions about the nature of the underlying distribution) and goodness-of-fit tests (which permit us to test some very strong competing hypotheses about the profiles displayed by individuals as well as groups).

SCYLLA: THE CASE AGAINST GROUP STUDIES

An old debate in psychology and neuroscience has been revived in the last few years, regarding the merits of group versus single-case studies. One of the most influential proponents of the single-case approach is Alfonso Caramazza, who presented a series of logical arguments against a widely practiced research strategy in neuropsychology and cognitive neuroscience, in which the results obtained with individual patients are collapsed and analyzed according to diagnostic groups, based on some a priori set of behavioral criteria (e.g., Badecker & Caramazza, 1985, 1986; Caramazza, 1986; Caramazza & McCloskey, 1988; Miceli, Silveri, Romani, & Caramazza, 1989; see also Marshall, 1984; Morton, 1980, 1984; Tyler, Cobb, & Graham, 1992). Although these arguments are elegantly wrought, in unprecedented detail, they boil down (in our view) to two serious but long-recognized problems of measurement in research based on diagnostic groups:

1. *Nonrepresentativeness of the mean.* When data for individual subjects are collapsed, the resulting group means may represent no one at all.

2. *The importance of minority patterns.* Even if the group mean does faithfully represent performance by a majority of patients, summary statistics can still hide information about extreme scores and other minority patterns that are of great theoretical importance.

These two well-known problems are all the more pressing in research on brain-damaged patients, where within-group variance may be considerably greater than within-group variance in the normal population (e.g., Miceli et al., 1989). In fact, Caramazza has argued that group studies are meaningless in neuropsychology, because one can never assume homogeneity. This is the key point in Caramazza's argument. To drive this point home, he makes a number of additional assumptions that are far more controversial than the first two points:

3. *Homogeneity or universality in normals.* Although there are demonstrable individual differences in the behavior of normal individuals, Caramazza argued that we are entitled to assume homogeneity in the architecture that underlies normal cognition and language. Specifically, we can assume with some confidence that normal individuals all possess the same basic set of processing mechanisms or "boxes"—see Ellis (1982) and Badecker and Caramazza (1991)—and that these processing mechanisms are always configured in the same way (i.e., connected by the same universal set of pathways or "arrows"). Of course cognitive theories can vary in the number and type of mechanisms that they use to explain behavior, and in the kinds of pathways or connections that tie these mechanisms together in time. Indeed, the hope is that neuropsychological data can help to decide between different "box and arrow" models. However, the starting point for all such research must be the assumption of a universal architecture in all normal adults (and, by extension, in all normal children at a comparable point in development).

4. *Subtraction or transparency in the relation between symptoms and architecture in brain-damaged patients.* According to Caramazza and his colleagues, data from brain-damaged patients can only be used for the aforementioned purpose if we can assume a direct and discoverable relationship between behavioral symptoms and the underlying architecture that is responsible for those symptoms. In particular, we must assume that the behavior of a brain-damaged patient reflects the operation of a normal system

minus some damaged component. In other words, processes can be sub-tracted or removed from the system without changing the functions carried out by those mechanisms that remain. If it could be shown that brain-damaged patients develop new and idiosyncratic processes that are not present in normal individuals, then the classic methods of cognitive neu-ropsychology would be difficult if not impossible to implement. Caramazza argued that there is no basis for cognitive neuropsychology if qualitative adaptations exist; hence we should assume that they do not exist, and go on with our work (see Fodor, 1983, for some related arguments on the impossibility of a coherent science of mind if the mind is not a modular system).

5. *On the irrelevance of replication.* If we assume (a) structural homogeneity in normals, and (b) a transparent relation between symptoms and structure in brain-damaged patients, then we can use the patterns of breakdown in those patients to test for the difference between competing theories of cognitive architecture. If we can find a patient who is selectively impaired in Process A but spared in Process B, then we have evidence in support of any theory that handles A and B with separate mechanisms. The evidence would be even stronger if we could find a double dissociation, that is, a second patient who is selectively impaired in Process B but spared in Process A. Beyond this single-case approach, Caramazza and his colleagues argued there is nothing more to be learned. To be sure, replication is always a source of comfort. But we should not expect or require replications in cognitive neuropsychology, because it is quite unlikely that we will ever find patients with identical lesions. Group studies can only obscure the picture, by mixing together distinct profiles of brain and behavior.

6. *On the limited relevance of neurological information.* Like many practition-ers in the field of cognitive neuropsychology, Caramazza accepted a form of dualism: It is possible to describe and explain disruptions of mental (func-tional) architecture without invoking or in any way assuming a one-to-one relationship between this mental architecture and the neural system that supports it (see also Morton, 1984). To draw conclusions about mental structure, it is enough to show that certain behavioral disruptions are possible.

So far, the single-case crusade has had relatively little impact within developmental neuropsychology. But it has become quite influential in research on brain-damaged adults. For example, as Shallice (1988b) reminded us, this scientific philosophy has been stated as a requirement for one of the major journals in the field, *Cognitive Neuropsychology*.

Although Shallice (1988b) was quite sympathetic to the single-case method (and concerned about abuses of the group method), he pointed out some serious problems that the field will face if the radical proponents of single-case studies win the day: "For some . . . the emphasis on the individual case, a rejection of the group study, and a lack of concern with the neurological basis of behavior are becoming almost elements of a creed. There is also a tendency to reject as irrelevant the clinical aspects of a case. This general cluster of positions I will call ultra-cognitive neuropsychology" (p. 203).

We share Shallice's (1988b) concerns about ultracognitive neuropsychology. We do not dispute the value of single-case studies in neuropsychological research, but we are concerned about some constraints on this method that have been overlooked in recent applications. Human behavior is inherently stochastic, and measures of human behavior are never perfect. These two sources of uncertainty (i.e., uncertainty of measurement, and "true" uncertainty in the phenomenon to be measured) force us to consider the possibility that apparent patterns of dissociation occur entirely by chance, for reasons that have nothing to do with cognitive architecture or the neurological system that sustains it. This brings us to the next section.

CHARYBDIS: THE CASE AGAINST SINGLE-CASE AND SMALL-GROUP STUDIES

Although statisticians come in many varieties, and they disagree on many matters, there is one statement with which all statisticians clearly agree: The reliability of an estimate is directly related to the number of observations that it contains. If we choose to restrict our attention to a single case (or a small set of cases), then we must be even more scrupulous about the reliability and validity of our measures, to avoid errors of interpretation based on spurious patterns of association and dissociation. The major problems associated with the interpretation of single-case and small-sample studies can be summarized in five parts: (a) base rate performance in the appropriate control populations, (b) reliability, (c) the underlying shape of the distribution (d) the probability of obtaining dissociations by chance, given a range of measures and patients with the properties discussed in a–c, and (e) the questionable relevance of idiosyncratic findings—even when those findings prove to be a stable characteristic of the patient.

Base Rates and Expected Values.   Claims about single dissociations within a single patient, and double dissociations within two patients, typically rest on a nonparametric comparison of error rates on two or more tests. Such comparisons rest, in turn, on two crucial assumptions that are rarely met in single-patient studies: first, that the different errors produced by that patient are independent entities; second, that the expected distributions should be equivalent for both measures (i.e., both measures are equally difficult for the population at large). In fact, it is quite unlikely that the error produced by our patient at Moment A is independent of the error produced at Moment B. Even more important, we cannot always assume that the expected distribution is identical for both measures.

Consider the following example. Miceli and Caramazza (1988) reported a case study of an aphasic patient who shows a supposed selective impairment between two aspects of lexical/grammatical morphology. Specifically, this patient produces many errors of inflectional morphology (e.g., noun and verb suffixes), but virtually no errors of the derivational type (e.g., substituting "-tion" for "-ment" in words like *government* or *management*). Their conclusion that this profile represents a selective and theoretically important deficit is necessarily based upon the implicit assumption that inflectional and derivational errors should be equally likely when a patient starts to make mistakes.

This assumption may be incorrect. Using a very large sample of speech error data from normal adults, Dell (1988) reported that errors in inflectional morphology (though rare) are more common than errors in derivational morphology. This fact comes to light only when the normal sample is extremely large; in a smaller sample of normal performance, we rarely observe errors of either type. Nevertheless, the true base rate difference revealed in a larger sample of normals may become quite important when we observe errors in inflectional versus derivational morphology in aphasic patients. Indeed, we should expect to find that inflectional morphology is selectively vulnerable under a range of different conditions. This prediction is supported in a series of cross-linguistic studies by Bates and her colleagues (for reviews, see Bates & Wulfeck, 1989a, 1989b). In richly inflected languages with a great deal of inflectional morphology, supposed dissociations of the kind demonstrated by Miceli and Caramazza (1988) are quite common; they occur in receptive and expressive language, in several different forms of aphasia. This could occur because the two forms of morphology are handled by different processors; but it might also reflect quantitative differences between the two morpheme types within a single processor (in which, for some reason we do not yet understand, derivational morphemes are more "robust").

Reliability. Spurious single and double dissociations can also arise from differences in the internal reliability of measures. Suppose, for example, that we find two patients with the following complementary profiles: Smith scores at 80% on Task A, with a 45% score on Task B; Jones scores at 20% on Task A, with a 55% score on Task B. At face value, it seems fair to conclude from these patterns that Task A and Task B tap into mechanisms that can be doubly dissociated. However, there are alternative explanations for the same distribution. Figure 12.1 illustrates the true distributions that underlie our two hypothetical tasks. As we can see, although the two tests have similar means, they differ greatly in their internal reliability. Task A is extremely

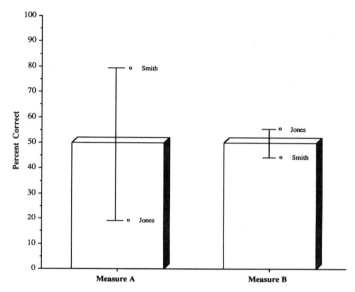

FIG. 12.1.   Hypothetical distribution for two patients against measures with markedly different standard deviations.

noisy, with a huge standard deviation; indeed, a single standard deviation can span the distance from 20% to 80%. Task B is much more reliable, with a single standard deviation that spans the distance between 45% and 55%. For present purposes, our point is that the double dissociation observed in Smith and Jones could have been obtained entirely by chance; in both cases, on both measures, the patients are within one standard deviation from the mean (see Miceli et al., 1989, for some claims about double dissociation based on distributions of this sort).

Researchers committed to the single-case method might dismiss these arguments by pointing out that normals make no errors at all on Tasks A and B. Therefore the true mean in the population at large is 100%. However, it is possible to obtain ceiling effects on two measures as different in their internal reliability as the hypothetical tests described here. Differences in the fidelity or noise inherent in two instruments may be evident only at certain points in the distribution, for example, in patients who are operating with global but severe resource limitations. When the entire system is subjected to stress or noise, we start to find double dissociations of the sort just described—patterns that may tell us nothing at all about the neurological underpinnings of cognitive processing.

Shape of the Underlying Distribution.   Shallice (1988a, 1988b) pointed out some related problems revolving around the assumptions of linearity and additivity that underlie so much research in this field, leading investigators to spurious conclusions about the dissociations responsible for contrasting performance profiles. To illustrate, consider the three performance functions illustrated in Fig. 12.2 (an adaptation and elaboration of a figure in Shallice, 1988b). Each function represents a relationship between performance on a given measure, and the amount of capacity or resources required for various levels of performance (we use the terms *capacity* and *resource* interchangeably in this discussion). Function 1 (f1) illustrates the kind of linear performance/capacity function that we typically assume (implicitly or explicitly) in drawing conclusions about single and double dissociations. Function 2 (f2) illustrates a nonlinear function that rises sharply from baseline, levels off around 90%, and rises slowly toward asymptote after that point. Function 3 illustrates another nonlinear relationship between capacity and performance (f3), the kind of S-shaped function that is in fact very common in the literature on attention and performance. If we assume a linear function when the task in question is really governed by a nonlinear distribution, there are at least three ways that we can be led to erroneous conclusions about differential patient profiles.

First, suppose we observe three patients (A, B, and C) on a single task, and obtain the following scores: 98% correct (2% error), 93% correct (7% error), and 75% correct (25% error). We typically conclude that Patient C is far more impaired than the other two (i.e., 3–10 times as many errors). This assumption

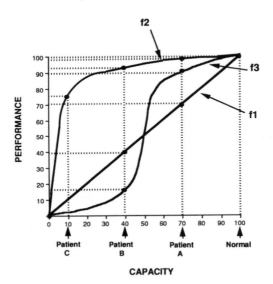

FIG. 12.2. Hypothetical linear and nonlinear distributions between performance and capacity.

would be warranted if there is a linear relationship between performance and severity of impairment (i.e., absolute amount of an underlying resource). However, let us suppose instead that the relationship between resources and performance is multiplicative rather than additive, as illustrated by the cur-vilinear function (f2) in Figure 12.2. As the reader can see by tracing these three performance scores (vertical axis) down to their corresponding capacity levels (horizontal axis), the amount of impairment necessary to drive error rates from 0% to 7% (i.e., a 60% loss of capacity) is actually twice as great as the amount of impairment required for a further increase in error rates from 7% to 25% (i.e., an additional 30% loss in capacity).

Now consider a case in which we are trying to establish a dissociation between two measures within a single patient (take Patient B). Unbeknownst to us, Task 1 follows the linear function (f1); Task 2 has a distribution closer to the nonlinear function (f2). Our patient displays a 60% error rate on Task 1, but commits errors only 7% of the time on Task 2. It is tempting to conclude that this patient suffers a selective deficit in the domain measured by Task 1. However, upon closer examination we can see that the deficits underlying this profile (i.e., absolute amounts of resource reduction) are equivalent for the two tasks (i.e., a 60% loss in capacity). In other words, there is no selective dissociation at the resource level. Presumably, the resource level is the one that is most relevant to the claim that processing mechanisms can be dissociated in brain-damaged patients.

Finally, as Shallice (1988a, 1988b) noted, differences in the performance/capacity functions that underlie two tasks can also create spurious double dissociations across patients, if these patients differ markedly along some global dimension of resource or capacity. Suppose we observe Patients A and B on Tasks 1 and 3. We are unaware of the fact that Task 1 follows a linear resource/performance function (f1), whereas Task 3 follows an S-shaped resource/performance function (f3). Patient A is functioning at a fairly high level overall, placing him in the 70% range on our hypothetical axis of resources; Patient B is more impaired across the board, falling at the 40% resource level on both tasks. Because of the underlying difference in resource/performance functions in Task 1 and Task 3, Patient A will perform better on Task 3 (90% correct) than Task 1 (70% correct); for the same reasons, Patient B will display the reverse pattern, performing better on Task 1 (40% correct) than Task 3 (16% correct). It looks very much as though there is a double dissociation between the processing mechanisms or knowl-edge systems that underlie each task; in this case, however, the supposed dissociation is actually produced by differences along a continuous dimension of capacity. In other words, we can be fooled—and fooled badly—if we do not understand the functions that relate performance to capacity for each and every task that we use with brain-damaged patients.

How Many Dissociations Should We Expect by Chance? Consider an abstract set of data, containing five variables for each of 20 cases. Assume that all the cells in this hypothetical data base contain scores that are sampled from the same population, a normal distribution with a mean of 0 and a standard deviation of 1 (i.e., assume that the standardized form of each variable follows an independent standard normal distribution). Let us define a dissociation between two variables as follows: Within the same case, the obtained score on one variable is one or more standard deviations above the mean, and on some other variable the obtained score is one or more standard deviations below the mean. On the basis of sampling error, there is a probability of approximately 0.32 that a score in any cell would be at least one standard deviation above or at least one standard deviation below the mean, and there is a probability of 0.16 that, for the same subject, some other cell would be one standard deviation above or below the mean, in the opposite direction as the first cell. Thus there is a probability of approximately 0.0512 (0.32 × 0.16) of finding a dissociation (as we have defined it previously) for any pair of variables for any subject. The total number of nonredundant pairs of variables that can be picked is "5 things taken 2 at a time," or 10, leading to an expected number of "dissociations" per subject of 0.512. Given that the data set contains 20 subjects, the expected number of chance dissociations is 0.512 × 20, or approximately 10. As the number of variables in the data set increases, so too does the number of expected chance dissociations. For 20 subjects, the expected number of chance dissociations for a data set with 10, 15, and 20 variables would be 46, 108, and 195 respectively.

This kind of analysis only applies when we know the number and range of patients from whom the cases with a putative dissociation were chosen. In many of the single-case studies reported in the neuropsychological literature, the situation is much worse. Indeed, we have no information at all on the number of patients that were screened before the "interesting" pattern appeared. If we can expect to find 195 dissociations in 20 subjects tested on 20 measures, how many dissociations would we expect to find if we were able to survey and measure the life's work of a practicing neurologist? What are the base rate probabilities that we might expect for a neuropsychological clinic that provides complete screening of 1,500 patients per year, using a detailed battery of neuropsychological measures? There are only three ways around this problem:

1. Adjust the alpha level for defining a true dissociation to an extremely conservative level, one that takes into account the number and range of patients that are screened to obtain the interesting case.
2. Avoid the use of bizarre and unpredicted patterns of dissociation.
3. If a bizarre and unexpected dissociation does emerge unexpectedly, be sure to replicate that dissociation across a number of different

tasks, preferably including tasks with different sources of chance variation (see also Shallice, 1988a).

Unfortunately, these recommendations are ignored in many current reports of "unusual" dissociations in brain-injured adults. As a result, it is hard to know which studies should be taken seriously.

The Questionable Relevance of Idiosyncratic Findings.   Imagine for the moment that we have found a rare and totally unexpected dissociation, one that appears to be very stable across many tasks and sessions. Furthermore, assume that the base rate probability of this pattern is exceedingly low. There are still serious limitations on the use that we can make of this case. Unusual patterns of association and dissociation in an individual patient may occur for idiosyncratic reasons that have no direct bearing on the organization of the brain and/or the organization of a normal language processor. The most obvious examples come from the psychiatric literature, where we find a vast array of peculiar and often unique obsessions, compulsions, phobias, and/or fixations in patients who are (as far as we know) neurologically intact. Most of us would agree that strong conclusions about the architecture of brain and mind would be unwise in such cases. And yet, when unusual deficits appear in a patient with focal brain damage (e.g., a selective impairment in naming fruits and vegetables—Hart, Berndt, & Caramazza, 1985), explanations of this sort are not uncommon. We certainly are not arguing for the equivalence of psychiatric and neuropsychological symptoms. But it is worth considering why we are so often willing to assume a transparent relationship between neural architecture and symptom patterns in one case, but not in the other.

One might argue that the transparency assumption is on firmer ground when patients who were normal prior to their illness display unique symptoms following focal brain damage. And yet, might we not expect a pathological adaptation to a pathological condition? A bored or frightened patient has many hours to worry and to analyze his disease, developing his own particular self-fulfilling theory of those things that are "hard" or "easy" for him; hence, unusual symptom patterns could in principle reflect an adaptation (positive or negative) that is related only indirectly to the disease process itself (Heeschen, 1985; Kolk, 1985; Kolk & van Grunsven, 1985). The notion of adaptation is rendered all the more plausible by increasing evidence that aphasic patients retain knowledge of linguistic structure, and (in many cases) the ability to reflect consciously on that structure (e.g., recent studies documenting preservation of grammaticality judgments in Broca's aphasics; see especially Linebarger, Schwartz, & Saffran, 1983; Shankweiler, Crain, Gorrell, & Tuller, 1989; Wulfeck, 1988). This fact forces us to recognize the further possibility that individual patients may shift their behavior in individual directions (adaptive or maladaptive) as they gain experience with the effects of their disease. We cannot assume a transparent relationship between symptom patterns and the architecture of either brain or mind.

Fortunately for us, the problem of idiosyncratic adaptations is somewhat reduced for researchers working with rare populations of children. First, this is true because (as noted earlier) we usually choose our subjects on independent grounds. That is, the children are in our studies because they belong to a well-defined clinical group, and not because they showed up by accident in our laboratory with a peculiar and unexpected form of behavior. Second, young children are much less sophisticated than the mature adults under study in many neuropsychological clinics. They have less metalinguistic (or metacognitive) awareness, that is, less ability to worry, analyze, think about and redirect their symptoms in peculiar directions. To be sure, this is only a difference of degree. There are no guarantees against the appearance of idiosyncratic strategies, in children of any age. In the long run, protections against spurious results must be based on the twin pillars of theory and replication. Unexpected results should be used with extreme caution, until we have a theory in which they make good sense, and grounds for predicting a similar pattern in other individuals.

THE ODYSSEY: SOME RECOMMENDATIONS FOR SAILING THROUGH SCYLLA AND CHARYBDIS

The recommendations outlined next were developed for the University of California, San Diego, Neurodevelopmental Program, a research consortium[1] that is studying the development of language, cognition, and affect in children between 0 and 12 years of age. We have set out to compare and contrast patterns of development across several important but very rare populations: (a)"late talkers" and children with well-defined forms of specific language impairment, (b) children who have sustained specific forms of focal brain injury before 6 months of age, (c) children with Williams versus Down syndromes (contrasting forms of mental retardation), (d) children with prenatal exposure to cocaine and/or methamphetamine (a population in which sample sizes are quite small after we have controlled for a host of confounding factors), and (e) children with inborn errors of metabolism, including some exceedingly rare syndromes that permit us to study at most two to three cases at a time. These children are being followed longitudinally wherever possible, and we are using the same battery of standardized and

[1]This research consortium is funded by two large program project grants: NINDS "Center for the Study of the Neural Bases of Language," covering research with children from 4 to 12 years of age, and NIDCD "Program Project: Origins of Communication Disorders," sponsoring our research with children from 0 to 4 years of age.

experimental measures with all these populations. As a result, we can compare and contrast profiles of sparing and impairment within a particular development level, as well as trajectories of recovery and delay across developmental levels.

This comparative strategy provides far more information than we would obtain from any of these groups if they were investigated separately. However, the comparative strategy is no protection against the many methodological problems outlined previously. Indeed, because we are conducting comparisons across measures, across ages, and across clinical groups, all of these problems are magnified. The sample sizes are small and the statistical comparisons that we want to carry out are large in number. Furthermore, these groups often vary in the amount of within-group variance they display, and in the shape of the distribution (i.e., assumptions of normality and homogeneity of variance do not apply).

We have no magic bullets to provide readers who are faced with similar problems. But we have developed a set of partial solutions that hold these dangers to a minimum. Let us start with a list of homilies, precautions that are probably obvious to most investigators in this field, but worth listing nonetheless. Then we present a three-level approach to data analysis in a large comparative project, an approach that separates exploratory analysis from hypothesis testing in a very clear way, reducing the problem of "alpha explosion." Finally, we describe some applications of Maximum Likelihood Estimation and Randomization Tests, two very useful techniques that are not well known but have considerable potential for research with small but well-defined samples.

Six Homilies for Small-Sample Research

Deviations from the Normal Distribution in Risk-Based Samples.   This is the first and most important analytic concern in research with special populations. Often samples are small because they are defined by a state of risk; that is, membership in a special small sample is determined by a medical condition (e.g., a particular type of location of brain lesion), a condition of birth (e.g., born of a mother under 15 years of age), or some other special condition. In these cases, very special care must be taken in applying "normal" statistics because these samples display exactly those features that make the use of large-sample, normal theory statistical techniques problematic. The problem is not simply one of sample size. Suppose, for example, that the number of available cases of infants with focal brain injury were suddenly to increase a hundredfold, due to some unforeseen international disaster. Despite the resulting increase in sample size, it is quite likely that two important distributional problems would still remain: highly unusual variances (i.e., the range of variation observed in our special population is markedly different from the range observed in normal controls) and non-normal population kurtosis (i.e., a general "flattening" of the variance at the center of the distribution). When these two features are coupled with small sample sizes (situations under which the Central Limit Theorem cannot be relied upon), the result is that standard statistical techniques, even the highly robust t test, behave poorly. Later on we discuss two analytic procedures (maximum likelihood estimation and randomization tests) that are designed to get around these problems.

Missing Data.   Despite heroic efforts to minimize missing data, there will be missing data points in any complex multivariate longitudinal study—an issue that is even more likely to come up in research with special populations (i.e., children whose sessions often must be interrupted or rescheduled for reasons that are related to their disabilities, or to family stress). In those cases where the missing data points represent subject dropout, our decision has been to include subjects in longitudinal analyses up to the point of dropping out. In all such cases, comparisons of subjects who leave the study with those who remain should be conducted prior to any further group comparisons, to determine if there is any specific pattern to dropout. Second, where it is possible to do so (i.e., where sample size is large enough to warrant parametric tests), results can be backweighted (i.e., adjusted proportional to the amount and type of data that are missing) to permit conclusions across population-based categories; in these cases, reweighting must be done at each stage of the study to reflect changing subject attrition. In those cases where missing data represent single missing data points (e.g., a laboratory measure that could not be obtained because of subject "fussiness"), contemporary methods of missing data estimation (multiple imputation theory) can be used to estimate the missing data value (see Little & Rubin, 1987; Rubin, 1987). In all cases where an analysis involves missing data estimates, two analyses are run in parallel: The same analysis is performed on the data set with the filled data points and with the data set reduced by subjects with missing data. We recommend that results be reported only where consistent (but not necessarily identical) findings are seen in both analyses.

Protection Against Ad-Hoc Results.   Each of the methods that we have chosen for the Neurodevelopmental Program has a track record in at least one of our associated laboratories. Every procedure has a strong theoretical motivation, and it is associated with a particular set of questions and predictions (although these may differ from one study to another). We also know a great deal about the psychometric properties of our measures (a situation that will be enhanced by the procedures for exploratory analysis of primary data described next). Under these conditions, the likelihood of obtaining spurious and ad-hoc results is significantly reduced.

Protection Against Multiple Tests of Significance. In most of our studies, we are looking not for single outcomes but for patterns of performance across an array of measures, populations, and age levels. Because we will have a large number of data points for every child in the study, we must be sensitive to the "alpha error problem," that is, the problem of capitalizing on chance with multiple tests of the same hypothesis. Our solution to this problem lies in (a) constraints on the level of analysis to which a strong hypothesis applies, (b) methods for aggregating multiple variables into a single robust variable, and (c) constraints on the order in which hypotheses are tested, and/or constraints on the way that individual variables are used within a single complex model.

With regard to the first point, many of the measures that we use to test these hypotheses are full-blown experiments in their own right, each with its own statistical design. In these cases, the hypotheses associated with each experiment are tested within the experiment itself; individual data points are never "exported" for use in (for example) correlational analyses with other data sets. Hence the alpha-level problem for these variables applies only at the "local," experiment-specific level.

Regarding the second point, it is frequently necessary to apply several different measures of a single construct in order to maximize reliability and validity (e.g., several different tests of grammatical comprehension—an area of performance that is notoriously difficult to evaluate in young children). In the same vein, some of our most fine-grained individual measures yield a large number of separate scores (e.g., move-by-move analysis of performance on a block construction task; productivity indices for individual grammatical morphemes) that must be grouped together to represent an abstract construct (e.g., degree of spatial coherence in a block design task; a single metric of "morphological productivity"). To meet these goals, scores are aggregated into one number (or a small set of contrasting numbers) that is then used to answer major questions about a particular population (e.g., are cases of expressive language delay with preserved comprehension more common following left anterior damage, compared with other lesion sites? Is Williams syndrome associated with a degradation of spatial coherence in the block design task? Do the grammatical morphemes produced correctly by language-impaired children meet criteria for morphological productivity?) In cases like these, we have minimized the number of significance tests that have to be conducted to answer a complex question.

In the third case, we are looking for contrasting performance profiles that apply across several distinct data points. At the behavioral level, examples might include the Language > Cognition patterns that characterize Williams syndrome children at a relatively late point in development, and the Language < Cognition patterns that define specific language impairment at every stage; at the neural level, we may instead construct profiles that represent prototypical neuroanatomical configurations for a given population (e.g., differential ratios of vermal lobules 1–5 to vermal lobules 6 and 7 in the cerebellum for normals, Down syndrome, autism, and Williams syndrome). In addition to profiles associated with a single moment in time, we are also seeking trajectories of change on a single measure or a group of measures across a particular developmental window (e.g., the "catch-up" functions observed in some late talkers and infants with focal brain lesions after the one-word stage). In some respects, this search for complex patterns corresponds to the "bottom-up" search associated with exploratory use of regression, factor analysis, and discriminant function analysis. However, many of our projects are well beyond the exploratory stage and have embarked upon a "top-down," confirmatory approach to profile analysis. As we see in more detail below, several indices are often grouped together "by hand" to form a single model, and that model is in turn tested against group and/or individual performance with a single goodness-of-fit statistic. In cases like these, the alpha-level problem takes a very different form. The alpha problem is usually stated in terms of the number of opportunities the experimenter takes to test a single hypothesis (e.g., flipping a coin 10 times to ask a single 50/50 question); in the top-down model-fitting approach that we adopt in many of our integrative analyses, the situation is much more constrained (e.g., one opportunity to toss a 10-sided die).

Replication.   In building up the complex patterns that are the goal of our research (i.e., developmental trajectories and cross-domain profiles within and across populations), we are engaged in an iterative process. In earlier research, we began with a set of contrasting populations selected on theoretical grounds. The expected profiles for each population were tested in small groups of target individuals, using a range of representative measures. Population profiles were refined accordingly, to be tested in successive studies with a new set of measures and a new cohort of experimental and control subjects. This is an open-ended process of hypothesis generation and hypothesis testing; each individual case is treated as an opportunity to replicate the results obtained in previous single-case and/or small-group studies. This emphasis on replication protects us against the temptation to conduct a "fishing expedition."

Optimizing the Match Between Data Sets and Analytic Tools.   Finally, we can obtain the most from a high-quality but very expensive sample of data by ensuring a good match between the structure of the data set and the analytic tools at our disposal. There will of course be many situations in which conventional parametric and/or nonparametric statistics are quite appropriate for our work. The decision to apply these familiar tools will depend on (a) the size of the sample that we have assembled so far to ask a particular question, together with (b) detailed information about measurement reliability and the power needed to test hypotheses using those particular statistical tools. However, those of us who are forced to work with small sample sizes need to be on the alert for new procedures that get around the standard assumptions of normality and homogeneity of variance that underlie so many traditional techniques. Fortunately, statistics is not a static field. Thanks in part to the increase in computational power offered by the new generation of desktop computers, investigators can now take advantage of procedures that were far too expensive to apply to any data set (small or large) 5–10 years ago.

Three Levels of Analysis

To implement these six homilies, we have organized our statistical procedures into three distinct levels, handled by different members of the research team.

Level 1: Data Reduction and Exploratory Analysis

The earliest stage of data reduction, exploratory data analysis (EDA), plays two important roles: (a) in the preparation of data for use in the hypothesis testing mode, and (b) as a source of new hypotheses for future research.

Data Preparation. Before a new data set can be used to test strong hypotheses, it is important to determine whether those data meet the assumptions for a proposed parametric or nonparametric test. Are the data normally distributed? Is there sufficient homogeneity of variance between two groups to permit comparisons within a single analysis of variance? Does the trade-off between sample size and measurement reliability provide enough power to test a given hypothesis? Can we aggregate the data from two or more measures to obtain a more robust index of the construct in question?

Standard methods of outlier detection and influence assessment are employed in all analytic runs in order to detect the undue influence of outlying data points and/or ill-conditioned variable sets (Barnett & Lewis, 1984). Although these techniques can be computationally tedious, many of them have now been implemented within standard packages for statistical analysis.

Visual inspection also plays an important role in the preparation of data for use in this hypothesis-testing mode. Technologies are now available that bring researchers back in touch with their primary data for this purpose. For example, Data Desk (Vellman, 1988) is a powerful Macintosh-based system that permits visual display and manipulation of complex multivariate data sets (in up to five dimensions). These programs are liberating (everything is available at a glance), but they are also chastening (one cannot hide from outliers or from skewed distributions). Intimate knowledge of one's database can never hurt, but this kind of knowledge is particularly important when we are dealing with unusual populations and aberrant patterns of development. We are making programs of this kind available to all participating investigators, with tutoring sessions to bring individual researchers up to speed. If each of us knows our own data in extraordinary detail, the process of collaboration will be greatly facilitated, and it will stand on very firm ground. Above all, we can increase the validity of strong hypothesis tests at the next level, by assuring that the assumptions of conventional statistical procedures have been met.

As noted earlier, there are many situations in which the same construct will be evaluated with several distinct but correlated measures. Prior to detailed multivariate analyses of data sets of this type, data reduction techniques such as principal components analysis and redundancy analysis will be used to determine if the bulk of the individual differences variance (say 85%) can be captured in a reduced set of variables (of a latent constructed variety, or as a simple reduction in the number of "raw" measures). In such cases, we will compare analyses on the reduced variable set with analyses using the full set, and report results that are consistent (though not necessarily identical—see earlier section Missing Data) on both analytic runs. We should also emphasize that this data reduction process is always guided by theoretical concerns: We will not attempt a grouping of variables unless those variables belong together within some reasonable theoretical framework.

Hypothesis Generation. Although it is important to distinguish between hypothesis generation and hypothesis testing, both are critical to the success of any large-scale research endeavor. Indeed, there is a particularly rich tradition of exploratory and descriptive research in developmental psychology (from Piaget to Roger Brown) and neuropsychology (e.g., the rich case studies of Alexander Luria). Because our Neurodevelopmental Program represents the union of developmental psychology and cognitive neuroscience, we plan to continue the analytic traditions that have made those fields so strong.

Data Desk and related EDA programs (e.g., JUMP—Sall, 1989) are particularly useful in this hypothesis-generating phase, for post-hoc analysis of data that have already been subjected to a hard a priori test, and/or for ancillary explorations of measures that are relatively new within our laboratories. They permit investigators to perform simple inferential statistics (e.g., correlation and chi square), call up bar graphs and line graphs of primary data in an instant (with appropriate confidence intervals), construct two- and three-dimensional scatterplots on command (rotating the latter to permit an "eyeball" understanding of the latent factors hidden therein), perform regressions and factor analyses and plot the residuals—a series of exploratory data analyses that can give the individual researcher an intimate knowledge of the distribution that underlies any further analyses that she or he may wish to perform. The basic principles of exploratory data analysis have been expounded by Tukey (1977) and Mosteller and Tukey (1977).

Level 2: Parametric and Nonparametric Tests of Specific Hypotheses

Within each individual project, specific hypotheses have been outlined regarding the population (or linked set of populations) in question. For some between-group contrasts, it may be appropriate to use a standard between-group analysis of variance design (e.g., Late Talkers vs their age-matched and language-matched controls) and/or a multiple analysis of variance design (e.g., to evaluate the relative contributions of semantic versus grammatical information to success on a sentence comprehension task in children with specific Language Impairment compared with their two control groups). Other multivariate analyses may also be appropriate, including discriminant function analysis (testing the power of two to three well-chosen variables to distinguish between those late-talker children who catch up with their age mates and those who continue to lag behind).

We also realize that many of our data sets do not meet the assumptions of standard univariate and multivariate procedures; nonparametric tests will be required for many of our most important hypotheses. Most standard nonparametric procedures are limited to a relatively small number of contrasts; they cannot be used (for example) to test for the existence of a complex interaction among variables. However, nonparametric tests can be used in some fairly complex and interesting ways, to test the validity of whole profiles of performance across several different measures within a given population. Randomization tests (described in more detail later) can play an important role at this level of analysis.

Level 3: Integrative Analyses and Construction of Comparative Models

In addition to the more conventional uses of statistics at Levels 1 and 2, the overall design of the Neurodevelopmental Program permits a series of integrative analyses, comparing profiles of performance across domains and across populations. Here are a few examples.

Techniques for Evaluating Profiles Within and Across Populations. In many instances, we are interested in the extent to which the individual members of a target group fit the abstract profile that drew our interest to that population in the first place. For example, previous research with adult victims of focal lesion injury often leads us to formulate a typical left-hemisphere profile and a typical right-hemisphere profile for a given set of linguistic and/or nonlinguistic tasks. With these formulations in hand, we can then ask whether and/or to what extent either of these profiles provide a good fit to performance by individual children or groups of children with left-versus right-hemisphere injury. At another level of analysis, we may ask whether and/or to what extent the same group profiles fit the data for a population with a very different etiology. For example, our research to date suggests that Williams syndrome children more closely resemble adults with right-hemisphere injury in drawing and block construction task (i.e., local detail with no global coherence); conversely, the performance of Down syndrome children on the same tasks resembles performance by adults with left-hemisphere injury (i.e., preservation of the global properties of a target pattern, with absence of local detail). There are several techniques available that permit us to evaluate the fit of such profiles within and across populations (Maxwell & Delaney, 1990). Maximum likelihood estimation and related procedures (described in more detail later) can play a particularly useful role at this level of analysis.

Techniques for the Analysis of Developmental Change. At a theoretical level, we are also particularly interested in normal and abnormal trajectories of development and change. The patterns of interest include recovery from initial delays in some focal lesion children and late talkers, patterns of reorganization and compensation in victims of early brain injury, and the mysterious process by which children with Williams syndrome overcome initial delays in all aspects of cognition and evolve toward a pattern of language sparing in the face of nonverbal deficits. We ask these questions with a combination of cross-sectional and longitudinal data, and the number of data points and their spacing necessarily differs from one study to another. Hence we need a broad array of techniques for the analysis of change.

In many cases, we are interested in determining the onset point for a single developmental event (e.g., the onset of word combinations) against a background of other behavioral or neural developments (e.g., a change in the event-related potentials observed over the left vs. right hemisphere—Mills, Coffey, & Neville, in press). Time series analyses and survival analysis methods including but not limited to Probit and Logit permit us to examine the degree to which a given individual or group is off schedule in the achievement of a particular developmental milestone.

In some studies, depending on sample size and power, we may be in a position to test developmental profiles with the techniques of growth curve analysis. This class of techniques has been described by Appelbaum, Burchinal, and Terry (1989) as well as by Rogosa and his associates (Rogosa & Ghandour, 1991). It is also closely related to Hierarchical Linear Modeling (HLM; Bryk & Raudenbush, 1987). HLM is a two-stage model developed to study change and correlates of change. It is most appropriate for situations in which the predictor variable and the outcome variable fall along the same dimension (e.g., using initial state in vocabulary development to predict vocabulary size at a later point). Stage 1 is a within-subject analysis, where we model an individual's growth trajectory plus error (with explicit assumptions about the distribution of error around that trajectory). Stage 2 is between-subjects analysis, examining how individual trajectories vary as function of between-subject differences (including the population differences that are a major focus in our Program Project). Under optimal conditions, HLM permits the investigator to model individual growth patterns, predict future development, assess the quality of measurement instruments for distinguishing among growth trajectories, and study systematic variation in a growth trajectory as function of certain independent variables. There are a number of advantages associated with HLM, compared with (for example) repeated measures analysis of variance using age as an independent variable; for one thing, HLM can be used in situations in which the number of data points and the spacing between data points vary from one individual to another. However, this procedure must be used with considerable caution when sample sizes and the number of time points for each subject are small.

For the small-sample situation, randomization tests may prove useful once again, providing a nonparametric test of the probability that a given trajectory type occurs more often in a target population, compared with normal controls and with other groups. For example, we can evaluate the probability of obtaining a catch-up function in language development by children with left-hemisphere injury, compared with the probability of the same nonlinear function in children with right-hemisphere injury and/or in normal controls. This should become clearer when we examine randomization tests in more detail later.

To summarize so far, this three-level approach to data analysis represents our best effort to guard against the methodological dangers inherent in small-sample research. In the long run, however, the best assurance against misinterpretation of data must come from two old-fashioned sources: theory and replication. Assuming that these old-fashioned constraints are in place, some new techniques are available that can make the most of small-sample data under strong theoretical assumptions.

MAXIMUM LIKELIHOOD ESTIMATION AND RELATED TECHNIQUES FOR DETERMINING GOODNESS OF FIT WITHIN A MULTIVARIATE DESIGN

The various precautions described previously pertain to a situation in which we have a large number of variables, and a small number of subjects. If we try to analyze each variable separately, then we are forced to confront the alpha explosion described earlier. However, the situation is very different if we treat these variables together in a single test of a complex and theoretically specified profile. As noted earlier, this is analogous to the contrast between 50 tosses of a single six-sided die, and one toss of a single die with 50 sides. In this section, we describe some techniques for evaluating the goodness of fit between data for a single subject (or a small group of subjects) and the profile of results that we would predict for that subject across a broad set of measures. These procedures offer three distinct advantages for small-sample research: They reduce the alpha problem, they permit us to test complex hypotheses, and they do not require any assumptions about the underlying distribution.

Maximum Likelihood Estimation (MLE) belongs to a family of procedures for estimating parameters of a model, a family that includes path analysis, structural equation modeling, and multiple regression (among others). When parameters of a model have been estimated through MLE (or alternative procedures), general methods for testing goodness of fit can be applied to evaluate the degree to which the observations that we have obtained correspond to or deviate from this model. To illustrate how this procedure can be used, we offer one extended example from research with brain-damaged adults (Bates, McDonald, MacWhinney, & Appelbaum, 1991; see also McDonald & MacWhinney, 1989).

In this study, MLE was applied to the results of a single complex experiment with aphasic patients who were asked to interpret a series of simple sentence stimuli that represent orthogonal combinations of grammatical information (word order, subject–verb agreement) and semantic information (i.e., the contrast between animate and inanimate objects). These different cues to sentence meaning are set into competing or converging combinations, yielding grammatical sentences like "The horses are kicking the cow," as well as ungrammatical or semigrammatical stimuli like "The horse are kicking the cows," "The pencil the dog chases," and so on. By placing these cues in competition, we can determine the relative weights of each cue (i.e., which source of information is most important for the subject in deciding "who did what to whom"). Previous research using this technique has revealed very different patterns of cue utilization or weighting, depending on the native language, age, neurological status, and the number of languages to which the subjects have been exposed (see articles in MacWhinney & Bates, 1989). For example, we know that English adults rely primarily on word-order information (e.g., picking the pencil as actor in "The pencil is kicking the cow," and choosing the cow as the actor in "The cow are chasing the horses"); Italian adults show a very different pattern, relying primarily on animacy (choosing the cow in the Italian version of "The pencil is kicking the cow") and subject–verb agreement (choosing the horses in the Italian version of "The cow are chasing the horses").

The performance of Broca's aphasics in this experiment was particularly interesting, because it has been argued that these patients have lost the ability to use grammar in their receptive language (Caplan, 1981; Caramazza & Berndt, 1985; Caramazza & Zurif, 1976; Zurif, 1980). If this characterization of Broca's aphasia is correct, then predictions for the aforementioned experiment are clear: Broca's aphasics in all three language groups (English, German, Italian) should base their sentence interpretations entirely on semantic cues, ignoring word order and subject–verb agreement. Differences among the three language groups should be wiped out. But that is not what happened. Instead, Italian and German Broca's aphasics retained significant use of grammatical morphology (the strongest cues in their language) whereas English Broca's aphasics continued (like English normals) to base their interpretations on word-order information. In other words, these patients still know their language! This was the major result that was obtained using traditional analysis of variance techniques. However, the study yielded several additional pieces of information that are difficult to capture with analysis of variance. For example, even though German and Italian patients still make significant use of grammatical morphology, there were differences among individual patients in the degree of morphological impairment observed in this task. MLE permits us to reanalyze the same data, exploring the degree of fit between individual cases and group trends, within and across language groups. Furthermore, MLE permits us to test individual and group data against various idealized theoretical models of aphasia, to see which model fits the data best. Hopefully, the extended example that follows serves to illustrate the power and utility of MLE and related goodness-of-fit procedures for the analysis of individual case and small-sample data.

The particular implementation of MLE that we used to reanalyze these data is a program called STEPIT (Chandler, 1969; for some applications, see Massaro & Oden, 1980, Oden & Massaro, 1978). This MLE procedure assumes a situation in which we have n sources of information or cues available to predict a choice between two or more outcomes. The procedure is used in conjunction with a linear (additive) or nonlinear (multiplicative) mathematical model. The equation that we use in the simulations described later is an adaptation of the multiplicative model used by Massaro and his associates (Massaro & Oden, 1980). The probability that a subject will choose the first noun on a given sentence is given by the formula:

$$\% \text{ first-noun choice} = \frac{PS_i}{[PS_i + PS_j]}$$

where S = cue strength, i = cue favoring the first noun, and j = cue favoring the second noun. This formula can be paraphrased as follows: The product of the weights for order type, verb agreement, and animacy in favor of choosing the first noun as agent, divided by that same number plus the product of the weights for order type, verb agreement, and animacy favoring the second noun as agent.

STEPIT is applied iteratively, using this formula to locate that set of input strengths or cue weights that provides the best possible fit to the choice behaviors that are observed when the cues are combined in different ways. The procedure seeks one absolute weight for each cue; this value is entered into the equation to predict behavior in every cell of the design in which that cue is present. On each try, the program generates a goodness-of-fit statistic to compare the observed values with the values predicted by that particular set of cue weights. This process is repeated until the smallest possible deviation or discrepancy between the *observed distribution* and the *predicted distribution* is obtained. If the final fit is good, then we may conclude that our model predicts the data very well. If the fit is bad, we must assume either that the model is bad (in which case, we may seek a different mathematical model, and/or a different set of predictors), or we may conclude that the data are too noisy and unsystematic to be fit by any model (in which case, we may add subjects to increase the reliability of a group mean, or add data points to increase the reliability of an individual distribution).

Several different goodness-of-fit statistics are available for this purpose, each with slightly different theoretical consequences. These include rho—which estimates the linear correlation between the 27 observed cells and the 27 expected cells, regardless of their absolute magnitude—and root mean square deviation (RMSD)—which tries to keep the absolute deviation low across all cells in the design. Both of these techniques give equal importance to every cell; hence, in theory it is possible to obtain a relatively good overall fit despite very bad fits between observed and expected values in a few outlier cells. If those few cells are important for our theory, we may want to minimize outliers by choosing a higher polynomial for our goodness-of-fit statistic (e.g., root mean cubed deviation); in principle (but rarely in practice), we could also design a model in which cells that are particularly important on theoretical grounds are given greater weight. Although these alternatives are attractive, the most conservative and widely used technique for evaluating goodness of fit is RMSD. RMSD can vary between 0 (representing a perfect fit) and 1 (representing a maximally poor fit). Hence we are seeking models that will generate a low RMSD.

Exactly what constitutes a "good" fit, and how can we decide whether one model fits our data better than another? Suppose one model fits the data with an RMSD of .2500 whereas another yields an RMSD of .2480. Do we really want to conclude that the second model is better? The major disadvantage of MLE, compared with traditional parametric statistics, is that it offers no probability value to assess the reliability of the difference between two models. This is the case because the model compares absolute numbers, without taking into consideration the amount of variation that may be present around those numbers. If the numbers themselves are stable (e.g., if they represent reliable group means, or stable performance estimates from one patient), then the data will be more systematic and it should be possible to obtain a good fit with the "right" model; if the numbers themselves are unreliable, then it will be difficult to obtain a low RMSD with any set of weights.

On the other hand, the fact that MLE deals with absolute numbers also permits us to carry out comparisons that are not possible with parametric statistics. For example, we can use the same goodness-of-fit statistics to test the degree to which a given individual fits the distributions obtained for one or more groups (e.g., does this bilingual speaker behave more like a modal Italian or a modal German? Does this aphasic patient look more like a Broca or a Wernicke?). We can also use the goodness-of-fit statistic to compare the abstract distance separating two or more groups (e.g., is the German distribution more similar to English or to Italian?). Furthermore, if the data set is highly reliable, we can generate a meaningful comparison of the degree to which one individual patient fits the profile produced by another single case. Finally, as we see later, we can use MLE to create a series of theoretically specified models (e.g., different models of receptive agrammatism), and test the fit of each patient group and each individual patient to the patterns of performance predicted by each theory.

In our simulations of aphasic performance, we began by using MLE to uncover the pattern of cue weights that generated the best fit for normal speakers of English, German, and Italian, respectively. Then we calculated the goodness of fit for individual aphasic patients to each of these three models of normal performance. These comparisons clearly showed that all English patients are best fit by the English model, most Italian patients are best fit by the Italian model, and most German patients are best fit by the German model. In other words, agrammatic aphasics retain (at least to some degree) the specific pattern of cue weights utilized by normal speakers of their language. Nevertheless, the RMSD for all these comparisons was relatively high, proving what we already knew in advance: Aphasic adults suffer from some kind of comprehension deficit. To obtain more information about the nature of that deficit, we then "lesioned" the normal model for each language in accordance with several idealized theories of aphasia. These included the *agrammatism model* in which grammatical cues (word order and agreement) were reduced to random levels whereas semantic cues were left intact; the grammatical *morphology model*, in which the weights for subject-verb agreement were reduced to random levels whereas word order and semantics were left intact; and the *normalcy-through-noise model* in which all cues were set to operate at half their normal strength. Each of these models was applied to the data for each aphasic patient, and for the aphasics as a group. For most individuals and for the aphasics as a group, the normalcy-through-noise model actually provided a better fit to the data than any of the classic aphasia models. However, some individual patients were better fit by a model that assumes selective deficits in the ability to process the endings on nouns and verbs (i.e., agreement morphology). This shows that MLE can be used to compare the performance of individual patients with group data, and with the patterns of performance that we would expect to obtain based on various competing theories of the underlying deficit.

At this point, it may be useful to discuss (briefly) the different philosophy behind MLE and multiple regression, a modeling procedure that may be more familiar to many of our readers. MLE is what we might call a top-down procedure. An investigator specifies the model that he wants to test in advance; his choice of models is jointly determined by the experimental design (e.g., the $3 \times 3 \times 3$ design of the sentence enactment experiment), and the particular theory that he wants to test. For example, in the Bates McDonald, MacWhinney, & Appelbaum (1991) study we decided in advance to use nine parameters (three levels of word order, three levels of agreement, and three levels of animacy) and a multiplicative formula for combining those parameters. The nine-parameters approach is relatively conservative (e.g., it allows for the possibility that agreement may have a different effect when it occurs on the first versus the second noun in a sentence). However, it is still a small enough number that the model does not become trivial (e.g., we could predict all 27 cells in the design perfectly if we had 27 parameters to work with!). We could have made other assumptions (e.g., in other studies, including some using the same data set, we have tried a smaller set of parameters, and a comparison of multiplicative and additive formulae—see McDonald & MacWhinney, 1989, for a detailed discussion). For present purposes, the point is that these decisions do not emerge from the data themselves (e.g., they are not based on the results of an analysis of variance, or any other bottom-up procedure); instead, they are independently motivated and imposed on the data in a top-down fashion. Maximum likelihood estimation is a procedure that finds the best possible set of parameter values against which this model can be tested; we are not particularly interested in the parameter values themselves, but in the extent to which a whole theoretically determined model fits this particular sample of reality. By contrast, multiple regression is typically used as a bottom-up procedure, in which we are trying to determine a posteriori which parameters provide the best account for the data in question (e.g., which variables contribute significant and/or unique variance to a given outcome measure). In regression, the parameters themselves are of central interest, as opposed to the way in which those parameters combine. In principle, multiple regression could be used in the top-down mode we have just described, but it is not particularly well suited for this purpose. First, it is not clear that regression would be very useful for the understanding of individual subject data; in a sense, the advantages of regression over MLE (i.e., availability of significance tests) are part and parcel of its disadvantages (i.e., dependence on derivation from group data with a reasonably well-behaved distribution). Second, the only way to achieve the equivalent of a multiplicative MLE model using regression would be to specify and enter all the possible multiplicative combinations of predictors as variables in the design (i.e., interaction terms like *animacy* × *agreement*). This is mathematically feasible, but clumsy and difficult to interpret. Third, the least squares estimation principles of regression will not necessarily yield the same results that are obtained with MLE. In short, MLE is the method of choice for certain experimental designs, if we know the range of theories that we would like to test.

This example of MLE is ideally suited to the results of a single complex experiment, where a single outcome is predicted by several different sources of information. We can obtain some of the same advantages provided by MLE in a greatly simplified form, in analyses that contrast behavioral profiles for individual children and groups across a relatively large set of outcome variables, drawn from different tests and different experimental situations. Fig. 12.3 illustrates a hypothetical but representative data set. We begin with a set of 12 behavioral measures, including 6 different measures of language and 6 nonverbal indices (5 measures of visual-spatial analysis through drawing and/or construction, and a single test of face recognition). Based on previous research, we have selected these 12 measures for their potential in discrimi-

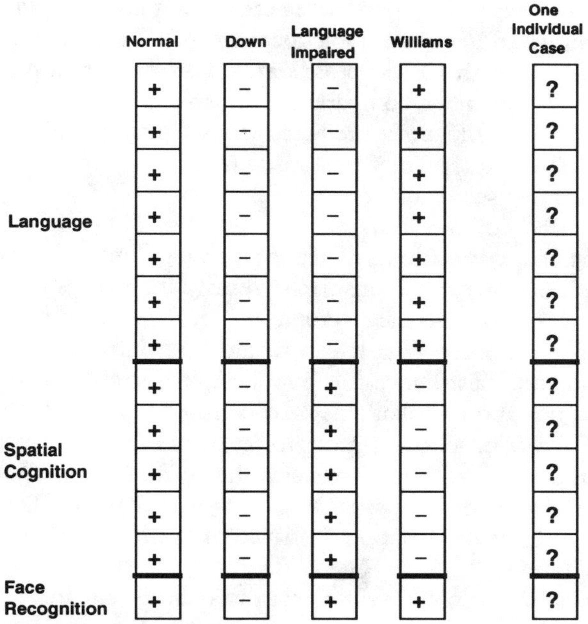

	Normal	Down	Language Impaired	Williams	One Individual Case
Language	+	−	−	+	?
	+	−	−	+	?
	+	−	−	+	?
	+	−	−	+	?
	+	−	−	+	?
	+	−	−	+	?
	+	−	−	+	?
Spatial Cognition	+	−	+	−	?
	+	−	+	−	?
	+	−	+	−	?
	+	−	+	−	?
	+	−	+	−	?
Face Recognition	+	−	+	+	?

FIG. 12.3. Idealized behavioral profiles for four populations and one individual case.

nating among four experimental groups (normal controls, LI, Williams syndrome, Down syndrome); plus or minus entries within each cell in Fig. 12.3 indicate the global level of performance we expect on each measure, within each group. In this simplified diagram, we expect reasonably good performance across the board by normals (where " + " indicates age-typical performance), poor performance across the board by Down syndrome children (indicated by " – " in every cell), a Language < Cognition profile in the language-impaired children (indicated by " – " entries in the language cells), and a Language > Cognition profile in Williams syndrome children (indicated by " + " in the language cells and " – " entries in the nonverbal cells, except for a predicted " + " entry in our test of facial recognition).

A matrix of this kind can be used to conduct confirmatory and exploratory research with individuals. At the confirmatory level, we can test the degree to which one or more individuals within a target population fit the profile that we have projected for that group (compared with the profiles that define other groups). At the exploratory level, we can take the data for a single case suffering from a rare syndrome that has never been described before in neuropsychological terms, and fit those data to alternative population profiles to determine (for example) if this syndrome is best fit by the assumptions of (a) normalcy, (b) general retardation, (c) specific language impairment, or (d) cognitive impairment with linguistic sparing. To obtain goodness-of-fit statistics, we replace the + / – entries in each cell in Fig. 12.3 with a score that represents mean and/or prototypic performance by each target group in previous research (with scores across tests transformed and normalized to a common scale). Then we compare the observed scores for our individual subjects with each of these predicted arrays, using one or two simple goodness-of-fit statistics. The rho statistic (rank order correlation) compares the ranking among scores observed in our target subject with the rank order predicted by each of the four reference groups. The winner is the group configuration that correlates most highly with data obtained from our target individual. Notice that rho is sensitive to relative differences among scores but not to absolute levels. This means, for example, that the overall rank order for cases of across-the-board retardation would be similar (in principle) to the rank order for normals; hence this goodness-of-fit statistic can tell us about deviance but not about global delay. By contrast, we can use RMSD to test the absolute deviation of our target subject from each comparison group; by definition, the group pattern that yields the smallest RMSD is the one that provides the best fit for our target subject. Notice that RMSD (unlike rho) is sensitive to the global retardation displayed by the idealized Down syndrome group.

These procedures provide a simple way to quantify the interpretive process that neuropsychologists carry out "by eye" when they evaluate unusual and deviant profiles in single-case studies. Unfortunately, like the eyeball procedure, these goodness-of-fit tests do not come with confidence intervals or p values. But they can be used to quantify conformity versus deviation on a case-by-case basis, until enough cases are available to apply a nonparametric test (e.g., a sign test to the number of instances in which our hypothesis was confirmed or disconfirmed). RMSD scores can also be used as the dependent variable in parametric analyses, when the conditions for a parametric test are warranted (e.g., a procedure adopted in Bates, McDonald, MacWhinney, & Appelbaum, 1991, where RMSD scores for individual aphasics were entered into an analysis of variance testing the overall predictive value of different aphasia models). Finally, we have begun to investigate procedures that take into account the variation around each predictor measure, seeking a cross-profile equivalent of a confidence interval that can also be used to evaluate individual patients (i.e., does the profile obtained for this individual LI patient fall outside the range of variation across this profile that we are likely to encounter in a normal sample?) Hence we can begin to combine goodness-of-fit procedures with the randomization tests described next.

RANDOMIZATION TESTS

The basic logical structure underlying randomization test methodology was first presented by Fisher (1935) in his description of the problem of the "Lady Tasting Tea." Although the logic of the approach is one of the oldest in hypothesis testing (and although one application of it, the Fisher Exact Test, is commonly known), only the availability of high-speed digital computers has made the widespread utilization of this technique possible.

The idea behind the randomization test is both elegant and simple, but is in some ways subtly different from that which forms the basis of much of contemporary "normal theory" hypothesis testing. Randomization test methodology begins with the simple idea of the null hypothesis and a well-formulated alternative hypothesis. The null hypothesis always encapsulates the idea that, absent a demonstration to the contrary, we, as scientists, have no basis for believing that a treatment makes a difference, that a classification scheme is anything more than a flight of our own fancy, that two attributes are related, and so forth. The null hypothesis will most often be stated in terms of a parameter such as the mean being zero, the difference of parameters being zero, a ratio being one, or a set of parameters being equal. The alternative hypothesis can be either the simple negation of the null hypothesis or a more restricted subset. For instance, the alternative could be simply that there is a difference among several groups with regard to the mean level of behavior exhibited in each or one which specifies that a specific group has a higher level of performance than one or more of the other groups. It is the purpose of the randomization test to determine the probability that empirical data would, by chance alone, lead us to think that the alternative hypothesis better characterizes nature than does the null hypothesis if the simple statement of the null hypothesis were, in fact, true.

Perhaps this idea and the derivative operations that define randomization tests can best be understood through an example. Suppose one were interested in the idea that the behavior of one group of individuals (children with Williams syndrome) were more variable on some specific task than that of another group of individuals (say children with Down syndrome). In order to empirically investigate this idea one would measure the behavior of children of these two types, perhaps having selected the exemplars of these two types to be equivalent with regard to gender or IQ or some other attribute. The resulting set of empirical observations is then taken to be the only source of information available to us in order to understand the variability of behavior among these two types of individuals with regard to the attribute of interest. Having obtained the data, one needs to determine an efficient way of indexing that aspect of the subjects' behavior that is of interest. In this case, we are interested in the variability of behavior of subjects and the differences between the two groups with regard to this characterization. We need to be able to characterize the data in a way consistent with this idea, or in technical terms, to establish an effect indicator.

In classical statistical applications, this specification of an effect indicator is done with two ideas in mind: one that characterizes the effect, the other dealing with the statistical distribution of the effect indicator under the null hypothesis. Were we to be approaching this problem from a classical view (rather than that of randomization tests), we would be likely to select as the effect indicator the ratio of the two sample variances

$$s^2\text{Williams}/s^2\text{Down} \tag{2}$$

not simply because there is a face validity to this ratio but because, under certain very restrictive assumptions, it is known that this ratio follows an F distribution. We would not, however, consider the equally "face valid" effect indicator

$$s^2\text{Williams} - s^2\text{Down} \tag{3}$$

not because it is not a perfectly valid indicator of the effect that interests us, but because its distribution under the null hypothesis is not known. We are not so restricted when using randomization test methodology, although we will be interested in whether different effect indicators result in equally powerful tests. Having established a numerical index that characterizes the effect of interest, it is a simple computational matter to estimate this effect indicator in our empirical data. But this estimate by itself tells us little, which leads us to conclude that the magnitude of the effect is due to real differences between Williams and Down children.

Indeed, the statement of the null hypothesis (there is no difference between the variability of the two groups for the targeted behavior) is the logical equivalent of saying that, in this limited regard, the labeling of children as Williams or Down is nothing more than random labeling constrained only by the number labeled as Down or Williams. It is, however, a rather easy matter to investigate the consequences of the *random labeling model*, which is exactly what the randomization test methodology does. Suppose in this example that there were nW Williams children and nD Down children in the sample actually studied, and further suppose that we assume, as the null hypothesis dictates, that the labeling of these children is nothing more than the random assignment of nW labels that say Williams and nD labels that say Down to the nW + nD ; = n children who make up the sample. There are then "n things taken nW at a time" ways in which we can randomly divide the sample of n children into two groups, nW of whom will receive the Williams label and the remaining n − n W of whom will receive the Down label. Although the number of such divisions of the sample into these random groupings can become very large as the total number of subjects increases, it is theoretically possible to consider this experiment with the effect indicator being calculated for each of the possible divisions (randomizations of subjects to "pseudogroups") of the sample. The collection of all values of the effect indicator resulting from the complete set of random assignments of subjects to groups is known as the randomization distribution and describes completely the consequences of the random labeling model; that is, it provides the complete description of what nature would be like if the null hypothesis were true.

Because the randomization distribution describes completely the consequences of the null model, one can easily determine the probability of a result such as the one empirically obtained if indeed the null model is correct. Suppose in our case that the null hypothesis stated that the two variances were equal and the alternative model stated that the Williams children were more variable than the Down children. Suppose further that we decided to use as our effect indicator the unusual statistic

$$s^2\text{Williams} - s^2\text{Down} \tag{4}$$

Let us call that statistic Q. Were the alternative hypothesis true, we would expect values of Q that would be larger than the value of Q were the null hypothesis to be true. As a consequence, obtaining an empirical value of Q which is large relative to the values in the randomization distribution would lead us to conclude that the model implied by the alternative hypothesis is a better representation of nature than that implied by the null hypothesis. The randomization distribution provides us with all possible values of Q that can occur from the random divisions of the population. The probability of getting an empirical result favoring the alternative hypothesis were the null hypothesis to be true is then the proportion of the randomization distribution with values as large or larger than the empirically observed value of Q, that is, the value of Q computed for the real labeling of the two groups. If this proportion (the ‡ value of traditional hypothesis testing) is sufficiently small, small often being taken as .05, we would be inclined to reject the null hypothesis in favor of the alternative. That is, we would conclude that the results we actually obtained were so unlikely if the null hypothesis were true (relative to the alternative hypothesis) that it is unreasonable for us to maintain belief in the null hypothesis as a viable model.

Historically, the difficulty in utilizing this simple and compelling logical approach to hypothesis testing has been in the formulation of the randomization distribution. The amount of computation required even for small sample sizes is staggering. In this day of high-speed computation, it is sometimes difficult to believe that there are bounds imposed by computation, but in the case of the complete randomization test these boundaries are genuine. If the total sample size in a two-group problem is 16, then there are 16! (or about 2.09×10^{13}) possible permutations of the data. If the computer could handle 2,000 of these permutations and accompanying statistical computation a second (about the speed reasonable for a 386-level machine), it would take 331 + years to do all of the computations. (In fairness, it should be noted that not all of these computations would be needed if one wrote efficient algorithms for the complete randomization distribution, but the magnitude is nevertheless correct within 100 years or so!)

Two breakthroughs, however, have made the utilization of randomization tests possible. The first, due to Edgington (1987), is the idea of an "approximate" randomization test, and the second is the widespread availability of high-speed, low-cost computers. It is, however, the first of these two advances that has truly brought randomization test methodology into the realm of the possible. Essentially, the idea behind the approximate randomization test is that one does not need to form the complete randomization distribution in order to produce a statistical test that maintains the validity (i.e., alpha control) of the randomization test. Rather, a random sample of the complete randomization distribution is sufficient to produce a test of adequate validity. In practice, a random sample of between 5,000 and 10,000 values from the complete randomization distribution is adequate for most purposes. Thus, rather than having to generate all possible randomizations and the accompanying values of the effect indicator, one produces a random selection of say 5,000 or so randomizations and estimates the required probabilities from that distribution.

Comparison with Normal Theory Statistics

The underlying logic of randomization tests and more familiar normal theory hypothesis testing is in a number of regards quite similar. The logical status of the null and alternative hypothesis, the idea of rejection rules, the concept of an ‡-level, are all virtually the same. The major point of departure between the two approaches is in the time-consuming and computationally intensive creation of the randomization distribution. In normal theory hypothesis testing, there is no need for the randomization distribution because of the assumption that observations are a random sample from a population with a known (and usually normal) distribution. By making this assumption (which is not made in randomization tests), it is possible to know analytically what the distribution of a carefully selected test statistic is under the null hypothesis. Thus, as opposed to the grossly empirical approach of the randomization test that takes the observed data as the best indicator of the nature of the attribute, normal theory adds an assumption about the nature of the attribute (its distributional form), thereby circumventing the need to generate the randomization distribution. Considerable statistical work has shown that, in many cases, the substitution of a distributional assumption for the randomization distribution is of little practical consequence (i.e., the normal theory approach is robust to violations of the distributional assumption base). The robustness of normal theory approaches is not, however, always the case. For example, tests of the homogeneity of variance (the test of interest in our illustration) are extremely sensitive to violations of their normality assumption and cannot be counted upon to yield valid results except in the most unusual cases. In small-sample cases, violations of the homogeneity of variance and normal kurtosis assumptions can and often do invalidate normal theory statistical tests. Thus, when dealing with hypotheses other than the equality of means or with small and unusual samples that are likely to have unusual variance characteristics or to exhibit nonnormal kurtosis, randomization test methodology (either alone or as a complement to normal theory statistical tests) is a highly useful analytic tool.

CONCLUDING THOUGHTS

Small samples are worth studying. Yet studying small samples obligates the investigator to collect and analyze data that clearly represent the nature of the problem. Furthermore, instead of assuming a normal distribution of scores in a small, unusual sample, we recommend that investigators be prepared to analyze their "observations of nature" (as the best definition of the population being studied) with the techniques we have described. By adapting such small-sample statistical techniques (e.g., randomization tests) and obeying the limitations of the inferences that can be made on the basis of these techniques, we can better understand the reliable between-group and individual differences that may lead to advances in our knowledge of how cognition maps onto brain.

ACKNOWLEDGMENTS

Partial support to the authors during preparation of this manuscript was provided by grants from NINDS "Center for the Study of the Neural Bases of Language" (NS-223-43-06A1), and NIDCD "Program Project: Origins of Communication Disorders" (PO1-DC01289), and by a grant from the John D. and Catherine T. MacArthur Foundation, Research Network on Early Childhood Transitions. Portions of this chapter have appeared in Bates, E., McDonald, J., MacWhinney, B. & Appelbaum, M.: A maximum likelihood procedure for the analysis of group and individual data in aphasia research, *Brain and Language, 40*, 231–265 (1991), and in Bates, E., Appelbaum, M. & Allard, L.: Statistical constraints on the use of single cases in neuropsychological research, *Brain and Language, 40* , 295–329, (1991).

REFERENCES

Appelbaum, M., Burchinal, M., & Terry, A. (1989). Quantitative methods and the search for continuity. In M. Bornstein & N. Krasnegor (Eds.), *Stability and continuity in mental development* (pp. 251–272). Hillsdale, NJ: Lawrence Erlbaum Associates.

Badecker, W., & Caramazza, A. (1985). On considerations of method and theory governing the use of clinical categories in neurolinguistics and cognitive neuropsychology: The case against agrammatism. *Cognition, 20*, 97–125.

Badecker, W., & Caramazza, A. (1986). A final brief in the case against agrammatism: The role of theory in the selection of data. *Cognition, 24*, 277–282.

Badecker, W., & Caramazza, A. (1991). Morphological composition in the lexical output system. *Cognitive Neuropsychology, 8*, 335–367.

Barnett, V., & Lewis, T. (1984). *Outliers in statistical data.* New York: Wiley.

Bates, E., Appelbaum, M., & Allard, L. (1991). Statistical constraints on the use of single cases in neuropsychological research. *Brain and Language, 40*, 295–329.

Bates, E., McDonald, J., MacWhinney, B., & Appelbaum, M. (1991). A maximum likelihood procedure for the analysis of group and individual data in aphasia research. *Brain and Language, 40*, 231–265.

Bates, E. & Wulfeck, B. (1989a). Comparative aphasiology: A cross-linguistic approach to language breakdown. *Aphasiology, 3*, 111–142, 161–168.

Bates, E., & Wulfeck, B. (1989b). Crosslinguistic studies of aphasia. In B. MacWhinney & E. Bates (Eds.), *The crosslinguistic study of sentence processing* (pp. 328–371). New York: Cambridge University Press.

Bellugi, U., Bihrle, A., Trauner, D., Jernigan, T., & Doherty, S. (1990). Neuropsychological, neurological and neuroanatomical profile of Williams syndrome children. *American Journal of Medical Genetics, S6*, 115–125.

Bellugi, U., Marks, S., Bihrle, A. M., & Sabo, H. (1988). Dissociation between language and social functions in Williams syndrome. In K. Mogford & D. Bishop (Eds.), *Language development in exceptional circumstances* (pp. 177–189). New York: Churchill Livingstone.

Bryk, A. S., & Raudenbush, S. W. (1987). Application of hierarchical linear models to assessing change. *Psychological Bulletin, 101*(1), 147–158.

Byng, S. (1988). Sentence processing deficits: theory and therapy. *Cognitive Neuropsychology, 5* (6), 629–676.

Caplan, D. (1981). On the cerebral organization of linguistic functions: Logical and empirical issues surrounding deficit analysis and functional localization. *Brain and Language, 14*, 120–137.

Caramazza, A. (1986). On drawing inferences about the structure of normal cognitive systems from the analysis of patterns of impaired performance: The case for single-patient studies. *Brain and Cognition, 5*, 41–66.

Caramazza, A., & Berndt, R. (1985). A multicomponent view of agrammatic Broca's aphasia. In M.-L. Kean (Ed.), *Agrammatism* (pp. 27–63). New York: Academic.

Caramazza, A., & McCloskey, M. (1988). The case for single-patient studies. *Cognitive Neuropsychology, 5*, 517–528.

Caramazza, A., & Zurif, E. (1976). Dissociation of algorithmic and heuristic processes in language comprehension: Evidence from aphasia. *Brain and Language, 3*, 572–582.

Chandler, J. (1969). Subroutine STEPIT finds local minima of a smooth function of several parameters. *Behavioral Science, 14*, 81–82.

Courchesne, E. (1991). Neuroanatomic imaging in autism. *Pediatrics, 87*(5), 781–790.

Dell, G. (1988, December). *Frame constraints on phonological speech errors.* Paper presented at the First Annual Conference on Language and Connectionism, Rome.

Edgington, E. S. (1987). *Randomization tests* (2nd ed.). New York: Marcel Dekker.

Ellis, A. W. (1982). Spelling and writing (and reading and speaking). In A. W. Ellis (Ed.), *Normality and pathology in cognitive function.* London: Academic.

Fisher, R. A. (1935). *The design of experiments.* Edinburgh and London: Oliver & Boyd.

Fodor, J. A. (1983). *The modularity of mind.* Cambridge, MA: MIT Press.

Hart, J., Berndt, R., & Caramazza, A. (1985). Category-specific naming deficit following cerebral infarction. *Nature, 316*, 439–440.

Heeschen, C. (1985, March). *The notion of "conventionality" of an expression in cross-linguistic research on aphasia.* Paper presented at the Conference on Cross-linguistic Studies of Grammatical Processing in Aphasia, Royaumont Conference Center, Paris.

Jernigan, T., & Bellugi, U. (1990). Anomalous brain morphology on magnetic resonance images in Williams syndrome and Down syndrome. *Archives of Neurology, 47*, 429–533.

Jernigan, T., Bellugi, U., & Hesselink, J. (1989). Structural differences on magnetic resonance imaging between Williams and Down syndrome. *Neurology, 39 (Supp. 1), 277.*

Kolk, H. (1985, March). *Telegraphic speech and ellipsis.* Paper presented at the Conference on Cross-linguistic Studies of Grammatical Processing in Aphasia, Royaumont Conference Center, Paris.

Kolk, H., & van Grunsven, M. (1985). Agrammatism as a variable phenomenon. *Cognitive Neuropsychology, 2*(4), 347–384.

Linebarger, M., Schwartz, M., & Saffran, E. (1983). Sensitivity to grammatical structure in so-called agrammatic aphasics. *Cognition, 13*, 361–392.

Little, R., & Rubin, D. (1987). *Statistical analysis with missing data.* New York: Wiley.

MacWhinney, B., & Bates, E. (Eds.). (1989). *The crosslinguistic study of sentence processing.* New York: Cambridge University Press.

Marshall, J. C. (1984). Multiple perspectives on modularity. *Cognition, 17*, 209–242.

Massaro, D., & Oden, G. (1980). Evaluation and integration of acoustic features in speech perception. *Journal of the Acoustical Society, 67*, 996–1013.

Maxwell, S., & Delaney, H. (1990). *Designing experiments and analyzing data.* Belmont, CA: Wadsworth.

McDonald, J., & MacWhinney, B. (1989). Maximum likelihood estimation in crosslinguistic studies of sentence processing. In B. MacWhinney & E. Bates (Eds.), *The crosslinguistic study of sentence processing* (pp. 397–421). New York: Cambridge University Press.

Miceli, G., & Caramazza, A. (1988). Dissociation of inflectional and derivational morphology. *Brain and Language, 31*(1), 24–65.

Miceli, C., Silveri, M. C., Romani, C., & Caramazza, A. (1989). Variation in the pattern of omissions and substitutions of grammatical morphemes in the spontaneous speech of so-called agrammatic patients. *Brain and Language, 36*, 447–492.

Mills, D., Coffey, S., & Neville, H. (in press). Changes in cerebral organization in infancy during primary language acquisition. In G. Dawson & K. Fischer (Eds.), *Human behavior and the developing brain*. New York: Guilford.

Morton, J. (1980). The logogen model and orthographic structure. In U. Frith (Ed.), *Cognitive approaches in spelling*. London: Academic.

Morton, J. (1984). Brain-based and non-brain-based models of language. In D. Caplan, A. R. Lecours, & A. Smith (Eds.), *Biological perspectives on language* (pp. 40–64). Cambridge, MA: MIT Press.

Mosteller, F., & Tukey, J. (1977). *Data analysis and regression*. Reading, MA: Addison-Wesley.

Oden, G., & Massaro, D. (1978). Integration of featural information in speech perception. *Psychological Review, 85*, 172–191.

Rogosa, D., & Ghandour, G. (1991). Statistical models for behavioral observations. *Journal of Educational Statistics, 16*, 157–252.

Rubin, D. (1987). *Multiple imputation for nonresponse in surveys*. New York: Wiley.

Rutter, M. (1978). Language disorders and infantile autism. In M. Rutter & E. Schopler (Eds.), *Autism: A reappraisal of concepts and treatment* (pp. 85–104). New York: Plenum.

Sall, J. (1989). *JUMP, version 2: Software for statistical visualization on the Apple Macintosh*. Cary, NC: SAS Institute.

Shallice, T. (1988a, December). *Connectionist modelling of aspects of acquired dyslexia*. Paper presented at the First Annual Conference on Language and Connectionism, Rome.

Shallice, T. (1988b). *From neuropsychology to mental structure*. New York: Cambridge University Press.

Shankweiler, D., Crain, S., Gorrell, P., & Tuller, B. (1989). Reception of language in Broca's aphasia. *Language and Cognitive Processes, 4*(1), 1–33.

Tukey, J. (1977). *Exploratory data analysis*. Reading, MA: Addison Wesley.

Tyler, L. K., Cobb, H., & Graham, M. (1992). *Language disorders: A psycholinguistic account of language comprehension deficits*. Cambridge, MA: MIT Press.

Vellman, P. (1988). *Data Desk*. Northbrook, IL: Odesta.

Wulfeck, B. (1988). Grammaticality judgments and sentence comprehension in agrammatic aphasia. *Journal of Speech and Hearing Research, 31*, 72–81.

Zurif, E. (1980). Language mechanisms: A neuropsychological perspective. *American Scientist, 68*(3), 305–311.

Part IV

COMMENTARY

Interpretations of a Behavioral Neurologist

Martha Bridge Denckla
Johns Hopkins University

RATIONALE FOR THE SYNDROME APPROACH TO BRAIN AND COGNITION RELATIONSHIPS

As a behavioral neurologist who has, for research purposes, taken the approach exemplified by this volume, it is appropriate for me to share the thinking that propelled such a choice. Embarking upon research into the mechanisms underlying learning disabilities, those "high-prevalence, low-severity" entities that exist in a gray zone between mental retardation and normalcy (and between syndrome and symptom), my neurological training motivated an attempt to reduce heterogeneity in the population to be studied. At which end of the selection process could such a reduction in heterogeneity be accomplished, given all the variables involved in the psychological and educational testing for learning disabilities? The decision was facilitated by the solicitation by certain groups with neurogenetic disorders to look into their learning disabilities. With this pragmatic push, it appeared logical to reduce heterogeneity in the learning-disabled population by sampling neurogenetic syndromes and thus proceeding from gene to brain to cognitive architecture to manifest learning disability. Turner syndrome (see relevant chapters in this volume) was an early example; a series of studies on the syndrome were pioneers in starting from biology and moving through neuropsychology into psychoeducational territory (Alexander & Money, 1966; Money, 1973; Shaffer, 1962). With the advances in imaging brain anatomy among the living with magnetic resonance imaging, it became possible to plan studies in which directly visualized brain architecture could be inserted in the causal chain.

THE EXAMPLE OF NEUROFIBROMATOSIS-1 (NF-1)

My experience with the first neurogenetic disorder that presented itself to me for study, neurofibromatosis-1 (NF-1), exemplifies several of the points that, as a neurologist, I see emerging as themes across this volume. These points, to be elaborated upon, are: (a) the value and the caution of using the syndromic approach, as contrasted with a focus on symptoms, or a dimensional approach; (b) the ways in which the assumptions of cognitive modularity and its structural affiliate, localization, are dynamically altered by development; and (c) the problem of controls and the vocabulary of "normality."

Now I return to the example of NF-1 as a neurodevelopmental underpinning to learning disability. Neurofibromatosis type 1 (NF-1), also known as Recklinghausen's disease, is one of the most common single-gene disorders of the human nervous system; it affects approximately 100,000 people in the United States. The disease is characterized by cafe au lait spots, neurofibromas of the skin, and iris hamartomas (Lisch nodules). The skeletal, central nervous, and endocrine systems may also be involved. Cognitive dysfunction and other developmental disabilities are said to occur in as many as 40% of patients. Parents of affected children complained that schools failed to recognize their children's learning disability because it was atypical, that is, spared reading but deficits in handwriting and mathematics. Despite many instances of preschool speech problems, NF-1 children were relatively good at the language arts. Speech usually improved, but general clumsiness, impairing athletics as well as handwriting, were evident during the elementary school years. The parents, organized into syndrome-oriented societies, wanted more information about their NF-1 offsprings' school difficulties.

During the late 1980s, three studies addressing the school-related problems of NF-1-affected children appeared. Despite methodologic differences, all three converged upon visuospatial disability as a distinctive weakness among NF-1-affected students (Eldridge et al., 1989; Eliason, 1987; Varnhagen et al., 1988). Two of the three studies reported deficient scores on the same test of spatial ability. The NF-1 deficiency on Benton's (1983) Judgment of Line Orientation was found in comparison to other, non-NF-1 (but heterogeneously nonspecific) attenders of learning disability (LD) clinic in one study (Eliason, 1987) and in the other study found in comparison to their own unaffected siblings (Eldridge et al., 1989). The third study used different measures of visual-spatial cognition and emphasized inattentive/impulsive dimensions of behavior based on rating scales in NF-1 children compared to their siblings (Varnhagen et al., 1988). The sibling pairs did not differ on Attention Deficit Hyperactivity Disorder (ADHD) ratings in the study of Eldridge et al., but a stricter criterion of two out of three ratings was used. Another finding was neuromotor disability in the NF-1 group study as reported by Eldridge et al.

Thus, by 1990, all the problems brought forth by Bender and colleagues (see chapter 10 of this volume) in the history of Turner syndrome research appear to be repeated with respect to NF-1 syndrome. The verbal domain is relatively unaffected, and therefore not in need of further explanation; but differences in what is assessed and who is the control group leave ambiguities about the nonverbal weaknesses. Constructs such as inattention/impulsivity are operationalized differently, visual tasks are conflated with task demands that override the visual element, and the motor factor is often ignored.

A further factor emerged from the histories taken in the Eldridge et al. (1989) study. Many parents unaffected by NF-1 were (or had been as children) "affected" by learning disabilities and/or hyperactivity. This factor, rarely made explicit in syndromic approaches to cognition, must be taken into account when such high-prevalence, low-severity disorders are foci of interest. Unaffected with respect to NF-1 does not mean unaffected with respect to cognitive and psychoeducational outcome. In fact, not only unaffected parents but unaffected siblings (by assessment) were as equally likely to be learning disabled as were NF-1-affected students. Only on neuromotor and spatial abilities were the NF-1-affected specifically and distinctively impaired.

The large gene region on chromosome 17 that underlies NF-1 has been mapped since these behavioral studies were published, and the hyperintensities, particularly in cerebellum and basal ganglia, on magnetic resonance imaging (MRI) in young NF-1-affected patients have become virtually pathognomonic of the NF-1 phenotype. The caution about the syndromic approach (refraining from attribution of complex psychoeducational outcome to the gene's effects per se) is now balanced by the value of investigating a well-mapped gene-based disorder that usually produces "lesions" or hyperintensities of as yet unknown pathologic origin visible in brain regions of great interest as convergence zones for complex behavioral integration. There is heterogeneity within the NF-1 population (starting with the fact that 50% are themselves new mutations, lacking parental NF-1 at all), but the localized brain lesions and the motor and spatial deficits can be related. More complex or global cognitive abilities are less susceptible to structure-function analysis in NF-1. Comparison of sporadic and familial cases, however, does afford another method of identifying non-NF-1 contributions to learning disability. Comparison-group strategies are crucial. Assessing the entire family is highly informative, and awareness of the role of assortative mating as well as the environmental context in the familial cases precludes naive oversimplification in the syndromic approach.

MODULARITY OF THE SPECIFIED DEFICIT

These points are as applicable to Turner syndrome (where there are multiple types, as chapter 9 informs us) as to NF-1. Similarly, the reformulation of the domain of deficit from spatial to a broader but still nonverbal one, which has happened in Turner syndrome (Waber, 1979) is in the process of happening with NF-1. The cognitive abilities subsumed under "executive function" (much like what Goldman-Rakic describes in chapter 1 of this volume as prefrontal capabilities) emerge as crucial in studying spatial skills. Common to the primate and clinical research on spatial ability is what may be termed *forward drift*, meaning greater appreciation of prefrontal involvement in tasks regarded as visuospatial. Frontal involvement in spatial cognition is illustrated by the Shepard–Metzler spatial rotation task. Mental rotations (choosing matches to a sample such that the matches are possible rotations of that sample) are accomplished in "real time," that is, as if the actual three-dimensional constructions were being manipulated by the problem solver (Shepard & Metzler, 1971). "Mental manipulation" brings into close affiliation the motoric and perceptual subdomains within the spatial cognition domain. To the best of my knowledge, however, the type of frontal (or prefrontal) role in spatial cognition elucidated by Goldman-Rakic (chapter 1) has not been addressed in human-clinical studies. That is, the elegant specification of working memory for location, with the dissociation between spatial localization guided by clear-and-present input and that guided by internal representations, is not yet to be found in human studies. Goldman-Rakic's "memory maps" need to be replicated in analogous human experiments where spatial localization is isolated from more complex verbal and motor components of tasks, and the sensory versus mnestic distinction is in clear focus. Conversely, it would help researchers who have been struggling with the possible motor-exploratory ontogeny of spatial cognition in humans to recruit, from developmentally oriented researchers using primates, data bearing on how early motor experience influences memory for location. Indeed, one of the more intriguing aspects of the NF-1 research is the developmental relationship between the neuromotor disability and the spatial disability. Certainly the common localization in brain (cerebellum, basal ganglia) and the evidence of motor dysfunction in preschoolers with NF-1 suggest an intriguing role for exploration of space during development (Acredolo, 1990; Nadel, 1990). As Waterhouse points out in chapter 8 of this volume, there is a "reorganizing effect that behavior itself has on brain mechanisms." When dealing with developmental disorders and localization, the traditional brain-behavior or structure-function approach needs to be modified by the notion that expressed behavior itself has an impact on neurological organization (chapter 8). This is an additional reason to exercise caution in using the syndromic approach to analyzing cognition, all the more so when explicit visible lesions are present. It would be naive to conclude from studies of NF-1 that basal ganglia or cerebellum are simply alternative localizations for spatial cognition. Rather, the visible lesions and the early motor dysfunction may in concert disambiguate for us something about the ontogenesis of spatial cognition.

SYNDROME VERSUS SYMPTOMS
(DIAGNOSIS VS. DIMENSIONS)

This brings us to the *symptoms versus syndrome* theme. For research, the syndrome is only a starting point. The symptoms, or dimensions, within the syndrome and, more particularly, the interrelationships among dimensions, are at a deeper level of interest to the researcher. Furthermore (to agree with Waterhouse in this regard) those symptoms or dimensions that appear to be brain based are the most likely to be focal points for productive investigation. Where findings from developmental and neurological sciences converge (on the "x," for developmental, and "y," for neurological, axes, as it were) there is a focal point or plane most likely to advance understanding of cognition.

AUTISM: ANOTHER KIND OF SYNDROME

In the case of autism, the phenotypes are acknowledged to be outcomes of multiple genotypes and epigenetic influences. With autism (or the autistic spectrum) certain central features of the syndrome are necessarily within the domain of social-interactive impairment, whereas features from other domains (two others, in *DSM–III–R* [Diagnostic and Statistical Manual of Mental Disorders (3rd ed., rev.) (APA, 1987)] terms) are, in a polythetic model, required to confirm the diagnosis. The social domain outweighs each of the two other domains two to one. Why is autism even discussed along with such syndromes as Turner and Williams (or my own NF-1 addendum) in this volume or the workshop from which this volume is derived? Heterogeneity in autism is far greater than in the "named" syndromes featured elsewhere in this volume. Nobody claims a chromosome, a gene, or a marker that defines autism as a syndrome. The sense in which autism is a syndrome is best appreciated in terms of the special needs common to all individuals diagnosed as suffering from autism. As Schopler (chapter 5) has concluded, the syndrome approach "serves important clinical and administrative purposes." The classification currently in official manuals, however, involves a cumbersome polythetic decision-making process in which, because no one characteristic is either necessary or sufficient, the syndrome is assuredly broad-based. In such an instance, quite opposite to that argued for Turner syndrome or NF-1, the syndrome of autism invites the researcher to analyze the collection of behaviors in search of core deficit(s). As Sigman (chapter 7 of this volume) eloquently comments, the investigation oriented toward core deficit(s) is complicated by the changes during development that the observable behaviors undergo. Thus, the clinical diagnosis of autism as syndrome is fraught with the dangers of wrongly identifying the set of behaviors that continue to belong to autism across development. The researcher is more interested in tracing and tracking what underlies changing behaviors in terms of basic abiding processes. The problem is to focus upon processes at the correct level of centrality and consistency; that is, what is core deficit and remains over the life span?

With the assumption that the core deficit is neurological, the focus upon relevant dimensions of autism is increasingly informed by neuropsychology and behavioral neurology. An example of the latter influence is Waterhouse (chapter 8) in her reflection upon autistic deficits in terms of Damasio's Convergence Zones model. Waterhouse advocates yet another meaning for the term *syndrome*, the intermediate meaning peculiar to neurology, in which certain localizations in brain (intermediate because neither etiologic nor clinical-behavioral) are identified as the source of a constellation of impairments. Exemplars of functional neurological syndromes are right parietal lobe syndrome or prefrontal syndrome. In this kind of model, one argues for a set of deficits that are dimensions, in the negative, of a certain brain regional capacity. It is not a model independent of empirical data, for clinical "clues" (often far from core deficits but pathognomonic of some localization) are usually the first steps in hypothesis generation. Over a decade ago, Damasio and colleagues used certain motor signs in autistic patients to raise questions about localization (Shopler reviews these in chapter 5). The point was not that these were core deficits (in Sigman's sense, the motor signs were epiphenomena) but that they suggested a brain region in which it would be reasonable to look for the source of core deficits. Courchesne's decision to look at the structure of the cerebellum on MRI was initially inspired by electrophysiological characteristics he identified in high-functioning autistic persons (see chapter 6). Whether or not those electrophysiological characteristics are "core" (in Sigman's sense) and whether or not cerebellum itself is the brain region to focus on for the "explanation" of autism (or some subtype thereof), I would argue for the heuristic value of allowing researchers to follow leads from symptoms or dimensions that suggest where to look in the brain. That Waterhouse, immersed in the heterogeneous manifestations of autism, can see in Damasio's Convergence Zone model (in which cerebellum does figure in Type II) a useful way to think about pathophysiology, is testimony to the manner in which progress in research occurs. Back and forth between syndromes and symptoms, or diagnosis and dimensions, we understand more as we engage in building models from both perspectives. I argue that we need both. We need to be told by the clinician that a core deficit or brain zone under study fails to account for certain features of the clinical syndrome and we need to be told by the researcher (who has evidence for a core deficit or a brain zone) that perhaps the clinician is misattributing certain features to autism per se that may emanate from comorbid conditions (e.g., mental retardation that so often accompanies autism).

What I read as remarkably consistent across the contributions of Schopler, Waterhouse, and Sigman, all experts on autism, is a willingness to take a dimensional approach to research without prejudice as to the source of the dimension. Research is free to generate hypotheses based upon tiny subgroups (Waterhouse), different age/intelligence cross-sections (Sigman), and, most consensually, upon brain modules/locales. This consensual position is facilitated by the availability of current neuroimaging techniques. It is a particularly gratifying consensus for a behavioral neurologist to comment upon, and so it is a pleasure to end this section with an example of model building from brain to behavior and back. This concerns the work of Reiss and colleagues. Inspired by Courchesne's findings on the posterior vermis of cerebellum in autism, and noting clinical similarities between autistic features and those seen in boys with Fragile X syndrome, Reiss and his group embarked upon MRI studies of the cerebellum. Strikingly similar hypoplasia was found (Reiss, Aylward, Freund, Bryan, & Joshi, 1991), linking autism and Fragile X at the neuroanatomic level. It is to be noted that Reiss, who is an advocate of a dimensional rather than diagnostic approach to childhood psychopathology, did not assume that Fragile X was a cause of autism. Reiss, in fact, has published on the ways in which Fragile X syndrome boys do/do not fit into the autism category as currently described (Reiss & Freund, 1990). Reiss and his group went on to investigate the anatomy of the cerebellum in females who have Fragile X chromosomes, but in whom learning disabilities and psychosocial problems, along with normal intelligence, have been identified. MRI findings indicate that cerebellar tissue volume in these females is intermediate between that of controls and that of males with Fragile X (Reiss, Freund, Tseng, & Joshi, 1991). Thus, a specific brain region became of interest due to research on normally intelligent autistic persons (of presumably diverse etiologic derivation); the brain region of interest was found to be of nearly identical reduced volume in mentally retarded Fragile X boys with autistic features. In female relatives who bear Fragile X and are of normal intellect but have selective cognitive and psychosocial impairments, there is some significant (but less drastic) tissue reduction in that same brain region, posterior vermis of cerebellum. Reiss and colleagues thus added to the work of Courchesne convergent evidence that the cerebellum may be more than a chronological marker of fetal brain development or an adventitious bit of anomalous anatomy but may be an underlying source of neuropsychological deficit. Whether it underlies the core deficit of autism remains to be seen, but it now appears to be an exciting research approach to pursue the role of the cerebellum in mental operations transcending its traditional motor affiliations.

The discussion of autism also illustrates the difficulty encountered by researchers when they stumble over vocabulary. The core deficit keeps resolving itself, like Russian nested dolls, into something more fundamental. The central social-interaction deficiency begins to resolve itself into process deficits that are its developmental precursors. Such analysis and behavioral reductionism is best guided by cross-referencing to known aspects of brain organization, as Waterhouse (chapter 8) has done in her modeling of information processing on Damasio's Convergence Zones theory. Psychological constructs alone (such as Frith's [1989] *theory of mind*) are in danger of replacing one complexity with another, rather than revealing the construction in the course of development of the complex from the simple. Finally, as Sigman (chapter 7) so beautifully reminds us, study of persons with deficits in development afford us opportunities to discover separate parallel strands that in more normal biographies cannot be unwoven.

WILLIAMS SYNDROME: THE MODULARITY OF COGNITION

The status of Williams syndrome as a probe into cognition differs yet again from that of Turner syndrome (chromosomal basis known) or autism (some brain localization tentatively proposed). Still of unknown etiology, Williams syndrome (WS) refers to an identifiable group of mentally retarded individuals. The special interest in this group resides in the phenomenon it presents in terms of striking sparing, within the context of mental deficiency, of linguistic capabilities. In this volume we learn of yet other islands of cognitive preservation, as well as some electrophysiological and neuroanatomic characteristics, of persons with Williams syndrome. Because it has been possible to study Williams syndrome in designs that use for comparison Down syndrome (a common and well-recognized cause of mental retardation with a chromosomal anomaly), powerful evidence for the modularity (and, by inference, localization) of linguistic competence has emerged. Bellugi and colleagues (chapter 2) have been able to match their Williams and Down syndrome study populations for measured intelligence; furthermore, their research explores the contrasting qualitative nature of the cognitive repertoires of the groups. This move beyond level of performance comparisons is valuable in the visual-perceptual domain. The linguistic competence of the Williams syndrome (WS) group is accompanied by extreme bias toward features or details rather than configurations. Within the visual-perceptual domain, WS subjects focus on "trees" but miss the "forest." This approach to copying tasks tempts neuropsychologists and behavioral neurologists to infer spared left hemisphere (or significant spared portions thereof) in Williams syndrome. Now Bellugi and colleagues (chapter 2) report that within the domain of visual discrimination involving noncanonical matching *faces* and visual closure tasks involving *faces* are intact modules for Williams syndrome subjects who are quite profoundly impaired in surrounding visuospatial modules of cognition.

Although the closure task is not one with which I am familiar, I have for years administered the Benton Facial Recognition Test upon which rests the discrimination/noncanonical face-matching findings in Williams syndrome, to normally intelligent learning-disabled young people. To my surprise, it has become clear that many dyslexic patients, generally excelling in visuospatial cognitive tasks and almost universally regarded as deficient in phonological (and perhaps syntactic) linguistic skills, are not competent in performance on Benton Facial Recognition Test. Thus, I see potential confirmation of an unsuspected relationship between certain linguistic skills and the particular requirements of facial recognition (i.e., discrimination and noncanonical matching of unfamiliar faces). Modules conjointly spared in Williams syndrome are impaired together in the far more heterogeneous group designated as *dyslexic*. When I attempted to replicate the association in a broader group of heterogeneous learning-disabled children it was not confirmed; only with the dyslexic subgroups did visuospatial task performance dissociate from face recognition. Generalized language disorders broader in scope than dyslexia did not correlate with poor face recognition (Denckla, 1992).

Suspecting that something comodular might be revealed by the linked behavior of certain linguistic competencies and face recognition, I began to reflect on whether these modules of cognition did imply left-hemisphere localization (or at least lateralization). Developmental considerations have thwarted such inferences in the past; for example, Gerstmann syndrome (syndrome in this usage meaning a collection of four signs—dysgraphia, dyscalculia, right–left confusion, and finger agnosia) does not localize to left parietal lobe in children who present with these phenomena (unless they have suffered illness or injury, in which case it is not developmental). Quite the contrary; the developmental Gerstmann syndrome presents in a context of right-hemisphere-based impairments.

One is struck by a nomenclature-related issue in the chapter on Williams syndrome (chapter 2). Where Spatial Cognition is a section heading, I would prefer Visual-Perceptual, with Spatial as a subdivision, rather than lump together the variety of visually presented tasks with some requiring hands-on motor responses like block design, some requiring pencil-controlling responses, and most evoking verbal mediation strategies. When such disparate tasks as Block Design, Design Copying, picture Drawing, Face Recognition, Judgment of Line Orientation, Tower Constructing, and so on, are all lumped under Spatial, then it is our collective defect as researchers when we "fail to fractionate" (paraphrasing from chapter 2) or lack "a broadly applicable nosology" (chapter 2) of spatial cognition. We need to follow the lead offered by Goldman-Rakic (chapter 1) in simplifying and clarifying spatial in basic terms of (a) two-and three-dimensional localization and (b) "clear-and-present" sensory versus "internally represented" conditions. We may search for spatial components in noncanonical object matching, in global aspects of Block Design or Face Recognition, but the complex nature of these tasks and the potential for compensatory nonspatial solutions is not adequately captured by subsuming them under Spatial Cognition. Bellugi (chapter 2) is well aware of the idiosyncratic strategies her WS group may be using to succeed. Rather, we must, like Goldman-Rakic, tease out what is spatial within what is visually presented or visually remembered.

If one reviews and discuss recent work on face recognition from the same Iowa department that produced the Benton Face Recognition Test (Damasio, Tranel, & Damasio 1990), one finds an expanded sophistication brought to the analysis of this task. First, Tranel (personal communication, 1991) pointed out the test is probably not as specific to faces as had originally been thought; that whatever specificity to faces it has must absolutely be distinguished from the neurological *prosopagnosia*, which refers to loss of recognition of previously familiar faces. The Iowa group documents prosopagnosia subtypes as follows. *Associative* and *amnesic associative* subtypes are traced to bilateral damage (inferior occipitotemporal for associative versus anterior temporal for amnesic associative). By contrast, the *apperceptive* type has a right occipitoparietal localizing implication (Damasio et al.). To the degree that the Benton Facial Recognition Test has anything to do with the neurological underpinnings of prosopagnosia, it is at the apperceptive end of the process. Tranel pointed out the need for detailed mapping of face features necessary to distinguish very similar unfamiliar faces and speculated that both inferior visual association cortices are necessary neural substrates for this processing of face data. Also, there is preliminary evidence that the left-sided inferior visual association cortex may be more specialized for static features whereas the right-sided cortex may guide visual scanning that creates the dynamic configurational map linking the features in faces.

At present it does not appear that we really understand enough about what is involved in the Benton Face Recognition Test to allow firm lateralization. Based on available neuroanatomic evidence (postmortem and MRI), *localization* (meaning what portions within hemispheres) bilaterally seems firmer, involving both inferior visual association cortices. It may be asked in future (with apologies to George Orwell) whether some such cortical areas are "more equal than others" in this face recognition task, but right now the answer is not clear. Neither neuroanatomic nor electrophysiologic data on Williams syndrome (chapters 3 & 4, respectively) appear to bear upon the lateralization issue within inferior visual association cortices. On the other hand, interpretation of the face-processing sparing in Williams syndrome may be related to relative brain tissue sparing (reported by Jernigan, chapter 3) in nonvisual regions such as mesial temporolimbic, cerebellar, and frontal subdivisions. This may be because "perception" is not so readily disambiguated from associative and mnestic processes (Damasio et al., 1990) especially in the dynamic process of perceptual development.

In summary, Williams syndrome (despite its still uncertain etiologic status) serves as a thought-provoking instance of the way in which preservation of cognitive modules against a background of mental retardation can illuminate (a) behavioral or functional relationships between cognitive modules, and (b) brain localizations implied by both the functional affiliations and the atypical cognitive profile. Study of entities such as Williams syndrome may lead us to rethink the underlying nature of certain cognitive processes and the structural components of brain networks contributory to these processes in a development context.

THE PROBLEM OF CONTROL GROUPS: WHO IS "NORMAL"?

The final theme to which I wish to address my discussion is a difficult one: Namely, if interested in atypical cognitive deficits in terms of the light they shed on brain architecture in a developmental context, then whose repertoire (by way of comparison) is typical? Williams syndrome research has had a felicitous comparison group in Down syndrome. It may be argued, however, that this was merely extraordinarily fortunate (Down syndrome being the most common and available form of mental retardation) or that Bellugi et al. (chapter 2) cannily made use of common clinical knowledge that persons with Down syndrome were at their very worst in linguistic aspects of cognition. This is not by way of negative criticism of what is brilliant research, but by way of illustrating that proactive choice of an "appropriate" control group may be a necessary subtext of hypothesis about the experimental group. What is already known by way of clinical anecdotal evidence is then subjected to more rigorous research design. That is as it should be; clinicians are excellent sources of hypotheses. Such was the case when neurofibromatosis-1 research moved into family studies because clinical histories strongly suggested that the contributions to cognition of the unaffected (with respect to NF-1) parent must be entered into the analysis of learning disabilities. Repeatedly, clinical work provides us with anecdotal evidence that cognitive deficits underlying learning disabilities often come from both sides of the proband's family. One of my favorite informal diagnoses is a pinch of linguistic deficit plus a dash of executive dysfunction, where the "pinch" may be maternally and the "dash" paternally derived. This sort of multifactorial causation is suggested so often in clinical experience with the learning disabilities of unknown etiology that we would be foolish to ignore the model when working on neurogenetic disorders, whether NF-1, Turner, or Fragile X syndromes. Siblings and parents are necessary comparison groups (or perhaps we need a new term like *contribution groups* in deference to multivariate statistical analysis) when we attempt to relate atypical cognitive deficits to particular identifiable syndromes. The more subtle and specialized the cognitive module under scrutiny, the less certain should the researcher feel about the normalcy of a control group matched for age/sex/IQ. This is because the finer grained, process-oriented description of a control group reveals heterogeneity of cognitive profiles in persons of unimpeachable adjustment and achievement. The neurocognitive terrain of a "control" approaches the individuality of a fingerprint or a face. Furthermore, what is normal cognition may change relative to societal demand or emphasis. For example, singing or drawing are optional aptitudes for normal status in our society; this special optional status may not be universal for all times and places. The closer in both genes and environment is the control group, the firmer is the interpretation of subtle cognitive deficit in the target group. Only rarely does one have the good fortune to meet twins identical except for one X chromosome, as has occurred with one case report of Turner syndrome (Reiss et al., in press). Another strategy would be to use multiple comparison groups, no one of which is the control group—in a sense, looking at atypicality from several noncanonical perspectives. Much help will be needed from sophisticated methodologists armed with statistics suitable to multidimensional matching with relatively small groups (see chapter 12). Waterhouse (chapter 8) is saying nearly the same thing when she advocates future studies of small numbers of similar members of subtypes within autism. In such studies the subtypes could be compared with each other along social, communicative, or imaginative dimensions as well as on hypothesized underlying deficits (e.g., sharing or shifting attention) and biological characteristics such as brain architecture. No normals would be required if, for example, a behaviorally homogeneous autistic subtype showed a distinctive attentional attribute and a correlated neuroanatomic anomaly. Schopler (chapter 5) volume) is heading in the same direction when he says that research may best profit from focus upon specific autistic dimensions. Sigman (chapter 7), who studies such dimensions in designs that utilize two control groups (normally intelligent, mental-age-matched controls and mentally retarded, chronological-age-matched controls), reminds us that linguistic ability is yet another problem in the match, confounded still further by developmental changes in the complex manifestations of intelligence, language, and social behaviors. Sigman, like Waterhouse, heightens the reader's awareness of the developmental aspects of atypical cognitive profiles, stimulating the comment that the best control for a subject is him or herself; that is, any cognitive deficit (and its underlying brain basis) that is considered a core module in the syndrome being studied ought to be present either at every critical and influential developmental stage or persistently. The challenges for research into atypical cognition and its implications for brain function are (a) to move beyond cross-sectional, univariate models and (b) to recognize that normalcy is quite heterogeneous with respect to cognitive profiles.

ACKNOWLEDGMENTS

Preparation of this article was in part supported by Grant P50 HD25806 from the National Institute of Child Health and Human Development, National Institutes of Health.

REFERENCES

Acredolo, I. (1990). Behavioral approaches to spatial orientation in infancy. In A. Diamond (ed.), The development and neural bases of higher cognitive functions. *Annals of the New York Academy of Science*, *608*, 596–612.

Alexander, D., & Money, J. (1966). Turner's syndrome and Gerstmann's syndrome: Neuropsychologic comparisons. *Neuropsychologia*, *4*, 165–273.

American Psychiatric Association. (1987). *Diagnostic and statistical manual of mental disorders* (3rd rev. ed.). Washington, DC: Author.

Benton, A. L., Hamsher, K. D., Varney, N. R., & Spreen, O. (1983). *Contributions to neuropsychological assessment: A clinical manual* (pp. 30–54). New York: Oxford University Press.

Damasio, A. R., Tranel, D., & Damasio, H. (1990). Face agnosia and the neural substrates of memory. *Annual Review of Neuroscience*, *13*, 89–109.

Denckla, M. B. (1992). Unpublished raw data.

Eldridge, R., Denckla, M. B., Bien, E., Myers, S., Kaiser-Kupfer, M. I., Pikus, A., Schlesinger, S. L., Parry, D. M., Dambrosia, J. M., Zasloff, M. A., & Mulvihill, J. J. (1989). Neurofibromatosis type 1 (Recklinghausen's disease): Neurologic and cognitive assessment with sibling controls. *American Journal of Diseases of Children*, *143* 833–837.

Eliason, M. J. (1987). Neuropsychological patterns; neurofibromatosis compared to developmental learning disorders. *Neurofibromatosis*, *6*, 1–10.

Frith, U. (1989). *Autism: Explaining the enigma*. London: Basil Blackwell.

Money, J. (1973). Turner's syndrome and parietal lobe functions. *Cortex*, *9*, 385–393.

Nadel, L. (1990). Varieties of spatial cognition. In A. Diamond (ed.), The development and neural bases of higher cognitive functions. *Annals of the New York Academy of Science*, *608*, 613–636.

Reiss, A. L., Aylward, E., Freund, L., Bryan, N., & Joshi, P. K. (1991). Neuroanatomy of Fragile X syndrome: The posterior fossa. *Annals of Neurology*, *9*, 26–32.

Reiss, A. L., & Freund, L. (1990). Fragile X syndrome, *DSM–III–R* and autism. *Journal of the American Academy of Child and Adolescent Psychiatry*, *29*, 885–891.

Reiss, A. L., Freund, L., Plotnick, L., Baumgardner, T., Green, K., Sozer, A., Reader, M., Boehm, C., & Denckla, M. B. (in press). The effects of x-monosomy on brain development: Monozygotic twins discordant for Turner syndrome. *Annals of Neurology*.

Reiss, A. L., Freund, L., Tseng, J. E., & Joshi, P. K. (1991). Neuroanatomy in Fragile X females: The posterior fossa. *American Journal of Human Genetics*, *49*, 279–288.

Shaffer, J. (1962). A specific cognitive deficit observed in gonadal aplasia (Turner's syndrome). *Journal of Clinical Psychology*, *18*, 403–406. Shepard, R. N., & Metzler, J. (1971). Mental rotation of three-dimensional objects. *Science*, *171*, 701–703.

Varnhagen, C. K., Lewin, S., Das, J. P., Bowen, P., Ma, K., & Klimek, M. (1988). Neurofibromatosis and psychological processes. *Journal of Developmental and Behavioral Pediatrics*, *9*(5), 257–265.

Waber, D. P. (1979). Neuropsychological aspects of Turner syndrome. *Developmental Medicine and Child Neurology*, *21*, 58–70.

Afterword: Behavior–Brain Relationships in Children

Jack M. Fletcher
University of Texas Medical School at Houston

When I was asked to write an afterword for the 1991 conference sponsored by the National Institute of Neurological Disorders and Stroke, my immediate thoughts were to simply summarize the major findings of articles and discuss some of these implications for the study of brain-behavior relationships in children. However, after reviewing the articles, I discovered that there were so many findings that any sort of systematic integration was difficult. It would be hard to extract general principles of brain-behavior relationships that would apply across these syndromes. This problem was compounded by the differences in the depth of research on the three syndromes. In Williams syndrome, there were three chapters focused on the same set of subjects from one center. These articles were nicely interwoven and well-integrated. The four autism articles, however, came from different centers. They reflected varying viewpoints, but accurately reflected the divergence of opinion characteristic of research on children with autism. The three chapters on Turner syndrome were quite disparate and not as well integrated theoretically or methodologically as the other two sets of chapters, reflecting the more rudimentary state of brain-behavior research on Turner syndrome. Goldman-Rakic's article at the beginning laid out elegant conceptual models for approaching childhood syndromes; Denckla's article at the end was integrative and actually the type of afterword I thought should be written.

Left without my original conception of an afterword, I chose to try and place the chapters in a broader context that addresses the history of research in these areas of child development and the contribution of these chapters to the longer term problems of understanding the development of children with significant handicapping conditions. The questions, of course, were what historical context and why these particular handicapping conditions? The historical perspective that seemed most appropriate involved acquired central nervous system (CNS) disorders of children, which have a long tradition. The factors underlying the selection of these three syndromes in a single volume were less clear. The etiology, genetic basis, and phenotypic presentation of the three syndromes are quite different. However, the syndromes do share in common an absence of a clear lesional basis in the brain despite significant effects on the development of most children afflicted with the syndromes.

One approach to understanding the relationship of the three syndromes is to examine them relative to other childhood syndromes characterized by CNS dysfunction. These types of questions involve *classification*, which is a set of scientific methods for addressing the similarities and differences among a group of entities (Fletcher, Francis, & Morris, 1988). Hence, this afterword represents an attempt to place the chapters in this volume in a broader historical context and from a perspective addressing the classification of childhood syndromes presumably characterized by brain dysfunction (see chapters 5, 8, & 13 of this volume). A brief review of some of the more pertinent historical influences on the study of CNS dysfunction in children is presented and the relationship of more recent studies of children with established CNS insults to the syndromes is evaluated. A major emphasis is placed on the continuity of research results across a wide array of syndromes and the importance of the types of methods described in this book. In addition, the critical importance of broad-based conceptualization of these syndromes and their relationships to other CNS disorders of childhood is stressed, reflecting the need for concepts and methods derived from classification research.

HISTORICAL CONTEXT OF RESEARCH ON BRAIN-BEHAVIOR RELATIONSHIPS IN CHILDREN

Any volume that attempts to summarize results from cross-laboratory studies of childhood syndromes involving behavior and the brain is remarkable for several reasons. The first reason is the ability to bring together a group of individuals conducting research in animal and human populations from clinical and basic science perspectives. The second remarkable feature is the commonality of purposes and methods across researchers, clinicians, and laboratories apparent in the presentations. A third is the similarity of observations, problems, and in some instances, results, that are present despite variations in the clinical samples under scrutiny. Finally, perhaps most remarkable is the ability to show that dissociations in the behavioral phenotype of children with various syndromes can be related to deviations in the development of the CNS. Throughout this volume, the study of behavior drives the search for neurobiological correlates; hence, these are studies of behavior-brain relationships.

These four remarkable features of this volume and the conference of origin take special meaning in the context of the history of the study of the consequences of CNS insult for the development of children's abilities. The syndromes in this book (Williams syndrome, autism, Turner syndrome) have in common an absence of consistent neuropathological lesions visible on neuroimaging studies. There are autopsy studies and considerable consensus that the CNS of these children has been altered, but few of these children would be considered candidates for neuroimaging studies just because of the syndrome. However, there is a long history of research on children with more clearly demonstrable neuropathological lesions to the brain. There is also a history of comparing these brain-injured children to children with developmental disorders of learning, attention, and behavior in whom a CNS basis remains a presumption (e.g., dyslexia, attention deficit-hyperactivity disorder).

When the syndromes in this book are compared and evaluated in light of the history of research on the neurobehavioral consequences of CNS insult in children, it is fair to state that dramatic shifts are apparent in the nature, quality, and direction of contemporary research. This history has at least four connected strands related to the articles in this volume that reflect the state of the art of understanding relationships between CNS insult and behavior in children prior to approximately 1980. The first strand represents studies of children with known CNS lesions (Fletcher & Levin, 1988). The second strand concerns concepts and studies (largely animal) of recovery of function after CNS insult in the immature animal (St. James-Roberts, 1979). The third historical strand is the concept of cerebral dysfunction, operating largely in conceptualizations of behavioral and learning disorders in children without known CNS pathology (Rutter, 1982). The fourth is the application of sophisticated theories and models of language and other areas of cognition developed in studies of normal children (and adults) to children with known and presumed CNS deviations (Dennis, 1988). A brief review of these four strands of history helps to place the state of the art as represented in this volume in a markedly different position. Indeed, through the first seven decades of this century, any attempt to study brain-behavior relationships in children with Williams syndrome, autism and other pervasive developmental disorders, and Turner syndrome, would generally have been met with firm skepticism—if not outright cynicism—because of the absence of known brain lesions as a basis for the syndromes.

Earlier Studies of Children with Known CNS Insult.
In the first seven decades of this century (and extending back into the 19th century), there

were numerous studies of children variously defined as (a) aphasic, (b) hemiplegic, and (c) unilaterally lesioned (see reviews by Alajouanine & Lhermitte, 1965; Annett, 1973; Dennis, 1988; Hecaen, 1976; Satz & Bullard-Bates, 1981; Woods & Teuber, 1978). In addition, there were studies of children who received hemispherectomies, usually for intractable seizures (Basser, 1962; Dennis & Whitaker, 1977; Smith, 1981). These samples were accrued with the presumption that all four groups met criteria for unilateral lesions to one hemisphere. The purpose of virtually all of these studies was to determine differences between children and adults in recovery of function after unilateral CNS insult, particularly language skills. The prevailing view was that children (a) were more likely to become aphasic than adults, (b) recovered better from aphasia than adults, (c) were more likely to show crossed aphasias than adults, and (d) could represent language in either hemisphere (Dennis, 1988; Dennis & Whitaker, 1977; Satz & Bullard-Bates, 1981).

It is now apparent that all four of these conclusions resulted from sampling problems that led to methodological artifacts producing these supposed differences (i.e., problems in classification). If children were selected as aphasic, there was usually an etiological confound. Many children had disease entities that would not be associated with unilateral brain disease (Aram, 1990). For example, the most common cause of aphasia in children is traumatic brain injury (TBI); in adults, vascular disease is commonly associated with aphasia. TBI is a multifocal, generalized insult to the CNS (Levin, Benton, & Grossman, 1982), so that the selection of adult and child cases did not reflect a comparison of unilateral lesions. Like TBI children, TBI adults rarely show long-term significant aphasic symptomatology (Levin, 1981). Similarly, selecting children with infantile hemiplegia, unilateral lesions, or even hemispherectomy provided no assurance of a unilateral lesion (Satz & Bullard-Bates, 1981; Woods & Teuber, 1978). Bilateral brain disease was often apparent, particularly before the advent of antibiotics (Woods & Teuber, 1978). One of the most ardent proponents of differences in childhood and adult aphasia recanted many of his earlier conclusions in an article prior to his death (Hecean, 1983). The results of these earlier studies reflected differences in the consequences of diffuse brain injury versus focal brain injury; children rarely show focal injuries and largely sustain generalized or multifocal insults to the CNS (Fletcher & Taylor, 1984; Levin, Ewing-Cobbs, & Benton, 1984).

A major lesson was learned in the hemispherectomy studies, which for years were touted as evidence of better recovery of language in children and for equal potential for two cerebral hemispheres in subserving language (Basser, 1962; Lenneberg, 1967; Smith, 1984). The lesson was that the null hypothesis of no differences was easy to support if the assessment of cognition was not thorough and not driven by hypotheses about the organization of cognitive skills in children (Dennis, 1980; Fletcher & Satz, 1983; St. James-Roberts, 1981). If hemispherectomy studies included children with globally poor cognitive development and assessments of cognitive functions restricted to general intellectual skills, no differences between right hemispherectomy and left hemispherectomy cases emerged. However, if children with global impairments were excluded and the assessments of cognitive skills addressed variables such as syntactic comprehension and production, and complex visual-perceptual processing, differences between the hemispherectomy groups would emerge (Dennis, 1980). As Dennis noted in her critically important studies, hemispherectomy is a rare and unusual event; it is difficult to extrapolate from these studies to children with other CNS abnormalities. Interestingly, Dennis moved from rare cases of children with hemispherectomy—probably as rare as Williams syndrome—in the direction of studies of children more broadly represented in the population of those with CNS insult (Dennis, 1985a, 1985b, 1987, 1988).

Why were studies conducted addressing issues of unilateral cerebral pathology when focal lesions are so rare in children? Concerns about unilateral lesions and recovery of function from aphasia are interesting primarily from the perspective of adults with CNS injury (Dennis, 1988; Fletcher & Taylor, 1984). This interest, however, may be misguided for children, who, depending on their level of development, vary in organization of behavior, CNS maturity, and etiology and pathophysiology of CNS deviance. As Bates and Applebaum (chapter 12 of this volume) noted, understanding the consequences of known and presumed CNS insults in children requires different questions, such as how learning and development proceed in the altered CNS. As Sigman (chapter 7 of this volume) exemplified for autism, assessments must be based on theories and research on the development of cognitive skills in children, not on their final representation in adults. Waterhouse (chapter 8 of this volume) also nicely outlined many of the issues involving how the CNS may reorganize to mediate behavior after early CNS insult. Finally, the studies must be on populations of children as they are actually represented in the state of nature—not on an artificial classification derived from adult neuropsychology (see Denckla, chapter 13 of this volume). Oftentimes the question must be along the lines put forward by Goldman-Rakic (chapter 1 of this volume): What are the consequences of a discrete CNS event or lesion for the processes underlying the development of complex mental processes?

Concepts of Recovery of Function. This historical strand needs only brief mention because it is well known and closely related to those studies in the previous section. The notions that children recover better from brain injury than adults—and the traditional concepts of plasticity and equipopotentiality as espoused by Lenneberg (1967) and Smith (1984)—were also fueled by a body of misinterpreted animal studies (e.g., the Kennard principle; Kennard, 1936) and the studies of language recovery discussed in the previous section (particularly Basser, 1962; Lenneberg, 1967; Smith, 1981). Although these concepts were still ascendent through the 1970s, they were addressed empirically by Goldman's (1974) animal studies and Dennis' studies of hemispherectomy (reviewed in Dennis, 1980), and conceptually by Isaccson (1975) and St. James-Roberts (1979). Goldman showed that performance on delayed alternation tasks in primates depended on several variables, including the maturation of the cerebral structure, type of task under investigation, and age of follow-up. Dennis showed that the intact right and left hemispheres of hemidecorticates were different in their organization of cognitive functions relative to normal right and left hemispheres. Issacson described the myth of recovery of function in children, noting (in part) all the children with mental retardation and cerebral palsy early in their development (and Williams syndrome, autism, Turner syndrome, etc.) who never develop normally. St. James-Roberts exposed traditional concepts of plasticity and equipotentiality hypotheses as the vague straw-people they were and pulled the pins from their foundations. Other studies also contributed significantly to this change in perspective (e.g., Lansdell, 1969; Woods & Teuber, 1978). Despite disagreement in the literature (Satz & Fletcher, 1981; Smith 1983) attention has turned toward a different set of questions involving the reorganization of behavior in the altered brain, reflected in the articles in this volume.

Concept of Cerebral Dysfunction.   This concept is simply the conviction that behavioral deficits in children reflect abnormal CNS functioning (Fletcher & Taylor, 1984). This concept may seem out of place in a book on syndromes, but is pertinent for two reasons. The first is the influence of this concept on current interest in measuring behavioral dissociations that may reflect CNS deviance (Benton, 1962). The second is that many studies of children with known CNS deviance—explicitly acknowledged by Denckla (chapter 13 of this volume)—have been influenced by studies of children with language, learning, and attention disorders in whom evidence for CNS deviation remains largely a hypothesis. These children were initially studied with the idea that studying patterns of dissociation in behavior and cognition would be informative of the CNS basis of these disorders (Benton, 1962; Rourke, 1975). This approach has now been applied to populations with documented CNS deviations, or at least populations where CNS deviance should be easier to document and relate to behavior than in children with developmental disorders of language, learning, and attention.

The origin of the concept of cerebral dysfunction was apparent in the Ghoolstonian lectures of Still (1902), an early British pediatrician. Still observed a population of children with no evidence of mental subnormality or history/physical evidence of CNS disease who had common behavioral characteristics—largely impulsive, acting-out behavior. He was unable to observe environmental factors that explained these patterns and also observed in these children (a) male preponderance, (b) an increased incidence of physical stigma and (c) greater probability of abnormal birth and perinatal histories. Because of these factors, Still expressed the conviction that the problems displayed by these children had a biological basis reflected by "a morbid failure of the development of moral control" (p. 1082).

Other influences on the concept of cerebral dysfunction can be described (see Fletcher & Taylor, 1984; Rutter, 1982). Kahn and Cohen (1934) described patterns of impulsive, acting-out behavior and concreteness in thinking in children as an organic drivenness syndrome relating these behaviors to a history of documented CNS encephalopathy. They emphasized that the history of encephalopathy was sufficient to explain this largely behavioral syndrome despite lack of evidence for CNS symptomatology in the physical examination. The Straussian Movement (Strauss & Lehtinen, 1947) further expanded this concept, emphasizing that the presence of certain behavioral signs was ipso facto evidence of CNS deviance even in the absence of a history or physical evidence of CNS disease. The term *minimal brain injury* (MBI) was used to describe these children, representing a contrast with "major" forms of brain injury that produced death or mental retardation. In the 1950s, the concept of MBI was expanded to include perceptual-motor problems and poor school achievement (Laufer & Denhoff, 1957). In the 1960s, the term MBI was redefined as *minimal brain dysfunctions* (MBD) in a legislative statement, emphasizing the conviction that there may be no physical evidence of CNS pathology, but that behavioral signs alone were sufficient to indicate CNS deviation (see Satz & Fletcher, 1980). Later in the 1960s, the term *specific learning disabilities* was formalized into a legislative definition, reflecting a simple nonetiological reworking of the MBD definition. The concept of MBD produced such a morass of confusion and concern about the heterogeneity of these children that a new emphasis on definition and classification emerged as the now well-known search for subtypes of learning and attention disorders (Doehring, 1978; Satz & Fletcher, 1980).

The notion of subtypes has certainly influenced the research reported in this volume, in particular by Schopler, Sigman, Waterhouse, Bender, and Denckla (chapter 5, 7, 8, 10, & 13, respectively). Perhaps more important is the notion that behavioral disorders reflect CNS deviance. Many neuropsychologists and behavioral neurologists studied disorders such as dyslexia with only a peripheral interest in the fact that these children had reading problems. Rather, the interest was in the difficulties that many of these children seemed to have with naming skills, finger agnosia, right–left confusion, and other problems often associated with brain disease in adults (Benton, 1975; Satz & van Nostrand, 1973). These associated features—which are now known to have little to do with the actual problem in reading—were studied as clues to brain dysfunction in these children. There was never any real intent to ignore language processing and phonological awareness as these skills relate to reading—only an attempt to understand biological factors in dyslexia. Many individuals who have developed hypotheses about the CNS basis of learning and attention disorders, and who actively study brain disease in children, have their roots in this tradition. In contrast, other researchers studied dyslexia from the viewpoint of cognition and reading, leading to curious controversies on the role of language and spatial skills in reading disability. In reality, the controversy represented different interests underlying the study of dyslexia. What is now widespread is the recognition of the need for careful attention to issues of classification, subtypes, and definition. This attention is reflected throughout the chapters in this volume and has its origin partly in the concept of cerebral dysfunction.

Application of Models of Language and Cognition in CNS-Impaired Children.   The final historical impetus underlying current research on children with known and suspected deviations of the CNS is the application of experimental models of language and cognition to these children. Much of this impetus—which characterizes cognitive neuroscience as a whole— stemmed from the development of hypothetical models of language in aphasic populations. This approach was fruitful and led to application of models of other areas of cognitive function in a variety of brain-injured samples. This process eventually became reciprocal, with studies of normal and brain-impaired samples informing the cognitive model builders of the weaknesses (and sometimes strengths) of their hypotheses. As this volume shows, studies of behavior actually drive the search for CNS correlations, consistent with the history of aphasiology (Benton, 1964).

Conclusions.   Dennis (1987) noted that "in neuropsychology, the units of mind or behavior, and the language used to describe them, have lagged behind the units and language of mainstream experimental and cognitive psychology . . ." (p. 728). The articles in this book—particularly those on Williams syndrome and autism—show that this situation does not always hold. In both areas, the psychology side of the behavior-brain equation is state of the art. For example, Bellugi et al. (chapter 2 of this volume) use contemporary models of language and spatial cognition to characterize the behavioral dissociations characteristics of Williams syndrome. Both Cour- chesne et al. and Sigman (chapter 6 & 7 of this volume respectively) use contemporary models of social interaction and attention to characterize children with autism. Interestingly, the "neuro" side of the brain-behavior equation is also well developed (see chapters 3, 4, 6, & 11 of this volume). Benton (1962) and Reitan and Wolfson (1992) no longer have to complain that the neuro side of behavior-brain studies of children is missing. This volume demonstrates that research on both sides of the behavior-brain equation is flourishing in children.

The Turner syndrome section in many ways is more typical of the current state of the affairs in what Bates and Applebaum (chapter 12 of this volume) term "cognitive developmental neuroscience" and what Dennis (1988) and Rourke (1989) would simply regard as child neuropsychology. Contemporary models of cognition have not been applied to children who have Turner syndrome. Rather, the bulk of the research on the behavioral phenotype consists of clinical studies of IQ scores and other more traditional measures. Similarly, notwithstanding the electrophysiological studies of Johnson et al. (chapter 11 of this volume), there is little evidence of applications of current neuroimaging technology in studies of children with Turner syndrome. This contrast is interesting and points out fruitful directions for research. Research on Turner syndrome should follow the approaches outlined in the studies of Williams syndrome and autism, reflecting the influence of cognitive neuroscience on these studies. Turner syndrome may be particularly interesting to study because the review by White (chapter 9 of this volume) suggests a higher prevalence than of Williams syndrome. In addition, Bender et al. (chapter 10 of this volume) imply variability and possible subtypes in the behavioral presentation. As we see, studying more prevalent syndromes from the viewpoint of within-group dissociations may be quite fruitful for elucidating CNS and environmental factors responsible for the presence of subgroups in a particular disorder.

MORE RECENT STUDIES OF CHILDREN WITH CNS DISORDERS

The Importance of Classification

The past 15 years or so of research on children with CNS-related syndromes has seen rapid growth. In addition to the studies of children with Williams syndrome, Turner syndrome, and autism reported in this volume, studies have been conducted of children with well-documented unilateral focal lesions (Aram & Whitaker, 1988), TBI (Fletcher & Levin, 1988), early hydrocephalus (Fletcher & Levin, 1988), viral and infectious diseases (Reye's syndrome, meningitis; Taylor et al., 1990, 1991), perinatal hypoxia (Broman, 1979, 1989; Broman, Nichols, Shaughnessy, & Kennedy, 1987), and other encephalopathic conditions. There are also studies of children with neurofibromatosis, hyperthyroidism, and other disorders where the pathophysiologic effects on the brain are less well understood—much like Williams syndrome, autism, and Turner syndrome. Many of these studies, particularly those involving clear changes in the cerebral white matter (e.g.,

TBI, early hydrocephalus, and the consequences of CNS irradiation in the treatment of cancer), show general patterns reflecting frequent preservation of some (varying) components of language, deficits in varying components of spatial cognition, and problems with attention, short-term memory, and executive functions. Some of the similarities across studies of TBI, hydrocephalus, and CNS irradiation are summarized in Table 14.1. This table represents broad generalizations from studies reporting group averaged data; substantial heterogeneity (i.e., subtypes) are likely within each disorder.

Much of this evidence was taken by Rourke (1989) and interpreted in terms of a "nonverbal learning disability syndrome," relating the cognitive dissociations in these syndromes to abnormal development of the cerebral white matter. Rourke provided a set of testable hypotheses at the level of the behavioral representation of syndromes characterized in part by dissociations in the development of language and spatial skills as well as the neural correlates of these syndromes. Of equal importance for this conference is the attempt to extract general principles about the relationship of behavior and CNS deviation in children by extrapolating across multiple disorders.

The importance of this type of effort was clearly acknowledged by Bates and Applebaum (chapter 12 of this volume), Waterhouse (chapter 8 of this volume), and Denckla (chapter 13 of this volume). However, extraction of these types of general principles requires another set of methods and derived from a research on how syndromes, or other entities, are related to each other. These are problems in classification and extend beyond questions of subtypes (Fletcher et al., 1988; Morris & Fletcher, 1988). In fact, questions about subtypes within a major group are generally secondary to questions concerning the definition and relationship of the major groups to each other. For example, Sigman (chapter 7 of this volume) worries about premature subdivision of children with autism into subgroups; Waterhouse (chapter 8 of this volume) suggests that subtypes with only a few members are important. Courchesne et al. (chapter 6 of this volume) seem to suggest that autism is a single syndrome characterized by cerebellar induced deficits in shifting attention. These questions cannot be resolved by only studying autistic

TABLE 14.1
Common Neurobehavioral Features of Closed Head Injury, Early Hydrocephalus, and CNS Irradiation Treatment in Children

1. Performance IQ Lower Than Verbal IQ
2. Complex and Speeded Motor Deficits
3. Preservation of Fluency, Automaticity, and Phonological Components of Language
4. Aphasia Rare
5. Deficits in Pragmatic Language
6. Arithmetic Computations Poorer than Reading Decoding
7. Deficits in Memory, Attention, and Executive Functions; Generally More Apparent on Nonverbal Tasks

children. Rather, extrapolations and comparisons to other groups of impaired children must be made. For example, if autism is a cerebellar disorder (Courchesne et al., chapter 6, this volume), how efficient is shifting attention in other childhood populations characterized by prominent cerebellar pathology (e.g., meningomyelocele, Dandy–Walker syndrome)? These could potentially represent a classification of children with cerebellar pathology. Similarly, comparisons of children with Williams syndrome and Down syndrome could be part of a classification of mental retardation. From this perspective, Rourke (1989) was arguing for a classification of children with disorders presumably based on deficits in motor, spatial, and executive function skills, with a common locus involving various abnormalities in the cerebral white matter.

The point of these comments is clearer at the end of this chapter. Basically, classification research offers not only a set of methods, but also a conceptual framework for extracting more general principles of behavior and brain. Classification is not simply a search for nosologies or subtypes. It is fundamentally an attempt to understand relationships among entities and how these entities are similar and different in relationship to each other and to external variables.

The value of orientations to childhood syndromes derived from classification are clearly apparent when more recent studies of children with acquired CNS disorders are examined. The bulk of these studies address children who have some form of generalized early insult to the CNS. The three syndromes covered in this book have an early insult that presumably caused pathophysiologic changes in multiple areas of the CNS. Comparisons of the results of studies of other populations characterized by generalized insult to the CNS is illuminating. Despite wide variability in etiology (and specific pathophysiologic changes in the CNS), there are common strands of behavioral variability across these disorders (see Table 14.1). These similarities are particularly interesting because they occur in children with documentable injury to the brain—visible to the radiologist's eye on current neuroimaging technologies and with expected distributions of lesions. In the next section, an overview of research approaches characterizing the study of children with brain injury is provided, with more detailed reviews of two "syndromes" that are particularly interesting in relation to the three syndromes included in this book.

Types of Studies

Research over the past 15 years on the behavioral consequences of CNS injury in children can be characterized as (a) *between-group* studies, (b) *across-group* studies, and (c) *within-group* studies. Between-group studies represent explicit comparisons of children with distinct disorders (e.g., Williams syndrome vs.

Down syndrome). Across-group studies basically combine children with various forms of known CNS pathology and search for behavior-brain correlations. Within-group studies are not particularly different from between-group studies except for the explicit attempt to understand variation within a particular syndrome. For example, if the comparison of Williams syndrome and Down syndrome represented an attempt to study mental retardation, it could be classified as within-group. The value of the distinction is in pointing out some of the alternatives possible in designing studies. For example, between-group studies of Turner syndrome and Williams syndrome would be interesting, but difficult because of the difference in average intellectual level. More meaningful for Turner syndrome would be comparisons among subgroups within Turner syndrome that show variations in ability profiles across a set of cognitive tasks. If data from Williams syndrome, Turner syndrome, and Down syndrome were placed into a data set with children who have TBI and early hydrocephalus, this would represent an across-group study. As the next section shows, application of appropriate methodologies makes this type of study entirely appropriate and valuable, just as appropriate methodology (see Bates & Appelbaum, chapter 12, this volume) makes studies of rare but small syndromes appropriate and valuable. All of these types of studies pertain directly to issues concerning the neurobehavioral classification of early CNS insult in children.

Comparisons Between Groups Varying in Etiology. Many between-group studies have been completed, including the studies of Williams syndrome and Down syndrome by Bellugi and her colleagues (chapter 2 & 3 of this volume), and the studies by Taylor on meningitis (Taylor et al., 1990; Taylor, Schatschneider, & Rich, 1991). These studies employ traditional contrasting group methodologies. As Denckla (chapter 13 of this volume) notes, a critical question for studies of children with CNS disorders is the nature of the appropriate comparison group. For example, the need to control IQ level led Bellugi et al. (chapter 3 of this volume) to the selection of Down syndrome children to compare with children with Williams syndrome. In contrast, Taylor et al. (1990, 1991) used sibling controls to deal with socioenvironmental effects on learning and behavior. Simply using "normal" controls and excluding comparison groups with related clinical disorders is usually not advisable. Most clinical groups always differ from normal and exactly what is controlled by recruiting normal children is not clear (see Denckla, chapter 13, this volume).

The between-group studies clearly illustrate the value and importance of an appropriate comparison group. Taylor et al.'s (1990, 1991) studies, for example, show that specific cognitive, motor, and behavioral deficits can be described for survivors of early meningitis relative to siblings. By using siblings, specific qualities of the environment in which the child develops can be described that separate psychosocial and disease influences on development. Taylor et al.'s studies provide an excellent example of the influence of the environment of the development of brain-impaired children, which did not receive much emphasis in this book. The phenotypic heterogeneity associated with syndromes of brain impairment are undoubtedly influenced by social, environmental, and family variables that deserve more attention.

Studies That Combine Groups of Brain-Injured Children.   Perhaps the best representation of across-group studies of brain-behavior relationships in children are several studies by Dennis (1985a, 1985b, 1987, 1988), which follow earlier studies with similar goals (e.g., Lansdell, 1969). To illustrate, Dennis (1985a, 1985b) systematically collected information on birth history, etiology, pathophysiology, early symptomatology, and other medical and sociodemographic variables on 407 children who sustained a variety of CNS insults during the first year of life. These insults were quite variable, including children with brain tumors, vascular accidents, hydrocephalus, hypoxic-ischemic encephalopathy, brain injury, and other disorders. The performance of these children on the three scales of the Wechsler Intelligence Scale for Children–Revised (WISC–R; Verbal IQ, Performance IQ, Full-Scale IQ) later in their development was added to the database.

Dennis (1985b) utilized regression methods to determine relationships of disease and sociodemographic variables with the Verbal, Performance, and Full-Scale scores from the WISC–R. Verbal IQ was related primarily to the presence of temporal lobe damage and to cerebral insults of abrupt onset (e.g., stroke). Performance IQ was related to a variety of diffuse, multifocal insults involving sensorimotor, subcortical, and midline structures of the brain. The presence of hemiplegia was related to all three IQ indices. Cerebral palsy was related primarily to Performance IQ. Most important, the correlates of each IQ scale were different.

For the second study, Dennis (1985a) used statistical methods to reduce the many medical variables to a set of 13 composites representing major dimensions of early brain disease. Cluster analysis, which is a statistical method that separates cases according to indices of similarity (e.g., in early medical factors), was then applied to the components to determine possible subtypes of early brain injury. This procedure produced 17 reliable subtypes that varied in their specificity. For example, one subtype was predominantly composed of children with closed head injury. A second represented children with several etiologies of early hydrocephalus. Another subtype was composed of children with sudden vascular accidents to the left hemisphere. Less specific subtypes included, for example, early hemisyndrome. This type was represented by multiple disorders, including hemiplegia, nonfebrile seizures, Sturge–Weber syndrome, and vascular pathology. A subtype labeled *congenital malformations* revealed similar variability.

Comparison of IQ scores across these subtypes was consistent with the correlational analyses. Verbal IQ was associated with disorders involving later, abrupt onset vascular disease and other sudden onset disorders. In contrast, Performance IQ was primarily related to disorders that were congenital, slowly emerging, and longer lasting. For example, children who sustained midline tumors showed greater impairment of Performance than Verbal IQ; any form of subcortical damage had primary effects on Performance IQ.

These types of studies are interesting for three reasons. First, this approach is clearly classification oriented. The effects of CNS insult in children on some index of cognition or behavior is studied in relationship to other children with CNS insult. The question of the covariation of a set of biological variables with a set of cognitive variables is the core of classification research in the neurobehavioral domain. Second, as Dennis (1985a, 1985b) showed, relationships emerged in these large-scale studies of heterogeneously impaired children that are consistent with studies that focus on more homogeneous groups of brain-impaired children. For example, the reduction in Performance IQ can be observed in a variety of disorders characterized by changes in subcortical white matter (see Table 14.1). These disorders include early hydrocephalus (Dennis et al., 1981; Fletcher, Bohan et al., 1992), head injury (Fletcher & Levin, 1988), CNS irradiation (Fletcher & Copeland, 1988), and other disorders characterized at a pathophysiologic level by significant manifestations in the cerebral white matter (Rourke, 1989). Whether these disorders represent a syndrome (Pennington, 1992; Rourke, 1989) is an open question, but a superficial relationship of white matter changes and spatial cognition is well established. The relationship may be superficial because as Denckla (chapter 13, this volume) suggests it is not clear how performance on spatial cognition tests relates to other domains of cognitive function (e.g., attention and executive functions). There is a major need for research addressing these relationships in clinical disorders, as in Williams syndrome.

This leads directly to the third reason that studies across heterogeneous groups are important. The deficits in spatial cognition bear some resemblance to those described in this book for Williams syndrome, and, to a lesser extent, Turner syndrome (and neurofibromatosis). Because Williams syndrome is rare, some understanding of how Williams syndrome children compare to children with brain injury—many of whom show major deficiencies in spatial cognition—would be informative. Of particular interest would be morphometric assessment of midline and white matter structures in Williams syndrome children. Jernigan and Bellugi (chapter 3 of this volume) tend to emphasize relationships of gray matter structures and temporal lobes to the language and affective development of the Williams syndrome children. However, some white matter structures were clearly reduced in volume in the Williams syndrome children relative to the Down syndrome children. It is interesting to speculate that these reductions could be related to the spatial cognition deficits of the Williams syndrome children.

Turner syndrome (and neurofibromatosis) are also interesting in relationship to studies of children with disorders involving the cerebral white matter. Because deficits in Performance IQ are commonly described in some (but not all) children with Turner syndrome (and neurofibromatosis), morphometric analysis of the cerebral white matter would also be interesting in these populations. These disorders are more prevalent than Williams syndrome and certainly vary in their phenotypic presentation: Spatial cognition deficits are apparent when averaged data are examined, but not all Turner syndrome (and neurofibromatosis) children show such patterns. Comparisons of cognitive functioning in relationship to biological variables within subgroups of Turner syndrome (and neurofibromatosis) children may be particularly illuminating.

Studies Within Etiologic Groups. The observations concerning phenotypic variability in various childhood syndromes lead directly to the third type of research study on acquired brain insult in children. These studies are basically comparisons of subgroups within a disorder. For example, studies of closed head injury (CHI) in children commonly divide cases into mild, moderate, and severe based on evaluations of depth and length of coma, initial neurological status, and neuroimaging studies (Fletcher & Levin, 1988). Similarly, studies of vascular accidents in children often compare left-and right-hemisphere lesions (Aram & Whitaker, 1988; Stiles-Davis, Janowsky, Engel, & Nass, 1988). Comparison of these two types of within-groups studies is interesting because the disorders are so different, but the underlying methodological approach is similar. Studies of both disorders can be difficult because of the question of the most appropriate comparison group. Simply obtaining normal children may lead to contamination because of unknown sociodemographic and developmental factors. In CHI, comparing mild versus moderate and severe cases is particularly strong because the mild cases usually have sociodemographic backgrounds that are similar to the more severe cases. If the injury to the brain is minimal, mild cases represent an ideal comparison to more severe cases. The most appropriate criteria for composing a mild injury group is to ensure only a brief loss of consciousness, no subsequent deterioration, normal neuroimaging studies, and an absence of premorbid learning and behavioral disorders (Levin, Fletcher, & Ewing-Cobbs, 1989). Such criteria will produce a group of children with generally good outcomes who perform at levels expected given the sociodemographic backgrounds of the children.

Studies of unilateral cerebral insult can also be conceptualized in this manner. The comparison is not only between clearly abnormal left and right hemispheres, but also relative to the presumably normal contralateral hemispheres in children with unilateral lesions. Because many children with unilateral cerebral insult have other disorders that ultimately lead to the insult (e.g., cardiovascular disease), such comparisons help control for less specific effects of disease and treatment. When a neuroimaging or electrophysiological component is added (see chapters 3 & 4 of this volume), the search for behavior-brain relationships becomes very powerful, particularly because of the use of appropriate comparison groups.

Two disorders in which research methods have been employed that examine variations in cognitive skills in relationship to quantitative neuroimaging are CHI and early hydrocephalus. Both disorders reflect generalized insult to the CNS; both disorders can be characterized by better development of verbal than nonverbal skills. In CHI, problems in the recovery of spatial cognitive skills are much more obvious than problems with the recovery of language capacities. Significant problems with attention, short-term memory, and executive functions are also apparent. The fact that CHI is a generalized, multifocal cerebral insult does not have to be an obstacle to the evaluation of behavior-brain relationships, particularly with the advent of MRI and morphometric analysis. In fact, CHI children vary in pathophysiologic characteristics of the injury and in neurobehavioral recovery (Levin et al., 1982). It may well be possible to relate different patterns of recovery to variations in the nature of the injury (i.e., within-group study). Similar observations can be made of children with early hydrocephalus (Fletcher & Levin, 1988).

Closed Head Injury. Many studies have observed slower recovery of WISC–R Performance IQ than Verbal IQ in children with CHI (see Figure 14.1). However, this slower recovery may not always reflect spatial processing deficits. Rather, these problems may reflect difficulties developing strategies on tasks that are novel and require new learning. As Denckla (chapter 13 of this volume) noted, there are major questions concerning the relationship of spatial cognition deficits to other areas of cognition. More recent investigations have begun to address executive function deficits in children with CHI and specific injury involving the frontal lobe relative to CHI children with extrafrontal and nonfrontal injuries.

To illustrate, Levin et al. (in press) obtained measures of concept formation/ problem solving, planning, word and design fluency, and verbal memory on 76 CHI children and adolescents at least 3 months postinjury. Each child also underwent magnetic resonance imaging (MRI) of the brain. The MRIs were subjected to morphometric analysis of lesion size and distribution in the frontal lobes and other areas of the brain. Many children undoubtedly sustained diffuse axonal injury in the cerebral white matter that is often visible only on autopsy (Levin et al., 1982). However, 75% of the children also had focal areas of abnormality on the MRI. In 26% of the sample, these areas were restricted to the frontal region; an additional 14% had predominantly frontal abnormalities that extended into other areas of the brain. About 15% of the

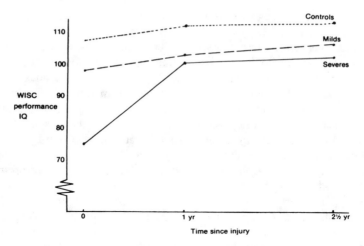

FIG. 14.1. Recovery of WISC–R performance IQ in children with mild and severe closed head injuries and orthopedic controls. Severely injured children show longer periods of recovery on performance IQ.

sample had predominantly extrafrontal abnormalities extending into the frontal region, whereas 20% had abnormalities only outside the frontal regions.

Levin et al. (in press) also measured the size of the frontal lesions and then subclassified cases using an anatomical atlas into orbital and dorsolateral areas. Results revealed that performance on executive function tasks more strongly related to depth of coma and other indices of injury severity. Adding the size of frontal lobe lesion to depth of coma also significantly improved the prediction of cognitive performance. There was also evidence for dissociations between tasks related to orbitofrontal versus dorsolateral injury within the frontal lobes. More generally, the degree to which the frontal lobes are injured may be a critical mechanism for recovery after CHI.

This study demonstrates the value of subdividing groups to evaluate dissociations within groups. These approaches may be particularly useful for studies of autism and Turner syndrome, where there may be heterogeneity in the behavioral presentation. For example, do all children with autism show the neocerebellar changes described by Courchesne et al. (chapter 6 of this volume)? Comparisons of attention-shifting skills in autistic children classified with different cerebellar findings may be informative. Similarly, comparisons of cognitive skills in Turner syndrome children classified according to genotypic or phenotypic variability may be useful. If Williams syndrome children were sufficiently prevalent and if it was the case that the phenotype described by Bellugi et al. (chapter 2 of this volume) was somewhat variable, within-group comparisons would be interesting. Such comparisons could be made, even in small subgroups if methods of the sort advocated by Bates and Applebaum (chapter 12, this volume) were employed.

The relationship of these types of studies to the within-group studies of unilateral cerebral insult is also interesting. As was discussed earlier in this chapter, studies of brain impairment during the first seven decades tended to focus on presumed unilateral injuries because of an interest in adult-based questions. Studies of more diffuse injuries were often disavowed because of the difficulties relating cognitive performance to the changes in the CNS. However, Levin et al. (in press) and other research in this chapter show that effects of injury to specific brain structures can be isolated in children who have focal lesions superimposed on generalized insults. It is also interesting to note that studies of unilateral lesions in children do not study parallel findings in adults, particularly if the nondominant hemisphere is involved. Neuroimaging studies (Eisle & Aram, 1992) suggest that depth (as opposed to side) of lesion is a central factor for prognosis, with lesions encroaching into subcortical regions of either hemisphere carrying a poorer prognosis. The value of studying questions relevant for children, who often present with generalized insult, is enhanced with a within-group approach.

Hydrocephalus.   As the example of CHI shows, there are populations of children with known CNS deviance that are larger than Williams syndrome. Early hydrocephalus is also a common form of cerebral impairment. Children with hydrocephalus, like children with CHI, are quite different from those described in this volume, particularly because their brains are visibly damaged. It may be argued that the nature of CNS encephalopathy in children with hydrocephalus is too "diffuse" for meaningful inferences between brain and behavior. However, the notion that brain disease in children is diffuse is actually another adultomorphic concept applied to children in the first seven decades of this century. In fact, neuropathologic lesion distribution in children with hydrocephalus (and CHI) varies considerably depending on etiology and early clinical management of the children. Focal lesions are rare, but as Fletcher, Bohan, et al. (1992) showed, cerebral structures can be measured and related to cognitive functions. The variability in neuropathology makes within-group comparisons of cognitive and behavioral functioning meaningful. A similar situation may hold for studies of children with neurofibromatosis and can also be bought to bear on children with the syndromes in this volume. Studies of children with hydrocephalus are especially germane for illustrating these principals.

Hydrocephalus is a common form of early brain insult. It often occurs in conjunction with a primary postnatal insult (e.g., TBI, meningitis), but is most often associated with prenatal and perinatal disorders. Three principal etiologies of early hydrocephalus are aqueductal stenosis, spina bifida, and prematurity. In any hydrocephalic child, commissural and midline white matter tracts can be affected by ventricular dilation. More lateral white matter tracts are generally less affected by hydrocephalus. In none of these disorders, however, are the CNS changes restricted to hydrocephalus, but include other neuropathological anomalies that may have an influence on development. Aqueductal stenosis is often accompanied by partial agenesis of the corpus callosum that most likely is not caused by hydrocephalus (Barkovich, 1990). Spina bifida represents several disorders that result from early defects in neural tube closure. These children have a spinal lesion, usually represented by a myelomeningocele or meningocele, at the caudal end of the neural tube. Many hindbrain and midline brain anomalies are present. Most prominent is the Arnold–Chiari II malformation, which represents a pattern of changes in the hindbrain including significant hypo- and hyperplasia of the cerebellum, generally more extensive than that described for autism by Courchesne et al. (chapter 6 of this volume). Most children with meningomyelocele also have partial agenesis of the corpus callosum as part of the defect in neural migration. This usually involves the rostrum and often includes the splenium and posterior body of the corpus callosum (Barkovich, 1990).

Some premature infants develop hydrocephalus because hemorrhages in the germinal matrix and parenchyma block CSF reabsorption. These hemorrhages also lead to destruction of the brain, leaving porencephalic cysts. Specific neurological deficits may depend on the laterality and severity of the hemorrhages and the porencephalic cysts (Volpe, 1989). Corpus callosum abnormalities can occur in these children because of stretching and thinning of the corpus callosum as the ventricles enlarge (i.e., as the hydrocephalus worsens).

Despite the significant injury to the CNS, children with congenital hydrocephalus infrequently present with frank mental retardation. However, many studies have shown poorer development of nonverbal cognitive skills relative to verbal cognitive skills in these children. Unfortunately, most studies addressing the question of discrepant development of verbal and nonverbal skills have been restricted to measures of psychometric intelligence (Fletcher & Levin, 1988). These studies generally showed lower scores on a Performance measure of IQ than on a Verbal measure.

To illustrate some of these studies, Dennis et al. (1981) compared Verbal IQ and Performance IQ scores from the WISC–R in three early congenital and perinatal and three postnatal acquired etiologies. The largest discrepancies occurred in children with congenital etiologies (aqueductal stenosis, spina bifida); children with perinatal and postnatal etiologies showed average but comparable scores on Verbal IQ and Performance IQ measures.

Fletcher, Francis et al. (1992) evaluated a large sample ($N = 90$) of 5- to 7-year-old children with hydrocephalus secondary to spina bifida, aqueductal stenosis, or prematurity-intraventricular hemorrhage. Comparison groups of children with spina bifida and no shunt, premature children with no hydrocephalus, and normal controls were also evaluated. Comparison of skill discrepancies at two occasions separated by 1 year revealed that hydrocephalic children, as a group, showed poorer nonverbal than verbal skills on measures from (a) the McCarthy Scales of Children's Abilities, (b) the WISC–R, and (c) composites of verbal and nonverbal neuropsychological skills. The neuropsychological results are displayed in Fig. 14.2. These discrepancies were not significantly different across etiologies and could not be attributed to the motor demands of the tasks.

Children with hydrocephalus are not without language deficiency. Historically, the term "cocktail party syndrome" has been used to describe the language of children with spina bifida, most of whom have hydrocephalus. This term was operationalized by Tew (1979), as follows:

1. A preservation of response, either echoing the examiner, or repetition of an earlier statement made by the child.
2. An excessive use of social phrases in conversation.
3. An overfamiliarity in manner, not normally expected in a 5-year-old child.
4. A habit of introducing personal experience into the conversation in irrelevant and inappropriate contexts.   Fluent and normally well-articulated speech.

The surface resemblance of these criteria to descriptions of language in Williams syndrome is clearly apparent. However, Tew (1979) compared a

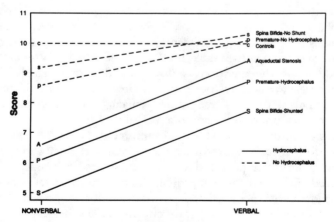

FIG. 14.2.   Performance on neuropsychological composites of verbal and nonverbal skills in children with hydrocephalus (premature-hydrocephalus, aqueductal stenosis, spina bifida-shunted) and comparison groups (normal, premature—no hydrocephalus; spina bifida—no shunt). Children with hydrocephalus show poorer performance on nonverbal skills than verbal skills ($M = 10$; $SD = 3$).

group of preschool children with spina bifida who met criteria for cocktail party syndrome with spina bifida children who did show cocktail party speech. A comparison group of children with cerebral palsy matched for age, gender, social class, and other demographic variables was also included. Results of several comparisons of language and other cognitive skills revealed that children who met criteria for cocktail party syndrome had significantly lower Wechsler IQ scores (M FSIQ $= 55.5$; $SD = 14.1$). They also scored lower on virtually any measure of language. Tew concluded that cocktail party syndrome was not specific to spina bifida and seemed related to lower intelligence test scores. However, the dissociations in language development in children with Williams syndrome and Down syndrome observed by Bellugi et al. (chapters 2 & 3 of this volume) are not consistent with this conclusion and probably reflect excessive reliance on psychometric assessments of language.

More recent studies based on contemporary cognitive models of language development in children with hydrocephalus by Dennis and associates clarify these issues. These studies have shown preservation of many language skills. For example, Dennis, Hendrick, Hoffman, Dennis, and Humphreys (1987) found preservation of word-finding ability, fluency and automaticity, sentence memory, and metalinguistic awareness. Consistent (but small) differences occurred on measures of the comprehension of complex syntactic structures (active–passive relationships). Dennis has also completed studies using narrative discourse methods. One recent study (Dennis, Jacennik, & Barnes, in press) showed that the discourse of children with early hydrocephalus was characterized by a smaller quantity of material that was also less cohesive and reduced in coherence. The narrations of the hydrocephalic children had more ambiguous material and conveyed less content, which was also often implausible, or irrelevant. When the knowledge base of the story was difficult to assess, fewer inferences were made; when the knowledge base was more accessible, stories were more verbose, hyperfluent, and less efficient in retelling. Dennis et al. (in press) argued that the difficulties experienced by hydrocephalic children in producing narratives that are rich in content reflected problems with the processing of pragmatic language. These problems were beyond hyperverbosity and enriched vocabulary. They reflected deficits in the textual use of language, not deficits in the social use of language because the interpersonal components of the narratives were preserved. Hence, Dennis et al. (in press) were able to use a group of children with multiple CNS anomalies to demonstrate fundamental dissociations between two components (textual and social) of pragmatic language.

Few studies have explored possible relationships of the spatial cognition and language deficiencies with the CNS anomalies characteristic of the population. Dennis et al. (1981) employed previously collectively air encephalograms in an attempt to correlate discrepancies in psychometric intelligence and changes in the hydrocephalic brain. This study showed that discrepancies in verbal and nonverbal cognitive functioning were related to greater posterior relative to anterior thinning of the cerebral white matter.

We recently completed a study employing assessments of verbal and nonverbal cognitive skills and morphometric evaluation of cerebral white matter structures and the lateral ventricles in age-matched children with meningomyelocele, meningocele, aqueductal stenosis, and normals (Fletcher, Bohan et al., 1992). The volume of each lateral ventricle, and the cross-sectional area of the corpus callosum and internal capsules were correlated with the measures of verbal and nonverbal cognitive skills used in Fletcher, Francis et al. (1992). Quantitative measurement of the MRI revealed that the corpus callosum in the meningomyelocele and aqueductal stenosis groups was smaller. In all patient groups, the lateral ventricles were larger, and the internal capsules were smaller, relative to normals. There were no differences in the size of the centra semiovale. Verbal and nonverbal measures correlated significantly with the size of the corpus callosum. However, the correlation was much higher for nonverbal measures. Nonverbal measures correlated with the right, but not the left, lateral ventricle and with the area of the right and left internal capsules. Verbal measures correlated with the left, but not right, lateral ventricle and with the left, but not right, internal capsule. These results showed a relationship between the corpus callosum and cognitive skills that was also influenced by hydrocephalus-related changes in the lateral ventricles and other cerebral white matter tracts.

These findings were consistent with current hypotheses suggesting that the development of nonverbal cognitive skills is dependent in part on the integrity of the CNS white matter. Corpus callosum abnormalities have not been emphasized in children with congenital hydrocephalus. When hypoplasia is included, most of the abnormalities involve the rostrum, splenium, and posterior body. The posterior body connects association areas involved in visual attention, sensorimotor integration, and other higher order cortical functions. The splenium connects visual areas of the occipital lobes. As Bellugi et al. noted (chapter 2 of this volume), the rostrum has been shown to connect areas of the frontal lobes involved in semantic language. The spatial cognition deficits are consistent with impairment of higher cortical functions commonly associated with the posterior parietal areas of the right hemisphere. These results imply a failure of such systems to develop because of reduced interhemispheric communication. The resulting lack of information would prevent normal specialization of the right hemisphere.

The spatial cognition deficits are not uniform in hydrocephalic children. Figure 14.3 presents a profile of performance on a variety of nonverbal processing tasks in children with early hydrocephalus (collapsed across the three hydrocephalus etiologies in Fig. 14.2) and comparison children (collapsed across the no-hydrocephalus group in Fig. 14.2). Traditional measures

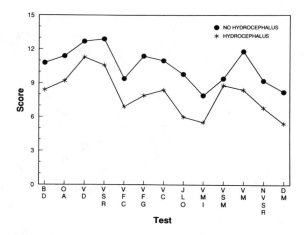

FIG. 14.3. Performance on a battery of spatial cognition tasks by hydrocephalic and nonhydrocephalic children. Hydrocephalic children show less impairment on simple visual-discrimination tasks (VD, VSR) and greater impairment on complex spatial tasks that are motor-free (JLO), involve copying (VMI), memory (NVSR), and both memory and copying (DM). Abbreviations: BD = WISC–R Block Design, OA = WISC–R Object Assembly, VD = Visual Discrimination, VSR = Visual Spatial Relationships, VFC = Visual Form Constancy, VFG = Visual Figure-ground, VC = Visual Closure, JLO = Judgment of Line Orientation, VMI = Beery Visual-Motor Integration, VSM = Visual Sequential Memory, VM = Visual Memory, NVSR = Nonverbal Selective Reminding, DM = Delayed Memory from the Wide Range Assessment of Memory and Learning. VD, VSR, VFC, VFG, VC, VSM, and VM are from the Test of Visual-Perceptual Skills (Gardner, 1988). For all tests $M = 10; SD = 3$.

of spatial cognition such as WISC–R Block Design and Object Assembly and simple matching-to-sample perceptual tasks (Visual Discrimination, Visual Spatial Relationships) are more preserved in hydrocephalic children relative to the comparison group. Complex motor-free spatial tasks (Judgment of Line Orientation), perceptual-motor tasks (Beery Visual-Motor Integration) and complex tasks with a memory component (Nonverbal Selective Reminding, Delayed Memory) are more impaired in the hydrocephalic children. The pattern, however, is quite variable. It would be interesting to use some of the measures of facial recognition and hierarchical processing showing preserved skills in Williams syndrome children in a population of children with early hydrocephalus. On the surface, there are similarities in the linguistic and spatial cognitive skills of many of the populations reviewed in this chapter. Evaluations of common skills across syndromes in relationship to pathophysiologic studies of the CNS would contribute significantly to the development of a cognitive neuroscience of children.

The spina bifida children are also interesting in relationship to the studies of autism summarized by Courchesne et al. and by Sigman (chapters 6 & 7 of this volume, respectively). The presence of hindbrain abnormalities (in-

cluding the cerebellum) in virtually all spina bifida children with meningomyelocele is particularly intriguing. Figure 14.4 shows an example of the
Arnold–Chiari II malformation. This figure, taken from a midsagittal MRI
slice, shows the significant changes affecting the entire cerebellum and other
parts of the hindbrain. The agenesis of the corpus callosum and some residual
hydrocephalus can also be seen. These children may well have deficits in
attentional skills that could be related to the hindbrain anomalies. They do
not usually have autism, but sometimes have interpersonal difficulties because
they are excessively social. It would be interesting to compare spina bifida
children with Arnold–Chiari II malformations on attention measures in
much the same manner as adults with cerebellar lesions were employed by
Courchesne et al. (chapter 6 of this volume). An obvious question is why a
group of children with neuropathology that included significant cerebellar
changes develops social functioning so differently from children with autism.
Do they have deficits in shifting attention? Children with spina bifida have
other CNS anomalies and cognitive problems, but these questions point out
the value of comparative studies of children with early brain impairments and
syndromes.

CONCLUSIONS: THE IMPORTANCE
OF CLASSIFICATION

The three types of studies in this chapter raise important issues concerning
classification that were also raised throughout this volume. Many articles
emphasized the importance of individual differences in subgroups of a

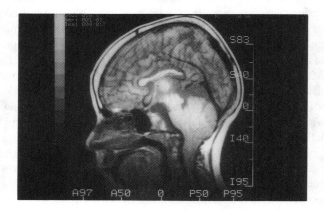

FIG. 14.4. Midsagittal slice from magnetic resonance imaging of child with meningomyelocele, showing Arnold–Chiari II malformation in the hindbrain, partial agenesis of the
corpus callosum, and mild residual hydrocephalus.

particular disorder. The complication is small sample size, but many of the methods outlined by Bates and Applebaum (chapter 12 of this volume) can help with these problems. The question more clearly apparent in studies of Turner syndrome and autism concerns the behavioral heterogeneity apparent within these groups. For example, not all women with Turner syndrome have a cognitive profile associated with discrepancies in language and spatial cognition. Similarly, as Sigman and Waterhouse (respectively, chapters 7 & 8 of this volume) both suggest, there is substantial variability in the phenotypic presentation of children with autism. Whereas Sigman worries over subdivisions of children into small subgroups, Waterhouse implies that such subdivisions may be essential to understanding neural reorganization in autistic individuals. This dilemma, of course, is exactly that represented by studies of children with language, learning, and attention disorders.

Any study comparing groups is ultimately a question of classification and definition. When sample size is adequate, such studies may directly address classification issues and provide a piece to the puzzle (e.g., Dennis, 1985a, 1985b, 1987, 1988). The ability to explain variability within a group of individuals with a particular syndrome according to variations in some type of CNS measurement is a particularly powerful method for establishing behavior-brain relationships. Interestingly, this particular methodological issue was not discussed in this book. Sample size aside, if behavioral dissociations are related to CNS measurement, there should be common sources of variability in the two levels of measurement. In other words, there should be correlations between behavioral and brain measurements. The critical problem, of course, is sample size. When sample sizes are small, the alternative is detailed and systematic analytic, hypothesis-driven studies of the sort described for Williams syndrome and autism. As the examples of CHI shows, behavior-brain relationships can be seen in children with focal lesions superimposed on generalized insult. The hydrocephalus example shows that such relationships are possible in cases characterized primarily by generalized insult.

Classification studies that address relationships within and across various childhood syndromes are clearly indicated. Because no single center would possess enough children of a particular disorder, multicenter studies employing a common methodology would enhance studies of single syndromes. Common assessment and measurement methodologies could be established that would include a set of core procedures as well as syndrome-specific assessments. Specific models of classification could be evaluated. For example, Waterhouse (chapter 8, this volume) actually invokes a particular theory of classification based on *prototypes*. Prototypes are actual or idealized entities that represent a relatively pure member of a hypothesized group (Blashfield, Sprock, Haymaker, & Hudgin, 1989). Other entities can be related to the prototype based on the degree to which resemblance occurs on a set of attributes, some of which are necessary for membership and others of which are not necessary but commonly co-occur within the population. Because the three disorders central to this book are cast as syndromes, this issue of whether these disorders are syndromes, collections of symptoms, or arbitrary groups could be systematically evaluated.

This type of work would also help establish the nature of cognitive processes characterizing these populations. As Denckla (chapter 13 of this volume) notes, the boundary between spatial cognition and executive functions is poorly established in the behavioral domain. Similarly, is attention a separable process or better subsumed under the rubric of executive function? For spatial cognition, major connections occur between the right posterior area of the brain and the frontal lobes. Similarly, as Courchesne et al. (chapter 6, this volume) notes, higher order mental activities mediated by the neocerebellum are richly connected to motor output and planning areas of the frontal lobes. Consistent with Goldman-Rakic (chapter 1 of this volume), behavioral dissociations may not reflect the nature and location of a CNS insult, but the effect on a complex set of sequenced events leading to an end product.

Classification also offers a general perspective for this research. The articles in this volume are not isolated studies, but occur in a broader research context. Questions about relationships across syndromes may lead to a set of principles concerning the relationship of behavior and the brain. It is not likely that a set of findings characteristic of children with Williams or Turner syndrome will only apply to these disorders. Rather, these findings may reflect more fundamental principles concerning how the brain mediates behavior after early disruption. It is the search for these principles that holds the keys to enhancing the development of children with early CNS deviations.

ACKNOWLEDGMENTS

Supported in part by National Institutes of Health Grants NS25368, Neurobehavioral Development of Hydrocephalic Children, HD27597, Neuropsychological Sequelae of Pediatric Head Injury, and NS21889, Neurobehavioral Outcome of Head Injury in Children.

REFERENCES

Alajouanine, T. H., & Lhermitte, F. (1965). Acquired aphasia in children. *Brain*, *88*, 653–662.

Annett, M. (1973). Laterality of childhood hemiplegia and the growth of intelligence. *Cortex*, *9*, 4–29.

Aram, D. M. (1990). Brain lesions in children: Implications for developmental language disorders. In J. F. Miller (Ed.), *Research on child language disorders. A decade of progress* (pp. 309–320). Boston: College Hill Press.

Aram, D. M., & Whitaker, H. A. (1988). Cognitive sequelae of unilateral lesions acquired in early childhood. In D. L. Molfese & S. J. Segalowitz (Eds.), *Brain lateralization in children* (pp. 417–436). New York: Guilford.

Barkovich, A. J. (1990). *Pediatric neuroimaging*. New York: Raven.

Basser, L. S. (1962). Hemiplegia of early onset and the faculty of speech with special reference to the effects of hemispherectomy. *Brain, 85*, 427–460.

Benton, A. L. (1962). Behavioral indices of brain injury in school children. *Child Development, 33*, 199–208.

Benton, A. L. (1964). Contributions to aphasia before Broca. *Cortex, 1*, 314–327.

Benton, A. L. (1975). Developmental dyslexia: Neurological aspects. In W. J. Friedlander (Ed.), *Advances in neurology*, (Vol. 7, pp. 2–44).

Blashfield, R., Sprock, J., Haymaker, D., & Hudgin, J. (1989). The family resemblance hypothesis applied to psychiatric classification. *Journal of Nervous and Mental Disease, 177*, 492–497.

Broman, S. H. (1979). Perinatal anoxia and cognitive development in early childhood. In T. Field (Ed.), *Infants born at risk* (pp. 29–52). Jamaica,NY: Spectrum Publications.

Broman, S. H. (1989). Infant physical status and later cognitive development. In M. Bornstein & N. Krasnegor (Eds.), *Stability and continuity in mental development*. (pp. 45–62). Hillsdale, NJ: Lawrence Erlbaum Associates.

Broman, S., Nichols, P. L., Shaughnessy, P., & Kennedy, W. (1987). *Retardation in young children: A developmental study of cognitive deficit*. Hillsdale, NJ: Lawrence Erlbaum Associates.

Dennis, M. (1980). Language acquisition in a single hemisphere: Semantic organization. In D. Caplan (Ed.), *Biological studies of mental processes* (pp. 159–185). Cambridge, MA: MIT Press.

Dennis, M. (1985a). Intelligence after early brain injury: I. IQ scores of subjects classified on the basis of medical history variables. *Journal of Clinical and Experimental Neuropsychology, 8*, 555–576.

Dennis, M. (1985b). Intelligence after early brain injury: II. Predicting IQ scores from medical variables. *Journal of Clinical Neuropsychology, 8*, 526–554.

Dennis, M. (1987). Using language to parse the young damaged brain. *Journal of Clinical and Experimental Neuropsychology, 9*, 723–753.

Dennis, M. (1988). Language in the young damaged brain. In T. Boll & B. K. Bryant (Eds.), *Clinical neuropsychology and brain function: Research measurement and practice* (Master Lecture Series) (pp. 85–123). Washington, DC: American Psychological Association.

Dennis, M., Fitz, C. R., Netley, C. T., Sugar, J., Derek, C. F., Harwood-Nash, M. B., Hendrick, H. B., Hoffman, H. J., & Humphreys, R. P. (1981). The intelligence of hydrocephalic children. *Archives of Neurology, 38*, 607–715.

Dennis, M., Hendrick, E. B., Hoffman, H. J., & Humphreys, R. P. (1987). The language of hydrocephalic children. *Journal of Clinical and Experimental Neuropsychology, 9*, 593–621.

Dennis, M., Jacennick, B., & Barnes, M. A. (in press). The content of narrative discourse in children and adolescents after early onset hydrocephalus and in normally developing age peers. *Brain and Language*.

Dennis, M., & Whitaker, H. (1977). Hemispheric equipotentiality and language acquisition. In S. J. Segalowitz & F. A. Gruber (Eds.), *Language development and neurological theory* (pp. 93–106). New York: Academic.

Doehring, D. G. (1978). The tangled web of behavioral research in developmental dyslexia. In A. L. Benton & D. Pearl (Eds.), *Dyslexia: An appraisal of current knowledge* (pp. 123–138). New York: Oxford University Press.

Eisele, J. A., & Aram, D. M. (1992, October). *The effects of lesion location, lesion size, and lesion age on developing language and cognitive functions*. Paper presented at the meeting of the Academy of Aphasia, Toronto.

Fletcher, J. M., Bohan, T. P., Brandt, M. E., Brookshire, B. L., Beaver, S. R., Francis, D., Davidson, K. C., Thompson, N. M., & Miner, M. E. (1992). Cerebral white matter and cognition in hydrocephalic children. *Archives of Neurology, 49*, 818–824.

Fletcher, J. M., & Copeland, D. R. (1988). Neurobehavioral effects of central nervous system prophylactic treatment for childhood cancer. *Journal of Clinical and Experimental Neuropsychology, 10*, 495–537.

Fletcher, J. M., Francis, D., & Morris, R. (1988). Methodological issues in neuropsychology: Classification, measurement, and non-equivalent group comparison. In F. Boller & J. Grafman (Eds.), *Handbook of neuropsychology* (Vol. 1 pp. 83–110). Amsterdam, Netherlands: Elsevier.

Fletcher, J. M., Francis, D. J., Thompson, N. M., Brookshire, B. L., Bohan, T. P., Landry, S. H., Davidson, K. C., & Miner, M. E. (1992). Verbal and nonverbal skill discrepancies in hydrocephalic children. *Journal of Clinical and Experimental Neuropsychology, 14*, 593–609.

Fletcher, J. M., & Levin, H. S. (1988). Neurobehavioral effects of brain injury in children. In D. Routh (Ed.), *Handbook of pediatric psychology* (pp. 258–296). New York: Guilford.

Fletcher, J. M., & Satz, P. (1983). Age, plasticity, and equipotentiality: A reply to Smith. *Journal of Consulting and Clinical Psychology, 51*, 763–767.

Fletcher, J. M., & Taylor, H. G. (1984). Neuropsychological approaches to children: Towards a developmental neuropsychology. *Journal of Clinical Neuropsychology, 6*, 39–56.

Gardner, M. F. (1988). *Test of Visual-Perceptual Skills.* San Francisco: Health Publishing.

Goldman, P. S. (1974). An alternative to developmental plasticity: Heterology of CNS structures in infants and adults. In D. Stein, J. Rosen, & N. Butters (Eds.), *Plasticity and recovery of function in the CNS* (pp. 149–174). New York: Academic.

Hecaen, H. (1976). Acquired aphasia in children and the ontogenesis of hemispheric functional specialization. *Brain and Language, 3*, 114–134.

Hecaen, H. (1983). Acquired aphasia in children: Revisited. *Neuropsychologia, 21*, 581–587.

Isaccson, R. L. (1975). The myth of recovery from early brain damage. In N. G. Ellis (Ed.), *Aberrant development in infancy* (pp. 1–26). New York: Wiley.

Kahn, E., & Cohen, L. H. (1934). Organic drivenness: A brain stem syndrome and experience. *New England Journal of Medicine, 210*, 748–756.

Kennard, M. A. (1936). Age and other factors in motor recovery from precentral lesions in monkeys. *American Journal of Physiology, 115*, 138–146.

Lansdell, H. (1969). Verbal and nonverbal factors in right hemisphere speech: Relation to early neurological history. *Journal of Comparative and Physiological Psychology, 69*, 734–738.

Laufer, M. W., & Denhoff, E. (1957). Hyperkinetic behavior syndrome in children. *Journal of Pediatrics, 50*, 463–474.

Lenneberg, E. (1967). *Biological foundations of language.* New York: Wiley.

Levin, H. S. (1981). Aphasia in closed head injury. In M. T. Sarno (Ed.), *Acquired aphasia* (pp. 427–458). New York: Academic.

Levin, H. S., Benton, A. L., & Grossman, R. G. (1982). *Neurobehavioral consequences of closed head injury.* New York: Oxford University Press.

Levin, H. S., Culhane, K. A., Mendelsohn, D., Lilly, M. A., Bruce, D., Fletcher, J. M., Chapman, S. B., Harward, H., & Eisenberg, H. M. (in press). *Cognition in relation to MRI in head injured children and adolescents. Archives of Neurology.*

Levin, H. S., Ewing-Cobbs, L., & Benton, A. L. (1984). Age and recovery from brain damage: A review of clinical studies. In S. Scheff (Ed.), *Aging and recovery of function* (pp. 169–205). New York: Plenum.

Levin, H. S., Fletcher, J. M., & Ewing- Cobbs, L. C. (1989). Neurobehavioral outcome of mild head injury in children. In H. S. Levin, H. M. Eisenberg, & A. L. Benton (Eds.), *Mild head injury* (pp. 189–216). New York: Oxford University Press.

Morris, R. D., & Fletcher, J. M. (1988). Classification in neuropsychology: A theoretical framework and research paradigm. *Journal of Clinical and Experimental Neuropsychology, 10*, 640–658.

Pennington, B. F. (1992). *Diagnosing learning disorders: A neuropsychological framework.* New York: Guilford.

Reitan, R. M., & Wolfson, D. (1992). *Neuropsychological evaluation of older children*. Tucson, AZ: Neuropsychology Press.

Rourke, B. P. (1975). Brain-behavior relationships in children with learning disabilities. *The American Psychologist, 30*, 911–920.

Rourke, B. P. (1989). *Nonverbal learning disabilities: The syndrome and the model*. New York: Guilford.

Rutter, M. (1982). Syndromes attributed to "minimal brain dysfunction" in childhood. *American Journal of Psychiatry, 139*, 21–33.

St. James-Roberts, I. (1979). Neurological plasticity, recovery from brain insult, and child development. In H. W. Reese (Ed.), *Advances in child development and behavior* (Vol. 14, pp. 253–319). New York: Academic.

St. James-Roberts, I. (1981). A reinterpretation of hemispherectomy data without functional plasticity of the brain: I. Intellectual function. *Brain and Language, 13*, 31–53.

Satz, P., & Bullard-Bates, C. (1981). Acquired aphasia in children. In M. T. Sarno (Ed.), *Acquired aphasia* (pp. 399–426). New York: Academic.

Satz, P., & Fletcher, J. M. (1980). Minimal brain dysfunctions: Current research concepts and methods. In H. Rie & E. Rie (Eds.), *Handbook of minimal brain dysfunctions* (pp. 699–714). New York: Wiley.

Satz, P., & Fletcher, J. M. (1981). Emergent trends in neuropsychology: An overview. *Journal of Consulting and Clinical Psychology, 49*, 851–865.

Satz, P., & van Nostrand, G. (1973). Developmental dyslexia: An evaluation of a theory. In P. Satz & J. Ross (Eds.), *The disabled learner: Early detection and intervention* (pp. 121–148). Rotterdam, Netherlands: Rotterdam University Press.

Smith, A. (1981). On the organization, disorganization and reorganization of language and other brain functions. In Y. Lebrun & O. Zangwill (Eds.), *Lateralization of language in the child* (pp. 51–70). Lisse, Netherlands: Swets & Zeitlinger.

Smith, A. (1983). Overview or "underview": A comment on Satz and Fletcher's "Emergent trends in neuropsychology: An overview." *Journal of Consulting and Clinical Psychology, 51*, 768–775.

Smith, A. (1984). Early and long-term recovery from brain damage in children and adults: Evolution of concepts of localization, plasticity, and recovery. In C. R. Almli & S. Finger (Eds.), *Early brain damage* (Vol. I, pp. 299–324). New York: Academic.

Stiles-Davis, J., Janowsky, J., Engel, M., & Nass, R. (1988). Drawing ability for young children with congenital unilateral brain lesions. *Neuropsychologia, 26*, 359–371.

Still, G. F. (1902). Some abnormal psychological conditions in children. *Lancet, 1*, 1077–1082.

Strauss, A. A., & Lehtinen, L. E. (1947). *Psychopathology and education of the brain-injured child*. New York: Grune & Stratton.

Taylor, H. G., Mills, E. L., Ciampi, A., DuBerger, R., Watters, G. V., Gold, R., McDonald, N., & Michaels, R. H. (1990). The sequelae of haemophilus influenzae for school-age children. *The New England Journal of Medicine, 323*, 1657–1663.

Taylor, H. G., Schatschneider, C., & Rich, D. (1991). Sequelae of haemophilus influenzae meningitis: Implications for the study of brain disease and development. In M. Tramontana & S. Hooper (Eds.), *Advances in child neuropsychology* (Vol. 1. pp. 50–108). New York: Springer-Verlag.

Tew, B. (1979). The "cocktail party syndrome" in children with hydrocephalus and spina bifida. *British Journal of Disorders of Communication, 14*, 89–101.

Volpe, J. L. (1989). Intraventricular hemorrhage in the premature infant—current concepts. Part I. *Annals of Neurology, 25*, 3–11.

Woods, B. T., & Teuber, H. L. (1978). Changing patterns of childhood aphasia. *Annals of Neurology, 3*, 273–280.

Author Index

Subject Index